ONCOLOGY NURSING
Advances, Treatments, and Trends into the 21st Century

Penny Ashwanden
Deputy Director
Division of Communications and Development
Columbia University Comprehensive Cancer Center
New York, New York

Anne E. Belcher, RN, PhD
Associate Professor
University of Maryland School of Nursing
Baltimore, Maryland

E. Anne Hubbard Mattson, RN, MS, MPH, ANP
Coordinator of Adult Health Sciences
Jefferson County Health Department
Birmingham, Alabama

Randi Moskowitz, RN, MS, MBA
Executive Director
Cancer Institute of Brooklyn
Brooklyn, New York

Nancy E. Riese, RN, MS
Research Nurse
Joint Center for Radiation Therapy
Boston, Massachusetts

AN ASPEN PUBLICATION®
Aspen Publishers, Inc.
Rockville, Maryland
1990

Library of Congress Cataloging-in-Publication Data
Oncology nursing : advances, treatments, and trends into the 21st
    century / Penny Ashwanden ... [et al.].
    p. cm.
  Includes bibliographical references.
  Includes index.
  ISBN: 0-8342-0168-2
  1. Cancer—Nursing. 2. Cancer—Nursing—Forecasting.
  3. Oncologic Nursing—trends. I. Ashwanden, Penny.
  [DNLM: 1. Acquired Immunodficiency Syndrome—nursing.
  2. Neoplasms—nursing. 3. Neoplasms—therapy. WY 156 0575]
  RC266.054 1990
  610.73'698—dc20
  DNLM/DLC
  for Library of Congress   90-648
                                            CIP

Copyright © 1990 by Aspen Publishers, Inc.
All rights reserved.

Aspen Publishers, Inc., grants permission for photocopying for limited personal or internal use. This consent does not extend to other kinds of copying, such as copying for general distribution, for advertising or promotional purposes, for creating new collective works, or for resale. For information, address Aspen Publishers, Inc., Permissions Department, 1600 Research Boulevard, Rockville, Maryland 20850

The authors have made every effort to ensure the accuracy of the information herein, particularly with regard to drug selection and dose. However, appropriate information sources should be consulted, especially for new or unfamiliar drugs or procedures. It is the responsibility of every practitioner to evaluate the appropriateness of a particular opinion in the context of actual clinical situations and with due consideration to new developments. Authors, editors, and the publisher cannot be held responsible for any typographical or other errors found in this book.

Editiorial Services: Ruth Bloom

Library of Congress Catalog Card Number: 90-648
ISBN: 0-8342-0168-2

Printed in the United States of America

1 2 3 4 5

Table of Contents

Contributors xi

Foreword xv

Preface xvii

Introduction xix

Chapter 1—The Oncology Nurse As Manager, Researcher, Care Provider, Teacher, and Consultant 1
Anne E. Belcher

    Study Questions 5

Chapter 2—Ethical Issues in Oncology Nursing Resulting from New Technologies 6
Penelope Buschman

    The Changing Role of the Nurse 7
    New Technologies 9
    Research Issues 10
    Conclusion 11
    Study Questions 12

Chapter 3—Health Promotion and Disease Prevention: Oncology Nursing in the Year 2000 13
E. Anne Hubbard Mattson

    Cancer Prevention Issues 15
    Community-Based Strategies for Cancer Prevention 28

Health Policy Advocates 29
Future Nursing Research 30
Conclusion 31
Study Questions 31
Appendix 3-A—National Cancer Institute's Cancer
 Control Objectives for the Nation, 1985–2000 35
Appendix 3-B—Risk Factors in Carcinogenesis 37
Appendix 3-C—Summary Table of Objectives To Reduce
 the Toll from Cancer by the Year 2000 39

PART I: CURRENT ADVANCES IN TREATMENT MODALITIES 43

Chapter 4—New Developments in Treatment Modalities 45
Anne E. Belcher

Delivery of Chemotherapy 46
Photodynamic Therapy 48
Reprogramming Therapy 50
Gene Replacement Therapy 50
Antisense RNA Inhibition of Oncogene Expression 51
New Chemotherapeutic Agents 51
Nursing Research Applications 55
Conclusion 56
Study Questions 56

Chapter 5—Technologic Advances in Radiation Oncology and Applications for Nursing Research 59
Glenda B. Kelman, Roberta A. Strohl, and Nancy E. Riese

Types of Radiation Therapy 61
Nursing Research in Radiation Oncology 67
Study Questions 73

Chapter 6—Biologic Response Modifiers: Therapies That Hold Great Promise for Cancer Patients 78
Brenda Shelton and Anne E. Belcher

Classifications of Biologic Therapy 79
Current Status of Specific Biologic Response Modifiers .. 81

	Nursing Implications of the Use of Biologic Response Modifiers	87
	Conclusion	95
	Study Questions	95
Chapter 7—Bone Marrow Transplantation		97
Sarina Petrolino-Roche and Ruth Nuscher Ford		
	Overview of the Application of Bone Marrow Transplantation	100
	Complications of Bone Marrow Transplantation	109
	Economic Issues in Bone Marrow Transplantation	116
	Future Trends in Bone Marrow Transplantation	117
	Study Questions	117
Chapter 8—Advances in Cancer Pain Management		122
Nessa Coyle and Russell K. Portenoy		
	Advances in Pain Evaluation	123
	Advances in Cancer Pain Treatment	127
	The Emerging Role of the Clinical Nurse Specialist in Pain Management	133
	Future Directions	134
	Study Questions	135
PART II: SIGNIFICANT POPULATIONS		139
Chapter 9—Cancer in the Older Patient		141
Susan Ann Derby		
	Perspectives on Aging	141
	Aging and the Natural History of Cancer	142
	Profile of the Older Population and Patterns of Disease ..	145
	Social Factors and Illness Behavior with a Cancer Diagnosis......................................	145
	Early Detection and Screening	146
	Age-Related Influences on Surgical Cancer Treatment ...	148
	Life-Threatening Infections Related to Cancer in the Older Patient	150
	Chemotherapy and the Older Patient	152
	Nursing Considerations for the Older Patient Receiving Radiation Therapy	154

Polypharmacy: Drug-Induced Illness in the Older
	Patient 155
Future Directions 158
Conclusion 159
Study Questions 159

Chapter 10—The Terminally Ill Cancer Patient **163**
Colleen Scanlon and Nancy Scannell D'Agostino

Assessment 165
Nursing Concerns for the Future: Ethical Issues 169
Conclusion 171
Study Questions 171

Chapter 11—Crucial Ambulatory Care Nursing Services: Detection and Management of Opportunistic Illness Related to Infection with Human Immunodeficiency Virus **173**
Kathleen M. McMahon Casey

Nature of the Acquired Immunodeficiency Syndrome 173
HIV Antibody Counseling and Testing 174
Early Detection of Aids-Related Disease 177
Conclusion 189
Study Questions 189

Chapter 12—Acquired Immunodeficiency Syndrome in Infants, Children, and Adolescents **192**
Margaret L. Fracaro

Epidemiology 193
Transmission 193
HIV Testing 194
Disease Process 194
Program of Care 197
Family Education 199
Immunizations 199
In-Hospital Precautions 200
Home Care 201
Chronic Disease Management 202
High-Risk Behaviors among Adolescents 204
Impact of AIDS 205
Children and Adolescents with HIV Infection 206
AIDS Education in the School and Community 208

Conclusion 209
Study Questions 209

Chapter 13—Home Care for the Patient with Acquired Immunodeficiency Syndrome and Drug Therapy for Human Immunodeficiency Virus-Related Infections and Neoplasms 212
Noreen Coyne

Issues Associated with AIDS 214
Case Management 216
Stress Associated with Caring for AIDS Patients 216
Home Nursing Care 217
Hospice Care 221
Drug Therapy 222
Into the 21st Century 231
Study Questions 231

Chapter 14—Acquired Immunodeficiency Syndrome Patient Handbook 234
Jeanne Kalinoski

Introduction 237
AIDS: What Is It? 237
Coping with the AIDS Experience 238
Your Body—Check It Out 239
How To Take Care of Yourself 240
Drug Use 245
Household Hints 246
The Care Giver at Home 247
Taking Care of the Care Giver 248
Nutrition and AIDS 249
Conclusion 256
Study Questions 256

PART III: SPECIALIZED HEALTH CARE DELIVERY SYSTEMS 257

Chapter 15—New Trends in Ambulatory Oncology Care 259
Randi Moskowitz

What Makes Ambulatory Care Attractive? 260
The Changing Role of the Ambulatory Oncology Clinical Nurse Specialist 262

Hospital-Based Ambulatory Care at a University-
    Affiliated Comprehensive Cancer Center 263
Study Questions 264

**Chapter 16—Freestanding Cancer Centers: New Trends in Nursing
    Care for Cancer Patients** **266**
Dolores M. Esparza and Nancy Bookbinder

Historical Events Leading Up to Modern Needs 266
Freestanding Cancer Centers 267
Current Trends in Ambulatory Cancer Center Health
    Management 268
Contributions of Freestanding Cancer Centers to Standards
    of Care 269
Reimbursement 269
Accreditation Requirements 270
Nursing Implications 271
Conclusion 274
Study Questions 275

**Chapter 17—Homelessness and Infection with Human
    Immunodeficiency Virus: What Are the Options?** .. **276**
Jo Anne Staats

Study Questions 280

Chapter 18—Cooperative Care for the Oncology Patient **281**
Melissa Meyers

Admitting 282
The Patient Room 282
Dining and Recreation 282
The Therapeutic Center 283
The Education Center 283
The Oncology Patient 284
Study Questions 285

Chapter 19—The Oncology Nurse in Business **287**
Joanne D. Hayes, Anita Nirenberg, and Randi Moskowitz

An Overview 287
The Nexus Group 290

The Oncology Nursing Agency	297
Computerization	301
Study Questions	301

Chapter 20—Home Care for Cancer Patients Including Chemotherapy Administration ... **303**
*Cecilia Wilfinger, Robin B. Brenner,
E. Anne Hubbard Mattson, Anne E. Belcher,
Penny Ashwanden, and Randi Moskowitz*

Educating the Patient and Family	304
Eligibility Requirements	305
Technologic Advances in Home Care	305
Financial Considerations in Home Care	306
The Role of the Nurse in the Home	307
The Home Care Nurse As Patient Advocate	308
Study Questions	308

PART IV: COMPUTERS, VIDEOS, AND THE ONCOLOGY NURSE ... **311**

Chapter 21—Computers and Oncology Nursing ... **313**
Janet B. Kelly, Gerry Hendrickson, and Luanne Citrin

General Capabilities of a Hospital Information System	314
Communicating Orders and Results between Nursing Units and Ancillary Departments	316
Nursing Process Application	318
Printouts and Reports	321
Confidentiality Issues	326
The Future	327
Conclusion	332
Study Questions	332

Chapter 22—New Instruction Technologies for Cancer Education: The Oncology Nurse Educator's Role ... **335**
Susan Bloch, Penny Ashwanden, and Dianne Howser

Computer-Assisted Instruction	336
Television and Video	340
Future Trends	348
Study Questions	349

**PART V: THE FUTURE: MOVING INTO THE
21ST CENTURY** 353

Chapter 23—What's Next for Oncology Nursing? 355
*Anne E. Belcher, E. Anne Hubbard Mattson,
Randi Moskowitz, Penny Ashwanden, Nancy E. Riese*

Oncology Nurses As Advocates 356
Quality Assurance 357
Specialist and Generalist 358
Oncology Nurses in Preventive Education 359
Oncology Nurses in Critical Care and Rehabilitation 360
Preparation for Oncology Nursing As a Specialty 361

Index 365

Contributors

Penny Ashwanden, BA
Deputy Director
Division of Communications and Development
Columbia University Comprehensive Cancer Center
New York, New York

Anne E. Belcher, PhD, RN
Associate Professor
University of Maryland School of Nursing
Baltimore, Maryland

Susan Bloch, MEd
Program Coordinator
Division of Communications and Development
Columbia University Comprehensive Cancer Center
New York, New York

Nancy Bookbinder, BA, BSN, MPH
Executive Director
Desert Hospital
Palm Springs, California

Robin B. Brenner, RN, BSN
Director of Clinical Services
PROTOCARE, Inc.
Elmsford, New York

Penelope Buschman, RN, MS, CS
Research Nurse Clinician
Babies Hospital
Assistant Professor of Clinical Nursing
Columbia University School of Nursing
New York, New York

Kathleen M. McMahon Casey, RN, MEd, OCN
Nurse Clinician II
Memorial Sloan-Kettering Cancer Center
New York, New York

Luanne Citrin, RN, MSN
Oncology Nurse Specialist
New York University Medical Center
University Hospital
New York, New York

Nessa Coyle, RN, MS, ANP
Director
Supportive Care Program
Pain Service, Department of Neurology
Memorial Sloan-Kettering Cancer Center
New York, New York

Noreen Coyne, RN, MS, ANP
Home Care Intake Coordinator
Visiting Nurse Service of New York
Memorial Sloan-Kettering Cancer Center
New York, New York

Nancy Scannell D'Agostino, RN, MSN
Calvary Hospital
Bronx, New York

Susan Ann Derby, RN, MA, OCN, CGNP
Nurse Clinician
Memorial Sloan-Kettering Cancer Center
New York, New York

Dolores M. Esparza, RN, MSN
President
Esparza Oncology Consultants, Inc.
San Antonio, Texas

Ruth Nuscher Ford, RN, OCN, MSN
Nurse Clinician
Bone Marrow Transplantation Service
Memorial Sloan-Kettering Cancer Center
New York, New York

Margaret L. Fracaro, RN, MA, CIC
Infection Control Coordinator, Epidemiology
Columbia-Presbyterian Medical Center
New York, New York

Martha E. Haber, RN, MA
Formerly, Vice President for Nursing
The Presbyterian Hospital
New York, New York

Joanne D. Hayes, RN, MA
President
The Nexus Group
Nutley, New Jersey

Gerry Hendrickson, PhD
Assistant Professor of Public Health
Center for Medical Informatics
Columbia University
New York, New York

Dianne M. Howser, RN, BSN, OCN
Special Assistant for Clinical Affairs
Medicine Branch
National Cancer Institute
Bethesda, Maryland

Jeanne Kalinoski, RN, MA
AIDS Education Program Coordinator and Assistant Director of Nursing, AIDS Team
Bellevue Hospital Center
New York, New York

Janet B. Kelly, RN, MA
Assistant Director
Hospital Information System-Nursing Coordinator
New York University Medical Center
University Hospital
New York, New York

Glenda B. Kelman, RN, MS, CS, OCN
Nursing Consultant
Cohoes, New York

E. Anne Hubbard Mattson, RNC, MS, MPH, ANP
Coordinator of Adult Health Sciences
Jefferson County Health Department
Birmingham, Alabama
Formerly, Assistant Dean and Acting Director, Master's in Oncology Program
Columbia University School of Nursing
New York, New York

Melissa Meyers, RN, MA
Oncology Nurse Specialist
New York University Medical Center
University Hospital
New York, New York

Randi Moskowitz, RN, MS, MBA
Executive Director
Cancer Institute of Brooklyn
Brooklyn, New York

Anita Nirenberg, RN, OCN, BSN
Director and President
Anita Nirenberg Out-Patient Agency Ltd.
New York, New York

Sarina Petrolino-Roche, RN, OCN, MSN
Nurse Clinician
Bone Marrow Transplantation Unit
Memorial Sloan-Kettering Cancer Center
New York, New York

Russell K. Portenoy, MD
Director, Analgesic Studies
Pain Service, Department of Neurology
Assistant Attending Neurologist
Memorial Sloan-Kettering Cancer Center
Assistant Professor of Neurology
Cornell University Medical Center
New York, New York

Nancy E. Riese, RN, MS
Research Nurse
Joint Center for Radiation Therapy
Boston, Massachusetts

Colleen Scanlon, RNC, MS, OCN
Psychiatric Nurse Clinician
Calvary Hospital
Bronx, New York

Brenda Shelton, RN, BSN, MSN
Research Nurse
Johns Hopkins Oncology Center
Baltimore, Maryland

Jo Anne Staats, RN, MSN, ANP
Nurse Practitioner
Bailey House/AIDS Resource Center
New York, New York

Roberta A. Strohl, RN, MN
Clinical Nurse Specialist
Department of Radiation Oncology
University of Maryland at Baltimore
Baltimore, Maryland

I. Bernard Weinstein, MD
Director
Comprehensive Cancer Center
Frode Jensen Professor of Medicine
Columbia University
President American Association for Cancer Research
New York, New York

Cecilia Wilfinger, RN, BS
General Manager
PROTOCARE, Inc.
Elmsford, New York

Foreword

As we enter the last decade of the 20th century, the fields of cancer and acquired immunodeficiency syndrome research—and the monumental task of caring for patients with these diseases—are at a major crossroad. Enormous changes have occurred in our understanding of the basic biology of these and related diseases, and exciting new technologies are being developed that will provide new strategies for more effective prevention, diagnosis, and treatment. At the same time, there have been major social, ethical, and economic changes, and the organization structures of our health care systems are undergoing vast changes. To an increasing extent the field of nursing plays a central role in all these areas and has become the bridge that links the various subdisciplines. At the same time, there is an urgent need in the nursing field in general, and in the field of nursing oncology in particular, to acquire new skills related to the above mentioned changes.

This book is therefore extremely timely. It represents a most useful manual for those who wish to take up these exciting challenges. The authors are experts in their respective fields, and the topics covered in each of the 23 chapters are well focused and highly relevant. Indeed, this book should become a standard reference not only for oncology nurses but also for other health care professionals concerned with meeting the new problems and challenges that we face as we lay the ground work for the 21st century.

I. Bernard Weinstein, MD
Director, Comprehensive Cancer Center
Columbia University
President, American Association for
Cancer Research
New York, New York

Preface

During the past decade, oncology nursing has emerged as an important and established specialty essentially because cancer has been recognized as a major public health problem. This is documented by the fact that the Oncology Nursing Society (ONS) has grown since its inception in 1975 from an organization with 250 members to one with more than 15,000 members. In 1986 ONS offered the first certification examination to nurses working in the field, which has helped lend credibility to those who practice cancer nursing.

In 1987, the editors of this book identified a need to provide information to practicing oncology nurses about the latest advances in relation to new technologies. A conference entitled Technological Advances in Oncology Nursing was planned. The positive response to this program led to the development of this book.

Although the book is written primarily for the practicing oncology nurse, its format and style make it an excellent text of readings for students in graduate nursing programs. At the end of each chapter, there are study questions that will help the student formulate ideas and concepts.

In selecting the 34 contributors, the editors sought nationally recognized oncology experts from various geographic locations. The contributors represent many nursing roles, such as clinical specialist, educator, administrator, consultant, and nurse practitioner. They bring leadership, creativity, and knowledge of standards of practice to this book.

The book is divided into five sections with an introductory overview that consists of three chapters. These first three chapters provide a framework for the remainder of the book, addressing important issues such as the role of the oncology nurse, ethical concepts related to new technology, and the importance of health promotion in cancer care.

The five chapters of Part I, Current Advances in Treatment Modalities, present current information about the latest developments in the treatment of cancer and the role of the oncology nurse in the management of patient care. Topics include advances in radiation oncology, chemotherapy, surgery and biologic response modifiers, bone marrow transplantation, and pain management.

Part II, Significant Populations, includes six chapters about those populations with special needs such as the older patient, the terminally ill patient, and infants, children, adolescents, and adults with acquired immunodeficiency syndrome (AIDS).

In Part III, Specialized Health Care Delivery Systems, six chapters address various creative approaches to the development of cancer programs. These include ambulatory oncology services, free-standing cancer centers, shelters for homeless patients with AIDS, cooperative care, oncology nurse business ventures, and home chemotherapy services.

Part IV, Computers, Videos, and the Oncology Nurse, is divided into two chapters dealing with computers in oncology nursing in the hospital setting and new instruction technologies for cancer education.

Finally, in Part V, The Future: Moving into the 21st Century, a summary of the text is presented. The editors have made every attempt to discuss those important economic, financial, and legal issues that have come to the forefront of the health care arena in recent years and will certainly have an impact on cancer care in the 1990s and into the 21st century. Many questions that arose in the compilation of the book but were not answered are also included as being of future concern.

The editors would like to express sincere appreciation to the contributors for their hard work and perseverance over the past year and a half. Without their expertise and good humor, this book could never have been published.

Special appreciation and thanks go to Deborah Kennington at Columbia University for her expert typing and computer skills and for her long hours of work in putting together this manuscript. Appreciation also goes to Daphine Miller for managing the typing at the University of Maryland.

Finally, the editors would like to thank their respective spouses and significant others, including Buzz Mattson, Carl Miller, and Marc Moskowitz, for their support through the many hours of meetings and preparation for this publication.

Penny Ashwanden
Anne E. Belcher
E. Anne Hubbard Mattson
Randi Moskowitz
Nancy E. Riese

July 1990

Introduction

As the field of oncology nursing continues to expand, the need for a comprehensive text with which to move this specialty into the 1990s and beyond is most apparent. This book not only provides a reference tool to expand the knowledge and practice of nurses already in the field but also serves to alert all nurses to the satisfactions of this dynamic and rewarding specialty.

The contributors are eminent in their respective fields and represent diverse centers of excellence throughout the United States in the care and treatment of people with cancer and acquired immunodeficiency syndrome (AIDS). Because these patients require care in various settings, from high-technology nursing to home nursing, experts who practice in complex medical centers, ambulatory care units, hospices, and homes share their knowledge of the nursing of adults and children with cancer and AIDS.

This book addresses the challenges of the future and explores trends and issues as nurse care providers, managers, researchers, teachers, and consultants utilize new technologies to advance the quality of nursing practice. As well as examining current advances in treatment modalities and patient populations of particular significance, the book reports on some interesting models of alternative health care delivery as well as on how computers and video technologies are being used in hospital and education settings. All the authors attempt to predict future directions and concerns for oncology nursing in the coming decades.

Martha E. Haber, RN, MA
Former Vice President of Nursing
Presbyterian Hospital in the City of New York
New York, New York

Chapter 1

The Oncology Nurse As Manager, Researcher, Care Provider, Teacher, and Consultant

Anne E. Belcher

> The roles of the oncology nurse—manager, researcher, care provider, teacher, and consultant—are being affected by various changes in care provision, health care, financing, and allocation of scarce resources. With each of these changes come challenges: maintaining quality of care, developing more cost-effective delivery systems, and recruiting and retaining health care providers. Each challenge has implications for the oncology nurse's roles.

Oncology nurses are practicing in a time of constant and rapid change that affects the way care is provided and financed as well as the resources available for providing care. With these changes come challenges: maintaining quality of care, developing more cost-effective delivery systems, and recruiting and retaining adequate numbers of health care providers.

There is no doubt that the restructuring of health care and the changing economics of health care are affecting the roles of the oncology nurse. The tremendous growth in ambulatory care and home care services has provided opportunities for nurses to develop collaborative practices among themselves or with other health care providers such as physicians; to function autonomously with or without physician-generated protocols; and to become entrepreneurs, especially in home care. The initiation of prospective payment by the Health Care Finance Administration, which is now being adopted by many third-party payers, has given oncology nurses the opportunity to document and cost out nursing care on the basis of patient acuity and nursing care hours.

As Baird (1988) emphasized, cancer care continues to use more hospital dollars than other diseases; hospital care expenditures account for 60% to 75% of the total direct cost of cancer care compared to 35% to 50% for all diseases. Tillman (1984) determined that the number of hours of nursing care per oncology patient day was significantly higher than that required by general medical-surgical patients. Specific areas of nursing care around which the hours clustered were medication administration, teaching, monitoring of the treatment response, and supportive care.

The emphasis on shortened hospital length of stay, which represents one effort to decrease this direct cost, has caused oncology nurses as care providers in acute care settings to assess more rapidly patients' potential problems, to emphasize self-care, to determine family/significant others' ability to assist the patient with home care, and to identify and coordinate necessary resources in preparation for discharge to the home or another care facility.

The oncology nurse as both care provider and manager can counteract many adverse cost-containment initiatives by quantifying the level of staffing on oncology units in terms of patient acuity, patient and family education needs, and the frequent changes in patient prescriptions (Baird 1988). Nurses at the unit level should be encouraged to monitor their use of supplies and equipment, to participate in product evaluation, and to collaborate with the departments responsible for supplying and maintaining equipment, treatment trays, and so on to generate supportive data.

New technologies have challenged oncology nurses to redefine standards of care, to revise staff development and patient education programs, and to develop expertise in the use of computers and other high-technology devices such as patient-controlled analgesia, venous access devices, and infusion pumps. The oncology nurse, functioning as care provider and manager, must maintain and update knowledge and clinical competence regarding these and other new technologies. As teacher and consultant, the nurse must educate staff, patients, and families regarding the use of the new technologies for improving the quality of care provided. As consultant and researcher, the nurse must test the efficacy of the new technologies for patient care, evaluate their impact on other activities of nurse and patient, and determine the resultant need for changes in standards of care.

Shrinking resources, specifically the declining numbers of nurses being educated and retained in the health care system, challenge the oncology nurse to design innovative care delivery modes, to create effective recruitment and retention strategies, and to enhance the public image of nursing. As Mayer (1989) recently stated:

> As a nursing specialty organization, the Oncology Nursing Society is committed to advancing the whole profession of nursing while we continue to improve our daily practices in cancer nursing.

She goes on to cite the findings of the final report of the Secretary's Commission on Nursing, which was released in December 1988 (Department of Health and Human Services 1988). The Commission's recommendations include provision of sufficient support services for nurses, use of the most appropriate mix of nursing personnel, adoption of automated information technologies to increase the productivity of the registered nurse, improvement of internal management of nurse resources in health care organizations, and increasing compensation with incremental and progressive salary adjustments throughout the nurse's career.

The nurse as consultant should assume a leadership role in the implementation of these findings in the care setting. There is no doubt that recruitment and retention of nurses will have a major impact on oncology nursing in the years to come. As teacher, the nurse can serve as a role model to prospective and enrolled nursing students, as preceptor to new graduates, and as mentor to nurses wishing to enhance their effectiveness as oncology nurses. As teacher in the community, such as a volunteer for the American Cancer Society, the oncology nurse reaches youth, who might develop an interest in nursing as a career, as well as the lay public, whose broadened perspective on oncology nursing might increase their likelihood of recruiting for and being supportive of oncology nursing.

The design of innovative care delivery systems provides the nurse as care provider and manager with the opportunity to reevaluate existing roles and relationships in both traditional and new settings. For example, nurses at such facilities as Johns Hopkins Oncology Center have developed a model of shared governance that addresses professional nurses' need for autonomy and accountability. Oncology nurses in various settings have developed collaborative practices with physicians (i.e., ambulatory care and physician's office services) and with one another as well as independent practices, home care services, and hospice services.

Yasko (1988) described the emerging role of the oncology nurse in the ambulatory care setting as that of care manager. In this role, the nurse would function as:

- the primary health care provider, to whom patients and family/significant others would relate when questions arise or problems develop
- the collaborator with medical, surgical, and radiation oncologists through caseload management (planning, teaching, and counseling for home care)
- the researcher in the areas of patients' self-care needs, effective teaching strategies, compliance, and third-party reimbursement

Another area of growth will be that of geriatric oncology, with the challenge being ensuring this population's access to costly new forms of health care. As Donoghue (1988, 3) noted, oncology nurses must respond strongly to ensure that in the 21st century persons older than 65 years who have cancer "will not be denied treatment with therapies made possible by today's developments in the pharmaceutical and biotechnology industries . . . can participate in clinical trials, [and] have access to the highly specialized services of Cancer Centers. . . ."

The image of oncology nursing must be addressed to attract nurses to the specialty. The oncology nurse as teacher and consultant can represent the specialty at all levels in the health care institution as well as among other health care professionals and in the broader community. For example, providing instruction and service in the areas of cancer prevention and early detection enhances the nurse's image as a knowledgeable and caring professional who is as concerned about the public's health as about its illness.

As the emphasis shifts from diagnosing and treating all patient problems in the scope of nursing practice to identifying only essential needs, nurses are going to become increasingly frustrated. As Baird (1988, 4) observed:

> If you can't address all needs, how and by whom will decisions be made about what is left unaddressed? When those decisions threaten the safety, adequacy, or ethical foundations of professional nursing practice, how will we proceed?

The federal government is defining quality of care in terms of both cost containment and efficient use of services (Mortenson and Kerner 1987; O'Leary 1987). The Joint Commission on Accreditation of Healthcare Organizations also develops criteria that are used to define quality of care in terms of documentation and evaluation of care. Oncology nurses should be actively involved in the formulation of definitions, criteria, and measurements for the evaluation of quality of care in the context of the regulating and accrediting agencies. The nurse as care provider, manager, teacher, consultant, and researcher is in a unique position to define nursing standards of care, to implement them in the practice setting, to gather data regarding their use, and to evaluate the degree to which they are attained as well as their relevance to practice.

A related issue brought up by Baird (1988) is the moral and ethical challenges confronting the oncology nurse. There is the need to analyze, study, and teach nursing staff how to deal with such issues as do not resuscitate (DNR) status, informed consent, euthanasia, and withholding of treatment. In the roles of teacher, consultant, and researcher, the oncology nurse has numerous opportunities to address these and other dilemmas caused by changes in health care delivery.

Oncology nurses must also address care for the caregiver. In the current environment of change and challenges, nurses must assist one another to cope effectively and to maintain a creative and positive perspective on the issues to be addressed.

There is in each oncology nurse a potential for growth—for giving to patients, families, the community, and one another—that is beyond imagining and is rewarded in many intangible ways: in learning, in leading, in teaching, and most of all in caring. This is oncology nursing, now and always!

STUDY QUESTIONS

1. What strategies are oncology nurses using to deal with the impact of shortened length of stay on patient care?
2. What are the implications of new technologies for the oncology nurse in each of his or her roles?
3. Develop a plan for implementing one of the recommendations of the Secretary's Commission on Nursing.

REFERENCES

Baird, S. 1988. The changing economics of cancer care: Challenges and opportunities. In *Cancer care within the context of change in health care*. Atlanta: American Cancer Society.

Department of Health and Human Services. 1988. *Final report of the Secretary's Commission on Nursing*. Government Printing Office: Washington, D.C.

Donoghue, M. 1988. 2001: Opportunity or ??? *Innovations* 4:3, 15.

Mayer, D. 1989. Press release. Pittsburgh, Pa.: Oncology Nursing Society.

Mortenson, L., and J. Kerner. 1987. Striving for excellence: Evaluating quality of care in oncology. *Journal of Cancer Program Management* 2:21–28.

O'Leary, D. 1987. Quality control challenges in the new competitive marketplace. *Journal of Cancer Program Management* 2:6–10.

Tillman, M. 1984. A comparison of nursing care requirements of patients on general medical-surgical units and on an oncology unit in a community hospital. *Oncology Nursing Forum* 11:42–44.

Yasko, J. 1988. Will oncology nursing survive or thrive in today's health care system? *Innovations* 4:1, 16.

Chapter 2

Ethical Issues in Oncology Nursing Resulting from New Technologies

Penelope Buschman

> With rapid advances in technology for the diagnosis and treatment of cancer and with marked changes in the role of the nurse, the oncology nurse is faced with the responsibility of updating clinical practice, of knowing the patient, and of advocating on his or her behalf. To do this, the oncology nurse must possess a sound knowledge base, highly polished clinical skills, a profound understanding of the patient and family, and the courage to think reflectively, to question aggressively, and to articulate clearly. Reflective thinking, which is the basis of ethical nursing practice, must influence all decision making with and on behalf of the patient and family.

Ethics as an area of philosophy refers to the study of our moral conduct, not what we actually do but what we ought to do. Hopefully, there is some congruence between what we actually do and what we ought to do.

(Aroskar 1987, 2)

Moral questioning in nursing practice certainly is not a new phenomenon. As long as there have been practicing nurses, there has been reflective thinking about the implications of the care being offered (Muyskins 1982). In recent years, the need for moral reflection has been felt more strongly and urgently. Perhaps the primary reason for this urgency is that nurses feel less sure about what ought to be done than they have in the past (Muyskins 1982).

There are two major factors that contribute to this state of uncertainty. One is the changing nature of the role of the nurse, and the other is the wider range of possibilities for patient care made available by new technologies.

THE CHANGING ROLE OF THE NURSE

From the late 1960s until the present, the role of the nurse has changed dramatically from that of surrogate parent and physician's handmaiden to that of patient and family advocate. Let us consider briefly why the traditional models have lost favor (Muyskins 1982):

- the sex role stereotyping with which these models are linked has been challenged and made obsolete by the feminist movement
- our notions of the traditional roles of family members has changed dramatically
- technologic advances have affected the practice and conception of the nurse's role
- the changing age distribution of the population in the United States has resulted in a greater need for the services best provided by nursing—caring not curing

Why consider this evolution of role at all? Simply stated, it is because the moral responsibilities one has as a dependent professional differ greatly from those one has as a patient advocate. The American Nurses' Association (ANA) Code for Nurses, which replaced the International Code of Ethics for Nursing of 1950, is based on the concept of the nurse as client advocate. The ANA code can be summarized as follows (ANA 1976):

1. The nurse provides services with respect for human dignity and the uniqueness of the patient and unrestricted by considerations of social or economic status, personal attributes, or the nature of the patient's health problems.
2. The nurse safeguards the patient's right to privacy by judiciously protecting information of a confidential nature.
3. The nurse acts to safeguard the patient and the public when health care and safety are affected by the incompetent, unethical, or illegal practice of any person.
4. The nurse assumes responsibility and accountability for individual nursing judgments and actions.
5. The nurse maintains competence in nursing.
6. The nurse exercises informed judgment and uses individual competence and qualifications as criteria in seeking consultation, accepting responsibilities, and delegating nursing activities to others.
7. The nurse participates in activities that contribute to the ongoing development of the profession's body of knowledge.

8. The nurse participates in the profession's efforts to implement and improve standards of nursing.
9. The nurse participates in the profession's efforts to establish and maintain conditions of employment conducive to high-quality nursing care.
10. The nurse participates in the profession's efforts to protect the public from misinformation and misrepresentation and to maintain the integrity of nursing.
11. The nurse collaborates with members of the health professions and other citizens in promoting community and national efforts to meet the health needs of the public.

In terms of patient advocacy, Muyskins (1982, 36) states the nurse's responsibilities as follows:

> The nurse's role is, at its fundamental level, a moral one of insuring the dignity and autonomy of the client in need. The fundamental question concerning the nurse's role is what conception of the nurse will likely result in the most effective and efficient exercising of this primary nursing responsibility to ensure humane, dignified care.

Advocacy, then, is at its simplest every nursing action that helps ensure the dignity and autonomy of the patient and family. Listening, knowing, informing, clarifying, and speaking for the patient or helping the patient speak all are examples of advocacy. As a patient advocate the nurse is in a position to know the patient and family system, that is, to know something about their preferences, their history, and their belief systems.

The nurse as patient advocate brings with him or her a concern for ethics in a professional relationship: "It is by knowing those we care for through a process of privileged intimacy that we can understand and respond to their needs" (Noddings 1984). There is potential for conflict here when the nurse's own personal ethical assumptions and moral reasoning differ from those of the patient and family or, for that matter, from those of nurse and physician colleagues. The following clinical example illustrates conflict in the ethical arena.

In a large urban cancer center, parents of a 4-year-old child with stage IV neuroblastoma agreed to additional experimental chemotherapy in the hope that the child's severe pain might be alleviated. The parents decided when the pain did not abate that they wanted no further treatment for their child. Indeed, they wished to care for him at home. This they conveyed to all staff. Physicians and nurses encouraged them to continue, however, implying that it was their duty as parents. One staff nurse allied with the family, feeling as powerless as they. The child died quietly in the hospital. The mother and father were with him at the time of death and waited for 10 minutes before calling a nurse. They left the hospital quickly, wishing to have no further contact with staff.

How might the nurses as patient and family advocates have provided better care for this child and family? The wishes of these thoughtful and caring parents might have been heard and respected. The nurse as patient advocate might have assisted her colleagues in understanding the parents' position so that some staff might have been supportive and comforting to them in their grief. These parents might have been listened to and supported by nurses willing to take the risk of advocating. (Nurses are not socialized to risk taking!)

NEW TECHNOLOGIES

The second factor that contributes to a kind of uncertainty in terms of the ethical issues that influence nurses' caregiving is the rapidly developing technology used for the diagnosis and treatment of cancer.

Technologic advances bring with them new capabilities to maintain and sustain life. Nurses are now forced to examine issues that were taken for granted in the past. What is meant by life and death? When is the shift from active to palliative care made? When is no further treatment appropriate? Technologic advances in cancer treatment make these questions difficult to answer.

There are two major areas in which technology has altered significantly the course of cancer care. Think of the changes brought about by high-technology infusions. With them, nurses have the capability to provide both palliation and active care in the form of continued chemotherapy and administration of antibiotics, nutrition, and blood products long after an oncology patient is considered terminal. This expanded capability makes it difficult to modify or stop treatment, that is, to focus on issues of terminal care.

How do nurses present this expanded capability to patients and families? Do they listen to the wishes of the patient and family members? Selected statements from the ANA Committee on Ethics' recently released Guidelines on Withdrawing or Withholding Food and Fluid (ANA 1988) must be considered carefully:

- It is morally as well as legally permissible for nurses to honor the refusal of food and fluid by competent patients.
- If a patient has never been competent (i.e., in the case of infants, children, and mentally retarded persons and mentally ill persons who were never competent), nurses and others have the moral and professional responsibility to decide whether provision of food and fluid is in the patient's best interest.
- The views and moral sensibilities of caregiving family members should be influential in decisions for such patients unless there is clear indication that the family does not wish to be involved in decision making or is not competent or substitutes its own interests for those of the patient.

- The good conscience, security, and sense of well-being among citizens rests in part on the knowledge that the vulnerable will be nourished and that carefully considered refusals of food and fluid will be respected.

Until the 1980s, technologic advances in cancer treatment and care had been confined to the hospital or outpatient treatment areas. When decisions were made to terminate active treatment, the patient frequently went home to be with his or her family. Some hospitals developed a "swinging door" policy, allowing terminal patients to return for pain control and palliative treatment. Patients were encouraged to tell staff where they wished to die, and staff attempted to respect those wishes, providing support and services.

In the past 10 years, however, specialized home care agencies that hire nurses with critical care hospital experience have moved technology into the home. For many oncology patients and families this development in the expanded use of technology in the home setting has been good and welcome. Patients have remained in comfortable, familiar settings. Family members have assumed enormous responsibility for care and have been supportive and accommodating. Hospital beds and dollars have been saved. Nevertheless, there are important questions to be raised. Are there patients and families who need to be at home without the burden of technologically complex care? Are there parents who need to draw close to their dying children without the encumbrances and the responsibilities of caring for lines, pumps, and monitors? Are there homes and families too chaotic to accommodate this precise and ordered care? Do nurses assess thoroughly the patient's and family's needs and wishes before offering (and then frequently during) a home care experience with this technology?

For example, a mother who was caring lovingly and well for her terminally ill child at home with the support of high technology said "I feel guilty for saying this but I am so tired. When will it be over?" Another mother and father who maintained active care at home when their child was dying of recurrent leukemia commented sadly "Our last days with him were spent monitoring lines and blood products. We never talked."

RESEARCH ISSUES

Practicing oncology nurses have been providing ethical leadership on oncology units, in terminal care facilities, and in hospice programs. Nursing educators have been incorporating the teaching of ethics into oncology nursing curricula. Nurse scholars have contributed to the growing body of professional literature on ethical dimensions of oncology practice. Even so, there has been little oncology nursing research in the areas of communication and moral psychology, where language, values, attitudes, and belief systems provide rich and fertile grounds for inquiry.

These areas influence, of course, every patient-nurse and colleague-nurse relationship, and further research on these aspects of patient care is required.

CONCLUSION

The changing role of the oncology nurse in the hospital and home care agencies and the development of new technology in the diagnosis and treatment of cancer care make it imperative for oncology nurses to:

- examine and reexamine their moral and ethical assumptions
- be knowledgeable about diagnostic and treatment options (and their sequelae)
- assess the patient's and family's wishes, beliefs, values, and ethical assumptions (i.e., advocate for the patient and family, and transfer patient care responsibility if the conflict in ethical issues is too great)
- be present with the patient and family when treatment options and plans are presented, and assess the patient's and family's understanding of new technologies for which they have given consent
- encourage the patient and family to consider and articulate the quality-of-life issues they deem important, and be informed about and inform patients of options such as organ transplantation and living wills
- communicate with colleagues the wishes, beliefs, values, and ethical assumptions of the patient and family
- seek our active participation in institutional committees that examine ethical issues in patient care

As the practice of oncology nursing moves into the 21st century, the examination and reexamination of ethical issues in the face of developing technology is at once the nurse's grave responsibility and exciting challenge. It is in this arena that the oncology nurse becomes expert caregiver, sensitive patient advocate, and full contributing member of the health care team. As Aroskar (1987, 2) states:

> The ethical dimension is an integral part then of practice, education, and research for individual nurses in relation to clients, research subjects, or students and collectively as members of a profession fulfilling the responsibilities of a social mandate to: promote health, prevent illness, restore health, and alleviate suffering according to the International Council of Nurses Code.

STUDY QUESTIONS

1. What is the impact of reflective thinking on nursing practice?
2. How have developing technologies and the changing role of nursing contributed to uncertainty in the practice of oncology nursing?
3. What attributes contribute to effective and ethical practice in oncology nursing?

REFERENCES

American Nurses' Association. 1976. *Code for nurses with interpretive statements.* Kansas City, Mo.: American Nurses' Association.

American Nurses' Association Committee on Ethics. 1988. *Ethics in nursing.* Kansas City, Mo.: American Nurses' Association.

Aroskar, M.A. 1987. Ethics in the leadership equation. Paper presented at the Dean's Distinguished Lecture Series, 24 September, Columbia University School of Nursing, New York.

Muyskins, J. 1982. *Moral problems in nursing.* Totowa, N.J.: Rowman & Littlefield.

Noddings, N. 1984. *Caring: A feminine approach to ethics and moral education.* Los Angeles: University of California Press.

SUGGESTED READINGS

Jameston, A. 1984. *Nursing practice: The ethical issues.* Englewood Cliffs, N.J.: Prentice-Hall.

Kohnke, M.F. 1982. *Advocacy: Risk and reality.* St. Louis, Mo.: C.V. Mosby.

Chapter 3

Health Promotion and Disease Prevention: Oncology Nursing in the Year 2000

E. Anne Hubbard Mattson

> Theories of carcinogenesis, which are so important to the understanding of why, where, how, and when to prevent and detect early cancer, are explored. Principles of public health, epidemiology, and nursing such as screening guidelines, cost effectiveness, high-risk populations, and incidence and trends in the development of cancer and acquired immunodeficiency syndrome (AIDS) are presented. A review of recommendations for a select group of cancers is included to lay the foundation for further nursing research, community health care planning, health policy initiatives, and financial and administrative considerations. Because preventive interventions also necessitate health counseling, the primary areas of nutrition, tobacco usage, sun exposure, AIDS prevention, and occupational-environmental exposures are also reviewed.

The essence of the practice of nursing is to promote health, whether it is the health of a person with a critical illness or the health of a carefree youth who has not yet contemplated his or her own mortality. The definition of the practice or act of nursing is as follows (New York State 1988, 62):

> The practice of the profession of nursing as a registered professional nurse is defined as diagnosing and treating human responses to actual or potential health problems through such services as case finding, health teaching, health counseling and the provision of care supportive to or restorative of life and well-being.

Whether the task is case finding, health teaching, or health counseling to maximize health and well-being, nursing practice *is* health promotion and disease prevention in the acute care setting, in the community, and in industry and business settings. It is within the independent role of oncology nursing to prevent and detect cancer and acquired immunodeficiency syndrome (AIDS) in their earliest and most treatable stages.

For the future, it is imperative that nurses adopt a well-conceived and well-thought-out vision of the health care system and the profession. As the 21st century nears, nurses involved in the health care system take with them the obligation to deliver cost-effective services to implement the professional nursing role. Nursing in general is charged with the continued development of cost-effective models of care that positively influence patient care. Measuring and accounting for those quality care outcomes are the goals toward which the entire health care system will be working. The cost-effective delivery of primary care services by nurses has been thoroughly reviewed and documented (Cosby, Ventura, and Feldman 1987; Stanford 1987). Oncology nurses are currently functioning as health educators in AIDS and cancer, screening and counseling coordinators, cancer control project consultants, health policy activists in the areas of primary and secondary prevention health services, prevention and detection specialists in nursing education, and expert clinicians in primary care services in a multitude of occupational, AIDS-related, and oncology health care delivery settings. The provision of primary and secondary preventive services in a profitable fashion will be the mandate for oncology nurses in the 21st century.

Primary, secondary, and tertiary prevention refer simply to the prevention of disease, further disease, and side effects from disease, respectively. Mausner and Kramer (1985) define primary prevention as the prevention of disease by altering susceptibility or reducing exposure for susceptible individuals, secondary prevention as the early detection and treatment of disease, and tertiary prevention as the alleviation of disability resulting from disease and attempts to restore effective functioning. Primary and secondary prevention are the two areas most commonly referred to in health promotion and disease prevention interventions; they are implemented before the onset of grave disease.

It has been estimated that between 80% and 85% of all cancers are caused through environmental exposure and can be prevented (Farber 1988). The prevention of the spread of AIDS relies solely on the informed and motivated public at risk to stop its spread. Oncology nursing is in the position to contribute significantly to the coordination and delivery of these cancer- and AIDS-related control services and thus to humankind's health and well-being.

Frank-Stromborg (1988, 1834) in her address at the American Cancer Society's (ACS) Second National Conference on Cancer Prevention and Detection, stated that when one looks at the epidemiology of cancer and the National Cancer Institute's (NCI) Cancer Control Objectives for the Nation: 1985–2000 (1986) (Appendix 3-A) to reduce cancer mortality by 50%

> It becomes readily apparent that these goals will only be achieved with the involvement of all health professionals (i.e., physicians, nurses,

respiratory therapists) and that it is unrealistic to expect attainment with only the involvement of physicians . . . . Nurses, the largest group of health professionals . . . have historically taken a leadership role in implementing activities and programs that were designed to improve the health of members of the community.

It is time that nurses responded to this important cause and effectively implemented their role as health care providers. Nurses possess the independent decision-making authority and autonomy of practice to develop and implement institutional programs as well as individualized plans of care. Collaborative efforts with occupational health nurses, social workers, physicians, lay groups such as the Gay Men's Health Crisis, and other members of the health care system will remain integral to the successful delivery and follow-through of primary and secondary prevention and detection services.

Referral patterns to medical facilities and collaboration with medical providers for those individuals who are screened or counseled for cancer or AIDS and are positively identified are necessary to meet the continuum of care needs of this population. The necessary medical support in health promotion and disease prevention protocol implementation is clearly a vital component. The importance of the team approach in screening and health counseling services remains paramount to quality programming. The elderly have been recognized as a significant population to target in health promotion and disease prevention activities (Albert 1987; Yancik, Kessler, and Yates 1988).

CANCER PREVENTION ISSUES

Carcinogenesis

Carcinogenesis is the process by which a normal cell becomes cancerous. It is a tripartite process that includes an initiation phase, a promotion phase, and a progression phase.

Initiation is usually due to agents that stimulate the mutagenic process, such as chemicals, radiation, and viruses. Initiation is frequently associated with a permanent change in the phenotype of the target cell as a result of DNA restructuring or gene rearrangement (Farber 1988). Once this cell has entered the initiation phase there are a number of situations that affect the physiologic milieu to which it is exposed, thereby promoting cell mutation. One of these is oncogenesis. The oncogene, a segment of chromatin, is somehow triggered by point mutation or gene translocation to communicate with other cells and promote their transformation into potentially cancerous cells (VandeWoude and Gliden 1985). Cancer promoters are usually hormonal, environmental, nutritional, or genetic. During the promotion phase targeted cells form focal proliferations that resemble benign neoplasms (Farber 1988). Progression to cancer of these focal proliferations is self-generating but can be modulated to cause the proliferation to regress to normal-appearing tissue (Farber 1988). Understanding the concepts of progression of cellular growth toward malignancy and the agents involved (Appendix 3-A) supplies the foundation of knowledge with which to intercede in many ways to prevent cancer development.

LeMaistre (1988, 1674) reminds us that "85% of the causes for cancer are found in our lifestyle and environment. Now that we know this, we must take action on it . . . . We must avoid carcinogens as much as possible . . . we must make our treatments in the future more effective." Prevention and early detection, including screening for risk factors and the seven warning signals of cancer promulgated by the ACS (1989) (Exhibit 3-1), are important steps toward improving interventions in the future.

Screening for Neoplastic Diseases

Primary prevention refers to steps that can be taken by the asymptomatic (or healthy) population to avoid risk factors that might lead to the development of cancer. Secondary prevention involves screening asymptomatic people who may have already developed risk factors or preclinical disease. It is, in essence, early detection to diagnose a cancer or precursor to prevent further disease. Obtaining a Papanicolaou smear to detect cervical dysplasia before the development of cancer and performing testicular and breast examinations are forms of secondary prevention (ACS 1989; Preventive Services Task Force 1989).

When a screening program is developed, there are a number of factors that need to be taken into consideration to validate the effort and the potential effectiveness of the preventive intervention. The first consideration is the prevalence of the disease in the population, which is an indication of the burden of suffering.

Exhibit 3-1 Cancer's Seven Warning Signals

1. Change in bowel or bladder habits.
2. A sore that does not heal.
3. Unusual bleeding or discharge.
4. Thickening or lump in the breast or elsewhere.
5. Indigestion or difficulty in swallowing.
6. Obvious change in a wart or mole.
7. Nagging cough or hoarseness.

Source: Reprinted from *Cancer Facts and Figures 1988* by the American Cancer Society, 1989.

Prevalence includes the proportion of the population affected by the disease at any one time and the incidence or number of new cases per year.

Second, one needs to consider the efficacy of the screening test. For the screening method to be efficacious, it must be accurate and have a high predictive value. Predictive value is a function of the test's sensitivity and specificity. Sensitivity is defined as the proportion of people with a condition who correctly test positive; poor sensitivity generates a high proportion of false-negative results. Specificity is defined as the proportion of people without the disease who correctly test negative; poor specificity generates a high proportion of false-positive results. Efficacy is also measured by the test's reliability, or its ability to provide the same result when repeated.

Third, one needs to evaluate whether or not there is any benefit to the patient in having been diagnosed early. If early detection offers no added benefit over conventional diagnosis and treatment it is said to have minimal effectiveness, and the purpose of the screening must be evaluated further. AIDS screening has been controversial because of this criterion. Because there is no effective treatment for AIDS, many have argued that screening for the human immunodeficiency virus (HIV) antibody is futile.

Finally, the potential adverse effects of the screening intervention must also be considered in assessing the overall health impact of the screening. For example, one must consider the incidence of colonic perforation, cost of procedure, sensitivity, and diagnostic yield, and emotional costs to the patient who is subject to the high rate of false-positive results when evaluating the use of sigmoidoscopy as a screening procedure for colorectal cancer.

The following is a summary of recommendations for screening of a select number of cancer types proposed by the ACS (1989), NCI (1986), the Department of Health and Human Services and the Institute of Medicine (Department of Health and Human Services 1989), the Preventive Services Task Force (1989), and others. These recommendations offer the most current synthesis of research and epidemiologic evidence and incorporate the principles of effective screening programs.

Breast Cancer

Risk factors. Risk factors contributing to cancers of the breast include age older than 50 years, personal or family history of breast cancer, nulliparity, and first childbearing after age 30 (ACS 1989).

Incidence and trends. Over the last 30 years there has been a slight increase (3%) in the incidence of breast cancer in women. An estimated 142,000 new cases occurred in 1989 in the United States, which means 1 of 10 women will be diagnosed with breast cancer during the lifetime (ACS 1989). The rate for men over the last 30 years has remained constant at 0.3 to 0.2 cases per 100,000 population (ACS 1989).

Recommendations. The Preventive Services Task Force (1989, 39) makes the following recommendation:

> All women over age 40 should receive an annual clinical breast examination. Mammography every 1–2 years is recommended for all women beginning at age 50 and concluding at approximately age 75 unless pathology has been detected. It may be prudent to begin mammography at an earlier age for women at high risk for breast cancer. Although the teaching of breast self-examination . . . is not specifically recommended at this time, there is insufficient evidence to recommend any change in current breast self-examination practices.

The ACS (1989) and NCI (1986) recommend monthly breast self-examination and regular clinical examination of the breast for all women, baseline mammography between the ages of 35 and 40 years with subsequent annual or biannual mammography from ages 40 to 49 years, and annual mammography beginning at age 50. These recommendations have been supported by other groups such as the American Medical Association (AMA) and the American College of Gynecology; the American College of Radiology, the Canadian Task Force on Periodic Health Examination (1979), and the American College of Physicians (1981) support annual clinical breast examinations for all women starting at age 40 but do not recommend beginning yearly mammography until age 50 (Preventive Services Task Force 1989). Dodd (1988) urges clinicians to educate the public about the decreased mortality of breast cancer associated with early detection. He maintains that mammography and physical examination have not been generally effective mainly because of underutilization. Owen and Long (1989) and Redeker (1989) have made significant contributions to the body of knowledge about breast cancer and have provided clinicians with tools to facilitate compliance with these screening guidelines.

The World Health Organization states that there is insufficient evidence to support the effectiveness of breast self-examination in reducing mortality from breast cancer. Thus it does not recommend self-examination screening programs as public health policy, although it finds equally insufficient evidence to change such programs where they already exist (Preventive Services Task Force 1989).

Colorectal Cancer

Risk factors. A high-fat, low-fiber diet has been recognized as a significant factor in the development of colorectal cancer. A family or personal history of polyps, inflammatory bowel disease, or colorectal cancer is also an associated risk factor (ACS 1989).

Incidence and trends. In 1989 there were an estimated 151,000 new cases of colorectal cancer (107,000 cases of colon cancer and 44,000 cases of rectal cancer) in the United States. Over the last 30 years there has been a slow but steady decrease in the incidence of rectal cancer and colon cancer in women. Men have shown an increase of 22% since the mid-1950s (ACS 1989).

Recommendations. There is insufficient evidence to recommend for or against fecal occult blood testing or sigmoidoscopy as effective screening tests for colorectal cancer in asymptomatic persons. There are also inadequate grounds for discontinuing this form of screening where it is currently practiced or for withholding it from persons who request it. It may be clinically prudent to offer screening to persons aged 50 years and older with known risk factors for colorectal cancer (Preventive Services Task Force 1989).

The ACS (1989) recommends three tests for the early detection of colon and rectum cancer in people without symptoms. The digital rectal examination, performed by a physician during an office visit, should be performed every year after the age of 40; the stool blood test is recommended every year after age 50, and the proctosigmoidoscopy examination should be carried out every 3 to 5 years in persons older than 50 years after two annual examinations with negative results. DeCosse (1988) offers further in-depth commentary on the ACS recommendations for the interested clinician.

Cervical Cancer

Risk factors. For cervical cancer, risk factors are multiple sex partners and early age at first intercourse. Epidemiologic studies have concluded that an infectious agent plays an etiologic role (Gusberg 1988). The human papilloma virus has been implicated as the prime initiating agent as well as herpesvirus type 1 and cigarette smoking (Gusberg 1988).

Incidence and trends. An estimated 13,000 cases of cancer of the cervix will occur in the United States in 1989 (ACS 1989). The incidence of invasive cervical cancer has fallen steadily over the years, but the incidence of cervical carcinoma in situ has risen in all groups. Low socioeconomic groups have a high incidence of disease (ACS 1989).

Recommendations. The Preventive Services Task Force (1989) concludes that regular Papanicolaou smear testing is recommended for all women who are or have been sexually active. Smears should begin with the onset of sexual activity and should be repeated every 1 to 3 years at the physicians's discretion. They may be discontinued at age 65 if previous smears have been consistently normal.

The ACS (1989) recommends that women who are or have been sexually active or have reached age 18 years should have an annual Papanicolaou smear and pelvic examination. After a woman has had three or more consecutive satisfactory normal annual examinations, the smear may be performed less frequently at the discretion of her physician.

Prostate Cancer

Risk factors. The risk factor contributing most significantly to the incidence of prostate cancer is age; about 80% of all prostate cancers are diagnosed in men older than 65 years (ACS 1989). There is some familial association, but it is unclear whether this is due to genetic or environmental factors (ACS 1989). Exposure to cadmium, lifestyle, and high dietary fat intake may be contributing factors in the development of prostate cancer (ACS 1989).

Incidence and trends. About 1 of 11 men will develop prostate cancer in the lifetime. An estimated 103,000 cases will have occurred in the United States in 1989. The 30-year trend for prostate cancer shows a slight overall increase of about 9% (ACS 1989).

Recommendations. The Preventive Services Task Force (1989) notes that there is insufficient evidence to recommend for or against routine digital rectal examinations as an effective screening test for prostate cancer in asymptomatic men. Routine transrectal ultrasonography and screening for serum tumor markers are not recommended in asymptomatic men.

The ACS and NCI recommend an annual digital rectal examination for both prostate and colorectal cancer beginning at age 40. The Canadian Task Force on Periodic Health Examination (1979) and others have advised against routine screening for prostate cancer. A technology assessment panel convened by the AMA recently concluded that the role of transrectal ultrasonography in screening for prostate cancer is investigational (Preventive Services Task Force 1989).

Lung Cancer

Risk factors. Cigarette smoking, particularly a history of smoking for 20 years or more, is by far the most common risk factor for the development of lung cancer. Asbestos, radon, and radiation exposure have also been recognized as contributing to the development of lung cancer (Department of Health and Human Services 1986, 1989). Passive or involuntary smoking also increases the risk (ACS 1989).

Incidence and trends. The most significant rise in cancer over the last 30 years has occurred in lung cancer, which has increased almost 400% in women and 161% in men. This steady increase is attributed most directly to cigarette smoking (ACS 1989). More than 155,000 new cases are estimated to occur in the United States in 1989, with an estimated 142,000 deaths being expected (ACS 1989).

Recommendations. According to the Preventive Services Task Force (1989), screening asymptomatic persons for lung cancer by performing routine chest radiography or sputum cytology is not recommended. All persons should be counseled about the use of tobacco products. There is a consensus of opinion that current evidence is insufficient to support routine screening for lung cancer among asymptomatic persons. This is the official policy of the ACS, NCI, Food and Drug

Administration, and others. Early warning signs include a persistent cough, sputum streaked with blood, chest pain, or recurring attacks of pneumonia or bronchitis (ACS 1989).

Skin Cancer

Risk factors. People with fair complexions, those who have had severe sunburn in childhood, and those who have occupational exposure to coal tar, pitch, creosote, arsenic compounds, or radium are at a high risk for developing melanoma (ACS 1989).

Incidence and trends. The incidence of melanoma is increasing at the rate of 3.4% per year (ACS 1989). Over the last 30 years there has been a 29% increase in all skin cancers, including basal and squamous cell types, in the male population and only slight fluctuations in the female population (ACS 1989). It is estimated there are more than 500,000 new cases of skin cancer per year, with 27,000 of those cases being melanomatous (ACS 1989).

Recommendations. Routine screening for skin cancer is recommended for persons at high risk, according to the Preventive Services Task Force (1989). Clinicians should advise all patients with excessive outdoor exposure to use sun screen preparations and other measures to protect their skin from ultraviolet rays. Currently there is no evidence for or against counseling patients to perform skin self-examination. The American Academy of Dermatology recommends an annual, complete skin examination by a physician, to be supplemented by monthly self-examinations of the skin. People should be taught to evaluate moles and skin for alterations such as scaliness, oozing, bleeding, change in size or color, itchiness, tenderness, or spread of pigment beyond the border. It also recommends advising patients to limit sun exposure and to use sun screens and protective clothing when exposed to sunlight. The ACS and NCI recommend including a complete skin examination as part of the routine periodic health examination. The Canadian Task Force advises against routine screening but recommends skin examinations for those in high-risk groups.

The ACS recommends using the "ABCD" method to remember the early warning signs of melanoma: asymmetry of mole, border irregularity, color not uniform, and diameter greater than 6 mm. The ACS recommends that adults at high risk should practice skin self-examination once a month (ACS 1989).

Testicular Cancer

Risk factors. History of atrophic cryptorchidism (undescended testes), orchiopexy, or testicular atrophy is associated with an increased incidence of testicular cancer.

Incidence and trends. Testicular cancer is the most common carcinoma in males 15 to 35 years old (Einhorn et al. 1985), although it accounts for only 1% of all male malignancies. An estimated 5,700 new cases will occur in 1989 in the United States (ACS 1989).

Recommendations. The Preventive Services Task Force (1989) states that periodic screening for testicular cancer by testicular examination is recommended for men with a history of cryptorchidism, orchiopexy, or testicular atrophy. There is insufficient evidence of clinical benefit or harm to recommend for or against routine screening of other asymptomatic men for testicular cancer. Clinicians should advise adolescents and young adults to seek prompt medical attention for testicular symptoms such as pain, swelling, or heaviness. Currently there is insufficient evidence for or against counseling patients to perform periodic self-examination of the testicles.

The ACS and NCI recommended that testicular examination be included as part of the periodic health examination of men. The Canadian Task Force, however, recommends that screening should be performed only on patients with a history of cryptorchidism, testicular atrophy, or ambiguous sex. Recommendations differ on whether patients should be counseled to perform monthly testicular self-examination. Clinicians have been advised to instruct their male patients in how to perform this examination, and some authorities believe that the technique should be reviewed at every periodic health visit beginning with puberty and continuing throughout life (Lindberg 1987).

Ovarian Cancer

Risk factors. Age greater than 65 years, nulliparity, history of breast or endometrial cancer, and history of colorectal cancer are risk factors for ovarian cancer (ACS 1989).

Incidence and trends. Approximately 20,000 new cases are estimated to occur in the United States in 1989. Over the last 30 years there has been a 9% decrease in the incidence of ovarian cancer (ACS 1989).

Recommendations. The Preventive Services Task Force (1989) does not recommend screening of asymptomatic women for ovarian cancer. It is prudent to examine the uterine adnexa when performing gynecologic examinations for other reasons.

Although there are no official recommendations to screen for ovarian cancer in asymptomatic women, the pelvic examination was mentioned in a recent consensus recommendation on Papanicolaou smear testing issued by the ACS and NCI. The pelvic examination and Papanicolaou smear are recommended annually for all women who are or have been sexually active or have reached age 18. Although Papanicolaou smears may be performed less frequently once three annual smears have been normal, the organizations did not specifically recommend reducing the frequency of the pelvic examination (Preventive Services Task Force 1989).

Pancreatic Cancer

Risk factors. Because there are no early warning signs of pancreatic cancer, risk factor avoidance is the best method of prevention. Cigarette smoking is the greatest known risk factor for pancreatic cancer, which occurs twice as often in the smoking population. An association with diseases of the pancreas such as diabetes or chronic pancreatitis has been suggested. Cirrhosis, high-fat diets, and coffee have also been implicated as risk factors in the development of pancreatic cancer, although these associations are not conclusive from current evidence (ACS 1989).

Incidence and trends. Pancreatic cancer ranks as the fifth leading cause of death due to cancer in the United States. Over the last 30 years there has been a steady increase in pancreatic cancer deaths, with a 12% change being noted in the male population and a 26% change in the female population (ACS 1989). An estimated 27,000 new cases are expected to occur in the United States in 1989, and 25,000 deaths from pancreatic cancer are expected (ACS 1989).

Recommendations. The Preventive Services Task Force does not recommend routine screening for pancreatic cancer in asymptomatic persons.

Oral Cancer

Risk factors. Cigarette, cigar, and pipe smoking, use of smokeless tobacco, and excessive use of alcohol are associated with 82% of oral carcinomas in the 15- to 91-year-old population (Silverman 1988) and are considered potential risk factors in oral cancer development (ACS 1989).

Incidence and trends. Over the last 30 years there has not been any change in the overall incidence of oral cancer (ACS 1989). An estimated 31,000 new cases will occur in 1989. In the United States the ratio of occurrence in men to that in women is almost 2:1 (ACS 1989).

Recommendations. According to the Preventive Services Task Force (1989), routine screening of asymptomatic persons for oral cancer by primary care clinicians is not recommended. It may be prudent for clinicians to perform careful examinations for cancerous lesions of the oral cavity in patients who use tobacco or excessive amounts of alcohol as well as in those with suspected symptoms or lesions detected through self-examination. All patients should be counseled to receive regular dental examinations, to discontinue the use of all forms of tobacco, and to limit their consumption of alcohol. Persons with increased exposure to sunlight should be advised to take protective measures to protect their lips and skin from the harmful effects of ultraviolet rays.

The Canadian Task Force (1979) recommends that an annual visual inspection of the mouth be made that includes an examination for oral cancer in men and in all smokers. Similarly, the ACS and NCI recommend that a complete oral examination for cancer be included in the periodic health examination.

Counseling

The most effective interventions available to clinicians for reducing the occurrence of the leading causes of cancer and AIDS are related to decreasing the incidence of smoking, improving nutrition, and modifying sexual practices (NCI 1986; National Academy of Sciences 1989). Sun exposure, alcohol and other drug abuse are lifestyle characteristics that have been addressed in preventive counseling with success (Holm et al. 1989; Love, Rodnick, and McPhee 1988; Schweitzer 1988). These personal behavior patterns can be effectively modified and eradicated from patients' lifestyles with appropriate attention to the principles of health education, counseling, behavior modification, and the health promotion model (Pender 1987; Shannon 1989; Weitzel 1989). Lifestyle changes will necessarily need to be addressed not only on an individual basis through counseling but also on a broader scale through alteration of cultural norms and societal appreciation of the effect of behavior on the potential outcome of disease. Public and private business, the media, and government sectors will need to be involved in and support good health. Oncology nurses can be at the forefront of these efforts through providing counseling and leadership in community cancer prevention programs.

Counseling To Prevent Tobacco Usage

Tobacco is the largest nonfood cash crop grown on the face of the earth. Cigarette smoking is not only the single most preventable cause of cancer; it is also the single most preventable cause of all disease. Ernster (1988) notes that about 30% of all cancers are related solely to cigarette smoking. An even greater cancer mortality figure is attributable to all tobacco product usage. Cancers of the lung, larynx and oral cavity, esophagus, bladder and kidney, pancreas, and cervix have all been associated with cigarette smoking.

The challenge to the clinician is great in this area of counseling because of the immense hurdles the smoker needs to surmount in breaking the habit. The powerful addictive powers of nicotine combined with the marketing powers of the tobacco industry create a never-ending, supported desire for the smoker to continue. Ernster (1988) cites the 1984 Federal Trade Commission's report to Congress pursuant to the Federal Cigarette Labeling and Advertising Act, in which it was reported that the tobacco industry spent about $2.1 billion to advertise and promote cigarettes. The entire budget of the NCI in 1985 was just under $1.2 billion. The populations in the United States that have been the focus of these advertising efforts through direct and indirect marketing measures have been the ethnic minorities, low socioeconomic groups, children and teenagers, and women. It is these groups that the clinician should recognize will benefit from continued antismoking counseling.

The Preventive Services Task Force (1989) has outlined the following strategies that will increase the effectiveness of counseling regarding tobacco use:

1. Direct, face-to-face advice and suggestions that give the patient a brief, unambiguous, and informative statement about the need to stop using tobacco. If possible, the clinician should also review the short- and long-term health, social, and economic benefits to quitting and foster the smoker's belief in his or her ability to stop. The message should address the patient's concerns and any barriers presented by age, social environment, nicotine dependence, and general health. The patient should be alerted about withdrawal symptoms and should be persuaded to contract a "quit date" with the practitioner. Patients can be supported by saying that if they relapse back to smoking it is just part of the process and that most smokers achieve long-term cessation only after many unsuccessful attempts.
2. Scheduled reinforcement in the form of scheduled support visits or follow-up telephone calls, especially during the first 4 to 8 weeks.
3. Self-help materials.
4. Referral to community smoking cessation programs that have demonstrated efficacy.

Studies have shown that providing the most effective program depends on using a combination of approaches, such as a certain number of support visits, a certain number of months for which clinician support is followed-through, personal face-to-face advice, self-help materials, and the involvement of all health practitioners (Preventive Services Task Force 1989).

Nutrition Counseling

The ACS and NCI as well as the Surgeon General have all made position statements identifying the positive relationship between nutrition and decreased incidence of cancer. Illustrative research findings are too numerous to discuss in this context, but the reader is referred to the *Surgeon General's Report on Nutrition and Health* for an extensive scientific and epidemiologic literature review (Department of Health and Human Services 1988). Points that the ACS (1989), NCI (Butrum, Clifford, and Lanza 1988), and the Surgeon General outline for a healthy diet include the following:

1. *Avoid obesity*. People who weigh 40% more than their recommended body weight are at an increased risk for developing certain cancers. Increased

rates of breast, ovarian, uterine, colon, prostate, and gallbladder cancers have been identified in this group of individuals, although statistical significance cannot be noted as a result of the high number of confounding variables. Investigators postulate that this relationship may occur because chemical carcinogens may be stored in body fat for mobilization and transport to target tissues or because available energy is one factor that controls cell growth and that an excess of available energy may increase cell multiplication and affect the promotion phase of carcinogenesis or shorten the latent period (Pardee and Bakshi 1983; Scott, Wille, and Wier 1984). Siiteri (1987) offers a third hypothesis that involves the influences of estrogens on cancers in women, in whom metabolism of hormones in fat cells may stimulate carcinogenesis. Counseling to decrease body weight is much more complex than recommending a diet and exercise program. Most people need ongoing support from clinicians to gain an appreciation of the effect of losing weight and to have their noncompliant behavior clarified to gain insights and strength to maintain a desirable body weight (Foltz 1988). Zifferblatt and Wilbur (1977) and Glanz (1986) have outlined key elements of the more successful strategies in dietary change counseling. They are to set realistic, achievable, and measurable goals; to tailor recommendations to individual lifestyle and dietary preferences; to use whatever social support systems are available to provide training in skills as well as to provide information; to establish good communication between educator and patient; and to provide systematic follow-up, reinforcement, and monitoring. These principles of changing behaviors can be applied in many cancers caused by lifestyle as well (Eriksen et al. 1988).

2. *Cut down on total fat intake*. Breast, colon, and prostate cancers have been associated with a high fat content of the diet. Patients should be encouraged to reduce their fat intake to 30% or less of their caloric intake.
3. *Eat more high-fiber foods such as whole grain cereals, fruits, and vegetables*. A decrease in the incidence of cancer of the colon has been associated with high-fiber diets. Fiber should be increased to 20 to 30 g daily with an upper limit of 35 g (Butrum, Clifford, and Lanza, 1988).
4. *Include foods rich in vitamins A and C in the daily diet*. Cancer of the larynx, lung, and esophagus may be decreased with intake of vitamin A from foods such as carrots, spinach, sweet potatoes, peaches, and apricots and intake of vitamin C from foods such as oranges, tomatoes, green and red peppers, and grapefruit.
5. *Include cruciferous vegetables in the diet*. Vegetables such as broccoli, cauliflower, cabbage, and kohlrabi contain indoles, which may have a protective effect against colon cancer and possibly benzo(*a*)pyrene–induced lung and stomach cancers (Enigbokan and Okafor 1988).
6. *Moderate intake of salt-cured, smoked, and nitrite-cured foods*. Cancers of the stomach and esophagus have been associated with these foods as a result of by-product formation once the food is ingested.

7. *Keep alcohol consumption moderate.* Cancers of the oropharynx and liver have been associated with heavy use of alcohol, especially when accompanied by cigarette smoking or use of smokeless tobacco.

Byers (1988) calls for an increase in the number of clinical trials that involve evaluation of nutrition supplements. He also notes that observational nutrition research, or "metabolic epidemiology," may be methodologically flawed and calls for controlled longitudinal studies of modified diets for the purpose of cancer prevention in individuals at high risk (Byers and Funch 1984).

Lifestyle Changes

Prevention of infection with HIV. It is incumbent on the oncology nurse to maintain current knowledge of the etiology and mode of transmission of the AIDS virus. Other chapters in this book review strategies for preventing the transmission of the AIDS virus, but it is appropriate to reemphasize the importance of counseling and other prevention measures. Samuel O. Thier, President of the Institute of Medicine, in defining the approach to the prevention of AIDS states "The only way to stem the spread of infection remains the public health approach of educating people about how to avoid infection or, if they are infected, how not to infect others" (National Academy of Sciences 1989, ii). Pugliese and Lampinen (1989) identify clinical forms of prevention that are widely accepted in the health care system and that health care clinicians can implement. These methods of prevention include the responsibility to interpret HIV antibody results, limiting sexual transmission, screening blood and blood products, reducing risk among intravenous drug users, avoiding perinatal transmission, practicing safety measures in health care settings, and implementing education goals. These investigators state that the goals of counseling and education are to help uninfected persons initiate and sustain behavior changes that reduce their risk of becoming infected and to help those who are infected avoid infecting others. It is the stated position of the Oncology Nursing Society that oncology nurses already possess the knowledge base and clinical expertise to be leaders in the care of AIDS patients (Halloran, Hughes, and Mayer 1988). It is therefore the responsibility of the oncology nurse to lead in the early detection and prevention of its further effect through the promotion of healthy behaviors.

Sun exposure. The ACS (1989) recognizes that most of the 500,000 cases of nonmelanoma skin cancer are ultraviolet light related. Sun exposure is a major factor in the development of melanoma. Cancers of the skin are the most common malignant neoplasms in humans.

Because the skin is readily examined clinically, Kopf (1988) suggests that early detection and prevention of skin cancers is a realistic and achieveable goal. Primary education of the public covers three areas. First is the need to avoid unnecessary exposure to solar radiation and to protect the skin from damaging rays by using sun screens and protective clothing. Second, health care providers are in a position to recommend that patients not use and not support the use of products containing pollutants that destroy the earth's protective shield of ozone, which blocks out a major portion of the sun's ultraviolet (B) radiation. Third is the need to counsel high-risk individuals to perform personal skin examinations (Lawler and Schreiber 1989) and to have a yearly skin examination by a trained clinician (Kopf 1988).

COMMUNITY-BASED STRATEGIES FOR CANCER PREVENTION

The number of community-based prevention and detection programs in the United States is growing (Holm et al. 1989; Love, Rodnick, and McPhee 1988; McKenna and Eyre 1988; Schweitzer 1988). The advanced practice oncology nurse is in the position to be an expert clinical consultant to the public health architects of the community education programs. Before a truly healthy public can develop, the structure and foundation that is the community need to have a continuous, clear, comprehensive, and integrated approach to prevention and detection.

The definition of a community is broad and covers everything from the workplace, to a neighborhood, to a church or school group, to the local automobile industry workers, to the whole of society. Community-based strategies for cancer prevention are therefore just as varied, covering screening for environmental and occupational exposure to carcinogens (Appendix 3-B), the implementation of educational campaigns in the medical center aimed at increasing the number of women older than 35 years who undergo mammography, smoking cessation programs in Chinatown, and a host of others.

There are four stages to a community-based prevention program: planning, development, implementation, and evaluation. Each stage depends on the thoroughness of the preceding stage for its success.

The planning stage consists of obtaining the epidemiologic information that allows the identification, measurement, and definition of the problem or condition. This information will aid in identifying the need for the program. When the need is clearly defined, the other components of the planning stage fall into place. Identification of the resources in the community that are able to assist in the program, the community's demographic characteristics, and those social and cultural components that are important in the success or failure of the program is necessary during the planning stage. It is also important to consider the history of the community during the planning phase; for example, what are the internal and external forces and political situations that have allowed the need for the program to exist? Without a clear understanding of the history and a sensitivity to the constituent forces that have an interest in the success or failure of the prevention program, the program director would be set up for failure. It is not until the strategic planning phase is complete that the prevention program can be defined and developed, for without thoroughness in the planning stage crucial information will be missing that would have aided in the program development.

During the development phase all the preliminary steps that will aid in the actual implementation of the prevention program are identified, explored, and expanded. These steps include, but are not limited to, developing a program staffing pattern; setting up a pert-chart or time frame; putting together a budget proposal; identifying what outcome criteria will be used to measure the successfulness and effectiveness of the program; pulling together a marketing plan; developing a nursing, behavioral, sociologic, and theoretical framework to guide the implementation and to give substance to the strategic planning process; conceptualizing the actual education or screening program; and contacting identified community resources such as churches, employers, and individuals to enlist their collaboration in the project.

The implementation phase is the operational phase. It essentially involves following the recipe created in the development phase. Revisions of the development plan will inevitably and necessarily occur during the implementation phase as unforeseen circumstances arise that will shape the future direction of the program. It is very important to maintain an open and flexible approach in this phase and to keep in a dynamic flux with the other phases.

Throughout the implementation phase evaluation and tracking of the program will be ongoing. In community-based prevention programs the experimental design and scientific rigor of the evaluation cannot always be perfect because of inherent conflict between the researchers' and program director's needs and the broad needs and realities of the community. For instance, an antismoking program in Chinatown may not be able to claim that the decrease in the number of smokers in Chinatown during the prevention program was due solely to the program. This could be concluded only if there was a control group, representative of the experimental group, that was exposed to the same macromedia and other forces influencing smoking behavior as the Chinatown group.

The essence of a community approach is the saturation of a community with a coordinated campaign to educate the public through a combination of mass media, printed materials, and face-to-face activities. Education materials and community events are designed after nursing and social science research has been conducted on the determinants of individual lifestyle change and social change. The oncology nurse is in the unique position to combine expertise in patient education, administrative and organization planning, and research and clinical knowledge to coordinate and direct community-based prevention programs.

HEALTH POLICY ADVOCATES

A number of cancer types and risk factors have been examined thus far, but this review of prevention and detection would not be complete without highlighting two of the initiatives at the national level that are underway to decrease the toll of cancer.

The Environmental Protection Agency's Office of Pesticides recommends that safeguards for pesticides become more stringent and that protective equipment, training for pesticide handlers, clean-up kits, verbal warning before spraying, blood tests for commercial applications, and Spanish-language translations for labels be offered (COPE 1988). Is this enough, or too much? Will it protect crop workers? Oncology nurses, with their expertise in patient education, cultural sensitivities, and understanding of the theories of carcinogenesis as well as their ability to weigh risks, costs, and benefits and their appreciation of local, state, and federal politics, could be the natural consultants and leaders in projects such as this.

The Department of Health and Human Services' Office of Disease Prevention and Health Promotion has put together a publication titled *Promoting Health/ Preventing Disease: Year 2000 Objectives for the Nation* (1989). These objectives focus on methods of cancer prevention and detection that have the highest probability for reducing cancer incidence, morbidity, and mortality (Appendix 3-C). Oncology nurses from all areas of practice, education, and research can focus their prevention and detection knowledge on these priority areas in this national cancer reduction effort.

FUTURE NURSING RESEARCH

The template for future research in the area of health promotion and disease prevention has just begun to be formed. This needed research is certain to guide many of the policies and interventions for the future. The research agenda that follows has been proposed to the ACS from the report of the Workshop on the Community and Cancer Prevention and Detection (McKenna and Eyre 1988).

1. Studies of cost effectiveness of cancer prevention and detection.
2. Studies of health and illness beliefs and behaviors to incorporate this knowledge in prevention and detection activities developed for use by health professionals.
3. Research on how to reach the public with prevention messages, especially the elderly, children, and the economically disadvantaged.
4. Studies to determine public compliance and incentives for behavior change such as smoking cessation.
5. Studies of primary care practice patterns to develop appropriate prevention and detection activities that fit primary care practice.
6. Studies to determine physician compliance and incentives for behavior change.

7. Research and development of computer software for use in primary care practice settings to assist in the implementation of prevention programs.
8. Training of prevention and detection research scientists.
9. Research to develop educational programs in preventive oncology.
10. Implementation of randomized trials for cancer prevention and detection.

The National Center for Nursing Research (1987) is supporting research studies that:

- identify risk factors that constitute a threat to the health status and the quality of life of study populations
- design and implement intervention strategies that reduce risk factors and increase an individual's capability for both improving and maintaining health as well as treating illness and injury
- investigate the cost effectiveness of health promotion programs

CONCLUSION

Nurses can be at the forefront of affecting the health of the nation by adapting their practice to include screening, counseling, planning, and implementation of community education programs and by serving as change agents in the health care system. Moving toward primary prevention and detection and maintaining an active participation in government and private sector activities that influence exposure to cancer-causing agents are incumbent on the medical profession and on oncology nurses in particular.

Over the next decade, as nursing moves from a cost center to a profit center, prevention and detection activities offer opportunities for entrepreneurial developments, and oncology nursing can generate revenue while minimizing cancer risk and incidence. The redesign of nursing practice plans and protocols to incorporate reimbursable primary care services and teaching and counseling for patients is just one way in which revenues can help bring oncology nursing into the 21st century (Lynaugh and Fagin 1988).

STUDY QUESTIONS

1. In a proposal to administration to design and implement a hospitalwide cancer prevention and detection program, what would you include?

2. What is your hypothesis about how this prevention and detection program would affect the number of patient visits to the employee health department? How would you go about designing a nursing research study to measure the cost savings to the institution? How long would this study last? Where would you apply for outside funding to support this important research project?
3. For those employees found to be at high risk for cancer or AIDS as a result of lifestyle characteristics, how would you design a program to support their behavior change? Be creative!

REFERENCES

Albert, M. 1987. Health screening to promote health for the eldery. *Nurse Practitioner* 12:42–58.

American Cancer Society. 1989. *Cancer facts and figures.* Atlanta, Ga.: American Cancer Society.

American College of Physicians Medical Practice Committee. 1981. Periodic health examination: A guide for designing individualized preventive health care in the asymptomatic patient. *Annals of Internal Medicine* 95:729–32.

Butrum, R.R., C.K. Clifford, and E. Lanza. 1988. NCI dietary guidelines: Rationale. *American Journal of Clinical Nutrition* 48 (supplement).

Byers, T. 1988. Diet and cancer: Any progress in the interim? *Cancer* 62 (supplement):1713–24.

Byers, T., and D. Funch. 1984. Towards the dietary prevention of cancer: Contributions of epidemiology. *Cancer Detection and Prevention* 7:135–46.

Canadian Task Force on Periodic Health Examination. 1979. The periodic health examination. *Canadian Medical Association Journal* 121:1193–1254.

Oncology news for professionals. 1988. *COPE Magazine.* 2:31.

Cosby, F., M.R. Ventura, and M.J. Feldman. 1987. Future research recommendations for establishing NP effectiveness. *Nurse Practitioner* 12:75–79.

DeCosse, J.J. 1988. Early cancer detection: Colorectal cancer. *Cancer* 62 (supplement):1787–90.

Department of Health and Human Services. 1986. *A citizen's guide to radon: What it is and what to do about it.* OPA Publication no. 86-004.

Department of Health and Human Services. 1988. *Surgeon General's report on nutrition and health.* DHHS (PHS) Publication no. 88-50210.

Department of Health and Human Services Office of Disease Prevention and Health Promotion. 1989. *Promoting health/preventing disease: Year 2000 objectives for the nation. Draft for Public Review and Comment.*

Dodd, G.D. 1988. Screening for the early detection of breast cancer. *Cancer* 62 (supplement):1781–83.

Doll, R., and R. Peto. 1981. *The causes of cancer.* New York: Oxford University Press.

Einhorn, L.H., J.P. Donohue, M.J. Peckham, S.D. Williams, and P.J. Loehrer. 1985. Cancer of the testes. In *Cancer: Principles and practice of oncology.* 2d ed., ed. V.T. DeVita, Jr., S. Hellman, and S.A. Rosenberg. Philadelphia: J.B. Lippincott.

Enigbokan, M.A., and K.C. Okafor. 1988. Anticancer components of diet. *Infusion* 12:6–14.

Eriksen, M.P., L.W. Green, and F.G. Fultz. 1988. Principles of changing health behavior. *Cancer* 62 (supplement):1768–75.

Ernster, V.L. 1988. Trends in smoking, cancer risk and cigarette promotion: Current priorities for reducing tobacco exposure. *Cancer* 62 (supplement):1702–12.

Farber, E. 1988. Cancer development and its natural history: A cancer prevention perspective. *Cancer* 62 (supplement):1676–79.

Foltz, A.T. 1988. Nutritional factors in the prevention of gastrointestinal cancer. *Seminars in Oncology Nursing* 4:239–46.

Frank-Stromborg, M. 1988. Nursing's role in cancer prevention and detection: Vital contributions to attainment of the year 2000 goal. *Cancer* 62 (supplement):1833–38.

Fry M.J.R. 1985. Principles of cancer biology: Physical carcinogenesis. In *Cancer: Principles and practice of oncology*. 2d ed., ed. V.T. DeVita, Jr., S. Hellman, and S.A. Rosenberg. Philadelphia: J.B. Lippincott.

Glanz, K. 1986. Nutrition education for risk factor reduction and patient education: A review. *Preventive Medicine* 15:721–52.

Gusberg, S.B. 1988. Detection and prevention of uterine cancer. *Cancer* 62 (supplement):1784–86.

Halloran, J., A. Hughes, and D.K. Mayer. 1988. Oncology Nursing Society position paper on HIV-related issues. *Oncology Nursing Forum* 15:206–17.

Holm, L.-E., E. Callmer, C.G. Eriksson, B.J.A. Haglund, L. Kanström, and P. Tillgren. 1989. Community-based strategies for cancer prevention in an urban area: The Stockholm cancer prevention program. *Journal of the National Cancer Institute* 81:103–106.

International Agency for Research on Cancer. 1982. International Agency for Research on Cancer Chemicals: Industrial processes and industries associated with cancer in humans. *IARC Monographs* (supplement 4).

Kopf, A.W. 1988. Prevention and early detection of skin cancer/melanoma. *Cancer* 62 (supplement):1791–95.

Lawler, P.E., and S. Schreiber. 1989. Cutaneous malignant melanoma: Nursing's role in prevention and early detection. *Oncology Nursing Forum* 16:345–52.

LeMaistre, C.A. 1988. Reflections on disease prevention. *Cancer* (supplement):1673–75.

Lindberg, S.C. 1987. Adult preventive health screening: 1987 update. *Nurse Practitioner* 12:19–41.

Love, R.R., J.E. Rodnick, and S.J. McPhee. 1988. Community models for cancer prevention and detection. *Cancer* 62 (supplement):1815–20.

Lynaugh, J.E., and C.M. Fagin. 1988. Nursing comes of age. *Image—The Journal of Nursing Scholarship* 20:184–89.

Mausner, J.S., and S. Kramer. 1985. *Mausner and Bahn—Epidemiology: An introductory text*. Philadelphia: W.B. Saunders.

McKenna, R.J., and H.J. Eyre. 1988. Report from the workshop on the community and cancer prevention and detection. *Cancer* 62 (supplement):1808–14.

National Academy of Sciences/Institute of Medicine. 1989. *Mobilizing against AIDS*, ed. E.K. Nichols. Cambridge, Mass.: Harvard University Press.

National Cancer Institute. 1986. *NCI monographs: Cancer control objectives for the nation: 1985–2000*, ed. P. Greenwald and E. Sondik. NIH Publication no. 86-2880 2.

National Center for Nursing Research. 1987. *Health promotion research underlying nursing practice*. NIH 16(37). Bethesda, Md.: National Institutes of Health.

New York State Education Department Office of the Professions. 1988. Education law, article 139: Nursing. *Nursing handbook*. Albany, N.Y.: New York State Department of Education.

Owen, P., and P. Long. 1989. Facilitating adherence to ACS and NCI guidelines for breast cancer screening. *Journal of the American Association of Occupational Health Nurses* 37:153–57.

Pardee, S., and K. Bakshi. 1983. Diet, nutrition, and cancer: Interim dietary guidelines. *Journal of the National Cancer Institute* 70:1151–70.

Pender, N.J. 1987. *Health promotion in nursing practice*. 2d ed. Norwalk, Conn.: Appleton & Lang.

Pitot, H.C. 1985. Principles of cancer biology: Chemical carcinogenesis. In *Cancer: Principles and practice of oncology.* 2d ed., ed. V.T. DeVita, Jr., S. Hellman, and S.A. Rosenberg. Philadelphia: J.B. Lippincott.

Preventive Services Task Force. 1989. *Guide to clinical preventive services.* Baltimore, Md.: Williams & Wilkins.

Pugliese, G., and T. Lampinen. 1989. Prevention of human immunodeficiency virus infection: Our responsibilities as health care professionals. *American Journal of Infection Control* 17:1–22.

Redeker, N.S. 1989. Health beliefs, health locus of control, and the frequency of practice of breast self-examination in women. *Journal of Obstetric, Gynecologic, and Neonatal Nursing* 18:45–51.

Schweitzer, R.J. 1988. A cancer education and prevention center: A community program. *Cancer* 62 (supplement):1821–23.

Scott, R.E., J.J. Wille, and M.L. Wier. 1984. Mechanisms for the initiation and promotion of carcinogenesis: A review and a new concept. *Mayo Clinic Proceedings* 59:107–17.

Shannon, M.T. 1989. Health promotion and illness prevention: A biopsychosocial perspective. *Health and Social Work* 14:32–40.

Siiteri, P.K. 1987. Adipose tissue as a source of hormones. *American Journal of Clinical Nutrition* 45:277–82.

Silverman, S. Jr. 1988. Early diagnosis of oral cancer. *Cancer* 62 (supplement):1796–99.

Stanford, D. 1987. Nurse practitioner research: Issues in practice and theory. *Nurse Practitioner* 12:64–75.

VandeWoude, G.F., and R.V. Gliden. 1985. Principles of cancer biology: Molecular biology. In *Cancer: Principles and practice of oncology.* 2d ed., ed. V.T. DeVita, Jr., S. Hellman, and S.A. Rosenberg. Philadelphia: J.B. Lippincott.

Weitzel, M.H. 1989. A test of the health promotion model with blue collar workers. *Nursing Research* 38:99–104.

Yancik, R., L. Kessler, and J.W. Yates. 1988. The elderly population: Opportunities for cancer prevention and detection. *Cancer* 62 (supplement):1823–28.

Zifferblatt, S.M., and C.S. Wilbur. 1977. Dietary counseling: Some realistic expectations and guidelines. *Journal of the American Dietetic Association* 70:591–95.

Appendix 3-A

National Cancer Institute's Cancer Control Objectives for the Nation, 1985–2000

Action	Target	Rationale	Year 2000 Objectives
Prevention	Smoking	The causal relationship between smoking and cancer has been scientifically established.	Reduce the percentage of adults who smoke from 34% (in 1983) to 15% or less. Reduce the percentage of youths who smoke by age 20 years from 36% (in 1983) to 15% or less.
	Diet	Research indicates that high-fat and low-fiber diets may increase the risk for various cancers. In 1983, the National Academy of Sciences reviewed research on diet and cancer and recommended a reduction in fat. More recent studies led NCI to recommend an increase in fiber. Research is underway to verify the causal relationships and to test the impact on cancer incidence.	Reduce the average consumption of fat from 37%–38% to 30% or less of total caloric intake. Increase the average consumption of fiber from 8–12 g/day to 20–30 g/day.
Screening	Breast cancer	The effectiveness of breast cancer screening in reducing mortality has been scientifically established.	Increase the percentage of women aged 50–70 years who have an annual physical breast examination coupled with mammography from 45% to 80% for physical examination alone and to 15% for mammography.

Action	Target	Rationale	Year 2000 Objectives
	Cervical cancer	The effectiveness of cervical cancer screening in reducing mortality has been scientifically established.	Increase the percentage of women who have a Papanicolaou smear done every 3 years from 79% to 90% for ages 20–39 years and from 57% to 80% for ages 40–70 years.

Source: Adapted from *NCI Monographs: Cancer Control Objectives for the Nation: 1985–2000* by P. Greenwald and E. Sondik (Eds.), NIH Publication No. 86-2880 No. 2, 1986.

Appendix 3-B
Risk Factors in Carcinogenesis

Risk Factor	Associated Cancer Type
Acrylonitrite	*Lung, colon, prostate
Aflatoxins	*Liver
Alcoholic beverages	Oral, liver, esophageal, *breast
Alkylating agents	Bladder, leukemia
Aromatic amines	Bladder
Arsenic	Lung
Asbestos	Lung, mesothelioma,* gastrointestinal tract
Auramine	*Bladder
Azathioprine (immunosuppressive drugs)	Lymphoma, reticulum cell sarcoma, skin, *Kaposi's sarcoma
Benzene	Leukemia
Beryllium (and its compounds)	*Lung
Betel	Oral
Bis(chloromethyl)ether	Lung
Boot and shoe manufacture	Nasal
Cadmium (and its compounds)	Lung, *prostate
Chloramphenicol	*Leukemia
Chlornaphazine	Bladder
Chromium (and some of its compounds)	Lung
Cigarette smoke	Lung, oral, laryngeal, esophageal, bladder
Dietary fat	Breast, colon, gallbladder, endometrial
Diethylstilbestrol	Vaginal (clear cell)
Premenopausal	Liver, *breast
Postmenopausal	*Endometrial
Furniture manufacture (hardwood)	Nasal
Halogenated hydrocarbons	*Liver
Hematite mining	Lung
High-calorie diet	Increased cancer incidence in general
Inorganic arsenicals	Skin, liver
Ionizing radiation	Increased cancer incidence in general
Isopropyl alcohol manufacture	Paranasal sinus
Methoxypsoralen with ultraviolet light	Skin
Multiple sex partners	Cervical

Risk Factor	Associated Cancer Type
Nickel refining	Lung, nasal sinus
Oxymetholone	*Liver
Phenacetin	Renal
Phenobarbital	*Liver
Phenoxyacetic acids and herbicides	*Soft tissue sarcoma
Phenytoin	*Lymphoma, neuroblastoma
Phorbol esters	Esophageal
Prolactin	*Mammary adenocarcinoma
Reproductive history	
Late age first pregnancy	Breast
Low parity	Ovary
Rubber industry	Leukemia, bladder
Saccharin	Bladder
Soots, tars, and oils	Skin, lung, bladder, gastrointestinal tract
Synthetic estrogens	Liver
Thorotrast (radiologic contrast agent)	Liver
Ultraviolet radiation	Skin
Vinyl chlorides	Liver

*Limited evidence for carcinogenicity based on findings reviewed by the International Agency for Research on Cancer (1982) and by Doll and Peto (1981).

Appendix 3-C

Summary Table of Objectives To Reduce the Toll from Cancer by the Year 2000

Health Status

1. Reduce breast cancer deaths to no more than 25.2 per 100,000 women (age-adjusted baseline: 27.2 per 100,000 in 1986).
2. Reduce deaths from cancer of the uterine cervix to no more than 1.5 per 100,000 women (age-adjusted baseline: 3.2 per 100,000 in 1986).
3. Reduce colorectal cancer deaths to no more than 18.7 per 100,000 people (baseline: 20.1 per 100,000 in 1986).

Risk Reduction

4. Reduce cigarette smoking to a prevalence of no more than 15% among people aged 20 years and older (baseline: 29.1 percent in 1987, 31.7% for men and 26.8% for women). Special population targets:
   - people with a high school education or less:
     22% (34.3% in 1987)
   - blue collar workers:
     22% (36.6% in 1987, 36.1% for men and 36.6% for women)
   - Blacks:
     18% (34% in 1987)
   - Hispanics:
     18% (33% in 1982–1984, 40% for men and 26% for women)
   - native Americans and Alaskans:
     20% (42% to 70% Northern Plains natives and 56% Alaska natives in 1979–1987)
   - Southeast Asian men:
     20% (estimated 55% in 1984–1987)
5. Reduce smokeless tobacco use to a prevalance of no more than 4% among men aged 18 to 24 years (baseline: 6.4% in 1986).

6. Reduce average dietary fat intake to no more than 30% of caloric intake and average saturated fat intake to no more than 10% of caloric intake among people aged 2 years and older (baseline: 36% of calories from total fat and 13.2% of calories from saturated fat in 1985).
7. Increase average intake of dietary fiber and complex carbohydrates in the diets of adults to five or more daily servings for vegetables and fruits and to six or more daily servings for grain products and legumes to provide between 20 and 30 g of daily dietary fiber (baseline: 2.5 servings of vegetables and fruits and 3 servings of grain products and legumes for women aged 19 to 50 years in 1985; approximately 10 g of dietary fiber in 1987, 11.5 g for men and 8.8 g for women).
8. Increase to at least 80% the proportion of women aged 40 years and older who have ever received a clinical breast examination and a mammogram (baseline: 36% in 1987). Special population targets:
   - Hispanics: 60% (20% in 1987)
   - income < $10,000 1987 dollars: 65% (22% in 1987)
   - education < 12 years: 65% (23% in 1987)
   - age > 70 years: 70% (25% in 1987)
9. Increase to at least 60% the proportion of women aged 50 years and older who received a clinical breast examination and a mammogram within the preceding year (baseline: 19% in 1987). Special population targets:
   - Hispanics: 50% (6% in 1987)
   - income < $10,000: 55% (12% in 1987)
   - education < 12 years: 55% (12% in 1987)
   - age > 70 years: 55% (13% in 1987)
   - Blacks: 60% (17% in 1987)
10. Increase to at least 95% the proportion of women aged 18 years and older with intact uterine cervix who have ever received a Papanicolaou smear, and increase to at least 75% the proportion who received a smear within the preceding year (baseline: 88% ever and 56% in the preceding year in 1987). Special population targets:
    - Hispanics: 80% and 65% (59% and 44% in 1987)
    - age > 70 years: 85% and 55% (69% and 38% in 1987)
    - education < 12 years: 90% and 60% (78% and 40% in 1987)
    - income < $10,000: 95% and 70% (80% and 48% in 1987)

Professional Education and Awareness

11. Increase to at least 35% the proportion of primary care providers in clinical practice who have received specific applied training in smoking cessation counseling, nutrition counseling, and the early detection of cancer (baseline: data unavailable).
12. Increase to at least 75% the proportion of primary care providers who regularly counsel patients about smoking cessation, diet modification, and recommended cancer screening guidelines (baseline: 52% of internists reported counseling approximately 75% of their patients about smoking cessation in 1986).

Services and Protection

13. Increase to at least 40% the proportion of adults aged 50 years and older visiting a health care provider in the preceding year who have been offered fecal occult blood testing (baseline: an estimated 19% underwent fecal occult blood testing during the preceding year in 1987; an estimated 25% had ever undergone proctosigmoidoscopy in 1987).
14. Increase to at least 40% the proportion of adults aged 50 years and older visiting a health care provider in the preceding year who have been offered oral, skin, and digital rectal examinations during one such visit (baseline: 27% received a digital rectal examination in 1987).
15. Ensure that Papanicolaou smears meet quality standards by monitoring and certifying all cytology laboratories.
16. Ensure that mammograms meet quality standards by monitoring and certifying at least 80% of mammography facilities (baseline: 11% certified by the American College of Radiology in 1989).
17. Increase to at least 30 the number of states requiring coverage of screening mammography by health insurance companies doing business in the state (baseline: 18 states in 1989).

Source: Adapted from *Promoting Health/Preventing Disease: Year 2000 Objectives for the Nation* by the Department of Health and Human Services, Office of Disease Prevention and Health Promotion, 1989.

Part I

Current Advances in Treatment Modalities

Chapter 4

New Developments in Treatment Modalities

Anne E. Belcher

> There have been numerous new developments in cancer treatment modalities, including the delivery of chemotherapy by regional perfusion or intrahepatic artery infusion, photodynamic therapy, hyperthermia, reprogramming therapy, gene replacement therapy, and antisense RNA inhibition of oncogene expression. Each new approach is described in terms of its therapeutic effect and nursing implications. In addition, the issues of informed consent for clinical trials and quality of life are addressed. Nursing research applications are also identified.

New developments in cancer treatment modalities are often greeted by the professional and lay communities with excitement and high expectations that frequently end in disappointment or reserved enthusiasm. This happens because each new development has to be vigorously tested and evaluated before it is determined to have a therapeutic value that overrides its potential risks. Thus the emphasis in recent years has been on refinements in already available surgical techniques, evaluation of new drug combinations with existing agents, construction of more powerful and precise radiation therapy delivery systems, and the identification and clinical study of biologic response modifiers.

The focus of this chapter is selected new therapeutic developments that reflect trends in the various fields not discussed elsewhere, such as delivery of chemotherapy through regional perfusion or intrahepatic artery infusion, photodynamic therapy (PDT), reprogramming therapy, gene replacement therapy, and antisense RNA inhibition of oncogene expression. Each development is described in terms of its therapeutic effects and nursing implications. Although the discussion is not inclusive of all new developments, those selected for examination reflect refinements in the traditional modalities of surgery, chemotherapy, and radiation therapy. In addition, each new development is being tested in combination with one or more of these therapies. As is the case with any new development in the treatment of cancer, the nurse has important roles in assessing the patient's response to the therapy and in intervening when problems occur.

DELIVERY OF CHEMOTHERAPY

Regional chemotherapy with surgical drug delivery systems has been found in prospective controlled studies to be of benefit to selected patients (Boddie 1989; Ghussen et al. 1985; Hohn et al. 1987; Krementz and Ryan 1972; McBride 1976; Stewart 1989; Taylor, Rowling, and West 1979). The two systems receiving renewed attention in recent years are isolated regional limb perfusion and intrahepatic artery infusion chemotherapy with surgically implantable pumps.

The rationale for the therapeutic use of regional chemotherapy is based on the observation that many solid tumors are unresponsive to drug levels that are safe for systemic administration; higher drug concentrations can be achieved by regional infusion. Systems such as isolated perfusion use agents that are non–cell cycle specific because drug exposure time is usually about 1 hour; systems that use arterial infusion allow a wider choice of drugs. Other factors that are considered in drug selection include whether the drug must be metabolized to an active form, where this occurs in the body, and whether the drug has an effect on the tumor to be treated when it is administered systemically. Regional chemotherapy should be applied primarily in tumors with a natural history of prolonged confinement to the treated areas (Boddie 1989).

Isolation perfusion combines tourniquet control of an anatomic region with pump oxygenator support of regional circulation by means of catheters inserted into the principal artery and vein supplying the region. Drugs are infused into the treated region through ports on the pump oxygenator. Only perfusion of the extremities is used regularly because such tumors as melanomas and sarcomas have a tendency to recur locally and regionally. Also, drug doses four to five times higher than those that can be tolerated systemically can be perfused, thereby increasing the therapeutic index. For example, isolated limb perfusion with phenylalanine mustard has been used to treat thick extremity melanomas with reported 5-year survival rates in the 80% to 95% range (Ghussen et al. 1985; Krementz and Ryan 1972; McBride 1976). Isolated limb perfusion has also been used for treatment of regional cutaneous recurrences of melanomas with or without regional node involvement.

The nursing care of the patient undergoing limb perfusion is focused on identifying and treating complications such as edema (treated with elevation of the limb and the use of elastic hose), cellulitis or wound infection (which require antibiotics and often rehospitalization with hydrotherapy), arterial insufficiency (a serious complication that requires prompt medical attention), and peripheral neuropathy (treated with active and passive exercises and protection from injury) (Stewart 1989).

Intrahepatic artery chemotherapy by means of bioimplantable, self-powered pump reservoir systems has been particularly useful in the treatment of metastatic colon cancer. Because only 5% of patients with hepatic metastases are eligible for surgical removal, the remaining 95% are candidates for regional chemotherapy if there is no evidence of extrahepatic involvement. Although not yet shown to be curative, this therapy does show evidence of prolonging time to disease progression (Applegate 1987). The physiologic advantages of this route are that administration of drugs through the hepatic artery preferentially concentrates them in tumors and that systemic toxicity is further reduced because the liver is the primary site of detoxification. In patients with hepatic artery occlusion, the portal vein has been used as an alternative route (Taylor, Rowling, and West 1979).

The factor that has been most limiting in the long-term treatment of patients with hepatic metastases is the toxic effects of intra-arterial chemotherapy on the liver parenchyma and the biliary system. Research to overcome this problem focuses on variable drug schedules and combinations.

Patient acceptance of the implantable infusion pump has been high because it allows the patient to be ambulatory and unencumbered by tubes or wires. Education of patients focuses on the importance of compliance with appointment schedules and reporting of pump complications and chemotherapeutic agent toxicities. Although catheter occlusion may result from complete emptying of the pump drug reservoir, the newer implantable pumps have low-reservoir alarms. Drug incompatibility with resultant precipitation in the drug chamber, another cause of catheter occlusion, is avoided with saline flushes between different drugs. If precipitate occlusion occurs, removal and replacement of the device may be necessary. Aspiration through the side port is contraindicated; if it is necessary, it should be followed immediately with a flush of 10 to 20 mL of heparinized bacteriostatic sodium chloride. If the occlusion persists, instillation of urokinase may be indicated.

The only restriction on patient activity is the need to avoid contact sports. Patients should report fever of 101°F or more or an extended stay in the high-altitude area. The greatest risk of infection is during the immediate postsurgical period, with the usual site of infection being the soft tissue pocket where the pump is surgically placed. Infection may also occur by way of the needle used to access the pump. The pump itself may, as a foreign body, cause inflammation or infection. Pump failure is rare and is caused by motor failure in old models or by the computer operating system or microcomputer circuits of the new, externally programmable pumps.

Automated drug delivery systems are being incorporated into outpatient and home care settings. According to Finley (1989, 5), "With multichannel programmable pumps, such refinements as crucial timing, overlapping schedules, and timing to coincide with circadian rhythm are all feasible on an outpatient basis." Pumps are programmed with software designed for IBM or IBM-compatible computers. Each channel (there are four) can be programmed to direct a prefilled syringe and to perform multiple functions over a 31-day period, including the initiation and discontinuation of infusions, administration of loading doses, and tapering of doses. An inexpensive, reusable chip powers the pump. Built-in alarms signal battery decline, pump malfunction, and difficulties with intravenous lines and syringes. Patients learn syringe replacement and device troubleshooting. The broader applications of this convenient, relatively cost-effective drug delivery system are limited only by the creativity of the nurse and pharmacist.

PHOTODYNAMIC THERAPY

Photodynamic therapy, an experimental approach to treatment of such tumors as recurrent cancer of the breast and head and neck, endobronchial tumors, bladder tumors in situ, skin malignancies, and early gynecologic cancer, involves the use of a photosensitizing agent, a special type of laser light, and oxygen. The interaction of the three components produces a localized fluorescence for detection and subsequent treatment of tumors and cell death. As noted by Pass et al. (1989), although PDT involves the use of a laser the mechanism of action is photosensitization rather than cutting, cauterizing, or vaporizing.

The photosensitizing agent most frequently used for PDT is dihematoporphyrin ether (DHE). DHE is a complex mixture of porphyrinoids: hematoporphyrin, hydroxyethylvinyldeuteroporphyrin (HVD), and a hydrophobic fraction (Pass et al. 1989). The commercially available form of DHE, known as PII, contains less of the inactive hematoporphyrin and HVD and allows for greater tissue penetration than does other agents. PII improves the light absorbence by such naturally present agents as hemoglobin. When injected, PII initially binds to albumin and lipoproteins but later associates almost completely with high-density lipoproteins. Although its serum half-life is relatively short (20 to 30 hours for a 5-mg bolus), the photosensitizing component will remain in the skin for at least 4 weeks. Large quantities of porphyrin are retained in reticuloendothelial cells, with the highest levels being retained in the liver, spleen, and kidney.

Lasers such as argon-pump dye lasers are used to excite Kiton red or rhodamine B to produce as much as 5 W of red light. The laser is coupled to one or more fiberoptic cables to transmit light to the tip; the tip can be split for forward light projection or bulb tipped for isotropic spheric distribution, or a cylindric scattering material can be applied to distribute light perpendicular to the fiber axis. The energy delivered depends on the amount of light and the duration of its delivery. The dose is always measured to prevent any hyperthermic effect.

When oxygen is not present or is present at levels less than 2%, cells are resistant to PDT. When light energy is absorbed, sensitizer in the ground state is excited to singlet sensitizer. With a high quantum yield, the sensitizer undergoes an intersystem crossover to the triplet state. The excited triplet sensitizer interacts with ground-state oxygen to produce singlet oxygen, which can then react with electron-rich substrates to produce oxidized products that lead to cell death.

PDT causes significant damage to membranes, especially the plasma membrane, with the formation of multiple membrane blebs that protrude from the cell membrane like balloons. Other structures at risk include the nuclear, mitochondrial, and liposomal membranes; the Golgi apparatus; and the endoplasmic reticulum. Mitochondrial damage in the form of inhibition of oxidative phosphorylation, decreased electron transport, and reduction of cellular adenosine $3',5'$-triphosphate levels is an important factor in PDT cytotoxicity. Others are the dose of sensitizer, the rate of delivery, and selective retention by tumor tissue. The mechanism of tumor tissue selective retention is unclear, but the clearance of the sensitizer seems to be slower from malignant tissue than from healthy tissue.

The patient receiving PDT is given intravenous PII (1.5 to 2.5 mg/kg) diluted in 50 mL of normal saline. The patient is then removed from direct contact with sunlight but may be exposed to fluorescent or incandescent light for as long as 8 hours each day. After 48 to 72 hours the patient is exposed to red light, such as that produced by an argon laser. The amount of energy indicated varies depending on the site of treatment, the method of treatment (surface illumination or interstitial implantation), the physician's familiarity with PDT, and the energy range (from 5 to 900 J/cm^2).

At the University of Kansas Medical Center, a carbon dioxide laser is used for the treatment of cervical intraepithelial neoplasia (CIN) when all boundaries of the lesion are visible on colposcopy and when endocervical curettage is negative (Declaration of Helsinki 1964). The laser instrument is attached to the colposcope; a suction device removes the fumes created by tissue vaporization. The major benefits of the carbon dioxide laser treating CIN include pinpoint precision for the removal of malignant tissue, minimal bleeding, reduced trauma, inherent sterility of the procedure, improved visibility, and reduced risk of metastasis. Ferenczy (1988) notes that laser vaporization is indicated for lesions larger than 3 cm. The disadvantage of this therapy is its expense; patients eligible for it should be referred to a medical center with a laser unit.

At the H. Lee Moffitt Cancer Center in Tampa, Florida, physicians have used the neodymium:yttrium aluminum garnet (YAG) laser to burn out tumor or scar tissue from the airway of patients with squamous cell carcinoma that is no longer resectable or responsive to radiation and chemotherapy (Goldman 1987). This laser delivers radiation with a wavelength of 1,064 nm that is conducted by a quartz monofilament through a flexible fiberoptic bronchoscope. Neodymium:YAG laser light is not absorbed by hemoglobin, so that it provides greater tissue penetration than other agents. Goldman's (1987) study of 13 patients indicated that palliation of symptoms did occur, but not without hazards such as perforation of a bronchus, severe hemorrhage, respiratory failure, pneumonia, or even the combustion of a fiberoptic bronchoscope or an endotracheal tube in the airway. The treatment nevertheless has value, according to Goldman, in treating such patients.

Nursing care of the patient receiving PDT includes education as to what it is, how it works, and what complications may occur. Patients receiving the treatment must be properly positioned, as must the probe that diffuses the light, for as long as 1 hour. Protective eye lenses must be worn to prevent red light damage to the cornea.

The primary complication is phototoxicity. After therapy, patients must be completely covered when exposed to the sun and must wear a sun screen or zinc oxide. They should not use lights of greater than 100 W for reading and should avoid exposure to lights in dentists' offices and operating rooms for approximately 30 days. After that period, a finger exposure test is performed; if still phototoxic, the patient is advised to remain covered 15 days more (Huether and Mooney 1987).

Although PDT has been used primarily to treat accessible cancers in various sites, there is hope that new photosensitizers will extend its use to more deeply seated tumors, the central nervous system, and cavitary spaces. A clearer understanding of the tumor retentive properties of photosensitizers is needed. Clinical trials should lead PDT into the mainstream of cancer therapy, although its use will require the institutional availability of optics, electronics, and bioengineering support (Russo et al. 1989).

REPROGRAMMING THERAPY

Reprogramming therapy includes strategies that are designed to remove or destroy neoplastic tissue. For example, growth regulatory factors are being cloned and produced in therapeutic quantities and intranuclear signals that mediate the activation and inhibition of gene expression are being purified and characterized.

The advantages of this therapy are the likelihood that (1) it is less toxic or functionally disabling than current therapy, (2) it is possible that drugs could be created that would amplify or inhibit the interaction of regulatory proteins with DNA, and (3) modulation of a single regulatory protein might be appropriate for many different types of mutations in tumor populations (Deisseroth 1989).

GENE REPLACEMENT THERAPY

Constitutional or acquired abnormalities in the function of structural genes can produce molecular diseases of the hematopoietic system that result in uncontrolled proliferation of abnormal differentiation. Thus the malfunction of specific genes causes neoplastic diseases; replacement of these malfunctioning genes with functional genes is being studied. Much research centers on viral and plasmid gene delivery systems (Deisseroth 1989).

Retroviral systems are offering the possibility of vectors that do not spread horizontally in the population, provide adequate levels of expression of the missing gene, do not recombine in the host cell to produce unwanted gene products, and persist in the settings of bone marrow transplantation, modification of hematopoietic cells, and organ or skin transplantation (Wong, Chung, and Nienhuis 1987).

Examples of growth regulatory molecules that have been cloned include colony-stimulating factor, interleukins (Boddie 1989; Ghussen et al. 1985; Hohn et al. 1987; Krementz and Ryan 1972; McBride 1976), oncogenes, tumor necrosis factor, and interferons (α, β, and γ). The implications of gene replacement therapy for biotherapy are limitless and exciting.

ANTISENSE RNA INHIBITION OF ONCOGENE EXPRESSION

Experiments are now underway to develop molecular strategies for down-regulating unwanted genes. For example, the generation of antisense RNA is being used to downregulate unwanted oncogene expression in cancer cells and to identify the biologic nature of genes. There is evidence that antisense RNA does inhibit oncogene expression and thus interrupts the reproductive cycle of certain viruses. Antisense RNAs may also be useful to target chemotherapeutic agents to certain cells. Other therapeutic uses are being studied (Stein and Cohen 1988).

NEW CHEMOTHERAPEUTIC AGENTS

As noted earlier, much of the current research in cancer chemotherapy is focused on testing new combinations of drugs, new schedules of drug administration, and new drug delivery systems. New chemotherapeutic agents are also being developed and tested (Table 4-1) (Loehrer 1989; Mastrangelo 1989a, 1989b; O'Dwyer et al. 1988; Speth, Minderman, and Haanen, 1989). The nurse may be involved in each phase of drug study depending on the practice setting and the involvement of physicians in various regional study groups. Two of the most important issues confronting the oncology nurse with regard to such research activities are informed consent and quality of life.

Informed Consent for Clinical Trials

The concept of informed consent has been described as the ethical underpinning of clinical research. Informed consent is also a process that implies voluntary,

Table 4-1 Selected New Chemotherapeutic Agents

Agent	Characteristics	Therapeutic Uses
Deoxycoformycin	Adenosine deaminase inhibitor (antimetabolite)	Indolent lymphoma, hairy cell leukemia. Being studied with mycosis fungoides and other lymphoid neoplasms.
Idarubicin	Anthracycline	Leukemias.
Ifosfamide	Structural isomer of cyclophosphamide (Cytoxan)	Testicular cancer, sarcomas, bronchogenic and gynecologic cancers, lymphomas.
Navelbine	Hemisynthetic Vinca alkaloid	Epidermoid cancer of lung. Breast cancer, Hodgkin's disease.
Carboplatin	Analog of cisplatin	Cancer of testis, ovary, bladder, lung, head and neck, prostate, esophagus, cervix; Hodgkin's and non-Hodgkin's lymphomas; melanoma; osteosarcomas.

educated decision making based on open and ongoing communication between the patient and the health professional, care provider, or researcher. The development of informed consent as a right reflects the individual's basic rights of privacy and freedom from injury.

Historically, the development of informed consent reflects the Nuremberg Code of 1949, the Declaration of Helsinki of 1964, and the report of the President's Commission for the Study of Ethical Problems in Medicine and Biomedical and Behavioral Research of 1982. In addition to these global statements from various political and government bodies, descriptions of informed consent are also given in the American Nurses' Association (ANA) *Code for Nurses with Interpretive Statements* (1985), the ANA *Human Rights Guidelines for Nurses in Clinical and Other Research* (1975), and the ANA–Oncology Nursing Society *Standards of Oncology Nursing Practice* (1987). In addition, the patient now receives *A Patient's Bill of Rights* (American Hospital Association 1972) on admission to a health care facility. This document delineates the individual's rights while he or she is hospitalized, one of which is "the right to receive from his physician information necessary to give informed consent prior to the start of any procedure and/or treatment" (American Hospital Association 1972).

The components of informed consent are disclosure, formation of a judgment, and agreement of the parties to an action. The elements of disclosure (Baird 1986) are:

1. explanation of the procedure
2. identification of the specific aspects of the procedure

3. identification of physical risks or discomfort
4. disclosure of threats to dignity
5. outline of benefits
6. description of anonymity and confidentiality
7. how to obtain more information about the study
8. how to withdraw from the study
9. coverage for complications

Applegate (1987) identified those elements that are essential to disclosure and should be present if consent is to be informed: the patient's legal capacity; the patient's mental capacity; voluntariness; freedom from coercion, deceit, or fraud; right to refuse; explanations given in comprehensible language; questions answered to the patient's satisfaction; and consideration of privacy and confidentiality.

Given these elements of disclosure and factors essential to disclosure, the patient should be accorded the time in which to make a decision and be supported by the oncology nurse as advocate. Once the patient has reached a decision, the health care professionals must accept it. The patient has the right of informed refusal as well as that of informed consent.

Because persons with cancer are often asked to participate in clinical trials, oncology nurses are frequently involved in ensuring that criteria for informed consent are met. Nealson, Blumberg, and Brown (1985) identified the following issues that result from clinical trials:

- Patients are under a great deal of physical and psychologic stress as a result of the cancer diagnosis and thus may have difficulty understanding and remembering information presented to them.
- Patients may have little or no idea as to what clinical trials are and thus may not know what questions to ask.
- Some patients fear that they will be used as "guinea pigs" in an impersonal health care system.
- Other patients view their participation as potentially helpful both to themselves and to future patients.

Consequently, patients need the basic information about clinical trials presented in a style that facilitates their understanding and retention. In response to these issues, the National Cancer Institute (NCI) has published *What Are Clinical Trials All About? A Booklet for Patients with Cancer* (1984). In addition to describing all aspects of clinical trials, the booklet provides a list of questions for patients to ask before agreeing to participate in one.

Bujorian (1988) focuses on the issues confronted by the patient during the clinical trial decision-making process: public attitudes, patient biases, patient comprehension of clinical research, treatment-related factors and quality of life, physician influence, and family attitudes. Each of these issues should be analyzed by the nurse in his or her roles of teacher, counselor, and advocate.

In a broad discussion of informed consent, Chamorro and Appelbaum (1988) address informed consent as a professional duty, review regulatory and statutory processes relating to human research, and address the following nursing issues: protection of the patient, witnessing a consent, legal accountability, depth of information provided, full disclosure and patient comprehension, ignorant consent, and strategies to aid patients' understanding of information.

Quality-of-Life Issues

As noted by Aaronson (1988, 69),

> While the traditional clinical markers of therapeutic success—tumor response, disease-free and overall survival, and control of major physical symptoms—maintain their primary position in [the efficacy of both standard and experimental cancer therapies], efforts have been mounted to assess systematically the extent to which cancer and its treatment affect the patient's functional capacity, psychological and social health, and overall sense of well-being [e.g., quality of life].

Aaronson identifies the following as reasons for the recent heightened interest in quality-of-life issues: patients, clinicians, and researchers are viewing cancer as a chronic disease with long-term functional limitations that must be acknowledged and assessed; clinical research is directed more toward the development of less toxic or less mutilating therapies than toward increasing survival time as such; the patients' rights movement is focusing on informed consent with an emphasis on the relative risks and benefits of alternative therapies; and much psychosocial oncology research has emphasized the value of ascertaining the patient's perspective when trying to understand cancer as a social phenomenon.

The oncology nurse serves as teacher, advocate, witness (to the patient's signature), and monitor of the patient's response to the protocol used should the patient agree to participate. In reality, the nurse is the health care provider most involved in helping patients make an informed decision about clinical trials.

Quality-of-life studies not only assist clinicians and researchers in monitoring the effect of standard treatments on patients' daily lives but also have the potential for guiding the development of norms for patients' short-term and long-term psychosocial adjustment. In looking toward the future, Aaronson (1988) and others see quality-of-life parameters being used for the redefinition and refinement of the best therapeutic approach among competing treatments. Nurses in ever-increasing numbers are designing and implementing quality-of-life studies as well as monitoring this aspect of the patient's response to treatment throughout the course of the illness.

NURSING RESEARCH APPLICATIONS

Kirchoff (1987) described the results of a survey at a large university medical center whose purpose was to assess the type and amount of research involvement by the nursing staff in medical projects. Several categories of nursing involvement were identified, but the most frequently occurring category was the involvement of nursing staff in data collection activities for medical studies, such as blood drawing or the collection of specimens. Recordkeeping, patient follow-up, instructing patients about tests, applying equipment, setting up for procedures, and so on often required additional nursing time. Although not limited to oncology units, the study findings could probably be replicated in such settings. The outcome of this study was the development of policies that focused on nurses' cooperating with medical research while maintaining quality of care for the patients. It would seem appropriate for studies involving nurses' time in data collection to be reviewed by nursing administrators to determine the amount of time required and its impact on patient care. In the context of financial constraint, nursing care time is a resource that must be used in a cost-effective manner.

Grant and Padilla (1983) determined that the factors that influence research productivity are qualified people, researchable questions, and support for research activity. In the specialty of oncology nursing, they examined the oncology nurse's characteristics, the oncology patient's characteristics, and the characteristics of the specialty. The characteristics of the oncology nurse that influence research productivity are:

- education background (i.e., exposure to what research is, how it is conducted, and how it can be utilized; 65% of the members of the Oncology Nursing Society have at least a BSN)
- clinical experience, particularly in a research apprenticeship role with a medical oncologist or a cooperative research group (oncology nurses have learned the problems of preparing a protocol for institution review board approval, the problems of identifying subjects and obtaining informed consent, the procedures necessary for valid and reliable data collection, and the development of manuscripts for submission to professional journals)

The characteristics of the person with cancer that influence research productivity are:

- distribution along the health-illness continuum
- location in acute care settings, long-term care facilities, and the home
- complex care problems

The specialty of oncology nursing has supported research productivity through Oncology Nursing Society congresses, its research committee activities, and its journal; American Cancer Society conferences, research grants, and scholarships; and NCI research grants.

Oncology nurses are in a unique position to design and implement collaborative research with physicians and other care providers, such as the recent quality-of-life studies that have been "piggybacked" onto chemotherapy protocols. Nurses are also working alone, with other nurses, and with other health care researchers in such areas as prevention and early detection, response to therapy and to the disease itself, overall quality of life and quality of care, and nursing care delivery systems. It is important that roles and relationships be defined, tasks be delineated, and authorship rights be negotiated (Mayer and Grant 1987). Addressing these aspects of organization before initiating the study will enhance the project and the sense of fulfillment of all involved.

CONCLUSION

The nurse's roles in the context of new cancer treatment modalities are those of assessor of the patient's response to therapy and intervener when problems occur. The nurse is also teacher, explaining what is known about the therapy, the rationale for its use, and expected outcomes. The nurse as advocate supports the patient's decisions regarding informed consent and quality-of-life issues. The nurse also functions as researcher, identifying nursing diagnoses for study, assessing patients' quality of life, testing selected interventions to solve treatment-related problems, and communicating the results to other professionals through presentations and publications. These roles enhance the patient's response to treatment and provide data that can be used to evaluate further the treatment modality's therapeutic value.

STUDY QUESTIONS

1. What is the rationale for the therapeutic use of regional chemotherapy? isolation perfusion? What are the nursing implications of each?
2. What are the three components of photodynamic therapy? What special precautions must the patient learn to prevent phototoxicity?

REFERENCES

Aaronson, N. 1988. Quality of life: What is it? How should it be measured? *Oncology* 2:69.

American Hospital Association. 1972. *A patient's bill of rights*. Chicago: AHA.

American Nurses' Association. 1985. *Code for nurses with interpretive statements*. Kansas City, Mo.: ANA.

American Nurses' Association. 1975. *Human rights guidelines for nurses in clinical and other research*. Kansas City, Mo.: ANA.

American Nurses' Association and Oncology Nursing Society. 1987. *Standards of oncology nursing practice*. Kansas City, Mo.: ANA.

Applegate, M. 1987. Informed consent. In *Core curriculum for oncology nursing*, ed. C. Ziegfeld, 391–94. Philadelphia: W.B. Saunders.

Baird, S.B. 1986. Informed consent and legal issues. In *Issues and Trends in Cancer Care*. Pittsburgh: Oncology Nursing Society.

Boddie, A.W. 1989. Regional chemotherapy using surgical drug delivery systems. In *Nursing interventions in oncology: M.D. Anderson case reports and review*, 7–10. New Town, Pa.: Associates in Medical Marketing.

Bujorian, G. 1988. Clinical trials: Patient issues in the decision-making process. *Oncology Nursing Forum* 15:779–83.

Chamorro, T., and J. Appelbaum. 1988. Informed consent: Nursing issues and ethical dilemmas. *Oncology Nursing Forum* 15:803–808.

Declaration of Helsinki. 1964.

Deisseroth, A.B. 1989. Molecular and genetic approaches to cancer diagnosis and treatment. In *Cancer: principles and practice of oncology*. 2d ed., ed. V.T. DeVita, Jr., S. Hellman, and S.A. Rosenberg. Philadelphia: J.B. Lippincott.

Ferenczy, A. 1988. *Laser treatment of patients with condylomata and squamous carcinoma precursors of the lower genital tract*. New York: American Cancer Society.

Finley, R.S. 1989. Multichannel pumps: Expanding the scope of outpatient chemotherapy. *Outpatient Chemotherapy* 3:5.

Ghussen, F., et al. 1985. A prospective randomized study of regional extremity perfusion in patients with melanoma. *Annals of Surgery* 198:764–68.

Goldman, A.L. 1987. Laser and radiation therapy of obstructed airways in lung cancer. *Innovations in Oncology* 3:9–10.

Grant, M., and G. Padilla. 1983. An overview of cancer nursing research. *Oncology Nursing Forum* 10:58–69.

Hohn, D., et al. 1987. The NCOG randomized trial of intravenous vs. hepatic arterial FUDR for colorectal cancer metastatic to the liver. *Proceedings of the American Society of Clinical Oncology* 6:85.

Huether, S.E., and K.H. Mooney. 1987. Nursing management of cancer patients treated with lasers and photodynamic therapy. *Oncology Nursing Forum* 14 (supplement):135.

Kirchoff, K. 1987. Nurses and physicians must interact for valid clinical research. *Research in Nursing and Health* 10:149–54.

Krementz, E.T., and R.F. Ryan. 1972. Chemotherapy of melanoma of the extremities by perfusion: Fourteen years of clinical experience. *Annals of Surgery* 175:900–17.

Loehrer, P.J. 1989. Current developments and future direction with isofamide. *Seminars in Oncology* 16 (supplement 3).

Mastrangelo, M.J. 1989a. Navelbine. *Seminars in Oncology* 16 (supplement 4).

Mastrangelo, M.J. 1989b. Carboplanin (JM-8, CBDCA): A new platinum compound. *Seminars in Oncology* 16 (supplement 5).

Mayer, D.K., and M. Grant. 1987. Identifying and utilizing key personnel for cancer nursing research. *Oncology Nursing Forum* 14:91–93.

McBride, C.M. 1976. Regional chemotherapy by isolation-perfusion. *International Advances in Surgical Oncology* 1:1–9.

National Cancer Institute. 1984. *What are clinical trials all about? A booklet for patients with cancer.* NIH Publication no. 85-2706, December.

Nealson, E., B. Blumberg, and B. Brown. 1985. What do patients know about clinical trials? *American Journal of Nursing* 85:807–10.

Nuremberg Code. 1949. *Permissible medical experiments. Trials of war criminals before the Nuremberg Military Tribunals under Control Council Law no. 10: Nuremberg October 1946–April 1949.* Washington, D.C.: Government Printing Office.

O'Dwyer, P., et al. 1988. Deoxycoporomycin: An active new drug for indolent lymphomas and hairy cell leukemia. *Oncology* 2:17–22.

Pass, H.I., J. Mitchell, A. Russo, T. Delaney, and E. Glatstein. 1989. Photodynamic therapy. *Mediguide to Oncology* 9:1–8.

President's Commission for the Study of Ethical Problems in Medicine and Biomedical and Behavioral Research. 1982. *Making health care decisions: A report on the ethical and legal implications of informed consent in the patient-practitioner relationship,* vol. 1. Washington, D.C.: Government Printing Office.

Russo, A., J. Mitchell, H. Pass, and E. Glatstein. 1989. Photodynamic therapy. In *Cancer: Principles and practice of oncology.* 2d ed., ed. V.T. DeVita, Jr., S. Hellman, and S.A. Rosenberg. Philadelphia: J.B. Lippincott.

Speth, P., H. Minderman, and C. Haanen. 1989. Daunorubicin: Preclinical and clinical pharmacokinetic studies. *Seminars in Oncology* 16:2–9.

Stein, C.A., and J.S. Cohen. 1988. Oligodeoxynucleotides as inhibitors of gene expression: A review. *Cancer Research* 48:2659–2668.

Stewart, C.D. 1989. Nursing interventions in regional chemotherapy using surgical drug delivery systems. In *Nursing interventions in oncology: M.D. Anderson case reports and reviews.*

Taylor, I., J. Rowling, and C. West. 1979. Adjuvant cytotoxic liver perfusion for colorectal cancer. *British Journal of Surgery* 66:833–37.

Wong, P.C., S.W. Chung, and A.W. Nienhuis. 1987. Retroviral transfer and expression of the interleukin-3 gene in hematopoietic cells. *Genes Dev* 1:358–65.

Chapter 5

Technologic Advances in Radiation Oncology and Applications for Nursing Research

Glenda B. Kelman, Roberta A. Strohl, and Nancy E. Riese

> Current applications of radiation therapy and cancer nursing research specific to radiation therapy are reviewed, and suggestions are made for future nursing research. In addition, directions for dissemination, utilization, and conduct of research for radiation oncology nurses are presented.

Among the available modalities for cancer treatment, radiation therapy is one of the oldest. From the time of the discovery of X rays by William Roentgen in 1895, there have been attempts to treat cancer patients with radiation (Kaplan 1979; Stein 1985). Early clinical trials were limited by a lack of understanding of radiation biology as well as by inadequate equipment. The first treatment units were orthovoltage machines that delivered superficial radiation, with virtually 100% of the given dose being realized at the skin surface. Treatment in this manner was effective for skin cancers, but it was impossible to treat more deeply seated tumors without serious and permanent sequelae in normal tissues. The development of sophisticated equipment that had the ability to deliver the maximum radiation dose below the skin surface, along with an enhanced understanding of the biologic effects of radiation, heralded the modern era of radiation therapy. Radiation therapy is used in all phases of cancer management with treatment goals of cure, control, or palliation. It is estimated that 50% to 60% of all patients diagnosed with cancer will receive radiation at some point during the treatment of their disease (Kramer et al. 1984; Strohl 1988).

Radiation therapy can be delivered in several ways. Most patients are treated with external beam therapy or teletherapy. This consists of electromagnetic radiation in the form of X rays and γ rays or particulate radiation in the form of α, β, and γ rays. This radiation delivery system consists of a fixed source at a distance from the patient. The patient is positioned on a treatment couch and is exposed to the radiation. The patient is never radioactive when receiving external beam treatment (Yasko 1982).

Brachytherapy or implant therapy is the use of nonpenetrating, sealed sources of radiation that are implanted into the tumor or a cavity by means of seeds, needles, or ribbons. Because the sources are sealed, there is no contamination of body fluids.

Isotope or radiopharmaceutical therapy is the use of unsealed sources of radiation. Because the sources are unsealed, there is contamination of body fluids while the source is active. Sources with short half-lives are therefore used in this type of treatment. Isotopes may be selected that are preferentially absorbed by the organ of interest; an example is the use of radioactive iodine (^{131}I) in the treatment of thyroid cancers. Protocols are ongoing for the use of radioactive phosphorus (^{32}P), which is used intraperitoneally for the treatment of ovarian cancers. Patients may receive radiation therapy by only one of the available systems or in a combined approach (Glicksman 1987; Withers 1987).

The most significant factor in the biologic effect of radiation is damage to DNA. Radiation-induced cell death is predominantly mitotically linked. Cells function but die when division is attempted. The rate at which radiation causes cells, both normal and cancerous, to die is dependent on the mitotic activity of the cell. Cells that are sensitive to radiation are those with a high mitotic index and include normal tissues such as hair follicles, bone marrow, and gastrointestinal mucosa and tumors such as lymphomas, Hodgkin's disease, and leukemia. Because these cells divide frequently, it takes a short period of time for the radiation effect to be realized. Cells that divide slowly have a delayed response to radiation; these include normal tissues such as muscles, vessels, and nerves and tumors such as squamous cell cancers and cancers derived from muscle such as rhabdomyosarcomas. These tumors do respond to radiation but require a high dose (Schiffer 1987; Withers 1987).

Normal cells have a greater capacity for repair than cancer cells and are therefore less likely to be permanently damaged by radiation. There is, however, a documented maximum radiation dose for each tissue. Doses above this level have the potential to cause irreversible damage. Treatment planning has as its goal the delivery of an adequate radiation dose to the tumor with minimal damage to the surrounding normal tissue (Schiffer 1987; Withers 1987).

New advances in radiation oncology seek to enhance the effect of radiation while minimizing sequelae in normal tissue. The nurse caring for the patient receiving radiation therapy must have an understanding of the treatment to prepare the patient for the experience. This knowledge is also necessary before providing information related to new advances or unconventional therapy. Receiving radiation therapy is a frightening experience for the individual. The lack of concrete or tactile sensation makes the therapy mysterious, and the nurse must help the patient understand what to expect (King et al. 1985; Peck and Boland 1977). Benner

(1984) describes the nurse as a coach who takes what is foreign and fearful to the patient and makes it familiar and thus less frightening.

TYPES OF RADIATION THERAPY

Hyperthermia

Attempts to use heat to destroy tumor cells are far from new. It was noted as early as 1890 that some febrile patients receiving no cancer therapy had a regression of tumor mass. The clinical use of hyperthermia became possible as equipment was developed to deliver and measure heat. Hyperthermia may be administered in the form of total body heating, but more commonly it involves local or regional heating of the area surrounding the tumor by means of ultrasound or microwaves. Clinical trials are currently ongoing to study the enhancement of radiation effect with a combination of radiation and hyperthermia; promising results have been obtained in several tumor types. Third party insurance carriers will reimburse hyperthermia fees only if the treatment is given in combination with radiation (Arcangeli et al. 1985; Dragovic et al. 1989; Dunlop et al. 1986). The biologic effect of the combination of hyperthermia and radiation is currently being investigated.

It has been postulated that hyperthermia enhances radiation damage by several mechanisms. Hyperthermia prevents the repair of radiation damage. It also is able to kill cells in phases of the cell cycle during which they are resistant to radiation, such as the S phase. Heat is able to kill more cancer cells than normal cells; it may be that hypoxic cells are sensitive to heat, and cancer cells are likely to be hypoxic as they outgrow their blood supplies. Cancer cells may be metabolically deprived by reducing the pH of their environment, thereby rendering them sensitive to heat. Blood flow in tumor cells is reduced, so that they hold heat for longer periods of time than normal cells. The damage to cancer cell DNA by heat is thought to impair cell recovery (Perez et al. 1987).

Hyperthermia is a frightening concept for many patients. The notion of being "cooked" is conceptually disquieting. The nurse must use sensitivity in explaining the therapy, paying careful attention to the rationale for treatment. The temperature of the area is measured with thermistors, which are placed in catheters and implanted under the skin (Figure 5-1). The catheters are left in place throughout the treatment course and require care, as is the case with any implanted catheter. The hyperthermia unit is coupled to the skin, and a temperature of 41° to 45°C is achieved and maintained for approximately 30 to 45 minutes (Moore 1984). Patients generally receive hyperthermia once or twice a week in conjunction with radiation therapy (Figure 5-2).

62   ONCOLOGY NURSING

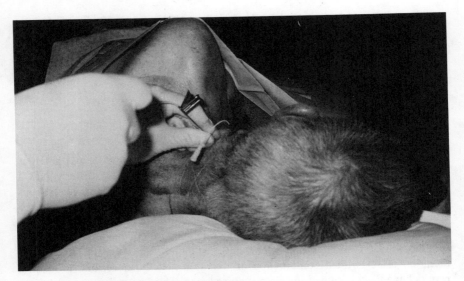

Figure 5-1 Catheters Being Inserted for Hyperthermia

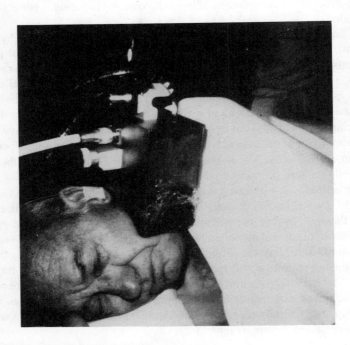

Figure 5-2 Patient Receiving Hyperthermia

Skin reactions are enhanced because of the combination of heat and radiation, and it is not uncommon for blisters to develop in the treated area. Skin care protocols should be followed meticulously. The patient must be taught good skin and hand washing techniques because breaks in skin integrity place the individual at risk for infection.

The treatment may cause discomfort, so that a short-acting narcotic may be necessary. The patient may note a burning sensation and the odor of burning; room deodorizers may minimize the latter. Patients may lie on a comfortable treatment couch and may bring tapes to listen to during the treatment. With these supportive measures, patients are able to undergo local or regional hyperthermia with minimal difficulty (Moore 1984; Perez et al. 1987).

Brachytherapy

Brachytherapy or implant therapy is the placement of a radioactive source directly into the tumor or a cavity. Nonpenetrating sources are used so that the maximum radiation dose is given to the tumor with a minimum dose to normal tissues. Implants are used in cases in which the tumor requires a higher radiation dose than the surrounding normal tissue can tolerate or when the patient has been previously treated (Glicksman 1987; Hassey 1987).

Innovations in surgical and radiation techniques now allow sites previously unsuitable for implantation to be managed by this modality. Brain implants (Figures 5-3 and 5-4) are being used for recurrent glioblastoma. The technique is known as afterloading because the catheters are implanted first and then the radioactive sources are loaded later, after radiography has verified catheter placement and the patient's condition has stabilized. The sources are generally left in place for 50 hours for brain implants and for 48 to 72 hours for other types. This allows a concentrated radiation dose to be delivered to the tumor while sparing the surrounding normal structures (Salcman et al. 1986).

Traditional implants have been used for gynecologic and head and neck cancers. Newer implants have been used in other tumor sites, including lung, bladder, and esophagus, and in early stage rectal cancers (Glicksman 1987).

It is beyond the scope of this chapter to present in detail the nursing management of patients treated with brachytherapy. The reader is referred to Withers (1987), Glicksman (1987), Hassey (1987), and McCarthy (1987) for more information.

Patients who have radioactive sources in place are radioactive for the period of implantation. The principles of time, distance, and shielding are therefore incorporated into the nursing care of brachytherapy patients. The sources are nonpenetrating, so that small differences in distances are significant, and all care should be delivered from as far away from the source as possible. If available, shielding should be used. The amount of time spent in the room should also be limited. Nursing care should be well organized so that care can be delivered

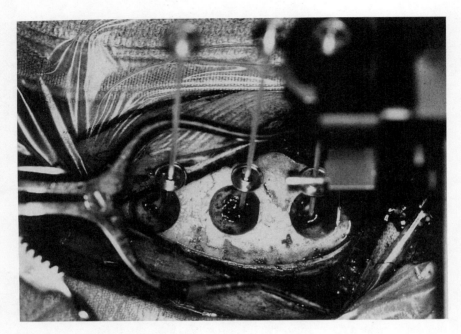

Figure 5-3 Insertion of a Brain Implant

effectively in an appropriate time frame. If the condition of the patient becomes unstable, the source may have to be removed until the patient's status allows it to be replaced. The nurse caring for the individual must be able to provide instruction and support for the patient and family during the time of implantation (Hassey 1987).

Altered Fractions

Conventional radiation therapy is delivered in equal doses, known as fractions, given 5 days per week until the prescribed dosage is achieved. This concept allows for tumor response and normal tissue recovery. Altered fractions are undergoing clinical trials for use in clinical situations in which tumors are resistant to radiation or for large tumors that do not respond well to treatment. Two forms of unconventional treatment include hyperfractionation and accelerated fractionation. In hyperfractionation two or more treatments are given each day, each fraction being smaller than the usual daily dose (the usual daily fraction for radical radiation is 180 to 250 rad/day). The total dose given for the treatment course is higher than the usual tumor dose. In accelerated fractionation the total dose remains the same but is given in a short period of time with more than one fraction per day or in a

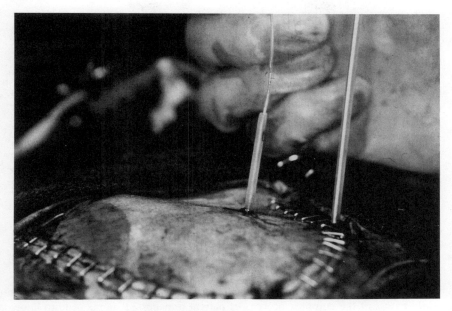

Figure 5-4 Brain Implant with Dummy Seeds in Place

higher daily dose. Patients receiving more than one treatment per day generally wait 4 hours between treatments. This means that the patient either has to make two trips to the radiation oncology department each day or must stay in the department for long periods (Cox et al. 1988; Cox and Vander Schueren 1988; Parsons et al. 1988).

The patient may be concerned about receiving more than one treatment per day. The rationale for this protocol must be carefully explained. Transportation may be difficult for two trips per day. If the patient elects to remain in the radiation oncology department, consideration must be given to meals and medications.

Intraoperative Radiation

Intraoperative radiation is a radiation treatment given during an operative procedure. The goal of this treatment is to deliver a single large radiation fraction. Doses generally range from 1,000 to 4,000 rad in one treatment depending on the tumor and site. The tumor bed is measured, and a sterilized Lucite cone is placed into the tumor bed and attached to the treatment machine. Radiation is given as a large single dose that is biologically equivalent to 2 to 2½ times the given dose. Tumors being treated in this manner include gastrointestinal, bladder, lung, pancreatic, and colorectal tumors (Goldson 1981; Haibeck 1988; Tepper 1987).

Intraoperative radiation provides the radiation oncologist with the ability to visualize the tumor and to move normal tissues out of the radiation field or to shield them. Superficial radiation delivered by means of an electron beam permits the irradiation of the tumor while sparing normal tissue (Tepper 1987).

The ideal method of treatment with intraoperative radiation is for a treatment machine to be in the operating suite, and there are several centers that have this capability. In most settings, however, the patient must be transported while under anesthesia to the radiation therapy department. The wound is temporarily closed, and the patient is transported to the treatment room in the radiation department, which must be cleaned and prepared accordingly. The wound is opened, and the patient is treated. The wound is then temporarily closed, and the patient returns to the operating room, where the surgical procedure is completed. Infection rates are not higher than usual in this group of patients.

Complications such as delayed wound healing and postoperative infection have not been significant problems. Rapid tumor lysis has resulted in perforation. Nausea and vomiting are seen when the abdomen is treated. The major limiting factor in the use of intraoperative radiation is the logistics of patient transportation (Goldson 1981).

The nurses in the radiation oncology department and the operating suite serve as coordinators of the complex process of patient transport. Patients need to know what to expect because the large dose of radiation is frightening to many. Assessment of the surgical site is crucial because radiation is known to influence wound healing, even though this has not been a problem. If the logistic difficulties of intraoperative radiation could be solved its application would be more widespread, and work is ongoing in this regard (Haibeck 1988).

Radiation Sensitizers and Protectors

There has been an ongoing search for compounds that act as radiation sensitizers and protectors. Sensitizers are compounds that are selectively taken into hypoxic cells to render them more sensitive to radiation by increasing their oxygenation. Misonidazole was among the first to be tested in clinical trials after showing promise in the laboratory. Its use has been restricted by dose limiting nausea and vomiting and peripheral neurotoxicity. Nonnitromidazole compounds, halogenated pyrimidine analogs such as bromodeoxyuridine (BUdR) and iododeoxyuridine (IUdR), and chemotherapeutic agents are undergoing clinical trials (Phillips 1981; Wasserman and Kligerman 1987).

Protectors are compounds that are selectively taken into normal tissues to protect them from radiation effects. Compounds such as vitamin E, vitamin C, and β-carotene have been studied. Most of the research has been related to WR-2721 CS-2 (3-amniopropylaminophosphorothioic acid). This protector is concentrated in all normal tissues except brain and spinal cord. Dose-limiting toxic reactions include hypotension, emesis, somnolence, and hypocalcemia. Studies are ongoing to identify nontoxic or tolerable compounds to serve as both sensitizers and protectors (Phillips 1981; Wasserman and Kligerman 1987).

Patients being treated with sensitizers and protectors require the same considerations as other individuals being treated in clinical trials. Patients need to understand what is known about the drug and also what is not known. Careful documentation of side effects is essential for the ongoing accumulation of information about these drugs. Patients and families need continuous support while they are undergoing clinical trials.

Summary of Radiation Therapies

The nurse caring for the patient receiving unconventional radiation therapy must be aware of the goals of the therapy and be able to explain them in words that the patient can understand. Radiation is a difficult modality for patients to comprehend, and time must be taken to clarify teaching and to correct misconceptions. The nurse must carefully document the physical and emotional responses of the patient to the new treatment because this valuable information is needed to plan further teaching and support. The nurse must be aware of the available nursing research related to individuals receiving radiation and incorporate these results into nursing care. Further research is clearly necessary to document patient response to unconventional therapy.

NURSING RESEARCH IN RADIATION ONCOLOGY

As described above, radiation therapy is used as primary and adjuvant therapy alone or in combination with surgery, chemotherapy, immunotherapy, and biologic response modifiers. It has been estimated that 50% to 60% of all individuals diagnosed with cancer will receive radiation therapy (Strohl 1988).

The goals of radiation therapy include cure, control, and palliation for the individual diagnosed with cancer. Expanded applications have included hyperfractionation, accelerated fractionation, particle radiation, isotopically labeled antibody therapy, hyperthermia, intraoperative radiotherapy, and radiosensitizing therapy in conjunction with chemotherapy (DeVita, Hellman, and Rosenberg 1989).

The rapid advances in technology have created a challenging learning environment for radiation oncology nurses. The practice of radiation oncology nursing has evolved into a clinical subspecialty. Application of theoretical frameworks and conceptual models will provide the structure for conducting research specific to radiation oncology nursing. In addition, utilization and application of proposed models will strengthen the position of radiation oncology nursing. Orem's model of self care, Pender's health belief model, Roy's adaptation model, Neumann's general systems model, and the Oncology Nursing Society (ONS)/American Nurses' Association outcome standards and nursing diagnoses have already served as foundations for nursing research in previous studies.

A 1988 ONS survey of research priorities was conducted by Funkhouser and Grant to update priorities previously identified by cancer nursing researchers (Funkhouser and Grant 1988; McGuire, Frank-Stromberg, and Varricchio 1984). The conceptual framework used for the study was the ONS's outcome standards for cancer nursing education (fundamental level), which divide theory and practice into five major areas: the individual and family, and health-illness continuum, the health care delivery system, the larger community and environment, and the nursing process (ONS Education Committee 1982). More than 200 members involved in research participated in this mail survey. Study results indicated that research priorities related to the conceptual framework were focused primarily on two areas: the individual and family and the health-illness continuum. Results indicated that respondents identified prevention and early detection, symptom management, pain control and management, patient or health education, and coping and stress management as their top five research priorities. The results were then submitted to the National Center for Nursing Research as the ONS's 1988 research priorities.

Prevention and (Early) Detection

Until the last decade the health behaviors and health-promoting activities of individuals with cancer had not been researched, although the concept of illness behavior (or sick role behavior) in individuals with cancer has been researched extensively. If health is defined as the fullest realization of human potential and as the ability to perform one's role, then having cancer does not negate being healthy (Frank-Stromberg 1986). Frank-Stromberg participated in a 3-year cluster grant funded by the Division of Nursing of the Department of Health and Human Services to Northern Illinois University School of Nursing entitled "Health Promoting Behavior: Testing a Proposed Model." The grant was composed of four projects that examined whether the cognitive-perceptual and modifying variables identified in Pender's health promotion model (Pender 1982) explain the occurrence of health-promoting behaviors in different populations.

The four areas investigated included exercise adherence among working adults, health-promoting behaviors among older adults, exercise adherence after myocardial infarction, and ambulatory cancer clients' health-promoting behaviors (Frank-Stromberg 1986). Because of the limitation of information about health-promoting behaviors of ambulatory cancer clients, one of the instruments developed by Frank-Stromberg (1988) was the health diary based on Pender's Health

Promotion Model (Pender 1982) and the six subscales contained in the Health Promoting Lifestyle Profile (Walker, Sechrist, and Pender 1987).

These subscales are exercise, self-actualization, interpersonal support, health responsibility, nutrition, and stress management. The surveyed ambulatory cancer clients included 108 individuals between the ages of 25 and 65 years, 91 of whom had received radiation therapy. The findings suggested that it is possible to be healthy at the same time that one has cancer and that individuals were participating in behaviors representative of the six dimensions of a health-promoting lifestyle (Frank-Stromberg 1986).

Although the studies discussed are not limited to the cancer patient receiving radiation therapy, future research could include replication of Frank-Stromberg's (1986) study with *only* cancer patients receiving radiation therapy (and further separation of patients into subcategories on the basis of type of radiation therapy and other variables). Winningham and MacVicar's (1988) study could be replicated only with individuals receiving radiation therapy to determine the effects of moderate aerobic activity on nausea. Additional studies investigating aerobic exercise in combination with other symptom-related strategies such as relaxation therapy could also be considered.

Symptom Management

There has been an increasing focus on research related to symptom management of acute and chronic reactions of individuals receiving radiation therapy. Fatigue may be the most frequent, cumulative, and bothersome side effect experienced by individuals receiving radiation therapy (King et al. 1985). Studies by Haylock and Hart (1979) indicated various patterns of fatigue as identified by patients, with individuals reportedly feeling better on some days than on others. More recent research has focused on developing a nursing theory about fatigue to develop a framework to guide nurses in fatigue assessments and interventions (Piper, Lindsay, and Dodd 1987). Most of the fatigue research has been conducted on healthy subjects, however, and may not be applicable to individuals with cancer (Gibson and Edwards 1985). Additional research to compare acute and chronic fatigue and to examine various patterns of fatigue in relation to diagnosis and patient-related variables is needed to enable nurses to identify individuals who may be at high risk and to prescribe appropriate intervention strategies.

Before 1986, the only known study investigating health-promoting activities of individuals with cancer was MacVicar's (1983) research on the effects of aerobic training on the functional status of women with stage II breast cancer who were undergoing chemotherapy (MacVicar 1983). A second study by Winningham and MacVicar (1988) suggested that moderate aerobic activity may be beneficial as an adjunctive self-care measure to antiemetic therapy in controlling chemotherapy-induced nausea and in promoting physical well-being.

Skin care during radiation therapy is a crucial need. There are many reported interventions for preventive skin care and management of skin reactions related to treatment, but few documented studies are available (Hassey and Rose 1982; Shell, Stanutz, and Grimm 1986). Additionally, studies have focused more on assessment of skin integrity than on intervention strategies (Miaskowski 1983). There is a significant need for nursing research to evaluate specifically preventive and treatment guidelines for skin care for the individual receiving radiation therapy.

Individuals receiving radiation therapy to the gastrointestinal tract complain of altered taste, anorexia, nausea, vomiting, diarrhea, and gastric distention. In addition, radiation to the oral cavity can also induce alterations in taste and smell, mucositis, and xerostomia. All these side effects have been consistently documented as common, persistent problems. The research issue is the lack of clear, concise, standardized, reliable, and valid symptom distress tools. Once such tools are established different intervention strategies can be compared for effectiveness, and individuals at risk can be identified. Progress, however, has been made specifically in developing tools to measure nausea and vomiting (Eilers, Berger, and Petersen 1988; Morrow 1984; Rhodes, Watson, and Johnson 1984).

Central nervous system toxicity related to radiation therapy and its effects on cognitive functioning have been investigated. A study by Moore, Kramer, and Arlin (1986) found that central nervous system prophylaxis by means of 2,400 rad of cranial radiation and intrathecal methotrexate can result in delayed injury to the brain. Findings suggest the need for ongoing evaluation of the child receiving radiation therapy for central nervous system cancer to detect and minimize late effects on cognitive functioning and academic performance.

Endocrine side effects of radiation therapy related to sexual and reproductive functioning may have a significant impact on the individual diagnosed with cancer. Variables such as self-concept, self-esteem, social support, body image, and sexuality are being studied to measure the impact of disease and therapy on the perceptions of individuals with cancer. Research, however, has been carried out primarily by the medical and psychologic professions. Nursing research focused initially on studies related to cancer patients and alterations in body image (due to mastectomies, ostomies, and amputations) but is beginning to explore additional concerns of cancer patients related to treatment and the impact on sexual and reproductive functioning (Dudas and Carlson 1988; Ruccione and Fergusson 1984).

Dyspnea has been reported to be an extremely distressing symptom (Brown et al. 1986). In addition, anxiety, which appears to increase dyspnea, may be a concern not only to the individual with cancer but to the family as well (Foote, Sexton, and Pawlik 1986). Research can test and compare various intervention strategies that may be used to decrease patient and family anxiety and to improve patient comfort.

Pain Control and Management

The measurement and evaluation of pain remains a challenge for researchers. Because of the subjective and complex nature of pain, the International Association for the Study of Pain (1979) developed a taxonomy of pain terms and definitions for use as minimum standard vocabulary. Other investigators agree that pain is a unique experience, that it represents a category of experiences, and that it exists when the individual states that it does (Ferrell and Schneider 1988; McCaffrey and Beebe 1989). Priorities in cancer nursing research for pain management focus on accurate assessment (i.e., using appropriate tools to assess and differentiate acute from chronic pain) and appropriate intervention strategies for different patient groups (adults, children, cultural background, sex, and the like) (Ferrell and Schneider 1988; Ferrell, Wisdom, and Wenzl 1989).

Studies reviewed are most often not specific to a single treatment modality or disease site. Recent nursing research has focused on the relationship between quality of life and cancer pain, including comparisons of short-acting and controlled-release analgesia (Brescia et al. 1987; Ferrell et al. 1989; Meed et al. 1987). Continued studies and research will create and test new alternatives for the ultimate goals of comfort and improved quality of life for the individual with cancer.

Patient or Health Education

Several studies specific to radiation therapy, patient perceptions, and patient teaching have been conducted. Lauer, Murphy, and Powers (1982) identified the rank order for importance of treatment information for radiation therapy. Purpose of treatment was ranked as most important and was followed by treatment schedule, duration of treatment, and side effects (including how to manage side effects). Studies examining patient fears and concerns regarding radiation therapy by Peck and Boland (1977) identified hearing the term *cobalt*, being left alone in the room during treatment, and having to undergo long periods of exposure to radiation as triggers of patient fears. Bricourt and McKenzie (1984) also identified similar concerns expressed by individuals receiving radiation therapy: being left alone in the treatment room, being crushed by the machine, being exposed to too much radiation, being burned, losing hair, experiencing nausea, and becoming sterile. In a study comparing different groups receiving radiation therapy for prostate cancer, the group that was given specific information about physical and temporal sensations and environmental aspects of the treatment reported less disruption of usual activities during and after radiation therapy than the group receiving routine information (Johnson et al. 1988).

Strohl (1988) recommends that the radiation oncology nurse act as Benner (1984) suggests: as a coach to help patients learn about and gain control over their situation. Dodd's (1984) findings also support the observation that patients receiving radiation therapy are interested in self-care activities but need further information to initiate these practices; that study identified a positive correlation between knowledge of radiation therapy and degree of self-care activities. In a more recent study by Dodd and Ahmed (1987) of preference for type of information among cancer patients receiving radiation therapy, patients preferred cognitive information (although this preference decreased over time); personal control, degree of anxiety, and demographic variables were significantly associated with preference for type of information. Further studies should include application of related concepts to learning, including self-efficacy and cognitive and sensory learning styles.

Coping and Stress Management

The diagnosis of cancer is probably the most disruptive and distressing life event that an individual and family experience. Cancer is a crisis for the entire family system, and life becomes an emotional roller coaster. No matter what coping method the individual or family uses, there is no escape from the reality of the diagnosis or the fear of the prognosis. The individual and family may need professional assistance to facilitate communication, to reduce stress, and to identify coping strategies (Lewis 1983; Thorne 1985).

A study by Tringali (1985) investigated perceptions of family members of cancer patients being treated with chemotherapy or radiation therapy as outpatients to determine needs that they perceived as important. Findings indicated that cognitive needs were most important. A review of family experiences of living with cancer indicated that family members' concerns vary with their roles in the family and whether they are patients or nonpatients (Woods, Lewis, and Ellison 1989). Concern varies with stage of illness and time since diagnosis. Families are a strong influence on the adjustment of the person with cancer. Concerns are not always shared among all family members. Family members cope in different ways, and coping patterns vary according to the disease status and role in the family (Woods, Lewis, and Ellison 1989).

A study by Hanucharurnkul (1989) that examined predictors of self-care in cancer patients receiving radiation therapy in Thailand suggested that socioeconomic status and social support are significant predictors of patient care; stage and site of cancer seemed to predict self-care indirectly through social support. Support groups conducted by professionals and lay groups warrant further study. Whitman and Gustafson (1989) suggest that most families can benefit from multifamily group therapy sessions. An evaluation of "I Can Cope" programs by Diekmann (1988) found that participants generally rate such programs positively. Topics that generated the most positive responses included learning about cancer, communication, and learning to like oneself.

Suggestions for Facilitation of Research

It is not uncommon for nurses who are employed in radiation oncology to be isolated from their professional colleagues. Many inpatient and outpatient settings employ only one oncology nurse. It is important that the oncology nurse develop a professional network to collaborate in establishing patient care standards, product evaluation protocols, quality assurance programs, and patient teaching materials and in initiating patient care studies. Suggestions for networking include national and local chapter membership in ONS, membership in the oncology unit or division of the American Cancer Society, and membership in the local chapter of Sigma Theta Tau International Nursing Honor Society. If the health care agency belongs to a community health consortium, the oncology nurse should find out whether there are other radiation oncology nurses and arrange to meet with them. Teaching days should be attended on local, regional, and national levels whenever possible.

Forming a research interest group will provide an opportunity to review and critique research. Information can also be shared regarding potential funding sources and developing grant applications and research proposals. Oncology nurses should also seek opportunities to participate in multidisciplinary research in their institutions and community.

Research provides a scientific knowledge base for practice; research tests and retests nursing behaviors with the ultimate goal of improving patient care and nursing practice. Utilization and application of research findings are essential to institute change and to provide high-quality, cost-effective care to the individual with cancer and the family.

STUDY QUESTIONS

1. List the three ways in which radiation therapy can be delivered to patients.
2. Identify the other forms of cancer treatments that may be combined with radiation.
3. According to nursing research, what are specific information needs of patients receiving radiation therapy?

4. Is moderate aerobic activity beneficial as an adjunctive self-care measure to antiemetic therapy in controlling treatment-induced nausea and vomiting and in promoting physical well-being? Why or why not?
5. In what ways are fatigue patterns similar or dissimilar in patients receiving radiation therapy?
6. What are the late effects of central nervous system toxicity related to radiation therapy and the effect on cognitive functioning?

REFERENCES

Arcangeli, Giorgio, Giancarlo Arcangeli, A. Guerra, G. Lovisolo, A. Cividalli, C. Marino, and F. Mauro. 1985. Tumor response to heat and radiation prognostic variables in the treatment of head and neck cancer. *International Journal of Hyperthermia* 1:207–17.

Benner, P. 1984. *From novice to expert: Excellence and power in clinical nursing practice.* Menlo Park, Calif.: Addison-Wesley.

Brescia, F.J., M. Walsh, J.J. Savarese, and R.F. Kaiko. 1987. A study of controlled-release oral morphine (MS Contin) in an advanced cancer hospital. *Journal of Pain Symptom Management* 2:193–98.

Bricourt, P., and J. McKenzie. 1984. Radiotherapy from the patient's viewpoint. In *Radiation therapy and thanatology*, eds. R. Torpie, L. Leigner, and C. Chang. Springfield, Ill: C.C. Thomas.

Brown, M., V. Carrier, S. Janson-Bjerklie, and M. Dodd. 1986. Lung cancer and dyspnea: The patient's perceptions. *Oncology Nursing Forum* 13:19–25.

Cox, J., and E. Vander Schueren. 1988. Time/dose/fractionation trials. *International Journal of Radiation Oncology, Biology, and Physics* 14(supplement):51–56.

Cox, J.D., C. Guse, S. Asbell, P. Rubin, and W.T. Sause. 1988. Tolerance of pelvic normal tissues to hyperfractionated radiation therapy: Results of protocol 83-08 of the radiation therapy oncology group. *International Journal of Radiation Oncology, Biology, and Physics* 15:1331–36.

DeVita, V.T. Jr., S. Hellman, and S.A. Rosenberg, eds. 1989. *Cancer: Principles and practice of oncology.* 2d ed. Philadelphia: J.B. Lippincott.

Diekmann, J. 1988. An evaluation of selected "I Can Cope" programs by registered participants. *Cancer Nursing* 11:274–82.

Dodd, M. 1984. Patterns of self-care in patients receiving radiation therapy. *Oncology Nursing Forum* 11:23–30.

Dodd, M., and N. Ahmed. 1987. Preference for type of information in cancer patients receiving radiation therapy. *Cancer Nursing* 10:244–51.

Dragovic, J., H.G. Seydel, T. Sandhee, A. Kolosvary, and J. Blough. 1989. Local superficial hyperthermia in combination with low-dose radiation therapy for palliation of locally recurrent breast carcinoma. *Journal of Clinical Oncology* 7:30–35.

Dudas, S., and C. Carlson. 1988. Cancer rehabilitation. *Oncology Nursing Forum* 15:183–88.

Dunlop, P.R.C., J.W. Hand, R.J. Dickinson, and S.B. Field. 1986. An assessment of local hyperthermia in clinical practice. *International Journal of Hyperthermia* 2:39–50.

Eilers, J., A. Berger, and M. Petersen. 1988. Development, testing, and application of the oral assessment guide. *Oncology Nursing Forum* 15:325–30.

Ferrell, B., and C. Schneider. 1988. Experience and management of cancer pain at home. *Cancer Nursing* 11:84–90.

Ferrell, B., C. Wisdom, and C. Wenzl. 1989. Quality of life as an outcome variable in the management of cancer pain. *Cancer* 63:2321–29.

Ferrell, B., C. Wisdom, C. Wenzl, and J. Brown. 1989. Effects of controlled-release morphine on quality of life for cancer pain. *Oncology Nursing Forum* 16:521–26.

Foote, M., L. Sexton, and L. Pawlik. 1986. Dyspnea: A distressing sensation in lung cancer. *Oncology Nursing Forum* 13:25–33.

Frank-Stromberg, M. 1986. Health promotion behaviors in ambulatory cancer patients: Fact or fiction? *Oncology Nursing Forum* 13:37–43.

Frank-Stromberg, M., ed. 1988. *Instruments for clinical nursing research*. Norwalk, Conn.: Appleton & Lange.

Funkhouser, S., and M. Grant. 1988. 1988 ONS survey of research priorities. *Oncology Nursing Forum* 16:413–16.

Gibson, H., and R. Edwards. 1985. Muscular exercise and fatigue. *Sports Medicine* 2:64.

Glicksman, A. 1987. Radiobiologic basis of brachytherapy. *Seminars in Oncology Nursing* 3:3–7.

Goldson, A. 1981. Past, present, and prospect of intraoperative radiotherapy. *Seminars in Oncology* 8:59–65.

Haibeck, S. 1988. Intraoperative radiation therapy. *Oncology Nursing Forum* 15:143–51.

Hanucharurnkul, S. 1989. Predictors of self-care in cancer patients receiving radiotherapy. *Cancer Nursing* 12:21–27.

Hassey, K. 1987. Principles of radiation safety and protection. *Seminars in Oncology Nursing* 3:23–30.

Hassey, K., and C. Rose. 1982. Altered skin integrity in patients receiving radiation therapy. *Oncology Nursing Forum* 9:44–50.

Haylock, P., and L. Hart. 1979. Fatigue in patients receiving localized radiation. *Cancer Nursing* 2:461–67.

International Association for the Study of Pain Subcommittee on Taxonomy. 1979. Pain terms: A list with definitions and notes on usage. *Pain* 6:249–52.

Johnson, J., L. Nail, D. Lauver, K. King, and H. Keys. 1988. Reducing the negative impact of radiation therapy on functional status. *Cancer* 61:46–51.

Kaplan, H. 1979. Historic milestones in radiobiology and radiation therapy. *Seminars in Oncology* 4:479–90.

King, K., L. Nail, K. Kreamer, R. Strohl, and J. Johnson. 1985. Patients' descriptions of the experience of receiving radiation therapy. *Oncology Nursing Forum* 12:55–61.

Kramer, S., G.E. Hanks, J.J. Diamond, et al. 1984. The study of patterns of clinical care in radiation therapy in the United States. *Cancer for Clinicians* 34:75–85.

Lauer, P., S. Murphy, and M. Powers. 1982. Learning needs of cancer patients: A comparison of nurse and patient perceptions. *Nursing Research* 31:11–16.

Lewis, F. 1983. Family level services for the cancer patient: Critical distinctions, fallacies, and assessment. *Cancer Nursing* 6:193–200.

MacVicar, M. 1983. Effect of aerobic training on functional status of women with breast cancer. Presented at the 8th ONS Annual Congress Conference, May 1983, Toronto, Canada.

McCaffrey, M., and A. Beebe. 1989. *Pain: Clinical manual for cancer nursing practice*. St. Louis, Mo.: C.V. Mosby.

McCarthy, C. 1987. The role of interstitial implantation in the treatment of primary breast cancer. *Seminars in Oncology Nursing* 3:47–54.

McGuire, D., M. Frank-Stromberg, and C. Varricchio. 1984. 1984 ONS Research Committee survey of membership's research interests and involvement. *Oncology Nursing Forum* 12:99–103.

Meed, S.D., P.H. Kleinmar, T.G. Kantor, R.H. Blum, and J.J. Savarese. 1987. Management of cancer pain with oral controlled-release morphine sulfate. *Journal of Clinical Pharmacology* 27:155–61.

Miaskowski, C. 1983. Potential and actual impairments in skin integrity related to cancer and cancer treatment. *Topics in Clinical Nursing* 2:64.

Moore, C. 1984. Nursing management of the patient receiving local or regional hyperthermia. *Oncology Nursing Forum* 11:40–45.

Moore, I., J. Kramer, and A. Arlin. 1986. Late effects of central nervous system prophylactic leukemia therapy on cognitive functioning. *Oncology Nursing Forum* 13:45–51.

Morrow, G. 1984. Assessment of nausea and vomiting: Past problems, current issues and suggestions for future research. *Cancer* 53:2267.

Oncology Nursing Society Education Committee. 1982. *Outcome standards for cancer nursing education, fundamental level*. Pittsburgh: Oncology Nursing Society.

Parsons, J.T., W.M. Mendelhall, N.J. Cassisi, J.H. Isaacs Jr., and R.R. Million. 1988. Hyperfractionation for head and neck cancer. *International Journal of Radiation Oncology, Biology, and Physics* 14:649–58.

Peck, A., and J. Boland. 1977. Emotional reactions to radiation treatment. *Cancer* 1:180–84.

Pender, N. 1982. *Health promotion in nursing practice*. New York: Appleton-Century-Crofts.

Perez, C., et al. 1987. Hyperthermia. In *Principles and practice of radiation oncology*, eds. C. Perez and L. Brady. Philadelphia: J.B. Lippincott.

Phillips, T. 1981. Sensitizers and protectors in clinical oncology. *Seminars in Oncology* 8:65–83.

Piper, B., A. Lindsay, and M. Dodd. 1987. Fatigue mechanisms in cancer patients: Developing nursing theory. *Oncology Nursing Forum* 14:17–22.

Rhodes, V., P. Watson, and M. Johnson. 1984. Development of reliable and valid measures of nausea and vomiting. *Cancer Nursing* 84:33.

Ruccione, K., and J. Fergusson. 1984. Late effects of childhood cancer and its treatment. *Oncology Nursing Forum* 11:54–61.

Salcman, M., W. Sewchand, P.P. Amin, and E.H. Bellis. 1986. Technique and preliminary results of interstitial irradiation for primary brain tumors. *Journal of Neuro-Oncology* 4:141–49.

Schiffer, L. 1987. Cellular proliferation in tumor and normal tissues. In *Principles and practice of radiation oncology*, eds. C. Perez and L. Brady. Philadelphia: J.B. Lippincott.

Shell, J., F. Stanutz, and J. Grimm. 1986. Comparison of moisture vapor permeable (MVP) dressings to conventional dressings for management of radiation skin reactions. *Oncology Nursing Forum* 13:11–16.

Stein, J. 1985. Some observations of the history of irradiation therapy. *Endocurietherapy/Hyperthermia Oncology* 1:59–65.

Strohl, R. 1988. The nursing role in radiation oncology: Symptom management of acute and chronic reactions. *Oncology Nursing Forum* 15:429–34.

Tepper, J. 1987. Intraoperative radiation. In *Principles and practice of radiation oncology*, eds. C. Perez and L. Brady. Philadelphia: J.B. Lippincott.

Thorne, S. 1985. The family cancer experience. *Cancer Nursing* 8:285–91.

Tringali, C. 1985. The needs of family members of cancer patients. *Oncology Nursing Forum* 13:65–70.

Walker, S., K. Sechrist, and N. Pender. 1987. Health promoting lifestyle profile: Development and psychometric characteristics. *Nursing Research* 36:76.

Wasserman, T., and M. Kligerman. 1987. Chemical modifiers of radiation effects. In *Principles and practice of radiation oncology*, eds. C. Perez and L. Brady. Philadelphia: J.B. Lippincott.

Whitman, H., and J. Gustafson. 1989. Group therapies for families facing a cancer crisis. *Oncology Nursing Forum* 16:539–43.

Winningham, M., and M. MacVicar. 1988. The effect of aerobic exercise on patient reports of nausea. *Oncology Nursing Forum* 15:37–43.

Withers, H.R. 1987. Biologic basis of radiation therapy. In *Principles and practice of radiation oncology*, eds. C. Perez and L. Brady. Philadelphia: J.B. Lippincott.

Woods, N., F. Lewis, and E. Ellison. 1989. Living with cancer: Family experiences. *Cancer Nursing* 12:29–33.

Yasko, J. 1982. *Care of the client receiving external radiation therapy.* Reston, Va.: Reston Publishing.

SUGGESTED READINGS

Cohen, L., T.E. Schultheiss, F.R. Hendrickson, J. Mansell, K.R. Sarota, and A. Lennox. 1989. Normal tissue reactions and complications following high-energy neutron beam therapy. *International Journal of Radiation Oncology, Biology, and Physics* 16:73.

Gibbs, F.A. 1983. "Thermal mapping" in experimental cancer treatment with hyperthermia: Description and use of a semi-automated system. *International Journal of Radiation Oncology, Biology, and Physics* 9:1057–63.

Hilderly, L.J. 1980. The role of the nurse in radiation oncology. *Seminars in Oncology* 7:42.

Hilderly, L.J. 1987. Radiation oncology. In *Cancer nursing principles and practices*, ed. S. Groenwald. Boston: Jones and Bartlett.

Luk, K.H., T.F. Pajak, C.A. Perez, R.J. Johnson, N. Donner, and T. Dobbins. 1984. Prognostic factors for tumor response after hyperthermia and radiation. In *Hyperthermic oncology, 1984: Proceedings of the 4th International Symposium on Hyperthermic Oncology*, vol. 1:353. ed. J. Overgaard. London/Philadelphia: Taylor & Francis.

Mayer, D.K., and R. Strohl. 1987. Investigational cancer treatment modalities. In *Core curriculum for oncology nursing*, ed. C. Ziegfeld. Philadelphia: W.B. Saunders.

Oleson, J.R. 1989. Hyperthermia. In *Cancer: Principles and practice of oncology*. 2d ed., ed. V.T. DeVita, S. Hellman, and S.A. Rosenberg. Philadelphia: J.B. Lippincott.

Oleson, J.R., D.A. Sim, and M.R. Manning. 1984. Analysis of prognostic variables in hyperthermia treatment of 161 patients. *International Journal of Radiation Oncology, Biology, and Physics* 10:2231–39.

Overgaard, L. 1989. The current and potential role of hyperthermia in radiotherapy. *International Journal of Radiation Oncology, Biology, and Physics* 16:535.

Perez, C.A., G. Nussbaum, B. Emami, and D. VonGerichten. 1983. Clinical application of irradiation combined with local hyperthermia. *Cancer* 52:1579–1603.

Slater, J., D.W. Miller, and J.O. Archambeau. 1988. Development of a hospital-based proton beam treatment center. *International Journal of Radiation Oncology, Biology, and Physics* 14:761–75.

Chapter 6

Biologic Response Modifiers: Therapies That Hold Great Promise for Cancer Patients

Brenda Shelton and Anne E. Belcher

> State-of-the-art biotherapy involves the use of biologic response modifiers that are capable of altering the immune system, which in turn mediates tumor destruction. Biologic response modifiers are described in terms of classifications, mechanisms of action, and current status of therapeutic use. Common side effects are delineated, as are specific toxic effects. Discussion of the nursing implications of biologic response modifiers includes nursing diagnoses, definition of characteristics, and nursing interventions.

The hypothesis that modulation of the immune system can result in regression of tumors in humans is not new, but it certainly has gained considerable popularity since the advent of sophisticated biologic technology. The first trials that applied this concept of immune modulation to the treatment of cancer took place in the 1960s and used bacille Calmette Guérin (BCG) and *Corynebacterium parvum* vaccines. This traditional concept of immunotherapy, known as active nonspecific therapy, has been extended to include molecular biology recombinant genetics, hybridoma technology, maturation factors, and artificial antagonists of neoplastic growth (Oldham 1985). Biologic therapy, as it is now called, is described as treatment with agents that alter biologic responses in the host-tumor interaction (Oldham 1985).

Early work with immunotherapy was discouraging and greatly limited by availability of active and pure substances. In 1979, when Weissman isolated and cloned the gene for human α-interferon, a new era of biologic therapy began (Spiegel 1986). Availability of large quantities of recombinant immunomodulator factors was the hallmark of the phenomenal growth of the field. Although there are significant uncertainties associated with the assumption that this therapy holds the greatest promise for curing cancer, many investigators hold a futuristic viewpoint of the merits of biologic therapy in cancer treatment as well as immune disorders (Simpson, Seipp, and Rosenberg 1988).

State-of-the-art biotherapy involves the use of biologic response modifiers (BRMs), which are defined as any soluble substance that is capable of altering (or modulating) the immune system by means of either a stimulating or a suppressive effect (Huffer, Kanapa, and Stevenson 1986). Through a clear understanding of how the body's immune system mediates tumor destruction, the physiologic origins of specific biologic agents can be identified. These are summarized in Table 6-1.

CLASSIFICATIONS OF BIOLOGIC THERAPY

Broad categories of biologic agents have been derived from the mechanism by which immune function is altered and from relationships among biologic agent, host, and tumor (Figure 6-1).

Active specific biotherapy involves the administration of tumor-related antigens (vaccines) that have been manipulated in vitro before use in vivo; thus the immune system can be stimulated, but the recipient does not develop intoxication with the agent. Although this therapy may hold the greatest promise for cure, it has been difficult to perform because of the individual nature of tumor cells and the mutations that commonly occur over time. Currently, there are no biologic agents of this nature commercially available or in phase III trials. The National Institutes of Health have developed a type of active specific technology in the form of tumor-infiltrating lymphocytes, whereby patient-specific tumor cells are the medium for production of sensitized lymphocytes that are infused back to the patient. Early studies of this method were promising, but more research is required before this therapy will become widely available.

Active nonspecific biotherapy has a long history of use as immune therapy. Biotherapeutic agents were first used in the late 1800s and were known as Coley's toxin (Groenwald, Fisher, and McCalla 1987). Early studies involved the administration of endotoxin to stimulate the individual's immune response, whereas current studies may include the administration of bacterial vaccines with the purpose of boosting the overall immune response. The most common examples of such vaccines include BCG, levamisole, *C. parvum,* and methanol extraction residue. Most trials with these agents demonstrated mixed results, with the most favorable responses occurring with minimal tumor burden. Many of these agents are now being used with other therapeutic modalities or as adjuvant therapy.

Passive biotherapy has been defined as the use of immune serum, active lymphokine substances, or antitumor lymphocytes given to individuals in the hope of transferring immunity or stimulating specific antitumor responses. Passive biotherapy has been further subdivided into specific, nonspecific, and adoptive. Specific passive therapy is the generation of tumor-specific antibodies that, when

Table 6-1 Tumor Immunology and Action of BRMs

Mechanism of Tumor Destruction	How Tumors "Escape" Immune Recognition	BRM Used To Restore
Humoral-mediated responses (antibody-dependent cellular cytotoxicity): antibodies kill tumor cells in the presence of a sensitized lymphocyte or macrophage	Antibodies interact with tumor antigens, creating immune complexes that prevent these same antibodies from acting on tumor cells	Monoclonal antibodies, tumor-infiltrating lymphocytes
Cellular-mediated response		
Macrophage activation with the release of nonspecific cytokines that directly kill tumor cells or activate specialized T cells	Tumor cells release antigens that cause excessive suppressor T-cell activity and a resultant lack of released cytokine	Tumor necrosis factor, interferon, interleukin-2, colony-stimulating factors
Sensitized T cells specific to the tumor (these have specific destruction mechanisms)	Tumor-specific antigen-antibody complexes block the antitumor mechanisms	Autologous tumor vaccines
Natural killer cells (antigen-nonspecific cells that directly lyse tumor cells)	Unknown	Lymphokine-activated killer cells

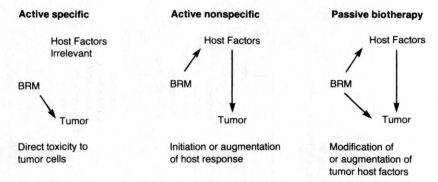

Figure 6-1 Mechanisms of BRMs. *Source:* Adapted from *Oncology Nursing Forum,* Vol. 9, No. 1, p. 47, by D. Scogna and C. Shoenberger, with permission of the Oncology Nursing Press, © 1982.

administered, will act as destructive agents to tumor cells. The classic example of this therapy is monoclonal antibodies (MoAbs). Nonspecific passive therapy implies the transfer of active immune substances that participate in the immunologic response in a more general fashion or at multiple sites during an immune reaction. Agents that stimulate the general immune response include interferon inducers such as poly-ICLC, tumor necrosis factor (TNF), γ-globulin, γ-interferon, and stimulation or growth factors. Adoptive immunotherapy refers to the transfer of extracts of or actual sensitized lymphocytes that participate in antitumor responses. Some of these agents are active in immunosuppression; others show activity in their effect on tumor response. Specific to antitumor activity are activated lymphocytes, immune RNA, interleukin-2 (IL-2), and α-interferon. The interrelationships and categories of the most common immunologic agents are outlined in Figure 6-2.

CURRENT STATUS OF SPECIFIC BIOLOGIC RESPONSE MODIFIERS

The biologic therapy of 1990 is very different from that of the early 1980s. Most therapy involves administration of active recombinant cytokines (cellular substances released during immune responses), or adoptive immunotherapy. The most common and clinically advanced technologies are addressed here.

Interferon

Interferon actually comprises many proteins, of which there are three distinct types—α, β, and γ. The major functions of interferons as a group are as follows (Higgins 1984):

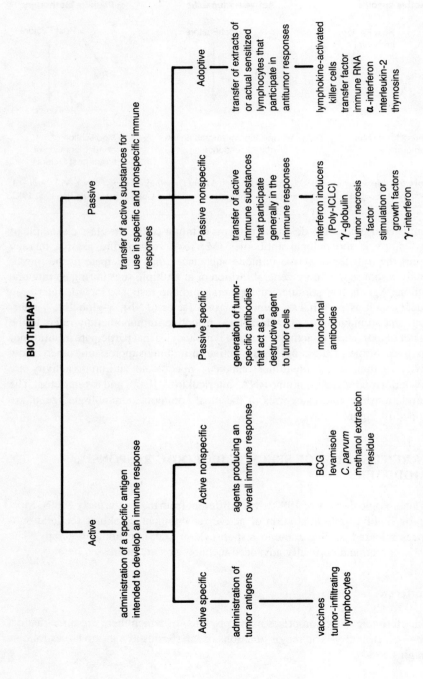

Figure 6-2 Classifications of Biotherapeutic Agents

- antiviral—inhibits the replication of DNA in a virus that has invaded a cell and protects the infected cell from invasion by another virus
- immunomodulatory—interacts directly with T lymphocytes to stimulate production of the cellular products that in turn signal monocytes, natural killer cells, and other T lymphocytes to recognize and destroy tumor cells
- antiproliferative—directly inhibits the division of tumor cells
- stimulatory—stimulates expression of tumor-associated antigens as well as human leukocyte antigen on tumor cell surfaces, which makes the tumor cells more recognizable to antibodies

Interferon activity is measured in terms of its ability to inhibit viral replication in tissue culture, (i.e., in units of antiviral activity), with the common unit of measurement being the megaunit (1 million units). Interferon has a demonstrated, dose-related, direct cytotoxic effect on renal cell carcinoma, Kaposi's sarcoma, and nodular lymphoma. The significant antitumor response in hairy cell leukemia seen with small doses has been attributed to an indirect immunomodulatory activity (Goldstein and Laszlo 1986). Specific actions, indications, and dose recommendations of the three major types of interferon are outlined in Table 6-2. Although human interferons produced in large cell cultures yield a blend of several subtypes, cloned interferons consist of only one purified protein with specific effects (Oldham 1985).

Side effects of therapy are notably dose-related and cumulative in nature. Acute toxicity usually occurs with doses of 1 MU/m^2 and becomes severe with higher doses. The toxicities noted with all BRMs are seen to a moderate or severe degree with interferon therapy. Side effects specific to interferons are few, although neurologic toxicities are common (70%), and cardiovascular toxicities have occurred as a result of acute ischemia, dysrhythmias, and hyperdynamics

Table 6-2 Interferons: Specific Actions, Indications, and Dosage Recommendations

Interferon Type	Maximal Dosage	Usual Route of Administration	Primary Effect	Specific Side Effects
α	30 MU/m^2 daily or 3 times per week	Intramuscular (IM) or subcutaneous (SC)	Antiviral	Neurologic toxicities, cardiovascular toxicities
β	150 MU/m^2 daily or 3 times per week	IM or SC	Antiproliferative	
γ	50 MU/m^2 daily or 3 times per week	Intravenous	Activation of macrophages	Prolonged systolic hypotension

(Quesada et al. 1986). An overview of toxicities seen with interferon and other BRMs is summarized in Table 6-3.

Tumor Necrosis Factor

TNF is a nonspecific macrophage product that acts by directly infiltrating the tumor mass and causing a hemorrhagic necrosis in the tumor itself. The activity is generalized; studies of its effects are still in initial stages, so that it is too early to demonstrate tumor specificity. The toxicities noted are similar to those of interferon, but with more severe fever and rigors (Maldawer and Figlin 1988).

Table 6-3 Common Side Effects of BRMs and Their Frequency

Side Effect	Interferon	TNF	IL-2	MoAbs	Colony-Stimulating Factors
Mental status changes	F*	F	F	N	N
Anxiety	F	F	F	N	N
Headaches	F	F	F	O	F
Dysrhythmias	F	F	F	N	N
Hypotension	F	F	F	N	O
Cardiac dysfunction	O	O	O	N	N
Angina	O	O	O	N	N
Fatigue	F	F	F	F	F
Fever	F	F	F	F	F
Chills	F	F	F	O	O
Respiratory distress	O	O	O	O	N
Weight gain/edema	F	O	F	O	O
Renal dysfunction	O	O	F	N	N
Hepatic dysfunction	O	F	F	O	O
Food/taste aversions	O	O	O	N	N
Anorexia	F	F	F	O	O
Nausea	F	F	F	O	O
Diarrhea	F	O	F	N	N
Rash/itching	F	F	F	F	F
Allergic symptoms	F	F	F	F	F
Anemia	O	O	F	N	N
Thrombocytopenia	O	O	O	N	N
Eosinophilia	O	O	F	N	N
Arthralgias	F	F	F	O	O
Myalgias	O	O	F	O	O
Bone pain	O	O	O	N	O

*F, frequently seen; O, occasionally seen; N, not seen.

Interleukin-2

IL-2 is a lymphokine produced by helper T cells after their stimulation by mitogens or specific antigens. IL-2 in turn mediates a wide range of immunoregulatory responses. In vitro, it has been found to act as a helper factor in T- and B-cell responses, to augment the generation of cell-mediated cytotoxic T cells, and to mediate the recovery of immune function of lymphocytes in certain immunodeficient states (Rosenberg 1986). In vivo, IL-2 has been observed to enhance natural killer cell function, to augment alloantigen responsiveness, to activate cytotoxic effector cells (lymphokine-activated killer [LAK] cells), and to improve the recovery of immune function in acquired immunodeficient states (Wanebo et al. 1986). The decision to utilize IL-2 has been based on the known existence of immunodeficient states associated with metastatic malignancy, evidence that in lymphoid tissue exposed to IL-2 in vitro fresh autologous and allogeneic tumor cells undergo lysis, and the ability of IL-2 with sensitized lymphocytes or LAK cells to increase the immune response in mice with metastatic tumors (Lotze et al. 1985).

Toxic effects of IL-2 therapy are dose and schedule related, with the most severe effects being related to lymphoid infiltration and an immunologically induced capillary leak syndrome. Fluid extravasation leads to hypovolemia, renal interstitial edema, pulmonary congestion, profound weight gain, and intracavitary fluid accumulation (ascites, pleural effusions, and pericardial effusions). Other side effects are the same as those of other BRMs, although they are usually more severe and related to immune stimulation. IL-2 toxicities have been most severe when IL-2 is given by bolus infusion at a dose of 100,000 U/kg. The use of lower doses and continuous infusion therapy are currently being studied to evaluate the ratio of potential toxicity to immunomodulation effects. This therapy has shown significant responses with renal cell carcinoma and malignant melanoma but is associated with considerable toxicity as well.

Lymphokine-Activated Killer Cells

Administration of LAK cells is a form of adoptive immunotherapy currently in use in combination with IL-2 infusion. Activated killer cells alone do not seem to precipitate an adequate immune response but, when used in combination with IL-2, have produced significant and durable responses with renal cell carcinoma (Rosenberg 1986). LAK cell administration alone does not seem to produce significant side effects other than fever and chills, but when LAK cells are given with IL-2 severe pulmonary and constitutional symptoms may develop. A multicenter trial is currently underway to evaluate the potential response benefit for use of LAK cells with IL-2 as opposed to IL-2 alone (Parkinson 1988).

Monoclonal Antibodies

MoAbs have been described as biologic tracers because of their target-specific nature. In addition to their uses in diagnostic and experimental therapeutics with cancer patients, MoAbs have been used to type blood, to monitor T cells at the sites of organ grafts, to detect serum antibodies to pathogens, to diagnose diseases such as herpes simplex and hepatitis, and to detect tumors serologically. Cells that have undergone malignant transformation often express tumor-associated antigens such as carcinoembryonic antigen; MoAbs to such antigens thus permit detection of cancer in undiagnosed patients or monitoring of the course of disease in patients receiving treatment (Rieger 1987).

Hybridoma technology has made possible the mass production of MoAbs, which can be created to bind with almost any antigen. The major difficulty in using MoAbs in antitumor treatment is their inability to remain specific to tumor cells. Tumors notably mutate, so that it is difficult to develop antibody clones against them. Two common therapeutic applications of MoAbs are use in a conjugate form with isotopes such as ^{131}I and use in the transfusion of donor marrow to prevent graft versus host disease in bone marrow transplantation (Rieger 1987). Immunoconjugate therapy with anticancer drugs, toxins, isotopes, and other BRMs is used in the hope of targeting cancer cells while bypassing normal cells. Some researchers predict that large doses of anticancer agents can be given with fewer toxicities resulting to normal cells (Lowder 1986). Much investigation is necessary to refine and specify these activities, and as yet no specific disease processes have been identified as being particularly susceptible.

Most side effects result from an allergic response to the foreign protein. Most are mild to moderate, but some individuals can exhibit anaphylactic symptoms and require intensive pharmacologic support with epinephrine, hydrocortisone, and diphenhydramine.

Colony-Stimulating Factors

The entire hematopoietic cell line is derived from stem cells, which can renew themselves as well as differentiate into progenitor cells. All progenitor cells require colony-stimulating factors (CSFs), which are produced by various cells. The most common CSFs are IL-3, which is manufactured by T lymphocytes; granulocyte-monocyte CSF (GM-CSF), which is also produced by T lymphocytes; granulocyte CSF (G-CSF), which is from monocytes; and monocyte CSF (M-CSF), which is produced by activated monocytes. In immune responses and negative feedback loops, IL-1 and TNF are produced by monocytes and precipitate the production of GM-CSF, G-CSF, and M-CSF (Foon 1988). Most clinical studies utilize GM-CSF or G-CSF to increase neutrophil counts in immune deficient states or during profound neutropenia associated with aggressive chemotherapy of solid tumors (Groopman 1988). Other studies that use these substances to shorten the duration of bone marrow aplasia with leukemia therapy and bone marrow transplantation are underway (Socinski et al. 1988).

Common side effects of CSFs are usually mild and transient and include fever, chills, and fatigue. Relatively uncommon side effects unique to CSFs include nausea, hepatotoxicity, and bone pain (Groopman 1988).

NURSING IMPLICATIONS OF THE USE OF BIOLOGIC RESPONSE MODIFIERS

Clinical trials with BRMs are still in their initial stages. Patients thus require extensive nursing monitoring, astute assessment for new or abnormally toxic effects, and evaluation of therapeutic efficacy. Many agents are still at the level of investigation where maximum tolerated dose, dose-limiting toxicities, and optimal immunomodulating dose are being determined. Because optimal immunomodulating dose may differ from the maximum tolerated dose, it is important to identify both to determine the most appropriate dose for phase II and III trials. Nursing plays an essential role in this data-gathering process.

The side effects of all biologic agents are similar in nature. Most cause constitutional symptoms of fever, chills, fatigue, myalgias, arthralgias, headache, and weakness to variable degrees. Because these effects are profound and more severe than with any other therapy, established toxicity grading criteria have not yet been established. This presents a unique challenge to nursing to develop useful and valid toxicity assessment tools that incorporate concepts involving subjective and objective quality of life in relation to tumor response. Some centers have sought to develop acceptable protocols for the management of these constitutional symptoms and common side effects; others have methodically detailed the precise nature and course of these effects. An overview of the common nursing diagnoses and strategies for management are outlined in Table 6-4.

Although much nursing time is focused on the assessment and management of acute toxicity, it cannot be forgotten that the best nursing care is anticipatory. A comprehensive baseline nursing assessment of risk factors for the development of specific toxicities may greatly reduce patient discomfort as well as morbidity during the course of therapy.

The first and most important evaluation that must be performed is an assessment of the patient's perception of the therapeutic plan: why this agent has been suggested, the anticipated response of the specific tumor to the agent, and the predicted side effects. It is common for individuals to have heard a great deal about immune therapy yet not to realize that the therapy they are about to receive is a phase I dose-finding study. In light of the tremendous media coverage that biologic therapy has received, this evaluation is essential to ensure informed consent. Some patients are able to describe the anticipated side effects but do not realize that for

Table 6-4 Nursing Management of Constitutional Symptoms with BRM Therapy

Nursing Diagnosis	Defining Characteristics	Nursing Interactions
Body temperature, altered	Warm; flushed skin; temperature > 100.4°F; tachycardia	1. Environmental control to avoid external sources of fever (i.e., blankets, warm room air, warmth from flow beds).
		2. Monitor intake and output considering potential losses from perspiration.
	Usually occurs within 1–3 hours of intravenous (IV) infusion or 8 hours of IM injection	3. Encourage tepid fluids to replace perspiration if indicated.
		4. Premedication and concurrent treatment with acetaminophen. Usually started at least 4–6 hours before the first treatment and continued throughout therapy. Naproxen or indomethacin may be given if fevers are refractory to acetaminophen.
	Lasts throughout therapy without evidence of tachyphylaxis	5. Ascertain the most accurate method of obtaining temperatures and monitor every 2 hours while febrile and every 4 hours otherwise.
		6. Administer BRM on a time schedule so that fevers interfere minimally with sleep and meals.
		7. Rigors may be treated with IV morphine or meperidine. Some centers may premedicate with these or plan to administer near the peak of patient's rigors (usually 1–3 hours after IV treatment and 8 hours after IM injection).
		8. Monitor for cardiovascular changes (e.g., tachycardia, irregular rhythms, angina).
		9. Monitor for central nervous system changes with high or prolonged fevers (somnolence, confusion, seizures).
Potential alteration in comfort	Myalgia, arthralgia, headache, bone pain	1. Acetaminophen or more potent agent with acetaminophen added is most often used. Nonsteroidal anti-inflammatory agents are often helpful. All steroid derivatives are CONTRAINDICATED, as they may abrogate immunologic benefits.

Biologic Response Modifiers   89

Early symptoms of headache or myalgias may occur within 1–3 hours of IV infusion

Arthralgias and bone pain usually occur after 1–2 days of therapy

Symptoms are often intermittent and schedule related, but residual symptoms may be present throughout therapy and up to several days after therapy

2. Administering of cool compresses to the head to reduce headaches.
3. A darkened room may be helpful in reducing headache, especially if photophobic.
4. Warmth may reduce arthralgias and myalgias. Occasionally warm compresses are used, but more often clothing covering involved areas is recommended.
5. Massage therapy may reduce myalgias or assist in relaxation and pain relief.
6. Relaxation therapy has been shown to be helpful at reducing many discomforts.
7. Diversional activities may be utilized to decrease the patient's focus on discomfort. These may include games, music, television, or activities.

Activity intolerance

Subjective fatigue; respiratory compromise with activity; tachycardia or chest pain with activity; vertigo, light-headedness with activity

Symptoms are greatly variable depending on agent used, dose, route of administration, and underlying medical disorders; onset is often 2–3 days after treatment begins and may extend for 2–4 weeks after therapy ends

1. Evaluate patient's normal sleep, activity, and rest patterns. Ascertain normal amount and time of sleep.
2. Obtain objective data on patient's baseline functional status.
3. Teach patient to monitor physiologic response to activity (e.g., pulse rate, shortness of breath, weakness).
4. Teach cognitive coping strategies (e.g., imagery, relaxation, controlled breathing).
5. Arrange more stressful activities after prolonged periods of rest (e.g., in the morning after sleep).
6. Encourage less physically strenuous activities (e.g., wheelchair for excursions, isometric exercises, recliner chairs in central locations, range of motion exercises if necessary).
7. Reinforce that fatigue is not necessarily related to tumor progression.
8. Give written material to reinforce verbal instruction.
9. Involve family in teaching or therapy planning conferences.

Table 6-4 continued

Nursing Diagnosis	Defining Characteristics	Nursing Interactions
Alteration in nutrition, less than required	Anorexia, nausea, vomiting diarrhea, glossitis/pharyngitis	1. Evaluate normal weight for patient, ideal body weight (IBW); weigh patient routinely during therapy. 2. Evaluate baseline and ongoing albumin levels. 3. Perform calorie counts when intake is less than normal. 4. Plan with patient desirable nutrition supplements and altering meal patterns so that they do not coincide with side effects of therapy. 5. Nausea and vomiting may be controlled by various agents that may be given either before meals or at the anticipated peak of the side effect. Agents and considerations for selection are phenothiazines (although these contribute to neurologic toxicity).

Table 6-5 Assessment Parameters for Patients Receiving BRMs

Assessment Parameter	Rationale	Frequency of Evaluation
Neurologic		
1. Psychiatric disease, particularly depression, manic-depression, or paranoid behavior	Clinical depression can result from interferon or IL-2; paranoid behavior seen with IL-2	Admission; daily evaluation of affect and behavior
2. Seizure disorders	These are a contraindication for therapy with interferon, TNF, and IL-2; even asymptomatic brain metastasis of tumors may cause seizures	Admission and daily
3. Anxiety at present or by history	Anxiety may be enhanced or precipitated by interferon, TNF, or IL-2	Admission and at least daily
4. Reasoning/memory/concentration	Baseline assessment will help identify subtle changes related to the drug rather than intellect, coping strategies, or other medical problems	Admission and at least daily
5. Coping	May be altered by severe side effects or neurotoxicities	Admission and at least daily
6. Sleep patterns	Insomnia or altered sleep patterns by interferon, TNF, IL-2	Admission and daily
7. Sexual activity	Fatigue greatly affects sexual performance and libido	Admission and as needed during hospitalization, at discharge
8. Migraine headaches	Headaches are a common side effect and may precipitate migraines	Admission and daily as needed

Table 6-5 continued

Assessment Parameter	Rationale	Frequency of Evaluation
Cardiovascular		
1. Dysrhythmias Spontaneous, medication-induced, or caffeine- or nicotine-related	These occur as side effects of interferon, TNF, IL-2; existing predisposition may enhance	Admission and every shift
2. Heart sounds	Abnormalities indicative of heart failure may occur with administration	Admission and daily
3. Angina	Fever, chills, increased metabolic rate, or capillary leak in heart may precipitate angina	Admission and daily
4. Edema Lymphedema or position-dependent	Baseline needed to ascertain whether this occurs with interferon and IL-2	Admission and daily
Respiratory		
1. Activity tolerance	Respiratory compromise may occur with interferon, TNF, IL-2; particularly important if tumor is in lung	Admission and every shift
2. Smoking history	Increases risk of respiratory side effects	Admission
3. History of respiratory problems (tuberculosis; asthma)	Increases risk of respiratory side effects and will help with differential diagnosis if respiratory distress occurs	Admission
4. Baseline room air arterial blood gas/oxygen saturation	Provides comparison information if respiratory distress occurs	Admission and as needed
Renal		
1. Prostate problems	Helps with differential diagnosis when oliguria occurs with IL-2	Admission
2. Recent weight changes/ideal body weight	Baseline with which to evaluate weight gain related to capillary leak with IL-2 and interferon	Admission and daily

3. Electrolytes	Changes occur with IL-2	Admission and as needed
4. Urination problems	Helps with differential diagnosis when patient becomes oliguric	Admission
5. History of gout	Increased uric acid and gout exacerbation occur with IL-2	Admission and as needed
Gastrointestinal		
1. History of gastrointestinal bleeding (gastritis, hemorrhoids, ulcerative colitis)	Tendency for exacerbation with interferon, TNF, IL-2	Admission and occult test as needed
2. Alcohol history	May be at increased risk for neurologic toxicities, cardiovascular toxicities, hepatic toxicities with interferon, TNF, IL-2, MoAbs, CSF	Admission
3. History of hepatitis	Increased risk for hepatic toxicities with all agents	Admission
4. Food intolerances/taste aversions	May become worse or change during all biologic therapy	Admission and daily
5. Anorexia	Greatly exacerbated by interferon, TNF, IL-2	Admission and daily
Integumentary		
1. Dermatologic disorders	Conditions exacerbated by interferon, TNF, IL-2; increased itching	Admission and daily
2. Allergies/nasal stuffiness	May be exacerbated by all biologic agents	Admission and daily
3. Presence/absence of scalp hair	Hair thinning noted with IL-2	Admission and as needed
Hematologic		
1. History of anemia	Exacerbated by interferon, TNF, IL-2; improved with CSF	Admission and as needed
2. Recent active infections	May worsen during biologic therapy	Admission and daily
3. Platelet problems/petechiae	May be exacerbated	Admission and as needed
4. Lymphatic involvement of disease	May note decreased disease during therapy	Admission and as needed

Table 6-5 continued

Assessment Parameter	Rationale	Frequency of Evaluation
Musculoskeletal		
1. Arthritis history	May be exacerbated with all biologic agents	Admission and daily
2. Orthopedic problems (previous broken bones, injured joints and ligaments)	May be exacerbated with all biologic agents	Admission and daily
3. Bone metastases	May be exacerbated with all biologic agents; particularly noted with CSF	Admission and daily
Metabolic		
1. Diabetes	Hyperglycemia occurs with interferon, TNF, IL-2	Admission and as needed
2. Hypothyroidism	Known to occur or be exacerbated by IL-2	Admission and as needed

some therapies the fatigue is so profound that continuance of work and household activities is virtually impossible. Being certain that the patient is well prepared for the specific side effects anticipated with each agent and particular regimen will reduce the risk of maladaptive coping during therapy, particularly with those agents that cause neurotoxicities and depression.

Admission assessment questions and physical assessment parameters should encompass a broad range of past medical history, functional status, and support systems. An outline of assessment cues and their rationales is given in Table 6-5. Daily physical, psychosocial, and cognitive assessment parameters may be derived from the specific agent being used, the dose being given, and the medication route and schedule.

CONCLUSION

In a relatively brief period of time, the field of biologic therapy in the treatment of cancer has grown tremendously. What seemed beyond comprehension 15 years ago is common practice today. Biotherapy has become as widely recognized by the public as chemotherapy or radiation therapy. Consumer support and interest have enhanced biotherapy development and investigation and may continue to provide the means by which to realize its full potential. The role of nursing in patient management with biologic therapy is evolving, much as the therapy has done. In the words of Durant (1987, 340), "While much is yet to be learned, the current successful manipulation of the cellular immune system may mean we are near the end of our search for a meaningful direction in the immunotherapy of cancer."

STUDY QUESTIONS

1. What two systems are most often negatively affected by interferon therapy? What nursing assessments will be useful in detecting side effects and toxicities at an early stage?
2. Identify three current uses of monoclonal antibodies. What is the major difficulty in using them in anticancer therapy?
3. Develop toxicity grading criteria for one of the constitutional symptoms experienced by patients receiving biotherapy.

REFERENCES

Durant, J.R. 1987. The immunotherapy of cancer—The end of the beginning. *New England Journal of Medicine* 316:339–40.

Foon, K. 1988. Biotherapy of cancer with interleukin-2, colony stimulating factors, and monoclonal antibodies. *Oncology Nursing Forum* 15:13–22.

Goldstein, D., and I. Laszlo. 1986. Interferon therapy. *Cancer Research* 46:4315–29.

Groenwald, S.L., S.G. Fisher, and J.L. McCalla. 1987. Biologic response modifiers. In *Cancer nursing: Principles and practices,* ed. S. Groenwald. Boston: Jones & Bartlett.

Groopman, J.E. 1988. Clinical applications of colony-stimulating factors. *Seminars in Oncology* 15:27–33.

Higgins, P. 1984. Interferons. *Journal of Clinical Oncology* 37:109–16.

Huffer, T.L., D.J. Kanapa, and G.W. Stevenson. 1986. *Introduction to human immunology.* Boston: Jones & Bartlett.

Lotze, M.E., Y.L. Matory, S.E. Ettinghausen, A.A. Rayner, S.O. Sharrow, C.A.Y. Seipp, M.C. Custer, and S.A. Rosenberg. 1985. In vivo administration of purified human interleukin-2: Half-life, immunologic effects and expansion of peripheral lymphoid cells with recombinant IL-2. *Journal of Immunology* 135:2675–85.

Lowder, J. 1986. The current status of monoclonal antibodies in the diagnosis and therapy of cancer. *Current Problems in Cancer* 10:490–551.

Maldawer, N.P., and R.A. Figlin. 1988. Tumor necrosis factor: Current clinical status and implications for nursing management. *Seminars in Oncology Nursing* 4:120–25.

Oldham, R. 1985. Biologicals for cancer treatment: Interferons. *Hospital Practice* 20:71–91.

Parkinson, D.R. 1988. Interleukin-2 in cancer therapy. *Seminars in Oncology* 15:10–26.

Quesada, J., M. Talpaz, A. Rios, R. Kurzrock, and J. Gutterman. 1986. Clinical toxicity of interferons in cancer patients: A review. *Journal of Clinical Oncology* 4:234–45.

Rieger, P. 1987. Monoclonal antibodies. *American Journal of Nursing* 87:469–73.

Rosenberg, S. 1986. Adoptive immunotherapy of cancer using lymphokine activated killer cells and recombinant interleukin-2. In *Important advances in oncology,* eds. V. DeVita, S. Hellman, and S. Rosenberg. Philadelphia: J.B. Lippincott.

Simpson, C., C.A. Seipp, and S.A. Rosenberg. 1988. The current status and future applications of interleukin-2 and adoptive immunotherapy in cancer treatment. *Seminars in Oncology Nursing* 4:3–9.

Socinski, M.A., S.A. Cannistra, A. Elias, K.H. Antman, L. Schnipper, and J.D. Griffin. 1988. Granulocytic macrophage colony-stimulating factor expands the circulating hemapoietic progenitor cell compartment in man. *Lancet* 1:1194–98.

Spiegel, R.J. 1986. Intron A (interferon alpha-2b): Clinical overview and future directions. *Seminars in Oncology* 13:89–101.

Wanebo, H.J., R. Pace, S. Hargett, D. Katz, and J. Sando. 1986. Production of and responses to interleukin-2 in peripheral blood lymphocytes of cancer patients. *Cancer* 57:656–62.

Chapter 7

Bone Marrow Transplantation

Sarina Petrolino-Roche and Ruth Nuscher Ford

> As more and more cancer centers develop bone marrow transplantation (BMT) programs for pediatric and adult patients, this once highly experimental procedure is becoming standard therapy for many diseases. Since 1970, by which time fewer than 100 BMTs had been performed, more than 10,000 BMTs have been performed in more than 100 centers. The chapter provides an overview of BMT procedures such as recipient-donor matching, marrow preparation and infusion, complications, and rejection as well as implications for nursing research and future nursing studies.

Bone marrow transplantation (BMT) is a process that involves infusion of marrow from a suitable donor to a properly conditioned recipient to treat a malignant or other life-threatening disease. Since the first successful BMT with identical twins in the 1950s (Thomas et al. 1959), the procedure has undergone continuous evolution. Presently, BMT is the most widely accepted therapy for some diseases but is controversial for others. Problems related to the patient's underlying disease and complications related to BMT prevent its broad application. Good prognostic indicators of successful BMT include the age of the patient, remission status, and clinical status at the time of BMT (Tables 7-1 and 7-2) (Kamani and August 1984).

BMT, which at one time was considered highly experimental, is now a common treatment for diseases such as aplastic anemia, severe combined immunodeficiency (SCID), various forms of leukemia, lymphoma, and several types of solid tumors (Exhibit 7-1). More and more cancer centers are developing BMT programs for pediatric and adult patients. In 1970 fewer than 100 BMTs had been performed at fewer than 10 centers, whereas by the end of 1988 more than 10,000 BMTs will have been done at more than 100 centers (Gale and Quinn 1989). Currently, for many diseases the question is no longer whether BMT should be

Table 7-1 Results of Allogeneic BMT

Disease	Long-Term Survival (%)	Relapse (%)	Reference
AA no tx	50–80		Kamani 1986; Thomas 1985; O'Reilly 1983
AA multiple tx	40–75		Kamani 1986; Thomas 1985
Thalassemia	75		Thomas 1985
ALL CR_1, CR_2	25–60	30–50	Kamani 1986; Santos 1984; O'Reilly 1983
ALL >CR_2, relapse	10–27	50–70	Doney 1985; Kamani 1986; Santos 1984
AML CR_1 <20yr	45–70	10–40	Santos 1984; O'Reilly 1983; Fefer 1986
AML CR_1 >40yr	25–35	10–40	Santos 1984; Fefer 1986
AML relapse <20yr	50–60	50–70	Kamani 1984; Thomas 1985
AML relapse 30–50yr	25–30	50–70	Kamani 1984; Thomas 1985
CML CP <30yr	60–75	30	Kamani 1984; Fefer, Clift, and Thomas 1986
CML CP >30yr	45	30	Fefer, Clift, and Thomas 1986
CML AP	10–40	38	Kamani 1984; Fefer, Clift, and Thomas 1986
CML BP	5–15	80	Kamani 1984; Fefer, Clift, and Thomas 1986

Abbreviations: AA = aplastic anemia; tx = transfusion; ALL = acute lymphocytic leukemia; AML = acute myelocytic leukemia; CML = chronic myelocytic leukemia; CR = complete remission; CP = chronic phase; AP = accelerated phase; BP = blast phase.

Source: Reprinted from *Seminars in Oncology Nursing*, Vol. 4, No. 1, pp. 3–8, with permission of W.B. Saunders Company, © 1988.

Table 7-2 Results of Autologous BMT

Disease	Long-Term Survival (%)	Relapse (%)	Reference
ALL CR_1	43	32	Gorin 1986
ALL advanced disease	15	>50	Gorin 1986
AML CR_1	48	32	Gorin 1986
AML advanced disease	30–43	>50	Gorin 1986; Yeager 1986

Source: Reprinted from *Seminars in Nursing*, Vol. 4, No. 1, pp. 3–8, with permission of W.B. Saunders Company, © 1988.

Exhibit 7-1 Types of Diseases Treated with BMT

Malignant disorders
  Acute and chronic leukemias
  Preleukemic states
  Hairy cell leukemia
  Lymphoma
  Multiple myeloma
  Neuroblastoma
  Selected solid tumors
    Testicular cancer
    Breast cancer
    Small-cell lung cancer
    Ovarian cancer

Nonmalignant disorders
  Bone marrow failure diseases
    Aplastic anemia
    Myelodysplastic syndrome
  Immunodeficiency diseases
    Severe combined immunodeficiency
    Adenosine deaminase deficiency
    Wiskott-Aldrich syndrome
  Hematopoietic disorders
    Fanconi's anemia
    Thalassemia major (β-thalassemia)
    Sickle cell anemia
  Congenital and hereditary disorders
    Mucopolysaccharidoses
    Gaucher's disease
    Diamond-Blackfan syndrome
    Infantile osteopetrosis

carried out but rather at what point in the disease course should the patient be considered for the procedure (Thomas 1987).

Historically, obstacles to transplantation have been the unavailability of a suitable donor, graft versus host disease (GVHD), bleeding, infection, rejection of the marrow graft, and relapse of disease. Currently many centers are focusing research efforts on eradicating these obstacles. Bone marrow registries are available to expand the donor pool. The application of T-cell depletion techniques, which remove the donor T lymphocytes that initiate the GVHD reaction in the host, has effectively decreased the risk of GVHD. The expanded availability of blood product support has been a significant advance. The use of broad-spectrum anti-infectious agents such as trimethoprim-sulfamethoxazole, acyclovir, and gancyclovir, commonly known as DHPG, has significantly decreased mortality related to infection in the posttransplant period. New protocols that use various combinations of chemotherapeutic agents and radiation therapy are targeted at eliminating the problems of rejection and relapse. Improved purging techniques used to eliminate the malignant cells in the marrow have also been developed in an attempt to decrease the relapse rate with autologous transplants.

Nurses must familiarize themselves with the BMT process to deliver comprehensive, quality care during the pretransplant and posttransplant periods. Nursing care entails a tremendous amount of patient teaching, physical care, and psychosocial support (Exhibit 7-2). The area of BMT is extremely challenging for nurses because much of the patient's physical and psychologic well-being depends on the delivery of highly skilled, sensitive nursing care.

OVERVIEW OF THE APPLICATION OF BONE MARROW TRANSPLANTATION

Rationale

The rationale for BMT is to "rescue" or reconstitute hematologic or immunologic function in cases of nonfunctioning, suppressed, or diseased marrow. BMT may be used to replace or stimulate nonfunctioning marrow (as in aplastic anemia or immunodeficiency diseases), to provide hematologic reconstitution to patients with malignancies who have been treated with high-dose chemotherapy or radiation therapy (as in neuroblastoma or lymphoma), or to replace diseased marrow (as in leukemia). High-dose chemotherapy with or without radiation is given before transplant to achieve marrow ablation and immune suppression. As a rescue technique, the patient's own marrow or that of a compatible donor is infused in an attempt to reconstitute the marrow and immune system.

Types of Donor Bone Marrow

There are three types of BMT: autologous, syngeneic, and allogeneic. Donor availability and the patient's disease dictate the type of BMT to be performed.

Autologous BMT may be used to treat malignant diseases. In autologous BMT, the patient's own bone marrow is harvested by means of multiple bone marrow aspirations, ideally when the patient is in bone marrow remission. The harvested marrow is cryopreserved (frozen and stored) and reinfused as an autograft after the patient receives high-dose chemotherapy or radiation therapy (or both) aimed at treating the underlying malignant disease. The autologous bone marrow may be treated with chemotherapy or monoclonal antibodies to purge the marrow of residual malignant cells. Relapse after autologous BMT is a significant problem. This may be due to pretransplant therapy that does not eliminate all residual

Exhibit 7-2 Frequently Used Nursing Diagnoses and Clinical Problems for BMT Patients

Information: knowledge deficit regarding
   preadmission work-up
   laminar airflow (LAF) germ-free environment/decontamination
   placement and care of long-term intravenous catheter
   autologous bone marrow harvesting
   daily routine related to mouth care, hygiene, nutrition, exercise
   radiation therapy (total body/total lymphoid irradiation, boost) and side effects
   chemotherapeutic protocol and side effects
   bone marrow infusion
   routine posttransplant interventions (total parenteral nutrition [TPN], blood product
      transfusions, antibiotics, *Corynebacterium* species group JK [CDC-JK] precautions)
   signs of engraftment
   discharge

Coping
   body image disturbance related to side effects of treatment plan
   fear
   powerlessness
   anxiety
   ineffective individual coping
   noncompliance
   sleep pattern disturbance

Comfort
   altered comfort related to nausea and vomiting secondary to cytoreduction
   potential alteration in comfort related to cytosine arabinoside (ara-C)–induced
      conjunctivitis/photophobia
   altered comfort related to chills, fever, nausea, vomiting, and/or odor of preservative
      secondary to infusion of bone marrow
   altered comfort related to fever, rigor, serum sickness secondary to antithymocyte
      globulin (ATG)
   altered comfort related to blood product transfusion
   pain
   altered comfort related to enlarged liver, pruritis secondary to liver dysfunction

Nutrition
   fluid volume excess related to inappropriate secretion of antidiuretic hormone secondary
      to cyclophosphamide
   fluid volume excess related to side effects of treatment plan
   fluid volume deficit related to side effects of treatment plan
   potential for electrolyte imbalance related to treatment plan
   actual electrolyte imbalance related to treatment plan
   altered nutrition: less than body requirements related to inability to ingest or digest food

Protective mechanisms
   immune function
      potential for infection related to neutropenia and/or compromised immune function
         secondary to disease process/cytoreduction
      hyperthermia

continues

Exhibit 7-2 continued

    hematopoietic function
        altered protective mechanisms related to thrombocytopenia secondary to cytoreduction
        altered protective mechanisms related to anemia secondary to disease process/
          cytoreduction
    hepatic function
        altered protective mechanisms: bleeding related to liver dysfunction
    integumentary function
        altered oral mucous membrane: stomatitis, xerostomia, esophagitis related to
          cytoreduction
        impairment of skin integrity related to side effects of treatment plan
    sensorimotor function
        impaired thought process related to high ammonia levels secondary to liver dysfunction

Mobility
    activity intolerance

Elimination
    diarrhea related to side effects of treatment plan
    potential for injury related to hemorrhagic cystitis secondary to interaction of
      cyclophosphamide metabolites with bladder epithelium

Sexuality
    altered sexuality patterns related to side effects of treatment

Role/relationship patterns
    impaired social interaction related to steroid therapy
    social isolation related to LAF environment
    altered family process
    ineffective family coping
    altered growth and development

Ventilation
    ineffective airway clearance
    ineffective breathing patterns
    impaired gas exchange

Circulation
    cardiac
        decreased cardiac output
    renal
        altered tissue perfusion
        potential for injury related to hypertension

malignant cells or reinfusion of tumor cells during the transplant (Santos and Kaizer 1982).

In syngeneic BMT the donor and recipient are identical twins. Thus the marrow from the donor is genetically identical and a perfect histocompatible match to that of the recipient. Syngeneic BMTs eliminate the obstacles of GVHD and bone marrow rejection, but in leukemic patients the risk of death from relapse is increased and is thought to be due to the absence of a graft versus leukemia effect resulting from GVHD (Kamani and August 1984).

Allogeneic BMT refers to the use of compatible donor marrow that is not genetically identical to the recipient's. Allogeneic transplants may be either conventional or T-cell depleted. With conventional allogeneic BMTs, the marrow is harvested from the donor and infused immediately into the patient. In T-cell–depleted BMTs, the harvested marrow is treated to remove T lymphocytes before infusion. The purpose of T-cell depletion is to prevent GVHD. Allogeneic BMTs require two tests to determine histocompatibility between the donor and recipient: human leukocyte antigen (HLA) typing and mixed lymphocyte culture (MLC). Both HLA-matched and HLA-mismatched transplants have been performed. Patients who do not have an HLA-matched donor may now have the option of an HLA-mismatched T-cell–depleted graft because T-cell depletion techniques have been used successfully to eliminate harmful mature T lymphocytes from the donor marrow. The donor for allogeneic transplants is most frequently a sibling but may also be a more distantly related family member or an unrelated person. Unrelated histocompatible identical donors may be identified through volunteer blood donor programs in which volunteers are tissue typed.

Pretransplant Period

Finding a Suitable Donor

To decrease the incidence of graft rejection and GVHD, it is crucial that the recipient of an allogeneic BMT be matched with a compatible donor. Tissue typing is the process of matching the donor tissue to the recipient tissue. The histocompatibility antigens (HLA) consist of five groups of alleles (A, B, C, D, and DR) that are located on chromosome 6. HLA typing involves obtaining blood samples to identify the HLA antigens at four of the five known loci. The HLA-D loci is determined by the mixed lymphocyte (MLC) culture assay, which establishes compatibility of lymphocytes of the potential donor with those of the recipient. A nonreactive MLC indicates compatibility, and a reactive MLC signals incompatibility.

Admission Process

Before being admitted for a BMT the patient usually meets with the transplant team, at which time a comprehensive teaching plan is initiated. Patient education booklets developed by a transplant center or national organizations supplement the teaching.

Because infection is a major threat to the immunocompromised patient undergoing BMT, a protective environment is necessary to decrease the risk of exogenous infections. On the day of admission patients are oriented to the protective environment, which may range from reverse-isolation clean technique to laminar airflow (LAF) sterile technique.

The degree of precautions taken to decrease the risk of infection varies on the basis of individual patient risk factors, the type of BMT, and institution policy. Most centers that have LAF germ-free isolation rooms reserve them for the patient at high risk for developing complications. LAF combined with procedures to rid the body of the normal flora on the skin, in the gastrointestinal tract, and in the vaginal mucosa can be used to achieve a total germ-free state for high-risk patients.

Exacting hygienic care is necessary to decrease the risk of endogenous infections. All patients are taught meticulous hygiene and oral care techniques on admission and are encouraged to perform self-care throughout the hospitalization.

Before BMT all patients have a long-term indwelling catheter inserted for intravenous access. Patient teaching includes the insertion procedure as well as care of the catheter.

Decontamination

As mentioned, patients at high risk of infection may benefit from LAF isolation to decrease the incidence of exogenous infection. These patients are also at risk for endogenous infection and may require decontamination. Antimicrobial soap is used to render the skin germ free. Oral nonabsorbable antibiotics are used to achieve a germ-free state in the gastrointestinal tract from the throat to the anus. Elimination of all bacterial flora, including normal flora, is determined by negative culture results. During gastrointestinal decontamination the patient receives a sterile diet. All food is rendered sterile by means of oven baking, irradiation, or autoclaving. Females also undergo vaginal decontamination, which consists of the administration of a mixture of antibiotics and an antifungal cream instilled vaginally through a catheter.

Preparative Treatment

The purposes of the immunosuppression given before BMT are to neutralize the patient's immune system and thus decrease the incidence of graft rejection, to remove all malignant cells, and to provide the bone marrow space for engraftment. Various combinations of high-dose chemotherapy and radiation may be used to achieve immunosuppression. Radiation may include total body irradiation (TBI) or total lymphoid irradiation (TLI). The use of a particular protocol depends on the patient's disease, prior therapies, the risk of rejection, and specific physical problems that may predispose the patient to complications (e.g., preexisting cardiac, renal, or hepatic problems). The most commonly used protocol for allogeneic BMT consists of the combination of TBI and high-dose chemotherapy, including cyclophosphamide (Cytoxan). Multiple chemotherapeutic agents may be used in the cytoreductive phase of BMT. Treatment regimens vary with respect to chemotherapeutic agents and dosages as well as sequence and timing of radiation therapy relative to chemotherapy administration.

TBI/TLI. TBI/TLI is usually given in fractionated doses. This means that the total amount of radiation is given in several small doses 2 to 3 times per day over 2 to 4 days. The total amount of radiation varies according to the patient's disease and institution protocol. As with any treatment, patient education is essential. The nurse focuses on rapid assessments and interventions related to the various side effects: bone marrow suppression, nausea, vomiting, diarrhea, skin irritation, sexual sterility, and alopecia. To decrease the patient's anxiety related to the therapy, it is important to review the TBI/TLI process and the environment in which the patient receives the therapy. Relaxation techniques are helpful, and their use is encouraged during the procedure. These techniques may be particularly useful to help patients stand or lie still during the TBI/TLI treatment. It is important to reinforce that jewelry, metal, and skin creams are not to come in contact with the skin during the radiation procedure because severe skin reactions may result. After TBI/TLI, alcohol-free skin creams may be applied to treat the dryness resulting from radiation.

High-dose cyclophosphamide. Cyclophosphamide is used in many BMT protocols because it is a potent immunosuppressive, antileukemic, and myeloablative drug. It is essential that patients receiving high-dose cyclophosphamide be well hydrated both before and immediately after treatment. Hydration decreases the incidence of hemorrhagic cystitis (irritation and sloughing of the bladder secondary to the metabolites of cyclophosphamide). Continuous bladder irrigation may be used to decrease the concentration of metabolites in the bladder and thereby diminish irritation to the mucosal lining of the bladder. Because cyclophosphamide can affect antidiuretic hormone secretion and thus serum electrolytes (particularly sodium), fluid balance and serum electrolytes are monitored closely. Hyponatremia from sodium depletion could result in seizure activity if undetected or untreated. High-dose cyclophosphamide may also affect the myocardium, so that daily electrocardiography and measurement of creatinine phosphokinase (CPK) level are performed to assess cardiac function before each dose and 24 hours after the last dose.

General Side Effects of Cytoreduction

The short-term side effects of cytoreduction may occur during treatment and continue during the immediate posttransplant period. These side effects include nausea, vomiting, diarrhea, mucositis, esophagitis, anorexia, and decreased white blood cell, red blood cell, and platelet counts (Exhibit 7-3).

Transplantation Period

Bone marrow transplantation occurs after the patient has been cytoreduced. The period immediately before the infusion of bone marrow can be an extremely

Exhibit 7-3 General Side Effects of Cytoreduction and Related Management

Mucositis
   Altered comfort: mouth pain
   Altered oral mucous membranes
      Administer meticulous oral care with oral sprays every 4 hours
      Apply topical anesthetics as needed
      Administer antifungal agents every 4 hours
      Administer systemic analgesics
      Perform oral assessments to note color and texture of mucosa and presence of lesions

Gastrointestinal symptoms
   Diarrhea
   Altered comfort related to nausea/vomiting
      Assess frequency, color, and amount of stool/emesis
      Administer antidiarrheal agents as indicated
      Assess level of comfort
      Administer antiemetics as indicated
      Administer antacids every 2–4 hours as indicated
      Assess hydration status

Fluid balance
   Fluid volume deficit/excess
      Assess intake and output
      Monitor weights every day or twice a day if indicated
      Auscultate lung fields for adventitious breath sounds
      Assess skin turgor and texture
      Administer fluids/supplements as ordered

Nutrition
   Altered nutrition: less than body requirements
      Assess caloric intake (3-day calorie count)
      Administer total parenteral nutrition as ordered
      Assess for hypoglycemia/hyperglycemia
      Encourage small, frequent feedings

Skin care
   Impaired skin integrity
      Assess skin integrity daily and note changes
      Provide individualized, meticulous skin care

Psychosocial
   Body image disturbance
   Anxiety
   Fear
   Powerlessness
   Altered sexuality patterns secondary to sterility
   Altered family process
      Consult supportive services as needed (psychologist/psychiatrist, psychiatric nurse specialist, social worker)
      Establish mutually set goals to offer patient control/independence
      Discuss patient's fears/anxieties and clarify misconceptions
      Offer clear, concise explanations before treatments
      Encourage verbalization and offer reassurance
      Meet with family members daily to discuss their concerns
      Teach patient relaxation techniques

emotional time for the patient, donor, and family. Once the rigorous preparative treatment is complete, concerns then shift to the donor's undergoing general anesthesia, the actual infusion of the marrow, and what may lie ahead for the donor, recipients, and family.

Marrow Donation

The day before the transplant, the donor is admitted for a preoperative work-up. Marrow harvesting is performed in the operating room under general anesthesia, although spinal anesthesia may be used. The marrow is usually taken from the donor's anterior and posterior iliac crests. If an insufficient amount is obtained from this location, the sternum is used. When the marrow is harvested, a bone marrow aspirate needle is inserted into the marrow space in four or five different skin sites around the crests of both the right and left iliacs. Several marrow aspirates may be withdrawn from each skin site with different depths and angles used to locate different marrow areas. The total number of aspirations is between 100 and 200.

The amount of marrow taken is dependent on the donor's size. Usually 10 to 15 mL of marrow per kilogram body weight is obtained from the donor; 600 to 800 mL of marrow may be taken from an average adult. The amount of marrow is not as important as its concentration or cell count (number of stem cells). A satisfactory cell count is approximately $(10 \text{ to } 20) \times 10^9$ nucleated marrow cells. The cell count is higher in conventional allogeneic transplants than in autologous or T-cell–depleted transplants.

Patient education for the donor includes an explanation of the harvesting procedure as well as expectations for the immediate and long-term postoperative period. The donor's immediate postoperative care focuses on postanesthesia assessment, wound care, and pain management. Mild to moderate analgesics may be needed for several days to control lower back pain. The donor is usually discharged 1 to 2 days postoperatively. Vitamin and iron supplements are prescribed by some physicians to enhance the replication of bone marrow cells and to replace the iron lost in donation. Many BMT centers also require the donor to be available during the posttransplant period for blood donation.

Although complications related to marrow donation are rare, the administration of general anesthesia and potential for pain and hematomas remain a risk for the donor. Family members find the day of transplantation to be a particularly stressful time because they have concerns about the recovery and well-being of both the donor and the recipient.

The psychosocial needs of the donor are of major importance. Donors frequently feel guilty when problems arise for the recipient or if the marrow fails to engraft. The BMT team should be aware of this potential effect on the donor and employ measures to reassure donors that they are not responsible for the success or failure of the transplant.

Marrow Preparation

After the harvesting process, all marrow is filtered to remove bone chips and fat globules. The preparation of the marrow depends on the type of transplant. In the conventional transplant the marrow is bagged immediately after the filtration process. The bagging is similar to that used for blood products; in fact, the marrow looks like a packed red blood cell transfusion. The filtration and bagging process takes approximately 15 to 20 minutes. If the donor and recipient are ABO incompatible, hetastarch may be added to the marrow. This procedure enables the red blood cells, which can trigger a severe transfusion reaction, to be physically removed from the marrow.

If the transplant is a T-cell–depleted transplant, the marrow goes through additional steps to remove T cells. These processes may include binding T cells to sheep red blood cells (E-rosetting) to remove mature T cells. Lectin separation techniques or monoclonal antibodies are used to remove more mature T cells. This procedure takes 6 to 10 hours.

In the autologous transplant procedure marrow is harvested from the patient, filtered, processed, and bagged. The treatment of autologous marrow may consist of bathing the marrow in various chemotherapeutic agents or monoclonal antibodies to remove any residual malignant cells. The aim is to eliminate malignant cells while sparing the early progenitor cells that are necessary for marrow reconstitution. The marrow is preserved, frozen, and stored for infusion after cytoreduction.

Marrow Infusion

Transplant day is anticlimactic in comparison to the pretransplant conditioning phase. It is usually an emotional time, with the patient and family experiencing mixed feelings of excitement related to possible cure and anxiety related to potential failure. The patient may need reassurance that these mixed feelings are normal, and verbalization should be encouraged.

If the patient is an adult and is receiving a conventional transplant, approximately 600 mL of marrow is infused over 3 to 4 hours depending on fluid tolerance. The procedure is similar to the infusion of a packed red blood cell transfusion, except that a blood filter is not used and the marrow is not irradiated. All patients must be monitored carefully for potential complications during the marrow infusion, including fluid overload, development of micropulmonary emboli, and reactions to the white blood cells in the marrow. The patient is monitored for vital sign changes, dyspnea, chest pain, chills, fever, and hives. To control reactions, acetaminophen, diphenhydramine, and hydrocortisone are administered as premedications. If rigors occur during the infusion, warm blankets and meperidine may be prescribed.

Recipients of an autologous transplant may experience symptoms specific to the autologous transplant and related to the preservation of the marrow. The patient may note a garlic taste in the mouth during the marrow infusion, and bodily secretions may have a garlic odor for several days, as a result of the preservative (dimethylsulfoxide) that is used for marrow cryopreservation. Red blood cell lysis may occur, as evidenced by the patient's urine becoming maroon in color. Hydration is an important prophylaxis against renal complications.

Engraftment Period

Engraftment occurs when the transplanted marrow gives rise to mature blood cells. Approximately 14 days after the BMT, early marrow engraftment may be evident as bone marrow precursors differentiate into red blood cell, white blood cell, and platelet precursors. Recovery of the lymphocytes usually occurs first and is followed by recovery of granulocytes. Erythrocytes recover next, and platelet recovery occurs last. Lymphoid recovery is necessary for immune reconstitution to occur; complete immune recovery may take from 9 to 18 months, B cell function usually being the last immune parameter to normalize. Patients who have had allogeneic BMTs may have HLA typing and marrow cytogenetic studies performed to confirm engraftment of donor cells. Patients who have had autologous BMTs may have prolonged recovery of their platelet counts.

COMPLICATIONS OF BONE MARROW TRANSPLANTATION

Immediate Complications

A number of acute complications occur in the immediate posttransplant period as a result of intensive chemotherapy, radiation therapy, and transplantation of bone marrow. These are related to the toxicity of the pretransplant treatment regimen, which causes bleeding and mild to severe stomatitis. Other common clinical problems after BMT include infection, GVHD, veno-occlusive disease, graft rejection, and relapse.

Bleeding

The hematologic side effects of BMT are due to the effects of intensive chemotherapy and radiation therapy on the bone marrow. Patients are at risk for bleeding complications as a result of low platelet counts, breakdown of mucous membranes, and gastrointestinal disturbances. When the platelet cell counts fall below 50,000/mm^3, patients are placed on bleeding precautions.

Aspirin-containing products are contraindicated because they increase bleeding by blocking the clotting mechanism of platelets. Invasive procedures, injections, rectal thermometers, rectal suppositories, and indwelling urinary catheters are also contraindicated. Medroxyprogesterone acetate may be prescribed to control the menses. Oral care consists of the use of soft toothettes and the application of thrombin powder to the oral mucosa to control bleeding. The patient is monitored closely for the presence of petechiae; ecchymosis; blood in the urine, stool, and emesis; epistaxis; vaginal bleeding; and other active sites of bleeding.

Blood counts are performed daily. Generally, blood product infusions are administered to keep the platelet cell count above a minimum of 20,000/mm^3, hematocrit above 25%, and hemoglobin above 8 g/dL. For the inactivation of lymphocytes, which otherwise may cause a potentially fatal graft versus host reaction, all blood products are irradiated (3,000 rads) before transfusion. Families may be requested to locate donors for the blood product donation especially for single-donor and HLA-identical platelet donations. Bleeding is a common and controllable side effect. Daily or twice-daily platelet infusions and as many as two packed red blood cell transfusions per week are necessary to maintain the hematopoietic system.

Infection

Bacterial, fungal, and viral infections from exogenous or endogenous sources are a threat to the granulocytopenic BMT patient during the immediate post-transplant period. These infections generally arise from flora colonizing the skin, upper airway, and gastrointestinal tract. Common pathogens are gram-positive and gram-negative (e.g., *Pseudomonas*) organisms and *Candida* organisms. Oral herpes simplex infections are also common. Acyclovir is administered to decrease the incidence of this complication. Protective isolation aimed at protecting the patient from potential sources of infection may range from minimal protection (i.e., masks and hand washing) to germ-free LAF isolation. Low bacterial or sterile diets are used to provide further protection from sources of infection.

Patients are monitored continually for signs and symptoms of infection. The site of infection is often difficult to locate because the patient's inability to exhibit an inflammatory response coincides with a severe decrease in neutrophils. If the patient's temperature is greater than 38.5°C, a chest roentgenogram as well as blood, throat, stool, and central intravenous line cultures are obtained before initiating broad-spectrum intravenous antibiotics. Broad-spectrum antibiotic coverage is initiated immediately because life-threatening septicemia may result if infection is not treated promptly. Acetaminophen and tepid sponge baths are administered to reduce the fever and to alleviate discomfort. Hypothermia blankets are useful when the patient's temperature is consistently higher than 40°C. If the patient continues to be febrile despite antibiotics, amphotericin B may be given to treat a potential fungal infection.

Prophylaxis with trimethoprim-sulfamethoxazole has virtually eliminated *Pneumocystis carinii* pneumonia among BMT patients. Other methods used to prevent interstitial pneumonia include cytomegalovirus (CMV) prophylaxis with

CMV immunoglobulin or γ-globulin, administration of only CMV-negative blood products to patients who are seronegative for CMV, and use of pentamidine aerosol.

Interstitial pneumonia is characterized by diffuse pulmonary disease with evidence of bilateral interstitial infiltrates and can be a consequence of viruses, protozoa, toxins, or TBI. The possibility of interstitial pneumonia warrants vital sign and lung assessments at least every 4 hours. Interstitial pneumonia occurs in 20% to 40% of BMT patients and may be fatal in 50% to 80% of these (Gale and Quinn 1989). More than half the cases are associated with CMV. In other instances drug or radiation toxicity may be involved, although patients receiving fractionated TBI have a significantly lower incidence of interstitial pneumonia than those receiving single-dose TBI. *P. carinii*, adenovirus, and herpes simplex viruses are involved in a small proportion of cases. Intravenous acyclovir may be given to prevent herpes infections.

If interstitial pneumonia occurs, it is treated with the appropriate antiviral or antiprotozoan drug. Despite the use of oxygen therapy and ventilator support to treat insufficient respiratory function, CMV interstitial pneumonia is associated with an extremely high mortality rate. Use of the combination of the antiviral drug gancyclovir and hyperimmune γ-globulin has reversed cases of CMV interstitial pneumonia, however.

Nursing interventions related to interstitial pneumonia include instructing and assisting the patient to cough and deep breathe and to use an incentive spirometer and ultrasonic nebulizer. Gentle postural drainage may be indicated. Ongoing assessment of the rate, depth, and pattern of respirations as well as the quality of breath sounds is crucial to ensure early detection of interstitial pneumonia.

GVHD

GVHD remains a major problem of transplantation and a nursing challenge to coordinate the care of patients with this complication (Exhibit 7-4). GVHD is a syndrome in which immunocompetent donor lymphoid cells react to a foreign immunosuppressed host (recipient). T lymphocytes from the donor marrow recognize foreign tissue in the host and attack it. There are three conditions necessary for GVHD to occur: the donor cells must possess mature T lymphocytes, there must be a certain degree of histoincompatibility between the graft and the host, and the host must be immunosuppressed. GVHD may occur in the immunosuppressed patient after an infusion of bone marrow or after a transfusion of a nonirradiated blood product.

The term acute GVHD has been used to describe a distinct syndrome involving the skin, gastrointestinal tract, and liver that develops within 100 days of allogeneic BMT. Acute GVHD may become chronic. Nevertheless, chronic GVHD may occur 2 to 12 months after BMT and may not be preceded by the acute phase. GVHD has been reported to occur in 20% to 65% of histocompatible and in

Exhibit 7-4 Nursing Diagnoses Related to GVHD

Skin
  Impaired skin integrity related to an immunologic reaction of the donor lymphocytes to the host tissue
  Impaired physical mobility related to skin scarring and contractures
  Pain related to GVHD of the skin
  Potential for infection related to impaired skin integrity

Gastrointestinal tract
  Diarrhea related to degeneration of intestinal mucosa and mucosal glands
  Potential fluid volume deficit related to diarrhea
  Pain related to gastrointestinal cramping
  Altered nutrition: less than body requirements related to gastrointestinal symptoms
  Potential for infection related to degeneration of intestinal mucosa

Liver
  Altered comfort related to enlarged liver, pruritis secondary to liver dysfunction
  Body image disturbance related to the biophysical effect of the disease

more than 80% of histoincompatible allogeneic recipients (Deeg and Storb 1986; Gale 1985; Storb et al. 1983).

Skin manifestations are the earliest and most obvious signs of GVHD. Diagnosis is confirmed by a skin biopsy, although the results are not always definitive. Involvement of the skin may range from a mild maculopapular rash to a generalized erythroderma with peeling that may be as extensive as a third-degree burn. Impairment of skin integrity may be treated with Aveeno® baths, A&D® and mineral oil mixtures, or Aquaphor® to alleviate local dryness and to keep the skin pliable and intact. Artificial saliva and tears may be necessary if the salivary and lacrimal ducts are affected. Systemic antipruritic medications, topical antihistamines, steroids, and lidocaine may provide localized pain relief. It is crucial to keep skin areas that are affected by blisters and peeling clean and free from infection. Comfort measures may include the use of air fluidized beds and bed cradles. Finally, active and passive range of motion exercises may be necessary to prevent contractures.

Gastrointestinal symptoms include abdominal cramping, diarrhea, and bleeding. In severe cases the characteristic green diarrhea can total 6 to 7 L per day. When GVHD manifests in the gut, a degeneration of the mucosa is seen. Meticulous assessment and rectal care are essential to prevent skin breakdown. Monitoring of fluid status and prompt treatment are important to prevent dehydration.

GVHD may progress to the liver, causing degeneration of the small bile ducts. GVHD of the liver is characterized by an increase in the liver function tests (serum bilirubin, serum glutamic-oxaloacetic transaminase, alkaline phosphatase, and lactic dehydrogenase). Manifestations are hepatitislike signs and symptoms.

Nursing interventions include monitoring the patient's liver function tests and coagulation studies, jaundice, abdominal girth, and level of comfort to assess the progression of liver dysfunction.

The commonly used grading systems for GVHD were developed by the Seattle transplant group (Tables 7-3 and 7-4). The degree of skin involvement is evaluated according to the severity of the rash. Gut involvement is graded according to the diarrheal quantity, and liver involvement is based on bilirubin elevations. An increase in grades is indicative of an increase in organ involvement and severity. Grade 1 reflects mild GVHD (limited to the skin and requiring no therapy), grade 2 indicates moderate multiorgan disease, grade 3 is severe multiorgan disease, and grade 4 is life threatening. Grades 2 to 4 develop in 30% to 50% of patients with marrow engraftment after a conventional allogeneic BMT (Sullivan and Parkman 1983).

Systemic treatment of GVHD is aimed at reducing the number of donor lymphocytes, thereby decreasing the immunologic reaction to host antigens. Patients with GVHD are conventionally treated with steroids initially. Many centers are exploring other types of treatment, however, including antithymocyte globulin, cyclosporine, and monoclonal antibodies. Treatment measures aimed at curing or controlling GVHD may also cause immunosuppression, which further predisposes the patient to infection.

Because GVHD remains a significant obstacle to successful BMT and because treatment measures historically have not been promising, many researchers are focusing efforts on methods to prevent GVHD. Efforts related to prophylaxis include the use of protective LAF environments, irradiation of all blood products to 3,000 rads, and administration of steroids, methotrexate, cyclosporine, antithymocyte globulin, or combinations of these agents. Recent research efforts have pursued the use of T-cell depletion in allogeneic BMT before marrow infusion by means of soybean agglutinin fractionation or monoclonal antibodies.

Table 7-3 Overall Clinical Grading of Severity of GVHD

Grade	Degree of Organ Involvement
1	+ to + + skin rash; no gut involvement; no liver involvement; no decrease in clinical performance
2	+ to + + + skin rash; + gut involvement or + liver involvement (or both); mild decrease in clinical performance
3	+ + to + + + skin rash; + + to + + + gut involvement or + + to + + + + liver involvement (or both); marked decrease in clinical performance
4	Similar to grade 3 with + + to + + + + organ involvement and extreme decrease in clinical performance

Source: Reprinted from *New England Journal of Medicine,* Vol. 292, p. 896, with permission of the Massachusetts Medical Society, © 1975.

Table 7-4 Proposed Clinical Stage of GVHD According to Organ System

Stage	Skin	Liver	Intestinal Tract
+	Maculopapular rash less than 25% of body surface	Bilirubin 2–3 mg/100 mL	More than 500 mL diarrhea/day
+ +	Maculopapular rash on 25%–50% of body	Bilirubin 3–6 mg/100 mL	More than 1,000 mL diarrhea/day
+ + +	Generalized erythroderma	Bilirubin 6–15 mg/100 mL	More than 1,500 mL diarrhea/day
+ + + +	Generalized erythroderma with bullous formation and desquamation	Bilirubin >15mg/100 mL	Severe abdominal pain with or without ileus

Source: Reprinted from *New England Journal of Medicine*, Vol. 292, p. 896, with permission of the Massachusetts Medical Society, © 1975.

Veno-Occlusive Disease

Veno-occlusive disease of the liver is a fibrous obstruction of small hepatic veins that can be caused by high-dose chemotherapy and radiation therapy. This syndrome can occur 1 to 3 weeks after transplant in approximately 20% of BMT patients. Patients older than 15 years of age and with underlying malignancy requiring vigorous pretransplant therapy and a previous history of liver disease are at risk (McDonald et al. 1984).

Veno-occlusive disease has no treatment other than resting the liver and supporting the patient in the acute phase of the disease. There is no known way to open the occluded vessels, but attention to the details of treating liver failure and fluid retention may allow the patient to live long enough for the liver to recover. The disease resolves in approximately 50% of cases; death results in the other 50% of cases (McDonald et al. 1984).

Graft Rejection

Graft rejection occurs when the recipient's body is unable to accept the transplanted marrow. The risk of rejection varies according to the type of transplant. The risk is usually less than 10% in allogeneic transplants and lower in autologous BMTs. Rejection may occur any time up to 4 months after transplant. Early signs of graft rejection include sudden changes in the total white blood cell count and the differential cell count. Bone marrow HLA or cytogenetic studies are useful in confirming that rejection has occurred. The treatment for rejection varies according to institution protocol. If subsequent allogeneic BMTs fail, the patient may receive an autologous infusion of marrow if one was harvested before the initial allogeneic BMT.

Relapse

Relapse after BMT is most likely to occur if the patient has reached an advanced stage of disease or is in relapse at the time of transplant. Relapse can occur in patients who have had autologous, allogeneic, or syngeneic BMTs if the preparative treatment (and in autologous transplants the marrow purging) was not sufficient to eliminate all malignant cells. Relapse may occur any time within 1 to 2 years of BMT. The signs of relapse vary according to the patient's disease.

If relapse occurs the transplant team reviews treatment options with the patient and family. The treatment plan depends on the patient's diagnosis, the extent of disease, tolerance to prior treatment, and the patient's and family's commitment to further treatment. Options for the patient include additional radiation therapy and chemotherapy, another BMT, or supportive care.

The nurse should reinforce the information that the BMT team has provided concerning the treatment options for patients who develop relapse or graft rejection and support the patient and family in their individual decision. Many patients and family members find psychiatric counseling and other support systems helpful during this extremely difficult time.

Long-Term Complications

Causes of delayed complications after BMT include the preparative regimen, problems from the original disease, or chronic GVHD. Patients require straightforward information regarding all potential long-term complications, which include chronic GVHD, infertility, cataracts, secondary malignancies, and alteration in growth and development (Table 7-5).

Table 7-5 Common Long-Term Complications of BMT

Potential Complication	Incidence
Bacterial, viral, fungal infections	>50%
Interstitial pneumonia (CMV, *P. carinii* pneumonia)	70%
Cataracts	
Fractionated TBI	20%
Single-dose TBI	50%
Impaired growth in children from irradiation	100%
Gonadal dysfunction (dependent on preconditioning regimen, age, sex)	
Chronic GVHD (multisystem disease; dependent on type of BMT)	

Source: Adapted from *Oncology Nursing Forum*, Vol. 13, No. 6, pp. 61–70, with permission of the Oncology Nursing Society, © 1986.

DISCHARGE

Discharge teaching and planning are initiated on admission day and continue throughout the patient's hospitalization. The primary nurse has an integral role in assessing the patient's and family's learning needs and in preparing patients for discharge when the BMT team determines that the patient is ready for discharge on the basis of assessment of discharge criteria. These criteria include peripheral blood and bone marrow studies, evidence of engraftment, nutrition intake, ambulatory status, and temperature and vital signs.

Patients who received gastrointestinal decontamination are recontaminated before discharge. Oral and vaginal decontamination medications are discontinued, as are the skin decontamination baths. The skin and mucosal surfaces are recontaminated with normal, nonpathogenic microbial flora or by skin touch to achieve skin recolonization; yogurt or Lactinex® is used to recolonize the oral-intestinal tract. Except for the recontamination process, discharge teaching and planning for BMT patients in both germ-free and clean isolation environments are identical and include specifics related to resuming life at home; observing for signs and symptoms of infection, bleeding, and GVHD; care of the long-term intravenous catheter; nutrition aspects; resuming sexual activity; discharge medications; dental care; and follow-up visits.

Patients and families are encouraged to discuss their particular concerns about discharge and possible long-term effects. Psychosocial counseling and follow-up are integral to the overall discharge preparation for transplant patients. Discharge is surely a happy time for patients and families, but it is also a time of ambivalence. Fears and concerns emerge in relation to leaving the security of the hospital environment and the staff, adjusting to home and family life, and reentering society. The feelings surrounding these issues require ongoing support from the transplant team. All patients require meticulous physical, psychologic, and psychosocial follow-up to monitor their state of health and to facilitate their readjustment after the rigorous transplant process.

ECONOMIC ISSUES IN BONE MARROW TRANSPLANTATION

BMT is extremely expensive because of the extended hospitalization (1 to 3 months or longer), intensive nursing and medical care, sophisticated technology, and pharmacologic agents and blood components necessary for supportive care. The inpatient hospitalization costs for the average BMT range from $50,000 to $120,000 (Durbin 1988; Thomas 1987). Expenses related to BMT are more than twice those of renal transplantation and rival those of heart transplantation (Durbin 1988). The vast majority of medical bills for BMT are paid by third party insurers and the government. Families rarely pay much for the direct medical expenses related to BMT (Durbin 1988). Nevertheless, these costs do not account for personal expenditures (transportation, housing, food, and the like) and income loss associated with a major illness in the family.

FUTURE TRENDS IN BONE MARROW TRANSPLANTATION

The expansion of nursing and medical research is crucial for the future development of BMT. At present, nursing research in the area of BMT has included issues related to psychosocial concerns of patients and families, oral care and mucositis, the protective isolation environment, measures to reduce the discomfort related to side effects of medications used during the transplant course, and survivorship issues. As transplantation evolves, so will nursing research in the transplant arena. Nurses are developing proposals for collaborative research among institutions to study common problems related to BMT nursing. The 21st century should be an exciting time for the development and completion of many nursing research projects that will serve to validate or change transplant nursing practice.

As advances are made in medical research, the application of BMT protocols will continue to evolve. Biologic response modifiers may be used to enhance the growth of stem cells, resulting in shorter marrow reconstitution time and thus decreasing infection and bleeding complications. Medical research continues to expand the unrelated donor pool and to eliminate GVHD and rejection and relapse problems while perfecting T-cell depletion and marrow purging procedures. Finally, advances related to antiviral therapy will have a profound impact on the successful outcome of BMT.

Bone marrow transplantation, once highly experimental and specific to only a few centers, is now becoming an addition to many hospitals. BMT is still in its evolutionary stages, and changes continue to occur as immunologic and pharmacologic advances are made. As protocols and treatments change, so do side effects and patient care needs. Nurses must constantly update their knowledge base in regard to transplantation. It is necessary for the nurse to incorporate new information into patient teaching as well as into the nursing care plan. Because BMT is an evolving specialty, nurses will continue to be challenged in caring for this patient population.

STUDY QUESTIONS

1. Differentiate between autologous, syngeneic, and allogeneic BMT.
2. Define the conditioning phase, and identify associated nursing diagnoses and nursing interventions.

3. Identify three potential complications of BMT and discuss the cause and treatment of these complications.
4. Discuss essential content to be included in donor, family, and patient education.
5. Discuss the ethical and psychosocial implications of BMT for the patient, family, and donor.

REFERENCES

Deeg, H.J., and R. Storb. 1986. Acute and chronic graft-versus-host disease: Clinical manifestations, prophylaxis, and treatment. *Journal of Clinical Investigation* 76:1325–28.

Durbin, M. 1988. Bone marrow transplantation: Economic, ethical and social issues. *Pediatrics* 82:774–83.

Fefer, A. 1986. Allogeneic marrow transplantation for acute nonlymphoblastic leukemia. *Journal of the National Cancer Institute* 76:1275–79.

Fefer, A., R.A. Cliff, and E.D. Thomas. 1986. Allogeneic marrow transplantation for chronic granulocytic leukemia. *Journal of the National Cancer Institute* 76:1295–99.

Gale, R.P. 1985. Graft-versus-host disease. *Immunology Review* 88:193–214.

Gale, R.P., and D. Quinn. 1989. The management of acute leukemias: Part I. Bone marrow transplants. *Clinical Advances in Oncology* 1:1–7.

Gorin, N.C. 1986. Autologous bone marrow transplantation in acute leukemia. *Journal of the National Cancer Institute* 76:1281–87.

Kamani, N. and C.S. August. 1984. Bone marrow transplantation: Problems and prospects. *Medical Clinics of North America* 68:657–674.

McDonald, G.B., P. Sharma, D.E. Matthews, H.M. Shulman, and E.D. Thomas. 1984. Venoocclusive disease of the liver after bone marrow transplantation: Diagnosis, incidence and predisposing factors. *Hepatology* 4:116–22.

O'Reilly, R.J. 1983. Review of allogeneic bone marrow transplantation: Current status and future directions. *Blood* 62:941–64.

Santos, G.W. 1984. Bone marrow transplantation in leukemia: Current status. *CA—A Cancer Journal for Clinicians* 54(supplement):2732–40.

Santos, G.W., and H. Kaizer. 1982. Bone marrow transplantation in acute leukemia. *Seminars in Hematology* 19:227–39.

Storb, R., R.L. Prentice, C.D. Buckner, R.A. Clift, F. Appelbaum, J. Deeg, K. Doney, J.A. Hansen, M. Mason, J.E. Sanders, J. Singer, K.M. Sullivan, R.P. Witherspoon, and E.D. Thomas. 1983. Graft-versus-host disease and survival in patients with aplastic anemia treated by marrow grafts from HLA-identical siblings. *New England Journal of Medicine* 308:302–306.

Sullivan, K.M., and R. Parkman. 1983. The pathophysiology and treatment of graft-versus-host disease. *Clinics in Hematology* 12:775–89.

Thomas, E.D. 1987. Bone marrow transplantation. *CA—A Cancer Journal for Clinicians* 37:291–302.

Thomas, E.D., H.L. Lochte, J.H. Cannon, O.D. Sahler, and J.W. Ferrebee. 1959. Supralethal whole body irradiation isologous marrow transplantation in man. *Journal of Clinical Investigation* 38:1709–16.

Yeager, A.M., H. Kaizer, G.W. Santos, R. Saral, O.M. Colvin, R.K. Stuart, H.G. Braine, P.J. Burke, R.F. Ambinder, W.H. Burns, D.J. Fuller, J.M. Davis, J.E. Karp, W.S. May, S.D. Rowley, L.L. Sensenbrenner, G.B. Vogelsang, and J.R. Wingard. 1986. Autologous bone marrow transplantation in patients with acute nonlymphocytic leukemia, using ex vivo marrow treatment with 4-hydroperoxycyclophosphamide. *New England Journal of Medicine* 315:141–47.

SUGGESTED READINGS

Autologous Bone Marrow Transplantation

Cogliano-Shutta, N.A., E.J. Broda, and J.S. Gress. 1985. Bone marrow transplantation: An overview and comparison of autologous, syngeneic, and allogeneic treatment modalities. *Nursing Clinics of North America* 20:49–65.

Dicke, K.A., S. Jagannath, G. Spritzer, C. Poynton, A. Zander, L. Vellekoop, C.L. Reading, U.W. Jehn, and S. Tindle. 1984. The role of autologous bone marrow transplantation in various malignancies. *Seminars in Hematology* 21:109–21.

Schryber, S., C.R. Lacasse, and M. Barton-Burke. 1987. Autologous bone marrow transplantation. *Oncology Nursing Forum* 14:74–80.

Donors

Kinrade, L. 1987. Preparation of sibling donor for bone marrow transplant harvest procedure. *Cancer Nursing* 10:77–80.

O'Rourke, A. 1986. Bone marrow procedure guide. *Oncology Nursing Forum* 13:66–67.

Early Complications

Champlain, R.E., and R.P. Gale. 1984. The early complications of bone marrow transplantation. *Seminars in Hematology* 21:101–108.

General Allogeneic Bone Marrow Transplantation

Cogliano-Shutta, N.A., E.J. Broda, and J.S. Gress. 1985. Bone marrow transplantation: An overview and comparison of autologous, syngeneic, and allogeneic treatment modalities. *Nursing Clinics of North America* 20:49–65.

Doney, K.C., and C.D. Buckner. 1985. Bone marrow transplantation: Overview. *Plasma Therapy and Transfusion Technology* 6:149–61.

Freedman, S. 1988. An overview of bone marrow transplantation. *Seminars in Oncology Nursing* 4:3–8.

Nuscher, R., L. Baltzer, D.A. Repinec, G. Almquist, J.E. Barrett, S. LoBombardi, J.D. DeMao, M.E. Diver, B.A. Field, M.C. Lee, J. Mamora, B. Pizzo, B.N. Sheehy, M. Sullivan, and J. Tierney. 1984. Bone marrow transplantation: A life saving option. *American Journal of Nursing* 84:764–72.

Spruce, W. 1983. Bone marrow transplantation. *American Journal of Hematology and Oncology* 5:287–306.

Thomas, E.D. 1989. High-dose therapy and bone marrow transplantation. *Seminars in Oncology* 12 (supplement 6):15–20.

Germ-Free Environment

Buckner, D. 1978. Protective environments for marrow transplant recipients: A prospective study. *Annals of Internal Medicine* 89:893–901.

Lindgren, P.S. 1983. The laminar air flow room: Nursing practices and procedures. *Nursing Clinics of North America* 18:553–62.

Graft-versus-Host Disease

de la Montaigne, M., J. DeMao, R. Nuscher, et al. 1981. Standards of care of the patient with "graft-versus-host disease" post bone marrow transplantation. *Cancer Nursing* 4:191–98.

Parker, N., and T. Cohen. 1983. Acute graft-versus-host disease in allogeneic marrow transplantation. *Nursing Clinics of North America* 18:569–78.

Harvesting

Holcombe, A. 1987. Bone marrow harvest. *Oncology Nursing Forum* 14:63–65.

Immunology

Dudjak, L. 1984. HLA-typing: Implications for nurses. *Oncology Nursing Forum* 11:30–36.

Infection

van der Meer, J.W.M., H.F.L. Guiot, P.J. van den Broek, and R. van Furth. 1984. Infections in bone marrow transplant recipients. *Seminars in Hematology* 21:123–40.

Lectin-Separation Bone Marrow Transplantation

O'Reilly, R.J., N. Kapoor, D. Kirkpatrick, S. Cunningham Rundles, M.S. Pollack, B. Dupont, M.Z. Hodes, R.A. Good, and Y. Reisner. 1983. Transplantation for severe combined immunodeficiency using histoincompatible parental marrow fractionated by soybean agglutinin and sheep red blood cells: Experience in six consecutive cases. *Transplantation Proceedings* 15:1431–35.

Long-Term Complications

Corcoran-Buchsel, P. 1986. Long term complications of allogeneic bone marrow transplantation: Nursing implications. *Oncology Nursing Forum* 13:61–70.

Nims, J.W., and S. Strom. 1988. Late complications of bone marrow transplant recipients: Nursing care issues. *Seminars in Oncology Nursing* 4:47–54.

Overview of Bone Marrow Transplantation

Blume, K.G., and L.D. Petz. 1983. *Clinical bone marrow transplantation*. New York: Churchill Livingstone.

Corcoran-Buchsel, P., and R. Rord. 1988. Bone marrow transplantation. *Seminars in Oncology Nursing* 4:1–81.

Hutchinson, M. 1983. Symposium on bone marrow transplantation. *Nursing Clinics of North America* 18:509–610.

Nuscher-Ford, R., V. McShane, K. McMahon, M. Siegler, S. McKeever, J. DeMao, M. de la Montaigne, and C. Stutzer. 1986. Bone marrow transplant. In *Standards of oncology nursing practice*, ed. M.H. Brown, M.E. Kiss, E. Outlaw, and C. Viamontes. New York: Wiley.

Patient/Family Education

Leukemia Society of America, Inc. 1987. Bone marrow transplantation: Questions and answers. New York: Leukemia Society of America.

National Cancer Institute. 1987. Bone marrow transplantation: Research report. NIH Publication no. 87-1178.

Psychosocial Aspects

Atkins, D., and A. Patenaude. 1987. Psychosocial preparation and follow-up for pediatric bone marrow transplant patients. *American Journal of Orthopsychiatry* 57:246–52.

Freund, B., and K. Siegel. 1986. Problems in transition following bone marrow transplantation: Psychosocial aspects. *American Journal of Orthopsychiatry* 56:244–52.

Pfefferbaum, B., M. Lindamood, and F. Wiley. 1978. Stages in pediatric bone marrow transplantation. *Pediatrics* 61:625–28.

Chapter 8

Advances in Cancer Pain Management

Nessa Coyle and Russell K. Portenoy

> Although the undertreatment of cancer pain continues to be an urgent problem of immense proportions, progress has been made in the past two decades in the areas of professional education, pain evaluation, treatment modalities, and continuing care. The chapter reviews the advances in these areas and describes their impact on the clinical management of cancer patients. As quality of life becomes increasingly viewed as an integral part of cancer therapy, the management of pain and other symptoms has become recognized as an essential element of care.

Cancer pain affects millions of people each year. In the United States alone, approximately 329,000 patients or two-thirds of the 494,000 people who died of cancer in 1988 had pain severe enough to warrant opioid analgesics (American Cancer Society 1989; Foley 1985; Coyle and Foley 1987; Daut and Cleeland 1982). For the individual poorly managed pain greatly augments suffering, and it exhausts the family, friends, physicians, and nurses who provide the necessary care and comfort (Coyle et al., in press). Pain undermines the quality of life of the patient and family and may be a major factor in a patient's wish for an early death (Angell 1982; Breitbart 1987; Coyle et al., in press; Daut and Cleeland 1982; Levin, Cleeland, and Dar 1985; Portenoy, in press).

The undertreatment of cancer pain continues to be an urgent problem of immense proportions. Nevertheless, this situation has become increasingly recognized during the last decade, and efforts are underway to enhance awareness of this issue on the part of the public and policymakers as well as professionals engaged in the treatment of cancer patients. Perhaps the most exciting of these efforts is the gradual development of statewide cancer pain initiatives. The first, the Wisconsin Cancer Pain Initiative (1988), was established through the efforts of a multidisciplinary work group that adopted the following as guiding principles: (1) the focus of legislative and educational efforts should be on cancer pain at all stages and not only among the terminally ill; (2) the problem is not due to lack of effective analgesics but rather to inadequate diagnosis and management with existing drug and nondrug therapies; (3) continuing education programs in pain management have not substantially improved the management of cancer pain; and (4) any program to improve pain management must address the need to change attitudes and behaviors in health professionals. Other factors that contribute to the undertreatment of cancer pain were similarly identified (Exhibits 8-1, 8-2, and 8-3), and the integrated approach to the resolution of these problems has become a model for the nation.

Improved awareness and education have also been the goals of the World Health Organization (WHO) Cancer Pain Relief Program, which was established in 1984. This effort evolved in response to the estimate that 25 million cancer patients worldwide die with poorly relieved pain (Foley 1985; WHO 1986). Expert committees sponsored by this organization have published guidelines for the effective use of drugs to treat cancer pain. These guidelines, which are based on a three-step analgesic ladder, are now being implemented around the world.

Thus, although the undertreatment of cancer pain continues, progress has been made, particularly in the areas of professional education, pain evaluation, treatment modalities, and continuing care. This chapter focuses on the clinical benefits that have accrued as a result of these advances. The emerging role of the clinical nurse specialist as a key figure in pain management and continuing care is emphasized.

ADVANCES IN PAIN EVALUATION

Recent advances in understanding of the basic physiology of pain have been dramatic. Increased recognition of the variable mechanisms of cancer pain has

Exhibit 8-1 Factors That Contribute to the Cancer Pain Problem: Health Professional Related

Lack of understanding of the pathophysiology of cancer pain
Lack of knowledge of the clinical pharmacology of opioid drugs
Lack of knowledge of the use of adjunct drugs and neurosurgical procedures for pain relief
Insufficient professional education in cancer pain therapy
Lack of knowledge of the difference between physical dependence on drugs and addiction
Excessive concern about the development of tolerance to opioid drugs
Excessive concern about the side effects of opioid drugs
The belief that cancer pain should be moderate to severe before patients receive medication
The belief that patients are not good judges of the severity of their pain
Assignment of low priority to pain management
Lack of thorough and frequent reevaluation of the patient's pain status

Source: Adapted from *Journal of Pain Symptom Management*, Vol. 3, No. 1, pp. S2–S5, with permission of the U.S. Cancer Pain Relief Committee, © 1988.

Exhibit 8-2 Factors That Contribute to the Cancer Pain Problem: Patient and Family Member Related

---

Lack of awareness that cancer pain can be managed, with the result that patients may suffer without staff awareness

Fear that the use of opioid drugs will lead to addiction

Fear that the use of opioid drugs will lead to mental confusion, sedation, disorientation, and personality changes

Failure to report pain because of the desire to be a "good patient" and not to distract the physician from the primary task of treating the disease

Underreporting of pain because increasing pain suggests that the disease is progressing

Source: Adapted from *Journal of Pain Symptom Management,* Vol. 3, No. 1, pp. S2–S5, with permission of the U.S. Cancer Pain Relief Committee, © 1988.

---

provided a rationale for various pain management techniques (Cleeland et al. 1986).

Classification of Pain Mechanisms

Basic and clinical researchers have begun to classify clinical pain by its underlying pathogenesis. Among cancer patients, the division of pain mechanisms into somatic, visceral, and neuropathic appears to have the greatest clinical utility (Payne 1987a).

Exhibit 8-3 Factors That Contribute to the Cancer Pain Problem: Health Care System Related

---

Lack of accountability for pain management because hospitals operate on the basis of an acute, disease-oriented model

Lack of continuity of care as patients are moved from one care setting to another

Fragmentation of care because of the highly specialized nature of cancer care and the multiple physicians and other care workers involved

Unwillingness of some pharmacies in large cities to stock narcotics because of the risk of theft; in other areas, resources for pain-relieving neurolytic and neurosurgical procedures are not available

Source: Adapted from *Journal of Pain Symptom Management,* Vol. 3, No. 1, pp. S2–S5, with permission of the U.S. Cancer Pain Relief Committee, © 1988.

Somatic pain is usually well localized and is described as aching, throbbing, or gnawing. Examples of somatic pain include pain from bone metastases, postsurgical pain, and musculoskeletal pain.

Visceral pain results from compression, distention, or stretching of abdominal or thoracic viscera, usually as a result of primary or metastatic tumor growth. When solid viscera are involved this pain is often described as deep, squeezing, or pressurelike; obstruction of hollow viscera usually produces a poorly localized cramping pain. The latter may be associated with nausea, vomiting, and diaphoresis, especially when pain is acute. Visceral pain is often referred to cutaneous sites remote from the site of the lesion (for example, shoulder pain from diaphragmatic irritation) and may be associated with tenderness in the referred cutaneous site.

Neuropathic pain results from neural injury, either peripheral or central. The injury may result from direct tumor invasion, surgery, radiation therapy, chemotherapy, or other factors. Examples of neuropathic pain include metastatic or radiation-induced brachial or lumbar plexopathies, epidural spinal cord compression, postherpetic neuralgia, and painful vincristine- and cisplatin-induced neuropathies. Pain resulting from neural injury is usually unfamiliar and often burning or stabbing in quality. Neurologic deficits may be associated.

Somatic and visceral pain are believed to be due to activation of nerve fibers sensitive to noxious stimuli that innervate somatic and visceral structures, respectively. These pains can also be termed nociceptive, a label that implies that the pain is commensurate with the degree of tissue damage present. Isolation of the painful part from the central nervous system, for example by neural blockade, may effectively relieve this type of pain. Somatic and visceral pain also usually respond well to the opioid drugs. Nonsteroidal anti-inflammatory drugs are particularly efficacious for somatic pain and are frequently used in combination with the opioids.

In contrast to somatic and visceral pain, neuropathic pains (particularly those due to deafferentation, in which aberrant somatosensory processing presumably develops in the central nervous system after neural injury) are nonnociceptive and appear to be less responsive to the opioid drugs. Combining an opioid with adjuvants, such as a tricyclic antidepressant or an anticonvulsant, is often more effective (Cleeland et al. 1986; Portenoy 1989). Abundant anecdotal data suggest that neuropathic pains, particularly those due to deafferentation, are not likely to be benefitted over the long term by isolation of the painful part from the central nervous system (Portenoy 1989).

In contrast to neuropathic pain, a second type of nonnociceptive pain, that due primarily to psychologic processes, is extremely uncommon among cancer patients. Although the psychologic state clearly contributes to both the experience and the expression of pain in this population, pain resulting from psychologic factors alone appears to be exceedingly rare (Bond 1979; Portenoy 1989).

Classification of Pain Syndromes

Advances in identifying common cancer pain syndromes have also yielded information useful in the management of these patients. Syndrome identification guides an appropriate evaluation to determine the underlying nociceptive etiology of the pain and may provide insight into prognosis.

Pain syndromes have been divided into three major categories: those associated with direct tumor involvement, those associated with cancer therapy, and those unrelated to cancer or its therapy (Foley 1985, 1987; Portenoy 1989). Pain associated with direct tumor involvement is most frequently encountered in patients with metastatic bone disease, hollow viscus involvement, or nerve compression or infiltration. Such pain syndromes account for more than three-quarters of pain problems in an inpatient population and for a somewhat smaller proportion in an outpatient pain clinic (Foley 1987; Portenoy 1989).

Pain syndromes associated with cancer therapy account for less than one-quarter of pain problems in an inpatient and outpatient population (Foley 1987). Included in this category are those patients in whom the pain occurs during the course of, or as a result of, chemotherapy, surgery, or radiation therapy. Each of these primary modalities of therapy may be followed by any of a series of specific pain syndromes. This group of chronic pain syndromes is growing because cancer treatment and systems of continuing care are becoming more effective and patients are living longer with their disease.

Cancer patients may also experience pain syndromes unrelated to the cancer or cancer therapy. The generally elderly population with cancer may describe pain associated with osteoarthritis, osteoporosis, postherpetic neuralgia, or many other conditions. Less than 5% of inpatients have pain unrelated to their cancer or cancer therapy; this figure increases to 10% when an outpatient cancer population is surveyed (Foley 1987; Portenoy 1989).

Classification of Groups of Patients with Cancer Pain

In addition to the classification of cancer pain into discrete syndromes, categories of pain patients can be discerned (Foley 1985). This classification may particularly contribute to an understanding of some of the psychologic and social factors that affect pain and its management.

Specifically, patients can be divided into five groups. The first includes those patients with acute cancer-related pain. This group can be subdivided into those patients with tumor-associated pain and those whose pain is associated with cancer therapy. As reflected in this latter distinction, the etiology of the pain is a key characteristic that not only determines the potential for primary treatment but is also potentially predictive of psychologic responses that may directly affect both pain tolerance and suffering. Pain that is tolerated by the patient when the hope is for cure or remission may become intolerable when it indicates progressive disease.

The second group includes patients with chronic cancer-related pain. As with acute pain, these patients can be further subdivided into those with chronic pain from tumor progression and those with chronic pain related to cancer treatment. The same issues related to the etiology of the pain and its meaning to the patient are evident.

The third group comprises patients with a history of chronic nonmalignant pain who develop cancer and pain. These patients and their families may already be psychologically and physically compromised because of chronic pain. With the added stress of cancer and pain of a different significance, they are at high risk for further deterioration. Early identification of this group of patients enables appropriate support mechanisms to be implemented.

The fourth group includes patients with a history of drug abuse who develop cancer-related pain. In this group are patients who are actively using street drugs, patients who are in methadone maintenance programs, and patients who have not used drugs for many years. The first subgroup strains the resources of the most sophisticated pain management team, and tight controls are needed on the way analgesics are dispensed, especially when the patient is discharged home. The second and third subgroups do not usually present a problem as long as it is recognized that the patient may be at risk for recidivism because of the added stress of cancer and pain and that additional psychologic and social support may be needed. It must be also emphasized that active users of street drugs and patients on methadone maintenance may be relatively tolerant to opioids and consequently may require higher doses than are normally anticipated. Any patient with a history of drug abuse is therefore at risk for having pain undertreated, particularly because the focus of therapy in these patients is often restriction of opioid use rather than adequate control of pain. For this group of patients, a multidisciplinary approach and continuity of care are essential.

The fifth group comprises patients with severe pain who are dying. At no time is pain more destructive. Fear of "hurrying" death and euthanasia has become a reason for poorly controlled pain in these patients (Coyle et al., in press).

ADVANCES IN CANCER PAIN TREATMENT

Cancer pain treatment has evolved as a result of new knowledge about the physiology of pain and increasing recognition of the diversity of clinical pain problems. Progress has been particularly notable in the development of new drugs, drug delivery systems, routes of drug administration, nondrug therapy, and continuing care.

Drug Delivery Systems and Novel Routes of Drug Administration

Although the oral route of drug administation remains the route of choice for most cancer pain patients, extensive survey data suggest that alternate routes are required by most patients at some point during their course (Coyle et al., in press; Sheidler 1987).

Oral Route

Advances in oral administration have focused on development of formulations that slowly release the drug as the tablet traverses the gut. This has been a major breakthrough for selected patients, relieving them of the necessity of taking analgesics on a 3- to 4-hour basis to achieve adequate pain relief. Morphine is now available in such a controlled release preparation, and a similar formulation of codeine is undergoing clinical trials (Brescia et al. 1987; Grandy et al. 1988; Lapin et al. 1989). A controlled release suspension of morphine is also under evaluation.

Sublingual or Buccal Route

The sublingual or buccal route is useful for patients who develop nausea and vomiting, dysphagia, or malabsorption of medication or for those who find the use of pills to be too burdensome. The enteric route is avoided, and concerns about bioavailability are obviated because hepatic first-pass elimination is bypassed. Studies have indicated that lipid-soluble drugs, such as methadone, fentanyl, and buprenorphine, are absorbed to a significantly greater extent than hydrophilic drugs, such as morphine sulfate (McQuay, Moore, and Bullingham 1986; Weinberg et al. 1988). Varying the intraoral pH may facilitate absorption. Contact time, but not concentration, has also been shown to affect sublingual absorption of methadone and fentanyl. There are currently no commercially available sublingual products in the United States.

Rectal Route

Although the rectal route of drug administration is well established as an alternative for patients who are unable to take drugs by mouth, few data are available on rectal absorption. It has been suggested that lipophilic drugs may be absorbed with greater ease by this route, but the smaller absorptive surface compared to the upper gut creates problems when the patient requires rapidly escalating opioid doses. Researchers in England are evaluating a sustained-release morphine suppository formulation that gives an initial bolus release and subsequent constant release for 12 hours. A sustained-release only preparation is also under clinical evaluation (Hanning and Smith 1988).

Intranasal Route

The use of the intranasal route to deliver opioid drugs for selected patients who require parenteral drugs for the management of either acute or chronic pain is undergoing clinical trials. Butorphanol, a lipophilic mixed agonist/antagonist drug, has a demonstrated ability when administered as an intranasal spray to provide analgesia, with side effects comparable to those seen after intramuscular or intravenous administration.

Transdermal Route

Fentanyl, a drug with high lipid solubility, is undergoing clinical trials as a transdermal product (Levy et al. 1988; Simmonds et al. 1988). The drug system consists of a patch that releases a controlled amount of the drug through a rate-limiting membrane. Patches can be changed approximately every 3 days. There is a delayed onset of action after the patch is applied, and the drug effect may continue for several days after discontinuation of the patch. Both phenomena relate to the development of a depot of drug in the subcutaneous tissue, from which absorption into the systemic circulation occurs. This delay in eliminating the drug from the body may be a disadvantage of this system should adverse effects develop.

Subcutaneous Route

Continuous subcutaneous infusion has been a major advance in the care of the cancer patient with chronic pain who is unable to take oral drugs (Bruera et al. 1987; Coyle et al. 1986; France and Krishnan 1988; Hanning and Smith 1988; Sheidler 1987). The opioid is delivered by means of a small portable pump with a 27-gauge pediatric butterfly needle. The technique is easily managed by patients and families in the home setting and does not impede mobility in the active patient. Morphine sulfate (in concentrations up to 60 mg/mL), hydromorphone, levorphanol, and methadone have all been used with this approach. Newer portable pumps have a patient-controlled bolus capability, a feature that is useful in managing the fluctuating severity of pain.

Intravenous Route

Although widely used in the management of postoperative pain and cancer pain, the intravenous route has poorly defined clinical indications and guidelines for use. Clinical experience suggests that the indications for the intravenous route can be distinguished from those for continuous intravenous infusions and that one-third of advanced cancer patients started on an intravenous infusion continue to experience severe pain despite rapid upward titration of the drug (Portenoy et al. 1985). The advent of patient-controlled analgesia and implanted intravenous access ports has allowed patients to use this route at home with greater ease

(Barkas and Duafala 1988; Citron et al. 1986; Kerr et al. 1988; Sheidler 1987). The new pumps allow the use of an intravenous bolus alone or the combination of an infusion with a bolus capability.

Epidural and Intrathecal Routes

The use of spinal opioids has become widespread in the hospital and home settings (Coombs et al. 1984; Cousins and Mather 1984; Payne 1987b). Various methods have been employed, the most popular of which is repetitive bolus administration of the drug into the epidural space through an implanted subcutaneous epidural access device. The bolus dose can be given by the patient, a nurse, or a family member.

Intrathecal administration is usually accomplished by means of continuous infusion delivered with a totally implanted pump. The pump consists of two chambers separated by a flexible metal bellows. One chamber is the drug reservoir, and the other contains the charging fluid. The vapor pressure of the charging fluid exerts a constant pressure on the bellows, forcing drug from the reservoir through a catheter into the intrathecal space. The pump is refilled by the physician or nurse through a percutaneous injection approximately every 3 weeks.

Further research is needed to define better the different indications for epidural and intrathecal drugs, the drug of choice, and the preferred method of delivery.

Old Drugs with New Uses

Clonidine, a centrally acting α-adrenergic drug commonly used to control hypertension, has recently been demonstrated to have analgesic properties. Epidural clonidine has been reported to be effective for some patients in the relief of postoperative pain, chronic nonmalignant pain, and deafferentation pain associated with spinal cord injury (Foley 1989). A trial in cancer pain is currently underway.

Capsaicin is found in hot peppers and other plants of the nightshade family. Its effect is first to stimulate and then to block the activity of small-diameter nociceptor afferent fibers in the skin. The topical application of capsaicin has been suggested to have an analgesic effect in some patients with postherpetic neuralgia (Watson et al. 1988).

Tricyclic antidepressants have analgesic effects independent of their antidepressant effects (France and Krishnan 1988). The mechanism of action is believed to involve enhancement of activity in descending pain modulating systems through increased levels of endogenous monoamines such as serotonin (Watson et al. 1988). They are most often used in cancer patients whose pain has a neuropathic component or in those with pain associated with depression or insomnia.

Anticonvulsants have analgesic effects in certain neuropathic pain syndromes, especially those in which the pain is neuropathic and described by the patient as sharp and shooting. Carbamazepine is the most frequently used anticonvulsant in this respect. The mechanism of action is believed to involve suppression of spontaneous neuronal firing (France and Krishnan 1988; Parkes 1978).

Methotrimeprazine is a phenothiazine with significant analgesic efficacy. In single-dose studies in postoperative pain and chronic cancer pain, 15 mg intramuscularly is approximately equianalgesic to 10 mg of morphine intramuscularly (Parkes 1978). Methotrimeprazine may be useful in the management of the patient who is highly tolerant to opioids or experiences dose-limiting side effects because the analgesic effects are not mediated through the opioid receptor system. The drug also has potent anxiolytic and antiemetic properties, which may be advantageous in selected patients. The major disadvantages are its sedative and hypotensive effects and the lack of an oral formulation. These factors usually relegate its use to the bedridden patient with advanced disease.

Neurosurgical Approaches and Anesthetic Techniques

Analyses of cost versus benefit of neuroablative procedures have become more focused and refined in this age of informed consent (Black 1985; Ferrer-Brechner 1985). Technologic advances combined with a clearer understanding of the physiology of pain transmission have reduced the technical difficulties involved in many procedures. As experience has been gained, however, the issues of patient selection and potential morbidity have become increasingly important. For example, painful dysesthesias, which may develop weeks or months after a neuroablative procedure, may become more problematic because patients live longer after treatment. Randomized comparative trials of the various neuroablative procedures and surveys of long-term follow-up with comprehensive assessment (including quality of life measures) are clearly needed.

Cognitive Behavioral Approaches

Cognitive behavioral interventions are psychologic techniques designed to modify the experience of pain and distress in patients with cancer pain (Chapman 1986; Fishman and Loscalzo 1987; Tan 1982; Turk and Rudy 1989). The major sources of distress in this population are uncertain medical status, fear of physical and functional deterioration, the threat of aggressive anticancer treatments, and fear of intensifying pain and death. The goal of the cognitive behavioral approaches is not only to ameliorate pain and to improve function, although these outcomes may occur, but also to diminish suffering and to help patients regain a sense of personal control, coherence, and meaning in their situation.

Cognitive techniques comprise interventions that enhance relaxation or reduce stress and those that modify dysfunctional thoughts. Stress reduction techniques include relaxation training and systematic desensitization, a method that is of particular importance to patients who avoid necessary medical procedures or treatment (such as bone marrow aspiration or chemotherapy) because they anticipate that the procedures will be painful or unpleasant. Techniques that modify dysfunctional thoughts include cognitive coping procedures, which are aimed at reducing the intensity and distress quality of the pain experience. This category comprises distraction procedures such as mental imagery, behavioral task distraction, hypnosis, music therapy, and cognitive modification. In cognitive modification, patients learn to identify dysfunctional thoughts and images, to monitor them, and then to replace them with more functional thoughts and images. For example, the cancer patient who thinks "This pain is getting worse and will never go away" replaces that dysfunctional thought and image with a more functional "self talk" such as "I have had pain like this before; it got better after I took my pain medications and practiced my relaxation techniques; I will do that now and wait for the pain to get better."

Behavioral techniques are designed to improve patient function through systematic efforts to increase physical activities or social interactions. These approaches are less often applied in cancer pain patients, particularly those with advanced disease. Returning a sense of mastery and control to the patient is an essential feature shared by all these techniques. They may also improve mood, activity, and sleep in addition to lessening pain severity.

Continuing Care

Patients are as varied in their responses to advanced disease as they are to other experiences in life. The common thread is the need for pain management, symptom control, and continuity of care. Such care must be offered in a framework that is consistent with the patient's philosophy of life and medical and psychosocial status (Coyle 1989a; Coyle et al. 1985; Ferrell and Schneider 1988; Morris et al. 1988; Parkes 1978).

Various models of continuing care have been developed. Such models include (1) hospice care, which may comprise home care with brief periods of hospitalization for symptoms that are poorly controlled at home or institutional care away from the hospital environment; (2) palliative care service in a general hospital, in which the resources of the hospital are readily available to the patient, family, and community; (3) a mobile van unit directed by the staff of a general hospital, in which frequent team visits are used to provide care for extremely ill and dying patients at home; and (4) supportive care, which can be developed as part of a pain service in a comprehensive cancer center and which attempts to integrate family and community resources to provide the patient with continuity of care from the home to the hospital.

Models of continuing care are influenced by the number of patients involved, the intensity and complexity of their needs, and the resources available. The major goal of future efforts to refine these systems is to allocate limited funds to the development of flexible models of continuing care that can be integrated into the standard medical system, bridge the gap between hospital and community, and have a strong education component.

THE EMERGING ROLE OF THE CLINICAL NURSE SPECIALIST IN PAIN MANAGEMENT

In few areas has the emerging role of the clinical nurse specialist had a greater impact on patient care than in pain management. This is reflected in the areas of consultation, research, and continuity of care (Coyle 1989b; National Institutes of Health 1987).

As a pain consultant, the nurse works with patients, families, and support networks and other health professionals. Frequently, consultation is requested by the medical or nursing staff to help with a specific pain management problem. The problem usually relates to the use of opioid drugs, the management of side effects or symptoms other than pain, methods of changing from one route of drug administration to another, or strategies to help the patient and family deal with the ongoing stress of chronic disease through the use of the cognitive behavioral approaches. Education is essential and is usually designed to change attitudes about opioid drugs, the effective use of which is greatly impeded by fears of addiction, respiratory depression, and tolerance (Charap 1978; Rankin and Snider 1984; Watt-Watson 1987).

Because of the multidisciplinary nature of pain assessment and management (Donovan 1987; McGuire 1987), the role of the nurse researcher falls into two areas: collaborator or coinvestigator in medical or psychosocial research and initiator of nursing research. By using patients and families with whom they work as their data base, nurses are undertaking clinical research in various areas. Examples include the effect of pain on quality of life (Ferrell, Wisdom, and Wenzl 1989), correlation of the patient's report of pain severity and the nurse's assessment of pain severity (Rankin and Snider 1984), and development and validation of assessment tools to predict the clinical course of patients with chronic pain.

As described, continuing care focuses on symptom management, pain control, and the changing psychologic and social status of the cancer patient and family. These areas are ideally suited for nursing practice, in which the integration of clinical work with nursing research occurs so naturally.

FUTURE DIRECTIONS

Many advances in the management of cancer pain have occurred, impelled by an increased understanding of the physiology of pain, recognition of the need for a multidisciplinary approach, and the development of systematic methods of assessing, classifying, and treating pain. Nevertheless, the barriers to adequate cancer pain management, as clearly outlined by the Wisconsin Cancer Pain Initiative (1988), continue to exist and must be continually addressed as a fundamental issue in the quality of life of the cancer patient.

Continued progress in the management of pain and other symptoms in patients with cancer will evolve from advances in three broad areas: education, assessment, and treatment. Although change is likely to occur slowly at first, the recent past suggests that growing awareness on the part of the lay public that deficiencies exist in these areas may accelerate clinical improvements through consumer demand for better symptom control. Public education, therefore, should be viewed as a cornerstone of future efforts to advance this area.

Clinical education is equally important and is likely to incorporate several key components: (1) recognition of the extent of the problem and barriers to management; (2) recognition of the need to include pain management in medical and nursing education; (3) proliferation of pain journals and texts on pain management; (4) establishment of interdisciplinary regional, national, and international associations for the study of pain; and (5) development of pain fellowship programs for physicians and nurses in comprehensive cancer centers. As noted, the goal of education includes the modification of attitudes as well as the acquisition of information about symptom control.

Future advances in pain evaluation will probably represent a broad spectrum ranging from continued progress in the elucidation of the basic mechanisms of clinical pain to the development of better assessment tools for monitoring the outcome of clinical interventions (Daut, Cleeland, and Flannery 1983; Fishman et al. 1987; Melzack 1983; Stromborg 1984; Ventafridda et al. 1986). Further efforts must be made to categorize cancer pain syndromes and to clarify the salient differences among patient subgroups.

Finally, it is very likely that clinical management will continue to improve, most notably as a result of pharmacologic advances. Specifically, the application of research findings to the clinical setting will probably occur most rapidly in the following areas: (1) development of more rational approaches to drug selection and administration in cancer pain management; (2) development of new drug formulations, such as controlled-release preparations, that allow a greater flexibility of dosing; (3) development of entirely new analgesic drugs; (4) increased recognition that the current level of concern about addiction, tolerance, and physical dependence does not reflect the true risks associated with opioid drugs and hinders proper management (Foley 1989a, 1989b; Porter and Jick 1980); and (5) development of novel routes of drug administration combined with increased attention to alternative techniques of pain control and development of models of continuing care for cancer patients with chronic pain. These advances are likely to have a substantial impact on the management of cancer pain.

The management of pain and other symptoms is a fundamental consideration in the quality of life of patients with cancer. As quality of life becomes increasingly viewed as an imperative of cancer therapy, recognition of the importance of pain and symptom control will continue to evolve. The advances of the past two decades provide a firm foundation for continued progress in the future.

STUDY QUESTIONS

1. Identify five factors that contribute to inadequate management of cancer pain.
2. List three areas of clinical practice in which nurses have made a significant impact on cancer pain management.
3. Identify three areas in which there have been major advances in cancer pain management over the past decade.

REFERENCES

American Cancer Society. 1989. *Ca—A Cancer Journal for Clinicians* 39:13.

Angell, M. 1982. The quality of mercy. *New England Journal of Medicine* 306:98–99.

Barkas, G., and M.E. Duafala. 1988. Advances in cancer pain management: A review. Patient controlled analgesia. *Journal of Pain Symptom Management* 3:150–60.

Black, P. 1985. Neurosurgical management of cancer pain. *Seminars in Oncology* 12:438–44.

Bond, M.R. 1979. Psychological and emotional aspects of cancer pain. *Advances in Pain Research and Therapy* 2:81–88.

Breitbart, W. 1987. Suicide in cancer patients. *Oncology* 1:49–53.

Brescia, F.J., M. Walsh, J.J. Savarese, and R.F. Kaiko. 1987. A study of controlled release oral morphine (MS Contin) in an advanced cancer hospital. *Journal of Pain Symptom Management* 2:193–98.

Bruera, E., M. Michaud, R. Bacovsky, and R. MacDonald. 1987. The use of subcutaneous infusions of narcotics for the treatment of cancer pain. *Pain* 28 (supplement 4):5343.

Chapman, C.R. 1986. Behavioral control of symptoms: Introduction. *Journal of Pain Symptom Managment* 1:36–38.

Charap, A.D. 1978. The knowledge, attitudes and experience of medical personnel treating pain in the terminally ill. *Mt. Sinai Journal of Medicine* 45:561–80.

Citron, M.L., A. Johnston-Early, M. Boyer, S.N. Krasnow, M. Hood, and M.H. Cohen. 1986. Patient controlled analgesia for severe cancer pain. *Archives of Internal Medicine* 146:734–36.

Cleeland, C.S., A. Rotondi, T. Brechner, A. Levin, N. MacDonald, R. Portenoy, H. Schutta, and M. McEniry. 1986. A model for the treatment of cancer pain. *Journal of Pain Symptom Management* 1:209–16.

Coombs, D.W., L.H. Maurer, R.L. Saunders, and M. Gaylor. 1984. Outcomes and complications of continuous intraspinal narcotic analgesics for cancer pain control. *Journal of Clinical Oncology* 2:1414–20.

Cousins, M.A., and L.E. Mather. 1984. Intrathecal and epidural administration of opioids. *Anaesthesiology* 61:276–310.

Coyle, N. 1989a. Continuity of care for the cancer patient with chronic pain. *Cancer* 63:2289–93.

Coyle, N. 1989b. The role of the nurse in pain management. In *Current therapy of pain*, ed. K.M. Foley and R. Payne. Toronto: BC Decker.

Coyle, N., J. Adelhardt, K.M. Foley, and R.K. Portenoy. In press. Character of terminal illness in the advanced cancer patient: Pain and other symptoms in the last 4 weeks of life. *Journal of Pain Symptom Management*.

Coyle, N., and K.M. Foley. 1987. Prevalence and profile of pain syndromes in cancer patients. In *Cancer pain management*, ed. D.B. McGuire and C.H. Yarbro. Orlando: Grune & Stratton.

Coyle, N., A. Mauskop, J. Maggard, and K.M. Foley. 1986. Continuous subcutaneous infusion of opiates in cancer patients with pain. *Oncology Nursing Forum* 4:53–57.

Coyle, N., E. Monzillo, M. Loscalzo, C. Farkas, M.J. Massie, and K.M. Foley. 1985. A model of continuity of care for cancer patients with pain and neuro-oncologic complications. *Cancer Nursing* 8:111–19.

Daut, R.L., and C.S. Cleeland. 1982. The prevalence and severity of pain in cancer. *Cancer* 50:1913–18.

Daut, R.L., C.S. Cleeland, and R.C. Flannery. 1983. The development of the Wisconsin brief pain questionnaire to assess pain in cancer and other diseases. *Pain* 17:197–210.

Donovan, M.I. 1987. Clinical assessment of pain. In *Cancer pain management*, ed. D.B. McGuire and C.H. Yarbro. Orlando: Grune & Stratton.

Ferrell, B.R., and C. Schneider. 1988. Experience and management of cancer pain at home. *Cancer Nursing* 11:84–90.

Ferrell, B.R., C. Wisdom, and C. Wenzl. 1989. Quality of life as an outcome variable in the management of cancer pain. *Cancer* 63:2321–27.

Ferrer-Brechner, T. 1985. Anesthetic management of cancer pain. *Seminars in Oncology* 12:431–37.

Fishman, B., and M. Loscalzo. 1987. Cognitive behavioral interventions in management of cancer pain: Principles and application. *Medical Clinics of North America* 71:271–87.

Fishman, B., S. Pasternak, S.L. Wallenstein, R.W. Houde, J. Holland, and K.M. Foley. 1987. The Memorial pain assessment card: A valid instrument for the assessment of cancer pain. *Cancer* 60:1151–57.

Foley, K.M. 1985. The treatment of cancer pain. *New England Journal of Medicine* 313:84–95.

Foley, K.M. 1987. Pain syndromes in patients with cancer. *Medical Clinics of North America* 71:169–84.

Foley, K.M. 1989a. Controversies in cancer pain: Medical perspectives. *Cancer* 63:2257–65.

Foley, K.M. 1989b. The "decriminalization" of cancer pain. *Advances in Pain Research and Therapy* 11:5–18.

France, R.D., and K.R.R. Krishnan. 1988. Psychotropic drugs in chronic pain. In *Chronic pain*, ed. R.D. France and K.R.R. Krishnan. Washington, D.C.: American Psychiatric Association.

Grandy, R., B. Oshlack, G. Thomas, N. Healy, R. Kaiko, P. Goldenheim. 1988. Bioavailability comparison of three controlled release codeine formulations vs. conventional oral codeine. *Journal of Pain Symptom Management* 3:S17.

Hanning, C.D., and G. Smith. 1988. Morphine hydrogel suppository. *Journal of Pain Symptom Management* 3:S19.

Kerr, I.G., M. Sone, C. De Angelis, N. Iscoe, R. MacKenzie, and T. Schueller. 1988. Continuous narcotic infusion with patient controlled analgesia for chronic pain in outpatients. *Annals of Internal Medicine* 108:554–57.

Lapin, J., R.K. Portenoy, N. Coyle, R.W. Houde, and K.M. Foley. 1989. Guidelines for use of controlled release oral morphine. *Cancer Nursing* 12:202–208.

Levin, D.N., C.S. Cleeland, and R. Dar. 1985. Public attitudes towards cancer pain. *Cancer* 56:2337–39.

Levy, S., S. Jacobs, J. Johnson, N. Schultz, C. Kowal, A. Meisler, J. Lee, K. Boggio. 1988. Transdermal fentanyl: Pain and quality of life effects. *Proceedings of the American Society of Clinical Oncologists* 7:292.

McGuire, D.B. 1987. The multidimensional phenomenon of cancer pain. In *Cancer pain management*, ed. D.B. McGuire and C.H. Yarbro. Orlando: Grune & Stratton.

McQuay, H.J., R.A. Moore, and R.E.S. Bullingham. 1986. Sublingual morphine, heroin, methadone and buprenorphine: Kinetics and effects. *Advances in Pain Research and Therapy* 8:407–12.

Melzack, R. 1983. The McGill pain questionnaire. In *Pain measurement and assessment*, ed. R. Melzack. New York: Raven.

Morris, J.N., V. Mor, R.F. Goldberg, S. Sherwood, D.S. Greer, J. Hiris. 1988. The effect of treatment setting and patient characteristics on pain in terminal cancer patients: A report from the National Hospice study. *Journal of Chronic Disease* 39:27–35.

National Institutes of Health. 1987. A report on the National Institutes of Health consensus development conference on the integrated approach to the management of pain. *Journal of Pain Symptom Management* 2:35–41.

Parkes, C.M. 1978. Home or hospital: Terminal care as seen by the surviving spouse. *Journal of the Royal College of General Practitioners* 28:19–30.

Payne, R. 1987a. Anatomy, physiology and neuropharmacology of cancer pain. *Medical Clinics of North America* 71:153–55.

Payne, R. 1987b. Role of epidural and intrathecal narcotics and peptides in the management of cancer pain. *Medical Clinics of North America* 71:313–28.

Portenoy, R.K. 1989. Cancer pain: Epidemiology and syndromes. *Cancer* 63:2298–2307.

Portenoy, R.K. In press. Pain and quality of life: Clinical issues and implications for research. *Oncology*.

Portenoy, R.K., D.E. Moulin, A.G. Rogers, C.E Inturresi, and K.M Foley. 1985. Intravenous infusion of opioids in cancer pain. *Clinical Cancer Treatment Reports* 70:575–81.

Porter, J., and H. Jick. 1980. Addiction rate in patients treated with narcotics. *New England Journal of Medicine* 302:123.

Rankin, M., and B. Snider. 1984. Nurses' perception of cancer patients' pain. *Cancer Nursing* 1:149–55.

Sheidler, V.R. 1987. New methods in analgesic delivery. In *Cancer pain management*, ed. D.B. McGuire and C.H. Yarbro. Orlando: Grune & Stratton.

Simmonds, M.A., C. Blain, J. Richenbacher, and M.A. Southam. 1988. A new approach to the administration of opiates (fentanyl) in the management of pain in patients with cancer. *Journal of Pain Symptom Management* 3:S18.

Stromborg, M. 1984. Selecting an instrument to measure quality of life. *Oncology Nursing Forum* 11:88–91.

Tan, S. 1982. Cognitive and cognitive behavioral methods for pain control: A selective review. *Pain* 12:201–208.

Turk, D.C., and T.E. Rudy. 1989. Behavioral approaches to pain management. In *Current therapy of pain,* ed. K.M. Foley and R. Payne. Toronto: BC Decker.

Ventafridda, V., M. Tamburi, S. Selmi, and R. De Canno. 1986. Pain and quality of life assessment in advanced cancer patients. In *Assessment of quality of life and cancer treatment.* ed. V. Ventafridda, F.S.A.M. Van Dam, R. Yancik, and M. Tamburini. Amsterdam: Excerpta Medica.

Watson, C.P.N., J.R. Evans, and V.R. Watt. 1988. Post-herpetic neuralgia and topical capsaicin. *Pain* 33:333–40.

Watson, C.P.N., J.R. Evans, V.R. Watt, and N. Birkett. 1988. Post-herpetic neuralgia: 208 cases. *Pain* 35:289–97.

Watt-Watson, J.H. 1987. Nurses' knowledge of pain issues: A survey. *Journal of Pain Symptom Management* 2:207–11.

Weinberg, D.S., C.E. Inturrissi, B. Reidenberg, D.E. Maulin, T.J. Nip, S. Wallenstein, R.W. Houde, K.M. Foley. 1988. Sublingual absorption of selected opioid analgesics. *Clinical Pharmacology and Therapeutics* 44:335–42.

Wisconsin Cancer Pain Initiative. 1988. The cancer pain problem: Wisconsin's response. A report on the Wisconsin cancer pain initiative. *Journal of Pain Symptom Management* 3:S2–S5.

World Health Organization. 1986. *Cancer pain relief.* Geneva: World Health Organization.

Part II
Significant Populations

Chapter 9

Cancer in the Older Patient

Susan Ann Derby

> Cancer in the older population is a major health problem. The incidence of cancer increases with age, and more than 50% of all cancer deaths occur in individuals older than 65 years of age. Because this group will constitute nearly 20% of the total population in future decades, the nursing profession must begin to recognize the developmental and individual needs of elderly patients with cancer. The physiologic changes of aging must be recognized and then placed in relationship to the various forms of cancer treatment. The effects of chemotherapy, radiation therapy, and surgery need to be evaluated in terms of their influence on aging. Nursing research in all areas of care of the elderly is badly needed. Some areas for nursing research in this population include the effect of age on chemotherapy toxicity, recovery from surgery, patient teaching, and ethical concerns. Polypharmacy remains a problem for the older population, especially when medications for management of chemotherapy toxicity are added to other prescribed medications. Future economic changes in the United States will influence the provision of comprehensive care. Prospective payment has caused a shift of care to the ambulatory setting, and the acuity level of patients who are hospitalized has increased. There is and will continue to be a demand on the oncology profession to meet the discharge and home care needs of this population.

PERSPECTIVES ON AGING

Demographics

It is both evolutionary and revolutionary in the American nursing literature to consider the older population a separate and special demographic group. This concern for the older population has existed in many European countries, as is reflected in the development of specialization in geriatrics. It is only in the past decade that the oncology nursing profession has become attentive to the age group older than 65 years.

Americans are living longer. The average life expectancy in the year 1900 was 47 years; in 1980 it was 73 years (Kovar 1977). According to Census Bureau projections people 65 years old and older, who now represent about 12% of the population, will represent about 21% of the population by the year 2030 (Fowles 1983). By that year, it is projected that 1 in every 11 Americans will be older than 85 years of age.

Cancer Incidence and Mortality in the Population Older Than 65 Years

Statistics reveal that not only are Americans living longer but that age is the greatest single risk factor for the development of cancer. Approximately 50% of all cancers occur in individuals older than 65 years, and close to 60% of all cancer deaths occur in this age group (Young, Percy, and Asire 1981).

Figure 9-1 shows the increase in cancer incidence with advancing age. Figure 9-2 reveals the leading sites of cancer and mortality rates in the older population. For 65- to 80-year-old men lung and bronchus malignancies are the major causes of death, and in men older than 80 years prostate cancer is the leading cause of death. For women older than 65 years, breast and colorectal cancer are the leading causes of death. Cancer of the uterus is one of the five leading causes of death in women 75 years and older.

Other cancers, despite their low incidence, occur primarily in the older population. Seventy-one percent of stomach cancers and 67% of bladder cancers occur in those older than 65 (Birdsell 1986). Seventy-six percent of all gallbladder cancers occur in people older than 65, as do more than 60% of multiple myelomas and chronic leukemias (Birdsell 1986). Although not a leading cause of mortality in the older population, basal cell or squamous cell carcinoma is the most common of all cancers.

AGING AND THE NATURAL HISTORY OF CANCER

Aging is a physiologic process that progresses steadily to a maximum lifespan of 80 to 110 years (King 1988). It is a genetic process associated with morphologic and functional changes in cellular and extracellular components that are aggravated by injury throughout life and result in a progressive imbalance of the regulatory systems of the organism, including the hormonal, autocrine, neuroendocrine, and immune homeostatic mechanisms (King 1988). Morphologically,

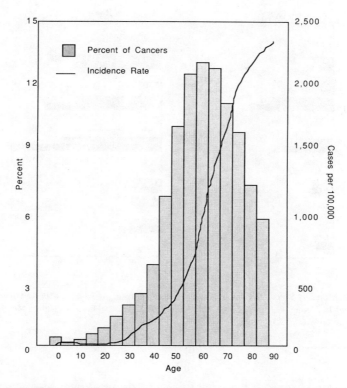

Figure 9-1 Incidence Rates for Cancer. *Source:* Reprinted from *Seer Incidence and Mortality Data 1973-77* by J.L. Young, C.L. Percy, and A.J. Asire (Eds.). National Cancer Institute Monograph 57, NIH Publication No. 81-2330, 1981.

---

there are lesions associated with aging. These changes are programmed at birth but are influenced either genetically or environmentally (King 1988). Table 9-1 lists the morphologic changes of aging. Lesions of atrophy and degeneration may produce hernias, cystocele, rectocele, bowel diverticula, and degeneration of ligaments and tendons (King 1988). Of special interest to the nurse involved in screening and early detection is the observation that compensatory hyperplasia sometimes progresses to premalignant lesions such as polyps.

There are many different theories of aging. Lamy (1988) postulates that aging is due to a steady accumulation of random and permanent damage resulting in malfunction and death. This classification places emphasis on cell injury and mechanisms that produce modification of the gene structure, including intrinsic mutagenesis, protein synthesis error, cross-linking of DNA, autoimmunity, slow virus infections, and free radical–mediated injury. Other theories speculate that

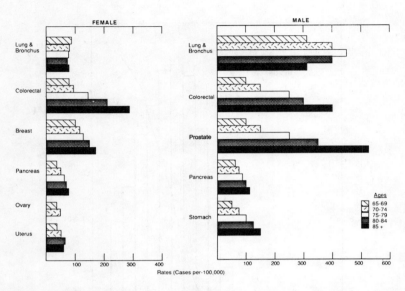

Figure 9-2 Mortality Rates for Cancer. *Source:* Reprinted from *Seer Incidence and Mortality Data 1973-77* by J.L. Young, C.L. Percy, and A.J. Asire (Eds.). National Cancer Institute Monograph 57, NIH Publication No. 81-2330, 1981.

---

aging is related to the mediation of lipofuscin (Beattie 1988), the so-called age pigment; to physiologic, progressive deterioration programmed at birth; and to age-related immunocompetence (Hersh et al. 1983), which places older individuals at risk for development of neoplastic disease.

Studies of experimental cancers have shown that there are both early and late stages in the development of cancer. The early or initiating events damage DNA irreversibly and produce chromosomal rearrangements. Examples include cigarette smoking and environmental carcinogens such as industrial pollutants, coal, and asbestos. Initiated cells need not develop into tumor if activity or exposure is stopped early.

Table 9-1 Morphologic Lesions of Aging

Cellular Lesions	Definition
Atrophy	Decrease in number and size of cells
Compensatory	Increase in number of those cells able to divide (e.g., liver, lung)
Hypertrophy	Increase in size of those cells unable to divide (e.g., heart)

Promoting agents produce tumors if cells have been initiated. Changes during the promotion phase occur on cell proliferation and differentiation rather than in DNA (Cairns 1983). Diet and hormones are postulated to influence the promoting phase, which is thought to be reversible. The role of diet and the development of certain cancers has yet to be established (e.g., low-fiber diet and colorectal cancer, alcohol consumption and esophageal cancer, high-fat diet and breast cancer), and further research needs to be done in these areas.

As educators, nurses need to become aware of new developments, especially as they relate to diet and cancer, and to incorporate these findings into their patient teaching. Screening and early detection methods with older patients should always include the following teaching: reducing alcohol intake to moderate amounts, stopping or minimizing smoking, increasing the intake of fresh or frozen vegetables, and minimizing the intake of nitrite-preserved foods.

PROFILE OF THE OLDER POPULATION AND PATTERNS OF DISEASE

In general, women live longer than men. In 1982 there were 80 men aged 65 to 69 years for every 100 women of the same age group and 42 men aged 85 years and older for every 100 women of the same age group (Lamy 1988).

The older patient who presents with cancer probably has at least one other chronic disease or sensory impairment. Most common chronic disorders are heart disease, hypertension, stroke, diabetes, arthritis, or chronic obstructive pulmonary disease. About 90% of all people older than age 65 have some visual impairment, and 50% have some hearing impairment (Pegels 1988).

In addition to multiple pathology in older people, Hodkinson (1973) identifies the need for careful observation in diagnosing common ailments because of the unusual, nonspecific presentation of disease in older patients. Diseases often lack definitive characteristics when presenting in an older patient. The classic presentations of disease are often replaced with nonspecific symptoms, including failure to thrive (eat or drink), confusion, and incontinence, and may further mask the symptoms of depression, drug intoxication, pulmonary embolism, congestive heart failure, alcoholism, infection, and cancer (Besdine 1980). This confusion in symptom identification may lead to delayed diagnosis of cancer or misdiagnosis.

SOCIAL FACTORS AND ILLNESS BEHAVIOR WITH A CANCER DIAGNOSIS

To understand the nature of cancer in the older population, one must begin to appreciate the psychologic and social dimensions beyond physical disease. Those factors include varying levels of education, retirement, and widowhood, which all add to the complexity of the older patient's understanding of normal aging changes and cancer symptoms. If, for example, an elderly person is dealing with the illness of a spouse, he or she may neglect his or her own health needs.

Nonmedical factors present in the older person's life can be significant in determining whether the person understands the importance of the symptoms. Hodkinson (1978) has stated that cancer warning signals often are unheeded because they are attributed to another disease. Weinrich and Weinrich (1986) found in their survey of 316, predominantly female, elderly residents living in a community house that most could name one or two of the American Cancer Society's seven warning signals and believed many cancer myths (i.e., that women can get breast cancer from being struck in the breast).

In addition, it is generally believed that older patients present with advanced disease more frequently than their younger counterparts. Hunt and colleagues (1980) studied 711 patients treated for breast cancer during 1955 to 1977 and found an average delay of 18 months between the time the patient recognized the disease and the time she sought medical care. Robins and Lee (1985), in a retrospective study of 152 women 50 years of age and older who had breast cancer, found a delay in seeking treatment compared with younger women. Approximately 25% of the older women presented with advanced disease.

EARLY DETECTION AND SCREENING

Historically, nursing and medical involvement in the older population as a target group for cancer screening and early detection has not been great. The current American Cancer Society (1989) estimate of cancer prevalence is 5 million individuals. This prevalence could increase to 9.6 million individuals by the year 2030 (Yancik et al. 1987). This increase is based solely on the expansion of the population comprising individuals older than 65 years. Clearly, the nursing profession needs to refocus its attention on these dramatic demographic changes.

Cancer Detection in the Older Population

Cancer detection in older people differs from detection in younger people. Early signs of cancer such as anorexia, fatigue, and weight loss may be easily overlooked by the patient and physician as natural parts of the aging process. Later signs of malignancy, such as blood in the stool and joint or bone pain, may also be attributed to the aging process.

Early detection and screening behaviors are found to be lacking in the older population. Older women are less likely to perform breast self-examinations than younger women (Celentano et al. 1982). For colorectal cancer it has been found that individuals younger than 65 are more likely to seek out screening procedures that might lead to early detection (Farrands and Hardcastle 1984).

Risk Factors and Screening Techniques for Common Cancers in the Older Population

Colorectal Cancer

The risk for colorectal cancer increases sharply with age. Winawer (1987) has identified average risk factor individuals as those 50 years of age or older and high risk factor individuals as those evincing inflammatory bowel disease, familial polyposis syndromes, family history of cancer, or past history of breast cancer, endometrial cancer, or radiation therapy.

Breast Cancer

Forty-three percent of all newly diagnosed breast cancers in the United States occur in women who are 65 years of age or older (Yancik et al. 1989). Cancer of the breast is the most common cancer in women of this age group. With the baby boom generation reaching age 65 in the next 20 years, it is anticipated that the expected incidence will increase. The American Cancer Society (1989) estimates that about 1 of every 10 women will develop breast cancer during her lifetime.

The literature reflects that most women discover breast masses themselves, that most older women do not routinely perform breast self-examinations, and that in general older women tend to delay seeking medical attention after a lump is discovered. Instruction regarding breast self-examination is not targeted toward older women, who have larger breasts than younger women and who may have visual or musculoskeletal difficulties that make self-examination difficult to perform.

Lung Cancer

In 1988 about 139,000 individuals died of lung cancer. Risk factors identified by the American Cancer Society (1989) include a persistent cough, history of cigarette smoking of 20 years or more, exposure to industrial substances such as asbestos, involuntary smoking, and radiation exposure. Almost 67% of lung and bronchus cancer are in individuals older than 65 years.

Prostate Cancer

The incidence of prostate cancer is rising. For whites, the incidence rate is approximately 50 per 100,000 persons; the incidence is 95 per 100,000 among black men (Perez et al. 1987). The overall 5-year survival is projected to be 63% in whites and 55% in blacks. American blacks have the highest incidence of prostate cancer in the world.

Prostate cancer remains the second leading cause of death in men. Most patients present with symptoms of advanced disease; in its earliest stages prostate cancer is often asymptomatic. Digital rectal examination remains the single most accurate test for early detection.

Risk factors for the development of prostate cancer include advanced age and benign prostatic hypertrophy. In addition, a positive family history may add to the risk of prostate cancer.

Skin Cancer

Skin cancers are the most common malignant tumors in humans. Basal cell carcinoma is an epithelical tumor that rarely metastasizes. Squamous cell carcinoma is derived from the squamous cells of the epidermis and may metastasize to regional lymph nodes and organs. The role of sunlight in the development of basal cell and squamous cell carcinomas has been supported in the literature (Urbach 1983). Risk factors for these types of cancers include advanced age and excessive exposure to sunlight. Those areas frequently exposed are the head, neck, arms, and hands; fair-complected people are particularly at risk.

Malignant melanoma is derived from the melanocyte, the pigment cell of the epidermis. Although 6% to 11% of malignant melanomas appear to be genetic, other risk factors include advanced age (Urbach 1983).

Nursing intervention includes instructions regarding the use of protective clothing and sun screens and limitation of skin exposure.

Implications for Nursing

Nurses caring for individuals older than 65 years are in an ideal position to provide education and instruction regarding risk factors and screening techniques. Various settings, including retirement communities, geriatric and community centers, and acute and ambulatory care facilities, can provide these vitally needed services. Nurse-directed cancer prevention programs have been shown to be effective in targeting high-risk individuals. Long-term compliance rates with breast self-examination have been reported, and nurse-directed clinics are generally accepted by the public (Marley 1982; Stromborg and Nord 1979).

AGE-RELATED INFLUENCES ON SURGICAL CANCER TREATMENT

The question of informed consent must be considered in terms of surgical risk, postoperative mortality and morbidity, and the goal of the surgical procedure. The issue of palliative compared to curative surgery needs to be clearly understood by the patient and family. If the intent is palliative and if the goal is to improve the quality of life of the patient and perhaps to add months or years to the patient's life, this intent must be clearly identified. Many older persons are fearful of surgery and may not fully understand the consequences of not undergoing surgery.

As an intervention, surgery is not contraindicated on the basis of chronologic age alone. Many cancers are best treated by surgery. The most important factor in determining morbidity and mortality related to a surgical procedure is the physiologic status of the older person.

Preanesthetic Evaluation

The older patient poses an anesthetic risk for several reasons, including concurrent medical conditions and their treatments. Anesthetic risks in the older surgical patient are dependent on normal age-dependent alterations in physiology. Alterations in lean body mass and hepatic and renal blood flow directly affect the metabolism and clearance of anesthetic drugs. The older person has a diminished ability to respond to heat or cold. Tissue necrosis can occur over bony prominences that are left unprotected during long surgical procedures.

The older person with multiple, chronic illnesses is probably on drug therapy, which may increase the risk of adverse reactions from anesthesia. Prior drug therapy may alter an older person's response to anesthesia in three major ways: depression of hemostatic reflex responses, intensification of anesthetic drug action, and shortening or diminution of anesthetic drug action (Eltherington 1983).

Surgical Risks in Older Patients

Cancer surgery is extensive and often radical. The surgical attempt is to remove all tumor tissue (or as much as possible) as well as regional lymph nodes for sampling. Surgical decisions regarding the extent of surgery should be based on the patient's preoperative physiologic status.

Elective surgery for cancer in older patients is far safer than emergency surgery. Multiple studies have shown that perioperative mortality in the older population is higher in emergency situations compared to elective procedures (Waldron et al. 1986). Howland (1987) found that elderly patients are at risk during emergency surgery because of a basic decline in organ function and an increased prevalence of concomitant diseases. He further found increased morbidity after emergency surgery to be associated with decreased immunocompetence.

Careful preoperative assessment of physiologic parameters and correction of fluid and electrolyte imbalance and nutrition deficiencies should be done as early as possible. All surgical procedures must be considered a major stress to the older patient.

Hypoxemia is the most common problem resulting from anesthesia in the older patient. Preexisting lung disease, advanced age, and obesity all tend to predispose the patient to the onset of hypoxemia. The older patient with decreased lung compliance is at greater risk for postoperative hypoxemia. In addition, postoperative hypoxemia is often associated with pulmonary edema, myocardial infarction, pulmonary thromboembolism, aspiration pneumonia, hypoventilation, low cardiac output, increased oxygen consumption, and a decrease in oxygen-carrying capacity of the blood (Hillary 1983).

Preoperative Nursing Assessment

If a thorough baseline assessment is done preoperatively and if patients are instructed regarding their postoperative care, many complications can be avoided. One of the biggest problems in early detection of postoperative complications in the older person is the lack of recognition that a change in the patient's condition has occurred. Continuity of nursing care from the preoperative to the postoperative period avoids such pitfalls. Primary nursing, beginning on admission and continuing through discharge, can provide this continuity.

Postoperative Confusion

A careful preoperative mental status examination of the older person will assist the nurse in determining whether a change in cognitive functioning has occurred. Family members should be questioned regarding the patient's preoperative cognitive functioning.

The mental status examination begins with the nurse's observation of the patient's general appearance and manner. Other areas to be evaluated include psychomotor activity, speech, mood and affect, intellect, thought processes, perception, judgment, and insight. Etiologic factors of postoperative confusion are multiple and include environmental isolation, sensory deprivation, drug reactions, infections, and vascular and metabolic alterations (Koin 1984).

LIFE-THREATENING INFECTIONS RELATED TO CANCER IN THE OLDER PATIENT

Pneumonia

Pneumonia occurs frequently in patients older than 50 years. Mortality due to pneumonia is significant. Pneumonia and influenza combined represent the fourth leading cause of death in persons older than 65 years (Siegel 1980).

The older cancer patient with underlying disease that adversely affects pulmonary function, cellular or humoral immune responses, or cardiovascular disease has a poor prognosis. The immunocompromised older patient has multiple risk factors for the development of pneumonia. Bacteremia, involvement of more than one lobe, and relative leukopenia (leukocyte count less than 5,000/mm^3) at the time treatment is begun are poor prognostic signs. Twenty-five percent of those patients will die (Hoeprich 1983).

Most of all community-acquired pneumonias are bacterial, being produced by *Streptococcus pneumoniae, Staphylococcus aureus*, or *Haemophilus influenzae*. Nosocomial or hospital-acquired pneumonias develop in the presence of general anesthesia or ventilating assistance, administration of immunosuppressive drugs, and systemic disease including malignancy (Graybill et al. 1973).

Signs and symptoms of pneumonia may not be obvious in older persons. Some older patients fail to present with fever or chills, dyspnea, rust-colored sputum, cough, and pleuritic chest pain. Instead, these patients may exhibit mental status changes or urinary incontinence. Because of this, long-standing, severe infections may go undetected.

Gram-Negative Bacteremia

Bacteremia caused by gram-negative infections is one of the most serious infectious diseases in the United States. The estimated mortality rate is 25%. There are 200,000 to 300,000 cases each year, resulting in 50,000 to 75,000 deaths (Wolff and Bennett 1974). Most cases are nosocomial and secondary to infections of the urinary tract, lung, surgical wounds, gastrointestinal tract, intravenous access, or catheter. The most common causative agents are *Escherichia coli, Klebsiella pneumoniae*, and *Pseudomonas aeruginosa* (Young 1978). Other pathogens include *Enterobacter, Serratia*, and *Proteus* organisms. The entire gastrointestinal tract serves as a reservoir for bacterial growth. *Escherichia coli* is the most common aerobic organism isolated from the blood and fecal flora. If untreated, gram-negative bacteremia in the older cancer patient can lead to disseminated intravascular coagulation, shock, respiratory distress syndrome, and multisystem organ failure.

Host-related and treatment-related risk factors have been identified by Zimmerman and Dietrich (1987). Host-related factors include malignancy, malnutrition, advanced age, chronic illness and an intact complement-mediated immune system. The most effective barriers for preventing bloodstream invasion are an intact gastrointestinal tract and an intact skin surface. The older cancer patient who is malnourished or who has a concurrent medical condition is at risk for gram-negative bacteremia. Contributing to this risk are immune deficiencies found in some cancers that occur most commonly in the older patient. Humoral defects are found in patients with multiple myeloma and chronic lymphocytic leukemia;

cellular defects are found in patients with Hodgkin's disease and lymphomas (Armstrong 1976; Meyers 1972; Young et al. 1974).

Treatment-related risk factors identified by Zimmerman and Dietrich (1987) include radiation therapy, chemotherapy, steroid therapy, surgery, hyperalimentation, and skin breakdown. Combined humoral and cellular defects are also found in patients receiving treatment with steroids and immunosuppressive drugs (Armstrong 1976; Meyers 1972; Young et al. 1974). Other sources of infection include contaminated inhalation therapy equipment with resulting colonization of the respiratory tract as well as contaminated indwelling vascular cannulas, intravenous monitoring devices, percutaneous catheters, and drainage tubes (LaForce 1981; Young 1985).

Impaired immunity coupled with advanced age may contribute to the development of gram-negative sepsis in the hospitalized older patient. The thymus atrophies with age, and both humoral and cellular immunity undergo changes with aging. Although there is no change in the number of circulating lymphocytes, the concentration of serum immunoglobulins (Igs), especially IgG and IgM, declines markedly after age 70 (Rowe and Besdine 1982). Skin testing reactivity (anergy) has been found to decline in older patients. Also, in tests with animals decreased ability of T-cell replication, decreased numbers of mitogen-responsive cells, and diminished proliferative capacity of those cells that respond have been noted. Cell-mediated killing, a function of T killer cells, has been found to be reduced in older mice (Chu et al. 1987). In addition to these humoral and cellular changes phagocytic capacity of polymorphonuclear leukocytes may diminish with age, and there may be a slower response to stimuli for the production of white blood cells.

CHEMOTHERAPY AND THE OLDER PATIENT

Physiologic Factors

Successful treatment of cancer with chemotherapy in the older patient depends on the antitumor activity of the chemotherapeutic agents and the management of potentially life-threatening toxicities (Table 9-2). Most clinical drug trials in oncology have an age cutoff of 65 or 70 years. Therefore, these drugs have not been adequately tested in older patients. Drug toxicity in the older patient affects organ systems already compromised by aging. Most notable are the bone marrow, lung, cardiovascular, respiratory, renal, and nervous systems. Chronologic age by itself does not adequately explain the older person's ability or inability to tolerate chemotherapy. The measurement of physiologic age is a critical issue when evaluating the impact of chemotherapy, so that various parameters of organ function should be evaluated before therapy.

In the past, oncologists were less aggressive in their approach to cancer in older patients because they believed the older patient to be less able to tolerate therapy.

Table 9-2 Chemotherapeutic Agents with Potential Increased Toxicity in Older Patients

Chemotherapeutic Agent	Toxicity
Cytosine arabinoside	Cerebellar toxicity with high doses
Bleomycin	Greater incidence of pneumonitis
Cisplatin	Greater incidence of nephrotoxicity, hearing loss, peripheral neuropathies
Methotrexate	Meningeal irritation, confusion, gait disturbances may occur with intrathecal administration; greater incidence of leukopenia, stomatitis, thrombocytopenia
Vincristine	Constipation, urinary retention, neurotoxicity
Methyl lomustine	Greater incidence of leukopenia, thrombocytopenia
Doxorubicin	Greater incidence of cardiomyopathy

Data from recent studies are proving that, within guidelines, chemotherapy can be safely administered. Chu and colleagues (1987) evaluated the process of care for older women with breast cancer who were treated in community hospitals. Most often the older women received less aggressive management (in terms of the number of lymph nodes evaluated and use of chemotherapy) than younger patients. Yancik et al. (1986) found that older women (65 years or more) with ovarian cancer were more likely to receive less aggressive therapy than younger patients.

In a retrospective review of older patients in the Eastern Cooperative Oncology Group protocols, chemotherapy toxicity rates were comparable in older and younger patients. In older patients, bone marrow toxicity was associated with the use of two drugs: methyl BCNU (carmustine) and methotrexate.

Tirelli et al. (1987) evaluated the results of treatment in older patients with non-Hodgkin's lymphoma; the median age of the patient was 75 years. Patients were randomized to either teniposide or etoposide and prednimustine. In both arms of the study toxicity was mild, and the investigators concluded that combination chemotherapy such as etoposide and prednimustine is well tolerated in older patients.

Fisher et al. (1986) evaluated 1,891 women with primary operable breast cancer and positive nodes. Patients were randomized to L-phenylalanine mustard and 5-fluorouracil with or without tamoxifen. Older patients (50 years or more) who received tamoxifen tolerated treatment better and had longer disease-free survival than younger patients.

Panettiere (1985) evaluated age and myelosuppression in 199 patients ranging in age from 17 to 85 years receiving methyl CCNU and 5-fluorouracil. Patients younger than 40 years demonstrated the lowest percentage of platelet toxicity, but there was no pattern of increasing platelet toxicity in patients 49 to 65 years. White blood cell nadir was also lowest in patients younger than 40 years, but there was no significant age-related effect in the older age groups.

The lung appears to be at risk for bleomycin fibrosis in patients older than 70 years (Hass et al. 1976). Adriamycin is thought to produce more cardiotoxicity in older patients (Praga et al. 1970), possibly because the incidence of concurrent cardiac disease is greater in the older population.

In another study of age and the treatment of multiple myeloma, older patients had responses and survival rates equivalent to those of younger patients, and hematologic toxicity was no greater in the older population (Cohen and Bartolucci 1985).

Psychologic and Psychosocial Factors

Although data on toxicity from chemotherapy are incomplete in the older population, it is known that when toxicities occur they may be more damaging to the older population because of factors unrelated to cancer. Social conditions of the aged patient and concurrent medical disease place the older patient in a sometimes limited capacity to manage and tolerate side effects. For example, an older patient who lives alone may be unable to tolerate anorexia or nausea and vomiting and may present with dehydration long before a younger patient does. An older diabetic with some mild peripheral neuropathy may have progressive toxicity from *Vinca* alkaloids.

In one study evaluating the psychosocial consequences of chemotherapy on older patients, Nerenz et al. (1986) found that elderly patients reported no more difficulty with treatment or emotional distress than younger patients. The population studied comprised patients receiving initial treatment for breast cancer and lymphoma who were evaluated in terms of emotional distress and life disruption due to chemotherapy.

NURSING CONSIDERATIONS FOR THE OLDER PATIENT RECEIVING RADIATION THERAPY

In older patients, radiation therapy may be given for cure or palliation. Palliative radiation therapy may be for pain relief from bone metastases or breast, lung, or prostate cancer; for prevention of bone fractures; or for prevention of spinal cord paralysis. Preoperative radiation therapy is generally used to reduce tumor bulk so that there is greater ease of surgical resection.

Strohl (1988) has defined the role of the nurse in radiation oncology as being multifaceted. The nurse prepares the patient for treatment by assessing fears and anxieties about this form of therapy. Common fears include being crushed by the machine, being burned, losing hair, and experiencing nausea (Bricourt and McKenzie 1984). The older patient presents a particular challenge to the nurse in

Table 9-3 Side Effects of Radiation Therapy and Age-Related Factors in Older Patients

Site	Side Effect	Age-Related Factors
Skin	Erythema, dry or moist desquamation	Decrease in subcutaneous fat, thinning of the dermis and epidermis, decreased elasticity of dermis, decreased effectiveness as a barrier against infection
Head and neck	Taste changes, skin changes in mouth, stomatitis	Decreased saliva, diminished ability to identify tastes, receding of gums, loosening of teeth
Esophagus	Pain, difficulty swallowing	Decreased motility of esophageal contractions, dilation of esophagus
Stomach	Nausea, vomiting	Decreased gastric acid secretion (achlorhydria), atrophic gastritis (may complicate nausea and vomiting)
Pelvis	Diarrhea	Decreased rectal tone (may further aggravate diarrhea)
Bone marrow	Blood count depression	Overall reduction in hematopoiesis (may increase blood count depression, especially if radiation therapy is combined with chemotherapy)
Lung	Pulmonary pneumonitis	Decreased lung compliance resulting in impaired oxygenation

terms of symptom management (Table 9-3). Generally, radiation effects on tissues and organs can be divided into early and late effects. Early effects occur during treatment or in the first 6 months after treatment and generally involve organs whose cells rapidly divide (skin, mucous membranes, and hair follicles). Late effects include vascular changes such as fibrosis and bone marrow depression. In managing the older patient the nurse must be cognizant of normal aging processes that may further aggravate the side effects of radiation therapy.

Meal preparation for the older, often debilitated patient may be difficult, especially if there is no family member to provide for meal preparation. Community resources such as Meals on Wheels may be helpful in this regard. Fatigue is another common complaint of older patients undergoing radiation therapy. The nurse can instruct the patient before treatment that this is a common side effect and can encourage activities that conserve energy. Frequent rest periods should be encouraged, and family members should be instructed to assume more responsibility in matters concerning shopping, meal preparation, and housekeeping.

POLYPHARMACY: DRUG-INDUCED ILLNESS IN THE OLDER PATIENT

Normal aging is associated with physiologic changes that influence drug response in the older patient. Although physicians prescribe and manage the drug regimen, initial identification of adverse drug reactions is often made by the nurse in the home, community, ambulatory, or acute care setting.

Adverse drug reactions have been defined by the World Health Organization (1970) as any response to a drug that is noxious and unintended and occurs at doses used in humans for prophylaxis, diagnosis, or therapy. The potential for drug adversity in the older population is staggering when one considers that (1) pharmacists dispense twice as many prescriptions to individuals older than 65 years compared to younger people, (2) individuals older than 65 years purchase 25% of all drugs sold in America, (3) the average older person may receive as many as 8 to 10 prescriptions per year, and (4) over-the-counter drug use and self-medication are common in older people.

The older cancer patient often presents with concurrent disease that is being treated pharmacologically. Medical management therefore must consider pharmacologic agents that further add to the risk of noncompliance and drug adverse reactions. Rates of adverse drug reactions rise steadily after age 50, and patients older than 60 years are twice as likely to develop adverse drug reactions as younger patients (Stewart and Cluff 1972).

Several factors contribute to drug vulnerability of the older person and are related to the normal aging process: body composition, drug absorption, drug distribution, drug metabolism, and drug excretion.

Body Composition

A decrease in the amount of muscle and an increase in the amount of fat per pound body weight is a normal part of the aging process. Thus a lipid-soluble medication has a greater effect in an older person than in a younger person. For example, benzodiazepines, which are commonly used to treat anxiety in older patients, may produce greater sedation because of the physiologic changes of aging.

Drug Absorption

The rate of drug absorption is dependent on the rate at which the stomach delivers the drug into the small intestine. Delayed gastric emptying, which is common in older people, may delay the onset of action of certain medications that should be absorbed quickly to provide maximal therapeutic effect and may increase degradation of drugs that are primarily metabolized by gastric mucosa. Short-acting analgesics such as acetaminophen, hydromorphone, meperidine, and levorphanol may have delayed onset of action in older patients requiring short-acting pain relief.

Drug Distribution

Distribution involves the transference of a drug from the bloodstream to the organs. Factors that contribute to drug distribution are body composition, water content, plasma protein concentration, and blood flow to regional organs.

The older patient with congestive heart failure treated with digitalis preparations requires blood monitoring for toxicity. The older patient is at greater risk for adriamycin toxicity requiring treatment with digoxin.

Low serum albumin levels in older people correlate with a decreased plasma protein-binding capacity of some drugs, and thus more free drug is delivered. Some drugs that bind with albumin, such as phenytoin and dicumarol, may be distributed in high concentrations because of increased absorption. Both these drugs are commonly prescribed to older cancer patients. The older patient on phenytoin needs careful serum monitoring of blood levels; the patient receiving dicumarol requires monitoring of prothrombin time.

Cardiac output, which declines with age, may decrease the rate of drug delivery to target organs and organs of excretion. Bronchodilators such as theophylline, which has a narrow therapeutic index, are often used to treat symptoms related to tumor involvement of the lung. Patients on bronchodilators therefore require careful blood monitoring.

Drug Metabolism

The liver is the major site of drug metabolism. With age there is a reduction in liver blood flow, which is probably related to reduced cardiac output and a decrease in liver mass. Drugs affected by hepatic blood flow include meperidine, morphine, and propranolol. All are commonly prescribed to older cancer patients.

Liver damage such as that caused by extensive metastatic disease from breast, colorectal, or lung cancer may further potentiate hepatotoxicity of drugs in older patients. Common drugs such as phenytoin, acetaminophen, and antithyroid medications may be extremely hepatotoxic in the presence of liver disease. Specific chemotherapeutic agents that may produce hepatotoxicity include methotrexate, mercaptopurine, L-asparaginase, and mithramycin.

Drug Excretion

The kidney is responsible for drug excretion. Advanced age is associated with morphologic and physiologic changes in the kidney, including decline in kidney volume and weight, reduction in renal blood flow, and reduction in glomerular filtration rate. Alterations in kidney function may affect the elimination of certain drugs and produce severe toxicity. Such drugs commonly used in the older cancer population include digoxin, nonsteroidal anti-inflammatory agents, allopurinol, aminoglycosides, triamterene, and vancomycin. Specific chemotherapeutic agents that are renally eliminated include methotrexate, cyclophosphamide, cisplatin, and streptozocin.

FUTURE DIRECTIONS

As the population ages, nurses will continue to see older patients seeking aggressive cancer treatments. Understanding the physiologic nature of aging and its relationship to cancer is just the beginning for future oncology nurses.

The prospective payment system (diagnosis-related groups) has shifted care to the outpatient setting and has created a decline in total inpatient hospital stays (Schaffer 1988). There has been and will continue to be a greater need for nurses in all areas as the inpatient acuity level increases and as more forms of treatment are given in ambulatory settings.

Research in areas of chemotherapy toxicity, impact of surgical procedures on older patients, determination of the effects of age on symptom management, patient teaching, fluid and electrolyte balance, discharge outcomes, and compliance with treatment regimens are just a few of the possible areas for nursing research. The economic impact of cancer care on older patients also needs to be addressed. Medicare presently does not reimburse for investigational treatment; thus the potential is great that many older Americans in the future will not have access to newer forms of treatment.

In the years to come the need for supportive services for older people will increase; improved transportation, home medical services, day care centers, and respite care services are a few areas needing attention in this regard. Home medical care for the oncology patient will include high technology services such as intravenous administration of chemotherapy, fluids, and analgesics. In terms of how older Americans will live, the future promises great changes. Combination residential and health care facilities will be able to provide basic medical care as well as screening and early detection procedures. Community-based outreach centers will provide such services as mammography, hemoccult testing, and education programs in areas of diet, exercise, medications, and various forms of health care practices.

Nursing and medical involvement in care of older cancer patients will continue to grow. Gerontologic social work, nursing, and medical programs have spread across the country. The number of states requiring geriatric education in their medical schools and involvement by physicians in community-based programs will increase.

CONCLUSION

As the population of older people increases, nurses will be faced with the complexities of caring for elderly cancer patients. There are many unknown areas relating to the older population, including the impact of aging on cancer surgery, chemotherapy, immunotherapy, and radiation therapy. The next two decades will bring the older patient into focus together with the social issues confronting this population. Issues of retirement, isolation, widowhood, and lack of financial security will affect how nurses intervene with this population. In addition, there are many ethical considerations for the nursing profession to consider, including informed consent, investigational treatment, and quality of life. Nurses in their role as health care coordinators will be in the forefront of managing these patients' care in the community and home.

STUDY QUESTIONS

1. Identify the most commonly occurring cancers in older adults.
2. Describe the effects of advanced age on various treatment modalities and the role of nursing in addressing these effects.
3. Identify risk factors for the development of cancer in older patients.
4. Describe areas of nursing research related to the older adult with cancer.
5. Identify future trends related to care delivery to the older adult with cancer.

REFERENCES

American Cancer Society. 1989. *Facts and figures*. New York: American Cancer Society.

Armstrong, D. 1976. Interstitial pneumonia in the immunocompromised patient. *Transplantation Proceedings* 8(4):657–661.

Beattie, D.S. 1988. Biochemical aspects of aging. In *Human aging research: Concepts and techniques*, ed. B. Kent and R.N. Butler. New York: Raven.

Besdine, R.W. 1980. Geriatric medicine: An overview. *Annual Review of Gerontology and Geriatrics* 1:135.

Birdsell, J. 1986. Cancer in the aged. In *Nursing considerations in geriatric oncology*, ed. D. Welch-McCaffrey. Columbus, Ohio: Adria Laboratories, 3–8.

Bricourt, P., and J. MacKenzie. 1984. Radiotherapy from the patient's viewpoint. In *Radiation therapy and thanatology*, eds. R. Torpie, L. Leigner, and C. Chang. Springfield, Ill.: Charles C Thomas.

Cairns, J. 1983. Aging and the natural history of cancer. In *Perspectives on prevention and treatment of cancer in the elderly*, ed. R. Yancik. New York: Raven.

Celentano, D., S. Shapiro, and C. Weisman. 1982. Cancer preventive screening behavior among elderly women. *Preventive Medicine* 11:454–63.

Chu, I., P. Diehr, P. Feigl, G. Glaefke, C. Begg, A. Glicksman, and L. Ford. 1987. The effect of age on the care of women with breast cancer in a community hospital. *Journal of Geriatrics* 42:185–90.

Cohen, H.J., and A. Bartolucci. 1985. Age and the treatment of multiple myeloma: Southeastern Cancer Study Group experience. *American Journal of Medicine* 79:316–24.

Eltherington, L.G. 1983. Complications of prior drug therapy. In *Complications in anesthesiology*, ed. F.K. Orkin and L.H. Cooperman. Philadelphia: J.B. Lippincott.

Farrands, P.A., and J.D. Hardcastle. 1984. Factors affecting compliance with screening for colorectal cancer. *Community Medicine* 6(1):12–19.

Fisher, R., C. Redmond, A. Brown, E.R. Fisher, N. Wolmark, D. Bowman, D. Plotkin, J. Wolter, R. Bornstein, and S. Legáult-Poisson. 1986. Adjuvant chemotherapy with and without tamoxifen in the treatment of primary breast cancer: 5 year results from the national surgical adjuvant breast and bowel project. *Journal of Clinical Oncology* 4:459–71.

Fowles, O. 1983. The changing older population. *Aging*, May/June, 6–11.

Graybill, J.R., L.W. Marshall, P. Charache, C.K. Wallace, and V.B. Melvin. 1973. Nosocomial pneumonia: A continuing major problem. *American Review of Respiratory Diseases* 108(5):1130–1140.

Hass, C.D., C.A. Coltman, A.J. Gottlieb, A. Haut, and J.K. Luce. 1976. Phase II evaluation of bleomycin: A Southwest Oncology Study Group. *Cancer* 38:8–12.

Hersh, E.M., C.R. Gschwind, and J. Frank. 1983. Host defense parameters in aging. In *Perspectives on prevention and treatment of cancer in the elderly*, ed. R. Yancik. New York: Raven.

Hillary, D. 1983. Hypoxemia and hypercapnia during and after anesthesia. In *Complications in anesthesiology*, eds. F. Orkin and L.H. Cooperman. Philadelphia: J.B. Lippincott.

Hodkinson, H.M. 1978. Cancer in the aged. In *Textbook of geriatric medicine and gerontology*, ed. J.C. Brocklehurst. Edinburgh/New York: Churchill Livingstone.

Hodkinson, H.M. 1973. Non-specific presentation of illness. *British Medical Journal* 4:94–96.

Hoeprich, P.D. 1983. *Bacterial pneumonias in infectious disease*. 3d ed., ed. P.D. Hoeprich. Philadelphia: Harper & Row.

Howland, W.S. 1987. Preoperative evaluation of the cancer patient for emergency surgery. In *Surgical emergencies in the cancer patient*, ed. A.D. Turnbull. Chicago: Year Book Medical Publishers.

Hunt, K.E., D.E. Fry, and K.I. Bland. 1980. Breast carcinomas in the elderly patient: An assessment of operative risk, morbidity and mortality. *American Journal of Surgery* 140:339–42.

King, D. 1988. *Pathology and aging*. New York: Raven.

Koin, D. 1984. Surgical concerns. In *Geriatric medicine. Fundamentals of geriatric care*, vol. 2, eds. C.K. Cassel and J.R. Walsh. New York: Springer-Verlag.

Kovar, M.G. 1977. *Elderly people: The population 65 years and over*. Department of Health, Education and Welfare Publication no. 77-1232.

LaForce, F.M. 1981. Hospital acquired gram negative rod pneumonias: An overview. *American Journal of Medicine* 70:664–69.

Lamy, P. 1988. Introduction to the aging process. In *Therapeutics in the elderly*, eds. J.C. DeLafuente and R.B. Stewart. Baltimore: Williams & Wilkins.

Marley, L. 1982. Knowledge of cancer facts among workers following an educational program. *Occupational Health Nurse* 30:16–17.

Meyers, B.R., S.Z. Hirschman, and J.R. Axelrod. 1972. Current patterns of infection in multiple myeloma. *American Journal of Medicine* 52:87–92.

Nerenz, D.R., R.R. Love, H. Leventhal, and D.V. Easterling. 1986. Psychosocial consequences of cancer chemotherapy for elderly patients. *Health Services Research* 20:961–76.

Panettiere, F.J. 1985. Age and chemotherapy: Myelosuppression data from a SWOG adjuvant study. *Proceedings of American Association of Cancer Research* 26:188.

Pegels, C.C. 1988. Vision, speech, hearing, and dental care. In *Health care and the older citizen: Economic, demographic, and financial aspects*, ed. C.C. Pegels. Rockville, Md.: Aspen Publishers.

Perez, C.A., W.R. Fair, D.C. Ihde, L. Labrie. 1987. Cancer of the prostate. In *Cancer: Principles and practice of oncology*. 2d ed., eds. V.T. DeVita, S. Hellman, and S.A. Rosenberg. Philadelphia: J.B. Lippincott.

Praga, C., G. Beretta, P.L. Vigo, et al. 1970. Adriamycin cardiotoxicity: A study of 1273 patients. *Cancer Treatment Report* 63:827–34.

Robins, R.E., and D. Lee. 1985. Carcinoma of the breast in women 80 years of age and older: Still a lethal disease. *American Journal of Surgery* 149:606–609.

Rowe, J.G., and R.W. Besdine. 1982. Immune system. In *Health and disease in old age*, eds. J.G. Rowe and R.W. Besdine. Boston: Little, Brown & Co.

Schaffer, F.A. 1988. DRGs: A new era for health care. *Nursing Clinics of North America* 123(3):453–63.

Siegel, J.S. 1980. Recent and prospective trends for the elderly population and some implications for health care. In *Second conference on the epidemiology of aging*, eds. S.G. Haynes and M. Feinleib. Bethesda, Md.: National Institutes of Health.

Stewart, R.B., and L.G. Cluff. 1972. A review of medication errors and compliance in ambulatory patients. *Clinical Pharmacology and Therapeutics* 13:463–68.

Strohl, R.S. 1988. The nursing role in radiation oncology: Symptom management of acute and chronic reactions. *Oncology Nursing Forum* 15:429–34.

Stromborg, M., and S. Nord. 1979. Nurse practitioner acceptance in a cancer detection clinic. *Nurse Practitioner* 4:110–12.

Tirelli, D., A. Carbone, V. Zagonel, A. Veronesi, and R. Canetta. 1987. Non-Hodgkin's lymphomas in the elderly: Prospective studies with specifically devised chemotherapy regimens in 66 patients. *European Journal of Cancer and Clinical Oncology* 23:535–40.

Urbach, F. 1983. Prevention and treatment of skin cancer in the elderly patient. In *Perspectives on prevention and treatment of cancer in the elderly*, ed. R. Yanick. New York: Raven.

Waldron, R.P., I.A. Donovan, J. Prumm, S.N. Mottram, and S. Tedman. 1986. Emergency presentation and mortality from colorectal cancer in the elderly. *British Journal of Surgery* 73:214–16.

Weinrich, S.P., and M.C. Weinrich. 1986. Cancer knowledge among elderly individuals. *Cancer Nursing* 9:301–07.

Winawer, S.J. 1987. Screening for colorectal cancer. In *Cancer: Principles and practice of oncology*. 2d ed., eds. V.T. DeVita, S. Hellman, and S.A. Rosenberg. Philadelphia: J.B. Lippincott.

Wolff, S.M., and J.V. Bennett. 1974. Gram-negative rod bacteremia. *New England Journal of Medicine* 291:733.

World Health Organization. 1970. International drug monitoring: The role of the hospital—A WHO report. *Drug Intelligence and Clinical Pharmacy* 4:101–10.

Yancik, R., L. Kessler, and J.W. Yates. 1987. The elderly population: Opportunities for cancer prevention and detection. *Cancer* 62(supplement):1823–28.

Yancik, R., L.G. Ries, and Y.W. Yates. 1986. Ovarian cancer in the elderly: An analysis of surveillance epidemiology and end results program data. *American Journal of Obstetrics and Gynecology* 154:639–47.

Yancik, R., L.G. Ries, and J.W. Yates. 1989. Breast cancer in aging women: A population based study of contrasts in stage, surgery and survival. *Cancer* 63(5):976–81.

Young, J.L., C.L. Percy, and A.J. Asire, eds. 1981. *Incidence and mortality data: 1973–77*. National Cancer Institute Monograph 57. Department of Health and Human Services Publication no. NIH 81-2330.

Young, L.A. 1985. Gram negative sepsis. In *Principles and practice of infectious diseases*, eds. G. Mandel, R.G. Douglas, and J.E. Bennett. New York: Wiley.

Young, L.S. 1978. Amikacin: Experience in a comparative clinical trial with gentamycin in leukopenic subjects. In *Proceedings of 10th Congress of Chemotherapy*, September 1977, eds. W. Siegenthaler and R. Lüthy. Washington, D.C.: American Society of Microbiology.

Young, R.C, J.E. Bennett, G.W. Geelhoed, and A.S. Levine. 1974. Fungemia with compromised host resistance. *Annals of Internal Medicine* 80:605–612.

Zimmerman, J., and C. Dietrich. 1987. Current perspectives on septic shock. *Pediatric Clinics of North America* 34:131–63.

Chapter 10

The Terminally Ill Cancer Patient

Colleen Scanlon and Nancy Scannell D'Agostino

> This chapter presents key areas for consideration in the care of patients with advanced cancer. A framework for a comprehensive biopsychosocial and spiritual assessment is presented along with a discussion of goal setting with this patient population. Finally, the ethical dimension of care of this nature is elucidated through a description of a forum established at Calvary Hospital, Bronx, New York, that is designed to assist nurses in addressing ethical issues and concerns specific to advanced cancer care.

The battle against cancer is a dramatic and challenging one, yet the responsibility for the care of patients with cancer does not end when response to therapy ceases. Although expertise in the delivery of active curative cancer care is necessary, the fact remains that many cancer patients will die as a result of their disease and thus will require care beyond the curative phase.

The point at which a designation of cancer in the advanced stage is made varies from patient to patient. For some patients, such designation may coincide with the initial diagnosis of cancer. For others, it may come after months and sometimes years of active therapy. Finally, some patients may be designated as having advanced cancer only when death is imminent. Despite the wide range, there are several characteristics that are generally descriptive of patients with advanced cancer.

First and foremost, patients can only be determined to be in an advanced stage of cancer when progressive disease is documented. Usually, but not always, metastases to one or more vital organs are present. Second, because the disease continues to progress despite treatment, patients in the advanced stage of cancer frequently experience various symptoms. Finally, in referring to patients with advanced cancer, one is speaking about those with a limited life expectancy.

Much of the discussion that follows is based on the patient care program at Calvary Hospital in the Bronx, New York. Calvary Hospital is a 200-bed specialty hospital accredited by the Joint Commission on Accreditation of Healthcare Organizations that cares solely for patients with advanced cancer. It is the only institution of its kind in the United States. Because it is an acute care hospital, patients are admitted for care related to the cascade of problems associated with advanced malignancy. There is great emphasis on amelioration of symptoms such as pain, infections, and nutrition disorders. Approximately 2,000 patients are cared for annually through inpatient, outpatient, and home care services. The underlying philosophy of care speaks to the nonabandonment of patients and families and to the maintenance of dignity and self-worth in the last few weeks of life. A strong multidisciplinary team effort is directed at meeting the complex, individual biopsychosocial and spiritual needs of this patient population and incorporates the unique expertise of many health care providers.

At the time of admission to Calvary Hospital, patient and family are introduced to the team of health care providers who are responsible for the development and implementation of the overall plan of care. Each patient is assigned to a primary attending physician who is on staff at the hospital and who sees the patient regularly throughout hospitalization. A social worker is available for direct assistance to the patient and family and to make referrals to family support groups (which are offered weekly in English and Spanish). A therapeutic dietitian works with the patient and family to plan a nutrition program that is enjoyable for the patient and accommodates any illness-induced difficulties. Representatives of various religious faiths are available around the clock to the patient and family through the pastoral care department. Religious services are held regularly and, although it is optional, many patients participate in these services. A recreational therapist is also available to engage the patient in one-to-one, small group, or large group activities that are planned to accommodate the special needs of this patient population. Support services such as laboratory, radiology, pharmacy, volunteers, music therapy, and patient advocacy are all designed to meet the complex and unique needs of patients with advanced cancer who are admitted to Calvary Hospital.

All this care is coordinated by the professional nursing staff, all of whom practice a modified version of primary nursing. In addition to conducting much needed ongoing assessment and planning of care, a major responsibility of the nursing staff is that of communicator. A great deal of necessary dialogue takes place between patient and nurse as new information as well as clarification of information is offered. There is always communication with family members, who are encouraged to call when they are not able to be at the hospital. Finally, it is the nurse who assumes major responsibility for interdisciplinary and intradisciplinary communication in an effort to ensure optimal planning and delivery of care.

Planning and delivering care to patients whose conditions are dynamic and generally deteriorating represents a great challenge for all health care professionals. Nurses are perhaps in the best situation to exert a positive influence on the quality of care rendered to those for whom the focus should not connote less active or less aggressive treatment but rather care of a different nature. The multisystem consequences of cancer and cancer therapy frequently seen in those in the advanced stages require creativity and flexibility as well as an ability to anticipate complications or problems as they arise.

A primary responsibility of care givers is to recognize that the overall goals of care may be quite different for those patients at the end of life compared to their counterparts for whom cure or remission is the expectation. The notion of restoring physical health is both unrealistic and unattainable for patients with advanced cancer, and it is futile to establish such goals.

In a palliative care setting, it is easy and convenient to identify the promotion of comfort and dignity as the overall goal of care for the dying. This may be appropriate, but it is probably not accurate or individual enough to reflect accurately the hoped-for outcome of care for the patient. The overall goals of care are primarily patient oriented, not nurse oriented. Nurse-oriented goals can be determined on the basis of the identified nursing needs and the designation of realistic expected outcomes. Nurse-oriented goals, however, have little value unless they are congruent with the patient's perceived idea of quality of life and what he or she expects or hopes for as the outcome of care. Although *quality of life* may seem to be a vague and nebulous term, when quality is defined by the patient the term loses its vagueness and becomes an individual perception that has meaning for the patient, the family, and the nurse.

ASSESSMENT

Crucial to appropriate planning of care for each patient is a comprehensive nursing assessment of health care needs. This assessment ideally takes place at the first meeting with the patient. Family members or significant others are included in this assessment process because they are often able to provide information valuable to the overall care planning.

Although it is impossible to assess individual aspects of a person without consideration of the person as a whole, individual components of a biologic, psychosocial, and spiritual assessment are presented here for the purpose of clarity. When analyzed, the nursing assessment, which represents the systematic collection of significant patient data, assists in the identification of actual and potential health problems; strengths, weaknesses, and patient resources; and priorities and expectations. This overall purpose is consistent for the assessment of care needs for all patients and thus remains the same for patients with advanced cancer.

Throughout a general assessment, there are areas of concentration that are specific to those with advanced cancer. These generic concepts recognize the general decline in patient functioning that is expected in advanced cancer and also acknowledge that patient perception and satisfaction are priorities of care. In assessing care needs of the patient with advanced cancer, one should concentrate on eliciting information that details any alteration in functioning and how this altered function compares to preillness status. It is also necessary to identify the patient's perception of and satisfaction with this level of functioning and the extent to which interventions have been effective.

With the above concepts recognized as basic to the assessment of patients with advanced cancer, an organized and complete assessment of biologic, psychosocial, and spiritual needs is then attempted.

Biologic Needs

Identification of needs related to biologic or physical functioning is usually made through interview and physical examination. It should be recognized that this process can be tiring for even the healthiest of individuals and can be thoroughly exhausting for the already debilitated patient whose emotional status may further discourage a detailed investigation of all systems. It is therefore necessary to prioritize areas of the assessment so that problem areas are given adequate attention. High-priority biologic areas are patient-expressed symptoms, disease-related symptoms, treatment-related symptoms, and systems affected by concurrent, non–cancer-related illness.

The identification of high-priority disease-related systems is dependent on the nurse's knowledge of cancer pathophysiology and the usual metastatic patterns and problems of site-specific cancers. Primary consideration is given to the systems of the primary and known metastatic sites as well as to those systems in which metastasis or problems may be anticipated. For example, the targeted systems for a patient in the end stage of lung cancer with spinal metastasis might be the pulmonary system (known primary site), the skeletal system (known metastatic site), the neurologic system (potential metastatic site), and fluid and electrolyte balance (potential problem area).

In terms of treatment-related systems, the primary concern in the assessment of the patient with advanced cancer is the identification of long-term consequences of cancer treatment, which may endure for the remainder of the patient's life and may negatively affect the quality of that life. Timely assessment of these consequences is dependent on nursing knowledge of the potential problems associated with each of the cancer treatment modalities. For example, a previous history of high-dose radiation therapy to the head should prompt an investigation of the functioning of salivary glands and taste perception. In the case of the patient with advanced cancer, it is necessary to recognize that some chronic problems initially resulting from cancer treatment may persist largely because of the patient's general condition. For example, declining general health and poor nutrition, which are common in advanced cancer, may preclude a patient's ability to recover from severe chemotherapy-induced stomatitis.

Because not all problems will be cancer related, priority must also be given to any systems affected by preexisting non–cancer-related illnesses. Cancer is largely a disease of middle and late adulthood (American Cancer Society 1989), so that many patients may present with secondary but important illnesses that can impede overall functioning and patient satisfaction with care. Illnesses such as diabetes mellitus, arthritis, peripheral vascular disease, and heart disease are not uncommon and, if present, should obviously be attended to in the overall assessment and care of the patient.

Finally, the concerns of the patient offer valuable information for the nursing assessment. Consideration of the nature of this patient population and the overall goals of care at this point in the disease process warrants giving highest priority to the patient's concerns. For example, the patient who complains of unrelieved constipation requires a complete analysis of the constipation problem as well as of the gastrointestinal system. There is no need for speculation in this area of assessment, and the nurse need only consistently acknowledge the patient's concerns and priorities of care.

Psychosocial Needs

The primary focus in the assessment of the psychosocial needs of the patient with advanced cancer is identification of what is presently of greatest concern and importance to the patient. Although the details of a comprehensive psychosocial assessment are not presented here, with the generic concepts for assessment serving as a point of reference the nurse should strive to identify alterations in function as well as patient perception of and satisfaction with this level of functioning.

An initial area for psychosocial investigation is the determination of the patient's mental status because this may greatly influence the course of care. Care is adapted according to the patient's orientation and level of alertness. Comparison of prior and present function is helpful, as is the determination of the patient's perception of changes.

Eliciting information regarding the patient's specific intrapersonal skills and coping styles may yield data valuable in the overall plan of care. Knowing how the patient has successfully dealt with stress in the past and how the patient views his or her present situation provides much-needed groundwork for assistance in dealing with present concerns or issues.

Finally, it is helpful to gather data about available support networks and resources. For some patients, families and friends may provide much in the way of emotional support. For other patients, these people may be a source of stress. It is not unusual for patients at this time in their lives to be quite concerned about significant others. Previously established patterns of communication, identified roles, and a perception of how the present situation may influence future functioning may greatly influence the patient's access to support systems.

Spiritual Needs

The role of faith and spirituality may take on greater emphasis in one's life when it is known that death is a reality in the not-too-distant future. For many patients, the last few weeks of life may be a time for introspection and clarification of one's beliefs and faith.

It is important to recognize the value of spirituality for every individual, regardless of whether he or she ascribes to any formalized religion. A distinction between spirituality and religion should be understood. "Spirituality refers to an inner religiosity, whereas religion refers to the behavioral expressions of that inner reality" (Corless 1986, 89). All patients, even those who have no belief in a spiritual being or an afterlife, can be helped to find meaning in their lives and thereby to ease any possible spiritual pain.

Although spirituality is, for most people, an individual and private part of their lives, health care professionals do have a responsibility to assist patients in attaining a level of spiritual comfort if this is viewed as important to the patient. This may be achieved through direct interventions or through referral to others after the identification of spiritual issues and concerns.

Initially, the nursing assessment should be directed at areas of concern and priority related to spirituality. Identification of religious affiliation and usual religious practices is essential because this may provide direction for the initiation of specific interventions such as a special diet or assurance of access to religious services.

It may take continued interaction with the patient to identify additional spiritual concerns and priorities. It is not uncommon for patients to be hesitant about voicing these issues at the first contact. Regardless of the time frame, it is important to continue to explore spiritual issues throughout the patient-nurse relationship because spirituality can be a great source of comfort (or distress) for patients. Patients frequently draw on their spiritual resources as they attempt to confront the complex issues that arise when life is time limited. Future plans have been interrupted, relationships may be strained, and other unfinished matters may need to be addressed in a shortened time frame. Throughout the patient-nurse relationship, attempts should be made to determine the patient's perception of the relationship (if any) between faith and illness. Additionally, beliefs about suffering and the death experience may be investigated. Many patients may also wish to discuss their preferences for post-mortem and funeral arrangements.

NURSING CONCERNS FOR THE FUTURE: ETHICAL ISSUES

Although ethical issues can arise in the course of any illness, the catastrophic ramifications of a diagnosis of advanced cancer heighten these concerns. The realization that life expectancy is limited adds a sense of urgency to decision making. The luxury of time in which to consider carefully all aspects of a situation is lacking. Further, because of the difficulty that many practitioners experience in discussing the diagnosis and prognosis of advanced cancer, many patients at this stage of illness lack the basic information needed to make informed choices. It is for these reasons that the ethical dimension of palliative care is recognized here. The following discussion is not meant to suggest that the concerns mentioned are the only concerns or that they are faced only by this patient population; nevertheless, they do occur more frequently with this group than others.

Do Not Resuscitate

Cardiopulmonary resuscitation can produce a dramatic reversal in the event of sudden cessation of life, yet it has not been successful in the case of patients with advanced cancer (Blackhall 1987). Despite this known fact, many patients with advanced cancer continue to be subjected to a "code" because the risks and benefits of resuscitation have not been explained to them, and in the absence of a do not resuscitate order full resuscitative procedures are employed. As stated previously, this is often a result of a failure to deal honestly and sensitively with the patient.

Withholding or Withdrawing Treatments (Including Food and Nourishment)

The devastating effects of advanced cancer and, at times, the effects of the treatments themselves can be more than an individual patient is able or willing to cope with. In some instances, patients may ask that therapy be stopped or may refuse to grant permission for treatments that are recommended. This can be upsetting for the practitioner who views the proposed therapy as being beneficial to the patient and thus in his or her best interest. An understanding of the patient's autonomy and a corresponding respect for that autonomy will enable the nurse to support the patient in his or her decision, even when it differs from that of the nurse.

Difficult as acting on this understanding may be in the case of medical therapies, many find it even more difficult in the case of withholding or withdrawing food and nourishment. Yet when the burdens imposed on the patient outweigh the benefits provided, this is a permissible alternative.

The Management of Pain

Adequate pain management of the patient with advanced cancer presents various challenges to the nurse, among them ethical ones. The control of pain often calls for the use of narcotics in dosages exceeding the safe limits defined by the manufacturer. This may present a dilemma for the inexperienced nurse who is educated in strict principles of safe practice. As a patient's death approaches, the nurse may be faced with a decision about whether to medicate a patient who is in obvious pain when the possibility exists that the medication may inadvertently hasten the patient's death.

No solutions are presented for these problems because it is important that all aspects of each individual case be considered thoughtfully. At times, the decision reached by the patient or family or the direction given to the nurse by medical orders may conflict with what the nurse believes is morally right and thus permissible. In these cases, it is important that the nurse be certain that the reason for the disagreement is based on a moral conviction and not on some other reason. If the nurse cannot in good conscience follow through with a patient's choices, he or she is under no obligation to participate; no one can be compelled to act contrary to conscience. It is essential that the patient's rights and wishes come first, however, and that the care be transferred to another practitioner so that the patient is never abandoned.

Decision Making

Decision making for the patient with advanced cancer can present ethical concerns for the nurse as well as for the patient and family. For some patients, the severity of symptoms or the extent of disease may interfere with the ability to think clearly and to make rational choices. For patients from whom basic information about the diagnosis or prognosis has been withheld, the process of deciding is flawed. How can one be expected to make intelligent decisions about treatment options and other crucial matters when basic information has been withheld?

The nurse has a critical role to play in assisting the patient (or person acting on the patient's behalf) in the decision-making process. It is here that the role of the nurse as patient advocate takes on special significance. Because of the unique bond that exists between the patient and nurse, the nurse is ideally suited to assist the patient and family in clarifying information and sorting out other dimensions that are crucial in reaching a sound decision. To be effective in this role, it is important that the nurse be well versed in ethical principles and their application to commonly occurring situations faced by patients with advanced cancer.

Nursing Ethics Group

Many of the concerns discussed above have the potential to present ethical dilemmas for the nurse as well as for the patient and family. The degree to which the nurse is prepared to address these dilemmas will be dependent in large part on his or her knowledge of ethical principles and their application to nursing practice. A nursing ethics group can be developed to assist nurses in this process. This model of ethical inquiry can assist nurses in all areas of health care in making decisions to ensure high-quality patient care. At Calvary Hospital a nursing ethics group has been active for several years, and its goal is "to promote responsible ethical nursing practice by increasing awareness of the ethical dimensions of nursing practice, facilitating communication among nurses, and familiarizing nurses with ethical principles and components of the decision-making process" (Scanlon and Fleming 1987, 46). The group meets monthly and is open to all nurses in the institution. Participants are encouraged to discuss concerns from their daily practice. Topics addressed have included informed consent, confidentiality, a patient's right to refuse care, suicide, the nurse as advocate, and the nurse-physician relationship. A model to assist nurses in ethical decision making was adapted and utilized in exploring the issues presented. The group has been effective in assisting nurses who care for patients with advanced cancer to address ethical matters. Nurses have moved from a strictly emotional type of response to a reasoned approach that is based on critical thinking.

CONCLUSION

Care of the patient with advanced cancer is a challenge to health care providers and requires an understanding of the expertise in the varied dimensions of palliative care. Nurses are in a key position to enhance this quality of care and to ensure the promotion of comfort and dignity in the final days of life.

STUDY QUESTIONS

1. Describe the role of the nurse in caring for hospitalized patients with advanced cancer.

2. What factors influence the establishment of goals of nursing care for patients with advanced cancer?
3. Discuss three ethical concerns commonly encountered when caring for patients with advanced cancer.
4. How might a forum for discussion of ethical issues assist nurses in decision-making in daily clinical practice?

REFERENCES

American Cancer Society. 1989. Cancer statistics, 1989. *Ca—A Cancer Journal for Clinicians* 39:8–9.

Blackhall, L.J. 1987. Must we always use CPR? *New England Journal of Medicine* 317:1282.

Corless, I.B. 1986. Spirituality for whom? Presented at colloquium, In Quest of the Spiritual Component of Care for the Terminally Ill, 85–96; May, Yale University School of Nursing, New Haven, Connecticut.

Scanlon, M.C., and C.M. Fleming. 1987. Nurses come together to face ethical issues. *Health Progress*, December, 46–48, 52.

SUGGESTED READING

Scanlon, M.C., and C. Fleming. 1989. Ethical issues caring for the patient with advanced cancer. *Nursing Clinics of North America* 24, 4:977–86.

Chapter 11

Crucial Ambulatory Care Nursing Services: Detection and Management of Opportunistic Illness Related to Infection with Human Immunodeficiency Virus

Kathleen M. McMahon Casey

> Care for patients with acquired immunodeficiency syndrome (AIDS) encompasses a vast territory. A crucial aspect of AIDS care is the early detection of illness and initiation of treatment. In the ambulatory care center, infection with human immunodeficiency virus (HIV) is often detected and treatment initiated. The steps in HIV testing and the program requirements necessary to ensure a quality care system are explained in this chapter. Early detection of AIDS-indicator diseases that signal progression of HIV infection are investigated, and areas of disease and symptom management are highlighted. With convincing data justifying early intervention in HIV infection, these two components of the total care needs of the patient with HIV infection and AIDS are extremely important.

NATURE OF THE ACQUIRED IMMUNODEFICIENCY SYNDROME

The acquired immunodeficiency syndrome (AIDS) was first defined in 1981 as the appearance of certain infections and cancers in previously healthy individuals without obvious underlying reasons for illness. This was before the discovery of human immunodeficiency virus (HIV), the cause of AIDS. AIDS was redefined in 1985 to account for the results of tests for HIV. Its definition was revised again in 1987 to include broader manifestations of HIV illness and to provide guidance for presumptive diagnoses. Generally, the Centers for Disease Control (CDC) define

---

The author gratefully acknowledges Kay Baxter for typing and James M. Casey for editorial reviews.

AIDS as an illness characterized by one or more opportunistic diseases (infections and cancers) that are moderately predictive of a T-lymphocyte–mediated immune defect. Opportunistic illnesses occur without known causes other than HIV infection. Unlike other illnesses, AIDS is a life-long illness with certain marker diseases recurring continuously or remaining constantly present. The patient then receives life-long care, much of which is provided on an outpatient basis. Testing for HIV enables the diagnosis to be established and treatment begun.

HIV ANTIBODY COUNSELING AND TESTING

Reason for Initiation of Testing

Counseling and testing of those individuals at risk for HIV infection is crucial in prevention and early detection of disease and initiation of medical intervention. The primary roles of HIV testing are to help uninfected individuals initiate and sustain behavioral changes to reduce their risk of infection and to help infected individuals avoid infecting others (CDC 1987). Whatever the reason for initiation of counseling and testing, the education perspective should not be overlooked in the care continuum (Becker and Joseph 1988; Glasel 1988; Fischl 1988; De Jarlais and Friedman 1988).

The following case study reflects the time and complexity that the steps of HIV testing add to a diagnosis. This is far from a routine test (Table 11-1).

> J.B., a 37-year-old Gay man, was recently diagnosed with testicular cancer. Because of known risk behaviors and a current cancer diagnosis, his physician requested HIV testing. HIV results could assist his physician in making treatment decisions and in determining how an underlying HIV infection might alter the course of the disease and response to therapeutics. Counseling focused on weighing the risks of disclosure of confidential data and the patient's anxiety about negative repercussions against the oncologist's desire to establish clarity about factors that influenced the patient's current health and illness. The risk reduction component was thoroughly addressed.

Types of Testing and Significance of Results

There are three major approaches to HIV infection detection: (1) analysis of viral cultures, (2) detection of serum antigens, and (3) detection of viral antibodies. The first two are used primarily in research settings and are costly in terms of staffpower and finances. Antibody testing by means of enzyme-linked immunosorbent assay (ELISA) and Western blot studies is the mainstay of detection today

Table 11-1 Common Reasons for the Initiation of HIV Counseling and Testing

Motivating Factor	Rationale
Behavior change	Guide decision making in the following areas: • safer sexual practices • safer drug use/needle sharing practices • entry into drug-free life • pregnancy termination • closely supervised prenatal and postnatal care • use of birth control • avoidance of breast feeding • avoidance of active virus vaccination • initiation of medical treatment for HIV and its clinical consequences
Anxiety reduction	Alleviate anxiety or uncertainty: • confirm a preconceived negative test • confirm a preconceived positive test • confront reality • ease an existential or interpersonal crisis
Diagnostic tool	Establish a need for medical care: • support a medical diagnosis in patients whose symptoms suggest an underlying HIV infection • confirm an AIDS diagnosis
Epidemiologic data	Provide data on HIV prevalence in certain subgroups of the population
Societal pressures or legislation	Enhance public health concerns and support gatekeeping purposes: • Department of Defense recruits and active duty personnel • ROTC candidates • immigrants • federal prisoners • licensed prostitutes

[National Institutes of Health (NIH) 1986]. A positive test is a repeatedly reactive blood sample that contains antibodies. This is determined with ELISA and an additional, more specific test (such as the Western blot). The significance of test results is summarized in Exhibit 11-1 (NIH 1986; McMahon 1988; Sandler, Dodd, and Fang 1988; Allen 1988). Because the virus can remain undetected in macrophages or in the infected T cells for years, however, these test results are not conclusive. Other tests, such as polymerase chain reaction and antigen testing are currently under investigation (J.W. Gold, personal communication 1989). These

Exhibit 11-1 Significance of HIV Antibody Test Results

Positive

- The individual is infected with HIV
- Most individuals infected with retroviruses such as HIV are infected for life
- All seropositive persons are considered infectious to others by blood and body fluid transmission
- HIV seropositivity is not synonymous with having AIDS
- It is not yet possible totally to prevent progression of illness from asymptomatic to AIDS; it is known that progression can be slowed, however
- It is not yet possible to identify with certainty which asymptomatic individuals will progress to AIDS

Negative

- No HIV antibodies were found
- The individual is in most cases uninfected
- The individual is not yet mounting antibodies but may still be infected
- The immune system may have declined to the extent that antibody formation is no longer possible

Inconclusive

- HIV infection is in its early stages
- Cross-reactivity to another retrovirus may be obscuring results
- ELISA may be positive but Western blot test may be negative or developing (i.e., bands are not yet positive)

tests may detect infection earlier than is currently possible (Grady 1988; McMahon 1988; Sandler, Dodd, and Fang 1988; Allen 1988).

Counseling Regarding HIV Infection

Counseling is a process through which a professional attempts to help a client in decision making and problem solving. Patient education and counseling form the basis of pretest HIV sessions. The required knowledge base (Miller 1987) and the necessary skills of the nurse counselor are summarized in Exhibit 11-2. Exhibit 11-3 outlines standard content areas included in these HIV counseling sessions (Matuszak et al. 1987; McMahon 1988).

Crucial Ambulatory Care Nursing Services 177

Exhibit 11-2 Knowledge Base and Skills of the Nurse HIV Counselor

---

Knowledge base

- Knowledge of HIV, immunopathogenesis, spectrum of infection, and clinical consequences
- Familiarity with standard care approaches, availability of clinical research trials, and referral resources
- Comprehension of applicable legal statutes in public health and confidentiality legislations
- Awareness of the potential psychosocial, spiritual, and legal ramifications of HIV and HIV testing
- Comfort with a wide range of lifestyles, substance abuse, sexual orientations, age-appropriate issues, and ethnic/cultural/economic influences

Skills

- Insight about countertransference issues
- Ability to discuss sexuality, substance abuse, health behaviors, pregnancy, and other emotionally laden topics in a culturally sensitive, tactful, nonjudgmental manner
- Ability to keep updated in this changing field
- Available time and supervision for providing this service
- Ability to decide when to refer to a specialist

Sample Programs of Antibody Testing in Ambulatory Care

If anonymous testing is an option, the patient is referred to an anonymous test site or to a private physician's office that has anonymous testing facility contacts.

In an ambulatory care setting, confidential counseling is done by nurses who augment the pretest education provided by the ordering attending physicians. These nurses establish a collaborative practice with medical, social work, and psychiatric services and undergo significant continuing education and supervised practice. Posttest results are given to the patient by the attending physician with the nurse providing counseling about the results. Counseling is tailored to the individual patient's needs (Van Devanter 1987; Christ et al. 1988).

EARLY DETECTION OF AIDS-RELATED DISEASE

Evidence of Progression

During clinic visits, the patient is monitored for progression of HIV infection (Table 11-2). Specific determinants are evaluated. Signs indicative of progression

Exhibit 11-3 Standard Content of Pre–HIV Antibody Test Counseling

1. Review of test
   - Significance of positive, negative, inconclusive results
   - Procedures for testing
   - Time frame for availability of results
2. Risk reduction education and counseling
   - Identification of risk factors
   - Education regarding:
     safe and safer sex practices
     safe drug use/needle sharing practices
     birth control measures; pregnancy continuation or termination decision making
     general health promotion behaviors
     transmission of HIV and illness spectrum
   - Counseling regarding:
     suitability of using risk reduction measures
     compliance issues, restraints, stressors, detractions, problematic areas
     available resources in agency or community; referrals as necessary
3. Confidentiality review
   - Legal statutes
   - Contact notification
   - Review of agency's confidentiality procedures
4. Potential psychologic, emotional, medical, existential, legal, social consequences of negative or positive results and of testing itself
   - Suicidal ideation
   - Relationship instability or crisis
   - Establishing contact with a primary care practitioner
   - Discrimination, stigmatization
   - Insurance difficulties
5. Availability of anonymous testing
   - Useful when seeking testing for anxiety reduction or personal behavior change
   - Not useful for times when result must be made known to others (e.g., medical team, Immigration Service official notification)
6. Availability of referrals, follow-up care
7. Planning for support while awaiting test results
8. When informed consent is obtained, appointment is made for notification of results in person; if more time is needed, second appointment is made for continued discussion of issues

of disease include decreasing percentage of T-helper cells; absolute number of T lymphocytes less than 200; development of persistent generalized lymphadenopathy (PGL) or the constitutional signs of weight loss, fever, fatigue, night sweats, and diarrhea; and the development of orofacial herpes zoster, oral thrush, or oral hairy leukoplakia. Preventive medications such as zidovudine (AZT) and aerosolized pentamidine or trimethoprim-sulfamethoxazole are initiated.

Table 11-2 CDC Classification: Spectrum of HIV Infection

Group	Category	Description
I	Acute infection	Mononucleosislike ailment Meningitis may occur Seroconversion to HIV antibody positive signals that infection has occurred
II	Asymptomatic infection	No detectable evidence of HIV infection except laboratory data (i.e., culture, antibodies)
III	Persistent generalized lymphadenopathy (PGL)	Palpable lymphadenopathy $\geq$ 1 cm at two or more extrainguinal sites; laboratory evidence of HIV infection
IV	Other disease:	Patients are subclassified into subgroups (A–E) without respect to the presence or absence of PGL:
	subgroup A*	constitutional disease (i.e., fever, weight loss, diarrhea) with evidence of HIV infection
	subgroup B	neurologic disease
	subgroup C	secondary infectious disease
	subgroup D	secondary cancers
	subgroup E	other conditions (i.e., clinical disease complicated by HIV infection)

*The term AIDS-related complex (ARC) is frequently used to denote subgroup A and, less commonly, group III.

Source: Adapted from *MMWR*, Vol. 35, p. 335, 1986.

AIDS Indicator Diseases

There are common, specific AIDS indicator diseases for which the patient is evaluated.

Opportunistic Infections

Opportunistic infections are the major identifiable cause of morbidity and mortality in AIDS patients. In an autopsy series, it was established that 90% of the fatalities were caused by opportunistic infections (Kovacs and Masur 1988; Macher et al. 1988). Therefore, extensive effort should be targeted to early detection and intervention of AIDS-related opportunistic infections.

The infections that AIDS patients develop reflect the specific immune defects caused by HIV, geographic location, age range, lifestyle, and habits of living. The illnesses are caused by a diverse group of infectious agents that are rarely single in occurrence and rarely curable. They are severe and require prolonged treatment. Although HIV can be transmitted from human to human, most AIDS-related opportunistic infections cannot be transmitted this way (McMahon and Sutterer 1988).

Protozoal opportunistic infections. Pneumocystis carinii pneumonia (PCP) is the initial manifestation of AIDS in 65% of those diagnosed (Kovacs and Masur 1988). Contrary to the typical picture of initial clinical manifestation in cancer patients as acute respiratory distress, PCP in AIDS patients develops in an indolent manner. Patients develop fever, exercise intolerance, a dry cough, and weakness over time. Early detection improves survival. Also, patients on PCP-suppressive or prevention regimens as well as AZT have mild courses of this infection.

Diagnosis is made by means of transbronchial lavage or sputum induction. Most PCP patients require hospitalization for intravenous therapy with pentamidine or trimethoprim-sulfamethoxazole for 10 to 21 days. Some patients, because of their less severe medical status, strong self-care ability, insurance coverage for home care nurses, and desire, are able to be treated at home. PCP recurs frequently, with most AIDS patients having another PCP episode within 7 months of the first. Continued intensive effort is directed at preventing or suppressing PCP (Table 11-3) (McMahon and Coyne 1989).

Cryptosporidiosis is detected in about 4% of AIDS patients (Kovacs and Masur 1988). The first human case was noted in 1976 and involved an immunocompetent veterinarian. In non-AIDS patients, it causes a self-limiting diarrheal episode. In AIDS patients, the diarrhea can be crippling (1 to 20 L/day). Medical intervention remains unsuccessful (Table 11-3) (McMahon and Coyne 1989, p. 296).

Toxoplasma gondii infection is common in the adult population, with 20% to 90% of healthy individuals demonstrating infection (Kovacs and Masur 1988). In the immunocompetent individual, the infection is silent. In AIDS patients, encephalitis develops over several weeks with symptoms that include headache, seizures, personality changes, altered mental status, and hemiparesis. The primary host of *T. gondii* is the cat; most infections in AIDS patients are reactivations of previous disease, however. The indicators or activators of this recurrence are unknown.

Toxoplasmosis is presumptively diagnosed by initiating a therapeutic trial of pyrimethamine and sulfadiazine. If the patient responds to treatment (as demonstrated by improved lesions and decreased symptoms), toxoplasmosis is assumed. If a definitive diagnosis is necessary, a brain biopsy is performed. Treatment is largely successful, but adverse effects (e.g., neutropenia, rash, and fever) may require cessation of treatment with ensuing relapse.

Bacterial opportunistic infections. Mycobacterium tuberculosis is an airborne organism; increasing numbers of tuberculosis (TB) cases are being reported in Africa, the Caribbean islands, and New York City's homeless population, presumably as a result of underlying HIV infection (Kovacs and Masur 1988). Unlike normal TB, AIDS TB is a disseminated form involving extrapulmonary sites. Clinical presentation is similar to that of normal TB in that patients demonstrate

Table 11-3 Symptom Treatment and Highlights of Nursing Care for PCP, Cryptosporidiosis, and Ulcerative Kaposi's Sarcoma (KS)

Common Symptoms	Occurrence	Nursing Care Highlights
PCP Dry, nonproductive cough; fever; shortness of breath; exercise intolerance; chills; chest pain; sputum production	Patients whose T-cell counts are less than 400 are most at risk for PCP. Patients with AIDS or ARC who are not taking PCP prophylaxis are at higher risk for the development of PCP. PCP recurs frequently.	Monitor patients closely for initial symptoms because early detection improves survival. Assist patient with administration of PCP prophylactic agents and ensure that patient is getting maximum benefit from drug therapy. Triage patient to urgent care for early diagnosis and intervention if PCP is suspected.
Cryptosporidiosis Diarrhea (1–17 L/day), abdominal pain, nausea, fever, anorexia, vomiting, weakness	30%–60% of AIDS patients develop diarrhea, which may not be attributable to one cause. Approximately 4% of AIDS patients develop this illness. Effective treatment has yet to be established.	Procure a containment system for profuse diarrhea. Suggestions include liners for underpants, adult diapers, soft Foley catheter in rectum, ostomy supplies. Provide nutrition fortification. Institute skin cleansing and protection regimen. Maintain and teach strict enteric precautions. Monitor fluid and electrolyte balance. Augment home care support or arrange for institutionalization.
Ulcerative KS Open, deep, foul-smelling lesions on lower extremities at end stage of illness	Prevention of suprainfection or containment of drainage are the major challenges and goals.	Maintain blood and body fluid precautions. Cover draining fluids with absorbent material; change coverings frequently. Cleanse wounds with potassium permanganate soaks and normal saline rinses if feasible. Consult with dermatologist about other cleansing regimens. Institute air-freshener, air-purifier interventions (vinegar, baking soda, trash odor agent) as needed.

weight loss, anorexia, fatigue, afternoon fevers, and night sweats. Diagnostically, the tuberculin skin test is unreliable because AIDS patients are unable to mount the immune response to demonstrate a positive reaction on the anergy panel. Sputum samples and cultures are relied upon to detect acid-fast bacilli. Patients respond well to the routine anti-TB drug regimens, but treatment may need to be maintained indefinitely because of relapse.

Mycobacterium avium-intracellulare infection occurs frequently in North American AIDS patients (Kovacs and Masur 1988). It manifests in a disseminated form causing fever, fatigue, weight loss, tremors, and a wide variety of gastrointestinal symptoms as well as hepatosplenomegaly. It is detected in 40% to 60% of patients. Medical treatment is largely unsuccessful. It is noncommunicable and acquired from the environment.

Fungal opportunistic infections. Although oral candidiasis is found in almost all AIDS patients and those HIV-infected patients who are experiencing progression of disease, candidiasis of the bronchi, lungs, trachea, or esophagus also indicates an AIDS diagnosis (CDC 1986). *Candida albicans*, the etiologic organism, is ubiquitous and can colonize where skin and mucous membranes are damaged. Unlike cancer patients, AIDS patients rarely develop systemic infections. If they do, they usually occur in relation to an indwelling vascular device. Diagnosis is made by means of microscopy or physical examination. Oral antifungal agents are instituted as well as ketoconazole or amphotericin B if needed. If there is no response, the diagnosis is evaluated by means of microscopy or biopsy. Treatment is usually life long because the HIV-induced cell-mediated immunity defect is not yet reversible and the condition recurs when therapy is stopped. A response to treatment is usually seen within 7 days.

Cryptococcus neoformans infection occurs in 7% of AIDS patients, with meningitis being the most common clinical presentation (Kovacs and Masur 1988). Symptoms develop subtly, with fever and headache being the most common. Other symptoms are nausea and vomiting, focal neurologic abnormalities, papilledema, and seizures. Extraneural disease is likely and includes skin lesions, pneumonitis, pericarditis with cardiac tamponade, arthritis, retinitis, pleural effusion, and abdominal pain due to peritonitis. *C. neoformans* has been identified in many organs. The organism is ubiquitous in nature, the chief vector being the pigeon. Transmission is airborne. The disease can also occur in normal hosts.

Diagnosis may depend on cultures or histopathology. Serum cryptococcal antigen is usually positive in patients with disseminated disease, however. Patients who are antigen or culture positive are routinely started on amphotericin B with or without flucytosine because they are at such high risk for infection. Fluconazole is now available for patients.

Histoplasma capsulatum is endemic in the central and southern United States. Most AIDS patients with histoplasmosis are from this region, Puerto Rico, or Central or South America (Kovacs and Masur 1988). Histoplasmosis can occur in immunocompetent patients but is usually asymptomatic or causes a limited pulmonary infection. In AIDS patients the clinical manifestations are a nonspecific disseminated disease that includes fevers, chills, sweats, weight loss, nausea, vomiting, and diarrhea. Other signs and symptoms commonly observed include pneumonitis, skin lesions, lymphadenopathy, leukopenia, thrombocytopenia, and liver dysfunction. Diagnosis is established by culture, histopathology, or serology. Blood and bone marrow cultures are routinely positive. Amphotericin B therapy is initiated, but the relapse rate is high after therapy is stopped. Continued suppressive therapy with low-dose amphotericin B at home or in the ambulatory care center or with ketoconazole is maintained.

Viral opportunistic infections. Herpes simplex infection is a frequent disease in HIV-infected patients. It may present as the patient's HIV infection is progressing, thus indicating further immunosuppression, or it can occur later, after the AIDS diagnosis is established. Because most adults have been previously infected with herpes simplex virus, it is commonly a reactivated infection in AIDS patients. It is transmitted by direct contact with infected secretions. Patients may also spread the virus to other areas of their bodies by their fingers. Disseminated herpes simplex infection has not been reported with HIV.

Genital or perianal ulcerations are the most common manifestations. Diagnosis is made by smears or culture of the lesion. Symptoms include itching, burning, pain, hematochezia, fever, or discharge. Viral cultures easily establish the diagnosis. Patients not responding to topical acyclovir require intravenous therapy. Long-term, oral, suppressive treatment may be required. Herpes simplex infection can also cause encephalitis, pneumonia, and esophagitis (Kocher and Roberts 1989).

Herpes zoster infection signals progression of disease and indicates worsening immunosuppression in an HIV-infected patient (Kovacs and Masur 1988). Herpes zoster is the etiologic agent of chicken pox and dermatomal zoster (shingles). It can also cause disseminated disease in HIV-infected patients. Clinical manifestations include herpes zoster ophthalmicus, head and neck zoster, and painful, severe lesions at other dermatomes, with disseminated zoster appearing cutaneously on the hands and feet. Diagnosis is made by clinical observations or by culture and biopsy. Acyclovir is administered intravenously as treatment, and the drug may be continued by mouth as suppressive therapy because of relapses. Patients may require hospitalization for intravenous drug therapy and strict isolation until lesions are crusted over. Other persons who have not had chicken pox and are therefore not immune need to avoid contact with these patients.

Cytomegalovirus (CMV) infection is common, with 45% to 80% of the general population being infected. It can be transmitted sexually, by blood, or congenitally. Asymptomatic HIV-negative persons can shed CMV. In AIDS, it is unclear in many clinical patient situations what role CMV is playing. It is the most common opportunistic pathogen noted at autopsy, however, and is frequently detected in AIDS patients (Kovacs and Masur 1988). The three clearly identified pathologies by which CMV heralds disease include retinochoroiditis, enteritis, and pneumonitis.

CMV causes more than 95% of the retinochoroiditis seen in AIDS. Diagnosis is established by an ophthalmologist, with the patient noticing blurred vision or decreased visual acuity. The infection progresses at a variable rate and can lead to blindness. Treatment with gancyclovir is effective, but the adverse effect of neutropenia can develop (Kocher and Roberts 1989). In that case, treatment may have to be stopped. Colony-stimulating factors are being investigated as a means to prevent neutropenia. Relapse is common, so that maintenance suppressive therapy is usually life long. Other routes (oral and intravitreous) and other agents (e.g., Foscarnet) are under investigation as possible therapies.

CMV colitis involves cramps, frequency of stools, watery or bloody diarrhea, or rectal discharge. Intestinal perforation or hemorrhage can occur. Biopsy or microscopy detects the presence of CMV inclusion bodies on histopathologic examination. Gancyclovir therapy is indicated.

CMV pneumonitis is difficult to diagnose. The cause of pulmonary dysfunction is difficult to establish. Gancyclovir therapy is not clearly effective in this manifestation of CMV disease.

Progressive multifocal leukoencephalopathy is a central nervous system disorder seen primarily in immunocompromised patients. The causative agent is generally identified as a papovavirus called the JC virus. Impaired cell-mediated immunity allows the usually nonpathogenic JC virus to invade the brain and to cause destruction. Although the virus is slow growing the patient exhibits rapid deterioration, with death resulting within 6 months of infection. The primary clinical manifestation is a progressive, slow decline in mental acuity. Symptoms may include limb weakness, headaches, tremors in the extremities, lack of coordination and balance, decreased visual acuity, and urinary incontinence. Neurologic symptoms may be present: slurred speech, wide-based gait, impaired concentration, and dementia. A diagnosis is established definitely by means of a brain biopsy or presumptively by computed tomography (CT), magnetic resonance imaging, or neurologic examination.

Epstein-Barr virus (EBV) has been isolated from the throat washings of more than 90% of AIDS patients (Kovacs and Masur 1988). It has been found in oral hairy leukoplakia along with papilloma virus and is implicated in the development of lymphoid interstitial pneumonitis in children with AIDS and of Burkitt-like lymphomas in adults and children with AIDS. It is unclear what role EBV plays in the symptomatology in AIDS, and there is no effective treatment.

Neurologic Disease

In the differential diagnosis of neurologic disease in AIDS patients, many illnesses or disorders need to be considered. They include opportunistic infections (particularly toxoplasmosis, cryptococcosis, and CMV), opportunistic cancers [primary central nervous system (P-CNS) lymphoma and malignant lymphoma], and other CNS disorders (cerebrovascular and metabolic diseases). All these can occur in AIDS patients. Baseline and continual neurologic assessments are crucial.

AIDS dementia complex (ADC) is the most prominent neurologic complication in AIDS (Brew, Rosenblum, and Price 1988). It is caused by the direct action of HIV in the brain; the patient is infected but asymptomatic from early in the course of HIV infection. It is presumed that the CNS is infected at the time of the initial infection. The infection usually remains asymptomatic until the patient is manifesting AIDS-related complex or AIDS. Early symptoms are impaired concentration and mental slowing. Besides cognitive changes, motor and behavioral symptoms develop: leg weakness, incoordination, apathy, social withdrawal, and depressionlike features. ADC can progress in an uneven course or wax and wane. Progression of ADC includes severe cognitive deficits: psychomotor slowing, global dementia, disinhibition, unawareness of illness, and disorientation. In end-stage patients, paralysis, hemiparesis, incontinence, and mutism can occur.

ADC needs to be distinguished from other neurologic phenomena. The HIV infection is detected and the HIV illness staged. A neurologic history complete with imaging studies and diagnostic procedures is performed. Neuropsychiatric testing is also indicated. The most sensitive tests include performance under time pressure, problem solving, visual scanning, visual-motor integration, and alteration between two performance rules or stimulus sets (Brew, Rosenblum, and Price 1988). These tests are more reliable and sensitive than the short mental status examination; but they do not stand alone in diagnostic value. Findings are integrated with clinical judgment and the total neurologic history.

Research continues on the use of AZT for ADC (Schmitt et al. 1988). Anecdotal reports and initial studies indicate improved cognition with a reversible component. Amitriptyline has alleviated the painful peripheral neuropathy in many patients. Exhibit 11-4 and Table 11-4 outline the severity of neurologic complications and suggested nursing interventions (McMahon and Coyne 1989).

AIDS-Related Malignancies

There are three types of malignancies associated with AIDS: Kaposi's sarcoma (KS), P-CNS lymphoma, and non-Hodgkin's lymphoma. They differ from non–AIDS-related cancers in a few ways: abnormal sites at presentation, an unusual pattern of spread, involvement of extranodal sites, and a marked lack of lasting response to chemotherapies. Additionally, the patient's course may be complicated by other concurrent HIV illnesses or prolonged side effects from treatment.

KS is the most common malignancy seen in AIDS (Krigel and Friedman-Kien 1988). Among AIDS patients, KS is usually seen in homosexual men and is rarely seen in women, children, and heterosexual men. In 1981, 30% of all AIDS pa-

Exhibit 11-4 Impact of Neuropsychiatric AIDS Complications

Contributes to patient's fear
Contributes to frustration, feelings of powerlessness
Increases risk of discrimination, including protective legal and social actions
Increases resource utilization
Adds burden to family's and care providers' responsibilities
Decreases interpersonal communication
Decreases patient safety
Decreases patient's ability to be compliant and responsible
Decreases functional abilities
    occupational ability
    community activities
    citizen responsibilities
    personal: activities of daily living and household safety
    social relationships
    leisure activities

---

tients had KS; that percentage has decreased to 10%. Reasons for this decrease are unclear but may include decreased use of "poppers" and the adoption of safer sex practices by Gay men.

KS, which is cancer of the lymphatic cell wall, can cause both structural and functional damage. Edema may result from lymphatic obstruction, or respiratory distress can occur as a result of bronchial blockage. It is usually not a painful condition unless the lesions are impinging on an organ or nerve. Lesions can develop on any skin surface and have various shapes, sizes, and colors. They can be red-brown to red and dark purple to violet. In advanced stages, the lesions can coalesce to form one large plaque. The most common extracutaneous sites are the gastrointestinal tract, lymph nodes, and lungs (Exhibit 11-5).

Diagnosis is established by biopsy. Treatment with interferon, radiation therapy, or chemotherapy may be indicated. Patients with KS generally live longer than other AIDS patients provided that they do not develop major opportunistic infections (see Table 11-3).

Non-Hodgkin's lymphoma was added to the case definition of AIDS in 1985. Lymphomas are primarily B-cell tumors of high-grade pathologic type such as small noncleaved lymphoma and Burkitt-like lymphoma (Levine 1988). B classification symptoms are commonly present, eg, fever, malaise, and sweating. The earliest sign is usually a unilateral enlarged cervical lymph node. As the disease progresses it spreads through lymphatic channels to other lymph nodes and to organ systems, including the spleen, liver, gastrointestinal tract, skin, lungs, CNS (leptomeningeal disease, not masses), and bone marrow. Diagnosis is made by means of tissue biopsy, and chemotherapy is initiated with curative intent. The tumor is responsive to chemotherapy because of its doubling time. After a rapid

Table 11-4 Critical Nursing Interventions in ADC Patients

Goal	Action
Maximize support network	1. Seek opportunities for enhanced socialization and discuss with patient. Suggestions include day care, recreation, leisure, phone calls, religious groups, community activities. 2. Provide ongoing spiritual and psychologic support in conjunction with managed care. 3. Refer to agency that provides "buddy" system. 4. Suggest home care training for nonprofessional care partners. This is available from the American Red Cross. 5. Call "team meeting" of friends and family if needed to update needs inventory and to elicit more help.
Enhance safety	1. Review prescriptions. Suggest pill box alarms, checklists, calendars. 2. Refer for home health services or institution care as indicated. 3. Consult with physical therapy if leg weakness is present. Obtain assistive devices. 4. Ensure uncluttered, safety-enhanced physical environment.
Reorient schedule to slower pace	1. Remind health team members to "take it slow." 2. Model thorough patient interactions with the ADC client. 3. Provide "to do" list or audiotape reminders. 4. Alert neurologist or physician to patient's dementia.
Prepare for future	1. Discuss plans and orientation to do not resuscitate orders, medical power of attorney, and wills. 2. Alert patient's social network that they will need to become increasingly more involved if dementia worsens. 3. Support respite care options. 4. Review on a regular basis the toll this illness is taking and revise plan accordingly.

remission is achieved, however, severe neutropenia may delay subsequent treatments. Additionally, if the patient has had a prior opportunistic infection, palliation or control is the realistic goal.

One risk factor for the development of lymphoma has been established clearly: HIV-infected patients with PGL have a greater risk. On the basis of incidence rates in America age-adjusted for lymphoma, patients with PGL have 850 times the expected rate of lymphoma development (Levine 1988).

P-CNS lymphoma has been described in patients with congenital or acquired immunodeficiency illnesses (Levine 1988). Initial signs and symptoms at presentation include headache, short-term memory loss, seizure disorder, cranial nerve palsies, altered mental status, and personality change. P-CNS lymphoma needs to be differentiated from other space-occupying brain masses, especially toxoplas-

Exhibit 11-5 Sites of KS in AIDS Patients

Skin	Lungs*
Buccal mucosa	Liver
Hard and soft palate	Pancreas
Lips	Adrenal glands
Gums	Spleen
Tongue	Epididymis
Tonsils	Testis
Conjunctiva	Heart
Sclera	Gallbladder
Lymph nodes*	Kidneys
Gastrointestinal tract* (includes esophagus, oropharynx, epiglottis, stomach, small and large intestine, appendix, rectum)	Brain† Bone marrow†

*Most common extracutaneous sites.
†Least common extracutaneous sites.

mosis. Diagnosis is established by a CT scan and brain biopsy. A delayed, double-dose contrast study may need to be performed. The P-CNS lymphoma space-occupying lesion is usually single and larger than 3 cm. It can develop in many localities, including basal ganglia, parietal lobe, frontal lobe, frontoparietal lobe, pons, and cerebellum. The cancer is somewhat radiation sensitive, and the prognosis is grave.

HIV and Other Malignancies

There have been numerous case reports about unusual courses or aggressive manifestations of solid tumors and Hodgkin's disease in HIV-infected or AIDS patients (Levine 1988). Currently, no epidemiologic data link the two; it is conceivable, however, that in the future, a correlation may be established. Other malignancies such as multiple myeloma, B-cell acute lymphocytic leukemia, T-lymphoblastic lymphoma, carcinoma of the anus, squamous cell cancer of the tongue, adenosquamous carcinoma of the lung, adenocarcinoma of the colon and pancreas, and testicular cancer have occurred. Some of these cancers are age appropriate for the 20- to 40-year age group, and lifestyle may play a role in others.

Wasting Syndrome

The unrelenting wasting syndrome or "Slim's disease" is a manifestation of AIDS in which the gastrointestinal symptoms predominate (Bartlett, Laughan, and Quinn 1988). Anorexia, nonbloody diarrhea, weight loss, and a change in taste are the major attributes. The disease is more common in Haiti and Africa than in America. Clinical trials investigating the therapeutic use of megestrol acetate have started. Although costly, total parenteral nutrition is being used in some cases. Limited studies report that patients remain in a negative nitrogen balance, which reflects a severe catabolic state. Aggressive efforts are made to fortify patients nutritionally early in the disease course.

CONCLUSION

In its position paper on AIDS, the Oncology Nursing Society urges its members to rise to the forefront of HIV-related care delivery (Halloran, Hughes, and Mayer 1988). Recognized needs in HIV-related care are HIV testing and counseling and early detection and treatment of illness. Other areas are also vastly important and overlap the areas mentioned: pharmaceuticals, substance abuse treatment programs, prevention education, various mental health services, prison care, respite care, hospice care, foster care, food and transportation services, health care professional preparation, social services, and case management. The New York City AIDS Task Force estimates that care of patients with AIDS or HIV infection will cost about $7 million over the next 5 years alone (New York City AIDS Task Force 1989).This figure does not cover the aforementioned services. It covers capital for construction of facilities; physician visits; care in acute, ambulatory, and skilled nursing facilities, health-related facilities; and housing. Ambulatory visits alone are projected to vary between $87.1 to $109.6 million per year. The consensus of New York City AIDS Task Force members is that care should be provided in a community-based setting whenever possible and incorporated into existing care delivery systems.

Two crucial components in the spectrum of HIV-related services have been outlined in this chapter. No longer should there be public debate about the utility of testing and early detection. Nurses need to be informed and share their understanding with their peers, patients, colleagues, and social network. AIDS nursing provides a real opportunity for personal fulfillment and comprehensive professional development for the oncology nurse. Because of its inherent nature, care for patients with AIDS broadens one's perspective and taxes one's skills and resources. We have the opportunity to be pioneers in the development of effective treatment.

STUDY QUESTIONS

1. How would you gain access to substance abuse programs for an HIV-infected patient at your facility? What patient advocacy work would you anticipate?

2. If your patient were to initiate a discussion about suicide, how would you respond? What interventions and exploratory discussions would you pursue?
3. You anticipate that your patient will be on his or her current regimen of maintenance treatment for life. What feelings does this provoke in you? How do you handle them currently? How do others?
4. Your patient is an HIV-infected woman who is 5 months pregnant. You are aware (and so is she) that the baby could develop AIDS. Identify the stressors in this situation. Discuss different approaches to the traditional nursing role of advocacy and teaching. What is the current medical knowledge base regarding the projected health of the baby?
5. Your patient develops AIDS dementia complex. What interventions would you apply? Provide case examples.
6. Your colleague asserts "Why bother treating them? They're going to die anyway." How do you respond? What attitudes and opinions do you presume your colleague to have? Do you agree? How is this situation different from cancer care? Are there historical insights or precedents to be explored?

REFERENCES

Allen, J. 1988. Screening and testing asymptomatic persons for HIV infection. In *AIDS: Etiology, diagnosis, treatment, and prevention*. 2nd ed., ed. V.T. DeVita, S. Hellman, and S.A. Rosenberg. Philadelphia: J.B. Lippincott Co.

Bartlett, J.G., B. Laughan, and T.C. Quinn. 1988. Gastrointestinal complications of AIDS. In *AIDS: Etiology, diagnosis, treatment, and prevention*. 2nd ed., ed. V.T. DeVita, S. Hellman, and S.A. Rosenberg. Philadelphia: J.B. Lippincott Co.

Becker, M.H., and J.G. Joseph. 1988. AIDS and behavioral change to reduce risk: A review. *American Journal of Public Health* 74:394–410.

Brew, B., M. Rosenblum, and R.W. Price. 1988. Central and peripheral nervous system complications of HIV infection and AIDS. In *AIDS: Etiology, diagnosis, treatment, and prevention*. 2nd ed., ed. V.T. DeVita, S. Hellman, and S.A. Rosenberg. Philadelphia: J.B. Lippincott Co.

Centers for Disease Control. 1986. Classification system for human T-lymphotropic virus type III/lymphadenopathy—Associated virus infections. *Morbidity and Mortality Weekly Report* 35:334.

Centers for Disease Control. 1987. Public health guidelines for counseling and testing to prevent HIV infection and AIDS. *Morbidity and Mortality Weekly Report* 36:509.

Christ, G.H., K. Siegel, and R.T. Moynihan. 1988. Psychosocial issues: Prevention and treatment. In *AIDS: Etiology, diagnosis, treatment, and prevention*. 2nd ed., ed. V.T. DeVita, S. Hellman, and S.A. Rosenberg. Philadelphia: J.B. Lippincott Co.

De Jarlais, D.C., and S.R. Friedman. 1988. Transmission of human immunodeficiency virus among intravenous drug users. In *AIDS: Etiology, diagnosis, treatment, and prevention*. 2nd ed., ed. V.T. DeVita, S. Hellman, and S.A. Rosenberg. Philadelphia: J.B. Lippincott Co.

Fischl, M.A. 1988. Prevention of transmission of AIDS during sexual intercourse. In *AIDS: Etiology, diagnosis, treatment, and prevention*. 2nd ed., ed. V.T. DeVita, S. Hellman, and S.A. Rosenberg. Philadelphia: J.B. Lippincott Co.

Glasel, M. 1988. High-risk sexual practices in the transmission of AIDS. In *AIDS: Etiology, diagnosis, treatment, and prevention*. 2nd ed., ed. V.T. DeVita, S. Hellman, and S.A. Rosenberg. Philadelphia: J.B. Lippincott Co.

Grady, C. 1988. HIV: Epidemiology, immunopathogenesis, and clinical course. *Nursing Clinics of North America* 23:683–96.

Halloran, J., A. Hughes, and D.K. Mayer. 1988. Oncology Nursing Society position paper on HIV-related issues. *Oncology Nursing Forum* 15:206–17.

Kocher, J., and R.B. Roberts. 1989. Treatment of opportunistic infections in patients with AIDS. In *AIDS and infections of homosexual men*. 2nd ed., ed. P. Ma and D. Armstrong. Boston: Butterworths.

Kovacs, J.A., and H. Masur. 1988. Opportunistic infections. In *AIDS: Etiology, diagnosis, treatment, and prevention*. 2nd ed., ed. V.T. DeVita, S. Hellman, and S.A. Rosenberg. Philadelphia: J.B. Lippincott Co.

Krigel, R.L., and A.E. Friedman-Kien. 1988. Kaposi's sarcoma. In *AIDS: Etiology, diagnosis, treatment, and prevention*. 2nd ed., ed. V.T. DeVita, S. Hellman, and S.A. Rosenberg. Philadelphia: J.B. Lippincott Co.

Levine, A.M. 1988. Reactive and neoplastic lymphoproliferative disorders and other miscellaneous cancers associated with HIV infections. In *AIDS: Etiology, diagnosis, treatment, and prevention*. 2nd ed., ed. V.T. DeVita, S. Hellman, and S.A. Rosenberg. Philadelphia: J.B. Lippincott Co.

Macher, A.M., M.L. De Vinatea, P. Angritt, S.M. Tuur, and C.M. Reichert. 1988. Pathologic features of patients infected with human immunodeficiency virus. In *AIDS: Etiology, diagnosis, treatment, and prevention*. 2nd ed., ed. V.T. DeVita, S. Hellman, and S.A. Rosenberg. Philadelphia: J.B. Lippincott Co.

Matuszak, D.L., E. Israel, J.T. Horman, et al. 1987. HIV antibody testing. *Maryland Medical Journal* 36:40–43.

McMahon, K. 1988. The integration of HIV testing and counseling into nursing practice. *Nursing Clinics of North America* 24:803–21.

McMahon, K., and N. Coyne. 1989. Symptom management in patients with AIDS. *Seminars in Oncology Nursing* 25:289–301.

McMahon, K., and M.G. Sutterer. 1988. Safety precautions and hospital practices in dealing with seropositive individuals. In *AIDS: Etiology, diagnosis, treatment, and prevention*. 2nd ed., ed. V.T. DeVita, S. Hellman, and S.A. Rosenberg. Philadelphia: J.B. Lippincott Co.

Miller, D. 1987. ABC of AIDS counseling. *British Medical Journal* 294:1671–74.

National Institutes of Health. 1986. Consensus development conference statement: The impact of routine HTLV-III antibody testing on public health. Washington, D.C.: Government Printing Office.

New York City AIDS Task Force. 1989. *The report*. New York: New York City Department of Health.

Sandler, S.G., R.Y. Dodd, and C.T. Fang. 1988. Diagnostic tests for HIV infection: Serology. In *AIDS: Etiology, diagnosis, treatment, and prevention*. 2nd ed., ed. V.T. DeVita, S. Hellman, and S.A. Rosenberg. Philadelphia: J.B. Lippincott Co.

Schmitt, F.A., J.W. Bigley, R. McKinnis, M.E. Scarola, R.M. Shipton, and C. Tendler. 1988. Neuropsychological outcome of zidovudine (AZT) treatment of patients with AIDS and AIDS-related complex. *New England Journal of Medicine* 319:1574–78.

Van Devanter, N.L., J.A.B. Grisaffi, and M. Steilen. 1987. Counseling HIV antibody positive blood donors. *American Journal of Nursing* 87:1027–30.

Chapter 12

Acquired Immunodeficiency Syndrome in Infants, Children, and Adolescents

Margaret L. Fracaro

> The incidence of acquired immunodeficiency syndrome (AIDS) in the pediatric population is increasing significantly. As the number of children with AIDS increases, so too does the need for nurses to provide comprehensive and compassionate care to them and their families. Early recognition and treatment of infection with human immunodeficiency virus is crucial for maintaining optimum health in these patients. Because there is no cure for AIDS, efforts should focus on preventive and restorative therapeutic interventions. Nurses are instrumental in the planning, initiation, monitoring, and evaluation of the various programs of care. The nurse is also a vital resource for the community and can provide current and rational public health information and education to the community.

Acquired immunodeficiency syndrome (AIDS) and infection with human immunodeficiency virus (HIV) in the pediatric population have become major concerns among medical, nursing, and public health professionals. Pediatric HIV infection now ranks among the most common fatal congenitally acquired infections in the United States. Complex issues arise whenever the diagnosis of AIDS is determined. These range from the impact of various stages of the illness on the child to the ability of the parents to cope with the stresses of the disease. Often the parents themselves may be infected with HIV or ill with AIDS. Frequently the diagnosis of HIV infection in the child may be the first indication that the mother or other household members are infected. A family that is fragmented by this illness may not have the medical or psychosocial support systems in place to cope appropriately or effectively. In addition, intravenous drug use, poverty, and homelessness further isolate the child and family from society.

This illness produces intense feelings of guilt, anger, remorse, fear, and isolation that can diminish compliance with programs of care and long-term follow-up. These are some of the barriers that must be overcome to provide a cohesive program of care.

EPIDEMIOLOGY

The incidence of AIDS in the pediatric population is increasing at an alarming rate: 85,590 cases of AIDS were reported to the Centers for Disease Control (CDC) from June 1981 to February 1989. Of the reported cases, 1,400 (1.6%) were children younger than 13 years of age who met the AIDS case definition (New York City Department of Health 1989; CDC 1989). The number of pediatric AIDS cases has tripled since 1986. By 1991, it is projected that there will be 10,000 to 20,000 HIV-infected children in the United States alone (Oleske 1988). Of the pediatric AIDS cases reported to the CDC, 50% were patients diagnosed as having AIDS during the first year of life, 83% by 3 years of age, and 90% by 4 years of age; 65% were fatal (CDC 1986).

Children who have less severe disease or who have not developed opportunistic infections have lower mortality rates, but the prognosis of these children is to a large extent unknown. It is likely that many children who were infected at birth have not yet developed AIDS or even AIDS-related complex (ARC) because of the virus' prolonged incubation period. As these children develop AIDS at older ages, the age distribution may change.

There is no gender predominance in the frequency of reported cases. Minorities are disproportionately affected, with over 75% of the pediatric cases occurring among Blacks and Hispanics (CDC 1989).

The geographic distribution of pediatric cases is similar to that of cases of women who use intravenous drugs or who are born in central Africa or the Caribbean, where heterosexual transmission is prevalent. Most pediatric cases have been reported from New York, New Jersey, and Florida.

TRANSMISSION

Children become infected by the AIDS virus perinatally, through receipt of contaminated blood or blood products, and on rare occasions through breast milk or sexual contact. The major risk factor for AIDS among children is maternal transmission associated with intravenous drug use. Of mothers of HIV-infected children, 79% are themselves infected and have a history of using intravenous drugs or having sexual contact with an intravenous drug user (CDC 1986). The mothers may have no symptoms of HIV infection and most often are unaware of their antibody status. Recent data indicate that the risk of perinatal transmission from an infected mother to her infant is not known, although a range from 0% to

65% has been reported. Women who are seropositive and give birth to an infected infant have a transmission rate of 65% in subsequent pregnancies (CDC 1986).

HIV TESTING

Serologic and immunologic testing of mothers and infants is important and should be performed whenever an AIDS diagnosis is considered. The procedure for HIV antibody detection uses two testing methods. The initial test is a screening for HIV antibody and is done by the enzyme-linked immunosorbent assay (ELISA). If ELISA is repeatedly reactive (positive), confirmation with another test such as the Western blot is performed to validate the results. A reactive or positive ELISA and a positive Western blot indicate that a person is infected with HIV and has detectable levels of circulating HIV antibodies.

A positive ELISA in infants may indicate passively acquired maternal antibodies, however, and the test can remain positive until the infant is 15 to 18 months of age (CDC 1987b). Follow-up testing over time is necessary to determine true HIV infection in these infants. New methods of diagnostic testing, including antigen testing (identifying the presence of HIV), will soon be available and should be able to detect HIV infection sooner and thus allow earlier therapeutic intervention.

DISEASE PROCESS

Infants and children with HIV infection have immunologic deficiencies unique to AIDS. Pediatric AIDS must be distinguished from other causes of primary immune deficiencies. Congenital infections such as toxoplasmosis, herpes simplex, or cytomegalovirus must also be excluded before an AIDS diagnosis can be made. Studies have confirmed that pediatric patients have profound abnormalities in humoral immunity (Exhibit 12-1). Dysfunction of both T cells and B cells contributes to poor specific antibody production in the patient, which results in a

Exhibit 12-1 Immunologic Abnormalities Characteristic of Pediatric AIDS

Hypogammaglobulinemia
Depressed T-lymphocyte helper cell: suppressor cell ratio
Decrease in T-helper cells
Decreased or absent peripheral blood mononuclear cell response to mitogen, antigen, alloantigen
Depletion of lymphocytes and Hassall's corpuscles in thymus

poor host response to infectious disease processes. In late stages of AIDS, the child may develop hypogammaglobulinemia. Treatment of children with AIDS or ARC with intravenous γ-globulin is currently under investigation and appears to yield clinical evidence of controlling infections, particularly bacterial sepsis (Gupa et al. 1986; Shannon and Ammann 1985).

In August 1987, the CDC issued a revised case definition for both adult and pediatric AIDS (CDC 1987b). The criteria required for an illness to be diagnosed as AIDS were greatly broadened, making the revision more effective for surveillance purposes. In addition, it provided clarification of which diseases were necessary to substantiate the diagnosis of AIDS in HIV infection (Exhibit 12-2).

The revised CDC case definition for children differs from that for adults in two ways. First, multiple or recurrent bacterial infections and lymphoid interstitial pneumonia/pulmonary lymphoid hyperplasia are two diseases that are indicative of AIDS in children but not in adults. Second, for children whose mothers had HIV infection during the perinatal period, the criteria remain stringent because the presence of HIV antibody in a child younger than 15 months of age may reflect passively acquired maternal antibodies. A classification system has been developed by the CDC for children younger than 13 years of age (CDC 1987a,b). Those 13 years or older are classified under the adult classification system.

There are two distinct definitions for infection in children: one for infants and children younger than 15 months with perinatal infection and one for infants and children younger than 13 years who acquired HIV infection by another means (e.g., by transfusion) (Exhibit 12-3). Additional classification is based on the presence or absence of clinical signs and symptoms. Subcategorization is based on the presence or absence of immunologic abnormalities and specific diseases. Indeterminate infection refers to those cases of children who have been exposed perinatally, are younger than 15 months old, and cannot be classified as definitely infected (Exhibit 12-4).

Children have clinical signs and symptoms of HIV infection that are similar to those of adults. The clinical presentation of AIDS can range from asymptomatic, mild, or serious symptoms to full-blown AIDS characterized by the presence of opportunistic infections as defined by the CDC. Both AIDS and ARC are characterized by the following common features: low birth weight, failure to thrive, generalized lymphadenopathy, organomegaly, interstitial pneumonitis, recurrent parotitis, chronic diarrhea, recurrent bacterial and viral infections (including sepsis and meningitis), fevers, oropharyngeal thrush, and various neurologic abnormalities (Exhibit 12-5).

Bacterial infections, both common and uncommon, are a constant threat to the child with AIDS. Infections tend to be severe and recurrent, and relapse often occurs when antimicrobial therapy is discontinued. Septicemia, meningitis, and pneumonia are common infectious disease processes that are frequently seen in these children. A child may have one or more infections at the same time. Several antibiotics may be necessary to achieve the appropriate therapeutic response.

Exhibit 12-2 Diseases and Conditions Indicative of Pediatric AIDS

Lymphoid interstitial pneumonitis or pulmonary lymphoid hyperplasia (or both)
Opportunistic infections
  Bacterial
    Mycobacterium tuberculosis (extrapulmonary)
    Atypical myobacteria (disseminated)
    Salmonella (nontyphoid; septicemia)
  Fungal
    Candida albicans (Tracheal, esophageal, bronchopulmonary)
    Coccidioidomycosis (disseminated)
    Cryptococcosis (extrapulmonary)
    Histoplasmosis (disseminated)
  Protozoal
    Cryptosporidium organisms (diarrhea > 1 month)
    Isospora organisms (diarrhea > 1 month)
    Pneumocystis carinii (pneumonia)
    Toxoplasmosis (cerebral)
  Viral
    Cytomegalovirus (in an organ other than spleen, liver, or lymph nodes in a patient > 1 month old causing a mucocutaneous ulcer)
    Herpes simplex (persisting > 1 month or bronchitis, pneumonitis, or esophagitis of any duration in a patient > 1 month old)
Bacterial infections, multiple or recurrent (any combination of at least two within a 2-year period), of the following type
  Septicemia
  Meningitis
  Pneumonia
  Bone or joint infection
  Abscess of an internal organ or body cavity (excluding otitis media or superficial skin or mucosal abscesses) caused by *Haemophilus, Streptococcus* (including *Pneumococcus*),
or
  other *pyogenes*
Progressive multifocal leukoencephalopathy
Malignancies
  Kaposi's sarcoma (patient < 60 years old)
  Primary lymphoma of the brain
  Non-Hodgkin's B-cell lymphoma
HIV wasting syndrome (loss > 10% of body weight)
HIV encephalopathy

Long-term antibiotic therapy may predispose the child to nosocomial infections if the child is hospitalized and particularly if the child is in the intensive care unit, where invasive procedures are performed.

Malignancies, although common in the adult AIDS population, are rarely reported in the pediatric AIDS population. Primary lymphoma of the brain has been described in 2% of pediatric AIDS cases, but malignancies such as Kaposi's sarcoma are rare.

Exhibit 12-3 Summary of the Definition of HIV Infection in Children

---

Infants and children younger than 15 months of age with perinatal infection
1. Virus in blood or tissues
   or
2. HIV antibody
   and
   evidence of both cellular and humoral immune deficiency
   and
   one or more categories in class P-2 (see Exhibit 12-4)
   or
3. Symptoms meeting CDC case definition for AIDS

Other children with perinatal infection and children with HIV infection acquired through other modes of transmission
1. Virus in blood or tissues
   or
2. HIV antibody
   or
3. Symptoms meeting CDC case definition for AIDS

Source: Reprinted from *MMWR*, Vol. 36, pp. 3–15, April 1987.

Central nervous system abnormalities are frequently reported in pediatric AIDS patients. Neurologic signs and symptoms are often detected early and tend to worsen with the progression of the immunodeficiency. The most common findings are cerebral atrophy, acquired microcephaly, intracranial calcification, acute and subacute encephalopathies, retinochoroiditis, and pyramidal tract signs (Belman et al. 1985). These children frequently have developmental and behavioral difficulties and often fail to meet established milestones; some exhibit regressive behavior leading to dementia (Ultmann et al. 1985).

A dysmorphic syndrome in the infant associated with HIV infection has been well described in the literature (Marion et al. 1986). The features include microcephaly, growth failure, and craniofacial abnormalities. Craniofacial abnormalities include ocular hypertelorism, prominent boxlike forehead, flattened nasal bridge, long palpebral fissures, blue sclerae, and patulous lips. This syndrome lends support to the probability that infection occurs early in fetal development (Figure 12-1). HIV infection can also cause premature labor, spontaneous abortion, and teratogenesis (Marion et al. 1986).

PROGRAM OF CARE

Infants and children and their families are often dependent on the hospital as the main provider of physical care and emotional support because there are few

Exhibit 12-4 Summary of the Classification of HIV Infection in Children Younger Than 13 Years

Class P-0	Indeterminate infection
Class P-1	Asymptomatic infection
Subclass A	Normal immune function
Subclass B	Abnormal immune function
Subclass C	Immune function not tested
Class P-2	Symptomatic infection
Subclass A	Nonspecific findings
Subclass B	Progressive neurologic disease
Subclass C	Lymphoid interstitial pneumonitis
Subclass D	Secondary infectious diseases
Category D-1	Specific secondary infectious diseases listed in the CDC surveillance definition for AIDS
Category D-2	Recurrent serious bacterial infections
Category D-3	Other specified secondary infectious diseases
Subclass E	Secondary cancers
Category E-1	Specified secondary cancers listed in the CDC surveillance definition for AIDS
Category E-2	Other cancers possibly secondary to HIV infection
Subclass F	Other diseases possibly due to HIV infection

Source: Reprinted from *MMWR*, Vol. 36, pp. 3–15, April 1987.

community programs available. The first wave of community services for AIDS patients originated through grassroots efforts predominantly organized by Gays and Gay rights activists to meet the social and emotional needs of the Gay population. The need for services for pediatric AIDS patients and their families has only recently been recognized, and many programs designed to offer support

Exhibit 12-5 Common Clinical Signs and Symptoms of Pediatric HIV Infection

Failure to thrive
Recurrent bacterial and viral infections
Thrush and candidal skin infections
Organomegaly
Parotitis
Cardiomyopathy
Diarrhea
Respiratory tract infections
Fever
Renal disease
Neurologic abnormalities

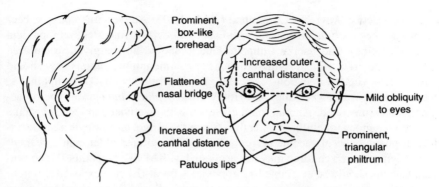

Figure 12-1 Fetal acquired immunodeficiency syndrome. These dysmorphic features have been observed in children infected in utero with HIV. The features differ from fetal alcohol syndrome and may be the first indication of fetal AIDS. *Source:* Reprinted from *American Journal of Diseases of Children*, Vol. 140, pp. 638–640, with permission of the author and the American Medical Association, © 1986.

services to families remain at the organizational level. Substance abuse prevention and rehabilitation services should be an integral component of AIDS services to the community and must be available in areas where AIDS is epidemic.

HIV-infected children and their families need a structured and supportive framework in which to manage and cope with the stresses of this illness on a day-to-day basis. Providers of care must identify the physical, psychologic, and social needs of the family and assess the home environment when preparing a plan for the child's discharge from the acute care setting.

FAMILY EDUCATION

Children who test positive for HIV are at risk for serious and potentially life-threatening infectious disease processes. One of the primary goals that the nurse must establish is providing the parent or care giver with the information needed to promote optimal health in these children. Regular follow-up visits to the physician is the first item that should be stressed to family members. Providing and maintaining a healthy environment, including sound nutrition and shelter, is equally important. Family members need to understand that it is crucial to avoid exposure of the child to communicable diseases and to report any exposure, especially to varicella and measles, to the health care provider.

IMMUNIZATIONS

Immunizations must be kept up to date and clearly documented. Guidelines for the immunization of HIV-infected individuals have been published by the Immunization Practice Advisory Committee (Table 12-1). Active virus and live bacterial vaccines such as OPV (oral polio vaccine), MMR (measles, mumps, and rubella vaccine), and bacille Calmette Guérin should not be given to children infected with HIV who are symptomatic. For routine immunizations they should receive IPV (inactivated polio vaccine). Immunization with DTP (diphtheria, tetanus, and pertussis vaccine) and HbCV (*Haemophilus influenzae* type b vaccine) is recommended. Annual immunizations with inactivated influenza vaccine are recommended for children older than 6 months of age, and a single administration of pneumococcal vaccine is recommended for children older than 2 years of age. Asymptomatic children may be vaccinated with MMR. Hepatitis B recombinant vaccine should be available for prophylaxis for at-risk and exposed children.

After significant exposure to measles or varicella, children should undergo passive immunization with immune globulin or varicella zoster immune globulin, respectively. The close contacts of children with HIV infection should receive IPV rather than OPV. It should be noted, however, that antibody response may be poor and that many of these children may not be protected.

IN-HOSPITAL PRECAUTIONS

HIV-infected children who are hospitalized or receiving follow-up care are maintained on blood and body fluid precautions. Blood and body fluid precautions are necessary when there is direct contact with the patient's blood or body fluids. Routine patient care practices such as measuring vital signs, feeding the patient, or providing hands-on comfort do not require these precautions. When starting intravenous lines, drawing blood, changing diapers, or cleaning surfaces soiled by

Table 12-1 Recommendations for Routine Immunization of HIV-Infected Children—United States

	Known HIV Infection	
Vaccine	Asymptomatic	Symptomatic
DTP	Yes	Yes
OPV	No	No
IPV	Yes	Yes
MMR	Yes	Yes*
HbCV	Yes	Yes
Pneumococcal	Yes	Yes
Influenza	No†	Yes

*Should be considered.
†Not contraindicated.

Source: Reprinted from *MMWR*, Vol. 38, pp. 205–27, April 1989.

blood or body fluids, however, disposable gloves are to be worn. The CDC has recommended that these precautions be used consistently for all patients; this is commonly referred to as universal precautions. Use of these precautions is also important when the infection status of a patient is unknown.

AIDS patients are often infected with other organisms, so that additional precautions must be taken. For example, patients infected with pulmonary tuberculosis need to be placed on respiratory precautions. The mode of transmission of the disease determines the additional precautions that need to be taken. Hand washing is important and should be done after any exposure to the child's stool, blood, or other body secretions. Children, once they are old enough, should be taught to wash their hands frequently, especially after using the toilet and before meals. Adolescents should be instructed in how to dispose of sanitary napkins and what to do for nose bleeds and other injuries in which blood is evident.

Sterilization and disinfection procedures currently recommended for use in health care facilities are adequate to sterilize or disinfect medical devices, instruments, or other items contaminated with blood or body fluids (Garner and Favero 1985). Environmental surfaces should be cleaned with soap and water to remove organic material (such as blood and mucus) and then rinsed with a fresh bleach solution (1 part bleach to 10 parts water). Certain medical devices may be corroded by repeated exposure to bleach; thus commercially available chemical germicides may be preferable. HIV is a fragile virus and is inactivated rapidly after exposure to commonly used chemical germicides. While the child is in the hospital, all disposable items contaminated with blood and body fluids should be placed in plastic bags and disposed of as infectious waste in accordance with the facility's infectious waste disposal policy.

HOME CARE

Nurses must explain and sometimes demonstrate routine infection control practices and principles to the families of HIV-infected children. The family needs to understand the various modes of transmission of HIV and be assured that items such as masks and gowns are not necessary in the home to render care to the infant or child.

Eating utensils, dishes, and laundry pose no risk to the family and should be washed in hot, soapy water. Bleach can be added to the laundry. Items such as toothbrushes, razors, pierced earrings, or personal care items should not be shared between the child and other family members. In the home, if plastic bags are not available, soiled disposable items can be wrapped in several layers of newspaper and disposed.

CHRONIC DISEASE MANAGEMENT

Failure to thrive, recurrent or chronic infections, fever, diarrhea, malabsorption, and painful oral lesions are the hallmarks of pediatric AIDS. Management of these chronic problems presents a unique challenge to the nurse when formulating a plan for the continuance of care.

Nutrition Concerns

Monitoring intake, output, and weight is crucial for infants and children with AIDS. Daily weights may be required with infants and with all hospitalized children. Causes of decreased intake or malabsorption must be identified and treated. Lactose intolerance is a complication of long-term antibiotic therapy and chronic gastrointestinal infections; implementation of a lactose-free diet benefits the patient in this situation. Soy formulas can replace milk. Supplements, in addition to meals, can provide extra calories. Food supplements that are high in calories and proteins and snacks that are full of nutrients, such as peanut butter or raisins, should be encouraged. Parenteral nutrition may become necessary in patients with critical weight loss. Soft or bland diets are better tolerated when painful mucosal lesions or oral thrush is present (oral thrush can contribute to difficulty in swallowing and eating). Frequent mouth care should be performed, and dental care should be carried out whenever indicated.

All diets and nutrition supplements must be tailored to the child's cultural and social background. Referrals to dietary services for a nutrition plan and to social services to ensure entitlement benefits to maintain a nutritionally sound program may be advisable or necessary in some situations. Diet teaching with the home care giver is important because nutrition knowledge among these individuals is frequently lacking. Care providers must be taught the difference between nutritious snacks and junk food.

Chronic or recurrent diarrhea contributes to the nutrition depletion of the AIDS patient. Stools should be cultured whenever there is an increase in frequency or change in consistency. Family members should be taught how to monitor stools and to prevent infection by using good perianal care and hand washing techniques.

Fever may accompany diarrhea or may occur alone. Parents or care givers must be knowledgeable about how to take the child's temperature and the implications of the findings. The axillary method is best for these patients. Thermometers should be available in the home. Use of sponge baths, administration of antipyretics, and maintenance of adequate hydration are fundamental for the management of elevated temperatures.

Respiratory Tract Infections

Respiratory tract infections are the most common infections in the pediatric AIDS population. The most frequently reported opportunistic infection is *Pneumocystis carinii* pneumonia. The next most common pulmonary disorder is pulmonary lymphoid hyperplasia. In most situations children with either of these disorders need to be admitted to the hospital.

Each entity has distinguishing characteristics that may be of assistance in the differential diagnosis and in choosing a therapeutic regimen. Patients with *Pneumocystis carinii* pneumonia have acute episodes characterized by rapidly progressive respiratory distress, fever, and cough. Patients with pulmonary lymphoid hyperplasia have a slow, progressive course with mild to moderate hypoxemia. Children with this disorder have a more favorable long-term prognosis (Rubinstein et al. 1986).

The patient needs frequent assessment of respiratory status. Supplemental oxygen or even mechanical ventilation may be necessary. Blood gas analysis, diagnostic testing, and therapeutic regimens with intravenous antibiotics are required. Family members need to be instructed in how to recognize the signs and symptoms of respiratory complications, including increase in cough, shortness of breath, change in respiratory rate, or change in activity level. Family members should be instructed to call the physician whenever the child's respiratory status changes.

When the patient is to be discharged, the medications should be reviewed with the parent, family member, or care giver. The correct dose, route, and schedule should be written down and reviewed several times before discharge and at each follow-up visit. Nurses must monitor untoward side effects of medications and collaborate with the physician regarding changing the dosage of medication or prescribing a new one.

Neurologic Abnormalities

As previously described, AIDS in both adults and children is frequently accompanied by neurologic dysfunction. As the encephalopathies progress, the child may lose some previously accomplished developmental milestones, plateau, or in some cases regress. The occurrence of progressive encephalopathy in HIV-infected children is a grave prognostic sign (Epstein et al. 1986). Neurologic assessments must be performed at each clinic visit, and any abnormalities warrant appropriate therapeutic interventions. Physical therapy may be helpful for patients who are hypotonic or hypertonic. Speech therapists and occupational therapists can provide assistance for speech difficulties and feeding problems. Volunteers or home health aides may be required to provide additional support in the home because the care of the child with neurologic abnormalities is time consuming and the parents may themselves be ill.

Nutrition and metabolic factors may also contribute to the child's developmental delays. Antimicrobial treatment of repeated bacterial and opportunistic infections can have adverse side effects. For example, aminoglycosides are known to affect hearing through sensorineural changes (Schuknecht 1974). Recurrent otitis media and serous otitis could also affect the child's ability to hear and therefore the acquisition of language skills (Sak and Rubin 1982).

There are also a number of psychosocial factors associated with chronic illness that may contribute to underdevelopment of cognitive skills. These include repeated hospitalizations and separation from the family or care giver as well as repeated exposure to isolation precautions and practices. In addition, the lack of an intact family may adversely affect the child's development at home.

Pain can be a major problem and may result from various causes. In infants or small children, nonverbal indicators of pain must be assessed. Behavior changes, irritability, crying, or restlessness can be important signs. Physical and emotional comfort measures should be encouraged as an adjunct to medications for pain control.

The clinical course of neurologic impairment or dysfunction in these children needs to be closely monitored to determine the progression of developmental changes and neurologic abnormalities.

HIGH-RISK BEHAVIORS AMONG ADOLESCENTS

A significant number of teenagers engage in behavior that increases their risk of becoming infected with HIV. Statistics regarding teenage pregnancy indicate that a large percentage of adolescents are sexually active. Approximately 25 million teenagers are infected with a sexually transmitted disease each year. Male homosexual intercourse is an important risk factor for HIV infection. In one survey conducted in 1973, 5% of 13- to 15-year-old boys and 17% of 16- to 19-year-old boys reported having at least one homosexual experience. Of those who reported having such an experience, most (56%) indicated that the first homosexual experience had occurred when they were 11 or 12 years old. Two percent reported that they currently engaged in homosexual activity (CDC 1988a).

Some teenagers are at risk of becoming infected through illicit intravenous drug use. Findings from a national survey conducted in 1986 in nearly 130 high schools indicated that, although overall illicit drug use seems to be declining slowly among high school seniors, about 1% of seniors reported having used heroin and 13% reported having used cocaine within the previous year. The number of seniors who injected each of these drugs is not known.

Only 1% of all persons diagnosed as having AIDS have been younger than 20 years. Most persons in this age group had been infected by transfusion or perinatal transmission. About 21% of all persons diagnosed as having AIDS have been between 20 and 29 years of age (CDC 1988a). Given the long incubation period between HIV infection and the onset of symptoms that lead to a diagnosis of AIDS (3 to 7 years or more), some fraction of those in the 20- to 29-year age group were probably infected while they were still teenagers.

Although teenagers are at risk of becoming infected with and transmitting the AIDS virus as they become sexually active, studies have shown that they do not believe that they are likely to become infected (Strunin and Hingson 1987). Adolescents frequently enjoy risk-taking behaviors. They have a lack of foresight and do not consider the consequences of their activities. Many of the adolescents who engage in high-risk behaviors have dropped out of school or are runaways and therefore have not participated in school or community programs that deal with AIDS and AIDS risk reduction activities. The increase in homelessness and prostitution, particularly among runaways in urban settings, has also contributed to the fear that AIDS will increase significantly in this population.

The CDC has been collecting data from high school students and states and cities with the highest cumulative incidence of AIDS since 1987 (CDCb 1988). Baseline data suggest that HIV-related beliefs, knowledge, and behaviors among the adolescents surveyed in 15 states and cities are similar. Many students incorrectly thought that HIV infection can be acquired from giving blood, using public toilets, or having a blood test or from mosquito or other insect bites. Most students knew that sexual intercourse and intravenous drug use could result in HIV infection. Departments of education should implement programs to correct misconceptions about HIV transmission and to reduce behaviors resulting in HIV infection and should assess on a periodic basis whether these misconceptions and behaviors change among high school students over time (CDC 1988a).

IMPACT OF AIDS

The diagnosis of AIDS has an immediate effect on the family and ultimately on the community. It is not unusual for more than one member of the family to be ill. A fragmented and disruptive home environment may increase the stress and anxiety of the affected child. Siblings are particularly affected because they may develop psychologic problems stemming from the fear of getting the disease themselves or because the parents are unavailable to them physically or emotionally (or both).

Parents may feel guilty when there has been perinatal transmission. Feelings of anger and frustration are inevitable when parents learn that their child has become infected with the AIDS virus through a transfusion of blood or blood components. Overwhelming feelings of helplessness and hopelessness can immobilize the family unit and strain interpersonal relationships. Frequently, the family feels isolated or rejected because friends, relatives, and neighbors no longer visit or avoid physical contact.

Parents are faced with considerable financial burdens that often extend beyond the cost of medical care. Frequently a parent will have to stay home to care for an ill child. The parent's income may be sacrificed if this occurs. The mother or father may be the only source of income as a single parent. On occasion, the mother, father, or both parents may be too ill to care for the child. Day care centers are often reluctant to extend care to these children, and foster care placement may be difficult. If the child is already in a foster home when the diagnosis is made, the foster family often has formed an attachment to the child and is committed to care for him or her.

Frequently, however, these children remain in the hospital and are commonly referred as "boarder babies." They simply have no place to go or no one to go home to. Hospital staff may attempt to provide needed emotional, physical, and psychologic support. Acute care settings are not conducive to addressing normal growth and development needs of the child, however, and staff must attend to acutely ill children first, so that boarder babies ultimately receive little attention.

Such a situation can demoralize the nursing staff, and it is especially difficult and stressful for the nurses who care for these children when one of them gets acutely ill or dies. As the day-to-day stresses of caring for these children increase, nurses must be aware of their own limitations and ability to cope. Administrative support is fundamental in providing resources to help nurses deal with children with HIV infection. Support groups, flexible scheduling, creative patient assignments, and conferences on stress management should be available.

CHILDREN AND ADOLESCENTS WITH HIV INFECTION

Children and adolescents with AIDS need to know about their infection. How the child copes with the illness depends on a number of factors, including age, cognitive development, parental involvement, and the response of others to the illness. To ensure a consistent plan of care, children must feel free to ask questions and in return must have their questions answered. They should be encouraged to verbalize and share their feelings and concerns.

Every effort should be made to minimize the isolation or confusion that the child may feel. These feelings of isolation are bound to increase when the hospitalized patient is maintained on blood and body fluid precautions. Children who are not allowed to attend school or play groups may experience rejection from peers or classmates, which may lead to anger, insomnia, or depression. Counseling or family therapy may help defuse stressful situations when they occur.

The numbers of children and adolescents with HIV infection will continue to increase in the years to come. These children have education needs and rights that must be acknowledged. The CDC has published guidelines for use by local and state education departments in developing policies relating to education, day care, and foster care of these children (CDC 1985). The CDC and the American Academy of Pediatrics (AAP) have recommended that most school-aged infected children be allowed to attend school (AAP 1986; CDC 1985). Because AIDS is not transmitted by casual contact, ordinary contact that would occur among school-aged children does not transmit HIV. There have been no reported cases of AIDS by casual transmission, nor has HIV been transmitted in school day care or foster care settings. Decisions regarding school, day care, or foster care should be made on a case-by-case basis. A more restrictive environment is advised for infected preschool children who may have risky behaviors such as biting. Extra caution must be used to minimize exposure of other children to blood and body fluids.

In the event that a problem should arise regarding an HIV-infected child, the case should be reviewed by a team knowledgeable about the transmission of HIV. The child's behavior, physical condition, neurologic status, cognitive capabilities, and interactive relationships with other children should be reviewed and discussed by team members.

On occasion, there are situations in which it is advisable that the HIV-infected child remain out of the classroom. One such situation is during an outbreak of measles or varicella (Exhibit 12-6). The school nurse should be involved in the formulation of guidelines regarding the exposure of HIV-infected children to the common communicable diseases of childhood and should provide input into decisions regarding the child's care in the school setting.

Privacy and confidentiality are critical issues when managing and caring for children with AIDS or HIV infection. The number of individuals who are aware of the child's HIV status should be restricted to those who need to know. Many states have mandates to protect the rights of HIV-infected individuals. Medical records

---

Exhibit 12-6 Infectious Diseases Occurring in Day Care Centers or School Settings

Meningitis, viral and bacterial
Varicella (chicken pox)
Diarrheal diseases caused by infection with *Shigella, Campylobacter, Salmonella*, and *Giardia* organisms
Diphtheria
Hepatitis A, hepatitis B
Measles
Mumps
Pertussis (whooping cough)
Rubella (German measles)
Pneumonia, epiglottitis, and acute infectious arthritis

are considered confidential, and the release of any information must be according to state regulations.

AIDS EDUCATION IN THE SCHOOL AND COMMUNITY

Education is the only means of AIDS prevention at this time. AIDS will affect every community in every state of the country in the not too distant future, so that it is vital that AIDS education reach every member of these communities. All age groups must be included in the education process. Nurses can act as professional and community resources in disseminating relevant and current information about AIDS. Nurses can help dispel misconceptions during the education process.

Although the issue is highly controversial, many believe that AIDS education should begin at the early elementary levels (*Time* 1986). While several authorities recommend that AIDS prevention be taught in the schools beginning no later than grade 7, the Surgeon General has recommended that AIDS education begin as early as grade 3 (Fulton et al. 1987; Department of Health and Human Services 1987; Yarber 1987).

An AIDS information program can frequently be incorporated into a sex education curriculum that is already in place. AIDS and HIV-infection prevention curricula should include discussion of the virus, modes of transmission, precautions for prevention, sexually transmitted diseases, and behaviors that reduce the possibilities of acquiring AIDS such as the proper use of condoms and reducing the number of sexual partners. Information about the risks of intravenous drug use should also be provided. Evaluation of content and effectiveness of class presentation is important and should be done on a periodic basis. Education programs should encourage student participation and provide a forum for students to ask questions. There may be anxiety or embarrassment over the discussion of sexual issues. The material should be presented in a straightforward fashion with an emphasis on the facts.

Parents who are interested in and concerned about what their children are being taught should be given the opportunity to review the curriculum and to express opinions or ask questions. Meetings can be arranged for parents, and information about AIDS can be distributed before the proposed curriculum is presented. Some parents may object to a program on AIDS being offered as part of a school curriculum. They may fear that teaching about sex implies condoning sex among teens. They may prefer that sex-related information, including AIDS information, be taught at home. Relevant and factual AIDS information should be given to these parents with the expectation that they will discuss these issues with their children at home.

CONCLUSION

AIDS has become a nationwide health crisis and is a number one public health priority. Nevertheless, the approach to planning and implementing the delivery of AIDS-related services has remained seriously fragmented. The cost of providing care for people with AIDS is expected to reach $8.5 billion in 1991 (Scitovsky and Rice 1987). This figure takes on added significance for the health care system when one realizes that most AIDS patients are poor and from unemployed families who have no medical insurance. The burden of an increase of patients with AIDS on urban public hospitals, who are already providing care to the indigent, may well become a financial disaster.

Many complex social issues have been brought to the forefront by the AIDS epidemic, including homosexuality, sex education, drug abuse, and various moral and ethical dilemmas, to name a few. These issues and the fear of the disease itself have frequently resulted in the rejection or isolation of persons with AIDS from the family and community.

Nurses have an opportunity to serve as health care planners in the existing health care system by promoting and facilitating an AIDS care delivery system. Creative, compassionate, and comprehensive services are needed. Such services should promote health and cost-effective utilization of all resources available. It is now the responsibility of nurses in all phases of practice to work collaboratively to implement, maintain, and evaluate these services.

AIDS presents nursing professionals with the health care crisis of the 1990s and beyond. Multiple and complex issues will confront nurses, but the opportunities to meet this crisis will be realized by dedicated and resourceful individuals who choose to meet the challenge of this epidemic.

STUDY QUESTIONS

1. Describe three ways to reduce the risk of infection in the child with AIDS during a hospitalization.
2. Explain the significance of a positive HIV antibody test in a 3-month-old infant.
3. Identify two nursing interventions for neurologic, respiratory, gastrointestinal, and comfort-related problems related to opportunistic infections.
4. Describe three areas of concern when teaching the care giver in preparation for the patient's discharge from the hospital.

REFERENCES

American Academy of Pediatrics Committee on School Health. 1986. School attendance of children and adolescents with HTLV-III/LAV infection. *Pediatrics* 77:430–32.

Belman, A.L., M.H. Ultmann, D. Horoupian, B. Novick, A. Spiro, A. Rubinstein, D. Kurtzberg, and B. Cone-Wesson. 1985. Neurological complications in infants and children with acquired immune deficiency syndrome. *Annals of Neurology* 18:560–66.

Centers for Disease Control. 1985. Education and foster care of children infected with HTLV-III/LAV. *Morbidity and Mortality Weekly Report* 34:517–21.

Centers for Disease Control. 1986. Immunization of children infected with human T-lymphotropic virus type III/lymphadenopathy-associated virus. *Morbidity and Mortality Weekly Report* 35:595–604.

Centers for Disease Control. 1987a. Revision of the CDC surveillance case definition for acquired immunodeficiency syndrome. *Morbidity and Mortality Weekly Report* 36:3–15.

Centers for Disease Control. 1987b. Classification system for human immunodeficiency virus infection in children under 13 years of age. *Morbidity and Mortality Weekly Report* 36:225–30.

Centers for Disease Control. 1988a. Guidelines for effective school health education to prevent the spread of AIDS. *Morbidity and Mortality Weekly Report* 37 (supplement S-2): 1–13.

Centers for Disease Control. 1988b. HIV-related beliefs, knowledge and behaviors among high school students. *Morbidity and Mortality Weekly Report* 37:717–21.

Centers for Disease Control. 1989a. General guidelines on immunization (ACIP). *Morbidity and Mortality Weekly Report* 38:205–27.

Centers for Disease Control. 1989b. Update: AIDS—United States 1981–1988. *Morbidity and Mortality Weekly Report* 38:229–35.

Department of Health and Human Services. 1987. *Public Health Service AIDS information/education plan to prevent and control AIDS in the United States.* Washington, D.C.: Government Printing Office.

Epstein, L.G., L.R. Sharer, J.M. Oleske, E.M. Connor, J. Goudsmit, L. Bagdon, M. Robert-Guroff, and M.R. Konigsberger. 1986. Neurologic manifestations of human immunodeficiency virus infection in children. *Pediatrics* 78:678–87.

Fulton, G.B., E. Metress, and J.H. Price. 1987. AIDS: Resource materials for school personnel. *Journal of School Health* 57:14–18.

Garner, J.S., and M.S. Favero. 1985. Guidelines for handwashing and hospital environmental control. Centers for Disease Control Publication no. 99-117.

Gupa, A., B. Novick, and A. Rubinstein. 1986. Restoration of suppressor T-cell functions in children with AIDS following intravenous gamma-globulin treatment. *American Journal of Diseases of Childhood* 140:143–46.

Marion, R.W., A.A. Wiznia, R. Gordon Hutcheon, and A. Rubinstein. 1986. Human T-cell lymphotropic virus type III (HTLV-III) embryopathy. *American Journal of Diseases of Childhood* 140:638–40.

New York City Department of Health AIDS Epidemiology and Surveillance Unit. 1989. AIDS surveillance update.

Oleske, J. 1988. Testimony presented to the Presidential Commission on the Human Immunodeficiency Virus Epidemic, January, Washington, D.C.

Rubinstein, A., R. Molecki, B. Silverman, M. Charytan, B. Krieger, W. Anaiman, M. Ziprkowski, and H. Goldman. 1986. Pulmonary disease in children with acquired immune deficiency syndrome and AIDS-related complex. *Journal of Pediatrics* 108:498–503.

Sak, R.J., and R.J. Rubin. 1982. Effects of recurrent middle ear effusion in preschool years on language and learning. *Journal of Developmental and Behavioral Pediatrics* 24:528–39.

Schuknecht, H.F. 1974. Aminoglycoside ototoxicity. In *Pathology of the ear*, ed. H.F. Schuknecht. Cambridge: Harvard University Press.

Scitovsky, A.A., and D.P. Rice. 1987. Estimates of the direct and indirect costs of acquired immune deficiency syndrome in the United States, 1985, 1986, 1991. *Public Health Reports* 102:5–17.

Sex and Schools. 1986. *Time Magazine* 54:60–63.

Shannon, K.M., and A.J. Ammann. 1985. Acquired immune deficiency syndrome in childhood. *Journal of Pediatrics* 106:332–42.

Strunin, L., and R. Hingson. 1987. Acquired immunodeficiency syndrome and adolescents: Knowledge, beliefs, attitudes and behaviors. *Pediatrics* 79:825–28.

Ultmann, M.H., A.L. Belman, H. Ruff, B. Novick, B. Cone-Wesson, H. Cohen, and A. Rubinstein. 1985. Developmental abnormalities in infants and children with acquired immune deficiency syndrome and AIDS-related complex. *Developmental Medicine and Child Neurology* 27:563–71.

Yarber, W.L. 1987. *AIDS, what young adults should know*. Reston, Va.: American Alliance for Health, Physical Education, Recreation, and Dance.

Chapter 13

Home Care for the Patient with Acquired Immunodeficiency Syndrome and Drug Therapy for Human Immunodeficiency Virus–Related Infections and Neoplasms

Noreen Coyne

> This chapter describes issues that make home care for patients with acquired immunodeficiency syndrome more complex and challenging than the traditional home care patient. These issues include the complex nature of the illness, concurrent and recurrent infections and diseases requiring frequent hospitalizations, the debilitating effects of the illness, and psychosocial problems that are frequently seen. Also discussed are insurance limitations for home care, substance abuse and infection with human immunodeficiency virus, high-tech therapy, and hospice care at home.

Acquired immunodeficiency syndrome (AIDS) is a chronic disease that progresses to a terminal stage with frequent episodes of acute illness. These episodes of acute illness may require hospitalization, but for most of the time the AIDS patient is maintained at home. In addition to helping a patient regain independence, it may be necessary for health care professionals to provide ongoing assistance in the home because of chronic problems or need for palliative care.

As of January 1990, 118,109 cases of AIDS were reported to the Centers for Disease Control (CDC 1989). National statistics on the number of patients requiring home care have not been determined. New York City's AIDS Task

Force, however, predicts that by late 1989 1,700 (23%) of the 7,300 AIDS patients living in the city will be enrolled in home care programs and that by late 1993 3,400 of the estimated 13,700 AIDS patients will be receiving home care. At the same time the need for acute care beds will increase from 2,420 in late 1989 to 4,990 by late 1993 (New York City AIDS Task Force 1989).

Home care services cannot substitute for inpatient hospitalizations for the diagnosis and treatment of acute problems. They can, however, significantly reduce the length of hospital stays by providing a range of nursing and supportive services at home, from homemaker and attendant services for assistance with activities of daily living (ADLs) to high-tech nursing intervention for the administration of intravenous (IV) hydration and antibiotic therapy and supportive care for dying patients.

Home care services are limited by the type and amount of services covered by insurance. Insurance coverage may be restricted to periodic nursing visits by a nurse when unskilled custodial care rendered by an attendant or homemaker is needed. The continuous skilled nursing care needed to manage safely a greatly impaired patient at home or to administer continuous IV infusion is usually not fully reimbursed. Although some patients can pay to supplement services covered by insurance, most have insufficient resources. Many are unemployed and uninsured when they are diagnosed with AIDS and quickly become indigent. A patient may qualify for Medicaid by meeting the income and disability criteria established by the Social Security Administration (National Academy of Sciences 1986).

New York City's Human Resources Administration, in responding to the growing number of AIDS cases, has developed a comprehensive case management approach for providing home and community-based care through the AIDS Home Care Program. Case managers assess a patient's or the support person's ability to direct care and the level of support services required as measured by the patient's functional status (e.g., the degree of assistance needed in ADLs and skilled nursing or rehabilitation needs) to determine the services to be rendered through the Medicaid program. These services include periodic visits by a registered nurse, physical therapist, or social worker and continuous hours of care by a registered nurse, licensed practical nurse, or paraprofessional service (e.g., homemakers, home health aides, or home attendants) (New York City AIDS Task Force 1988). Patients who are positive for human immunodeficiency virus (HIV) or have AIDS-related complex (ARC) but have not been diagnosed with AIDS are ineligible for the program.

To allow AIDS patients to remain in the community and to reduce the number, length, and cost of hospital admissions, all states must implement under Medicaid such expanded services and benefits for HIV-positive, ARC, and AIDS patients. Federal and state agencies must also develop innovative methods of combining public and private funds for more comprehensive insurance coverage for those patients who do not qualify for Medicaid.

ISSUES ASSOCIATED WITH AIDS

A Complex Illness

Issues that make home care for AIDS patients different from traditional home care are the complexity of the disease and the multiple psychosocial problems that frequently exist. The patient often develops concurrent multiple infections and diseases requiring frequent hospitalizations for work-up and treatment.

Pulmonary problems are common as a result of *Pneumocystis carinii* pneumonia, pulmonary Kaposi's sarcoma, and other opportunistic diseases and infections; progressive physical deterioration is also common in the AIDS patient (Lieberman 1988). Diarrhea is a frequent and often chronic problem resulting from gastrointestinal infections or pathogens such as *Cryptosporidium* organisms, cytomegalovirus, *Mycobacterium avium-intracellulare, Giardia lamblia,* and *Shigella, Salmonella,* and *Campylobacter* organisms. Diarrhea can result in malnutrition, dehydration, electrolyte imbalance, skin ulceration, and fecal incontinence (Lieberman 1988). The patient may develop progressive cognitive and motor deficits associated with AIDS-related dementia or infection and neoplasms involving the central nervous system. As a result of these deficits, the patient becomes increasingly dependent on others for care at home.

The complexity of the disease poses a challenge to the advanced practice nurse. To provide home care for these patients, one needs skill in assessment and intervention for the prevention of opportunistic diseases and management of AIDS-related symptoms, patient education, infection control, nutrition, IV therapy, and hospice care. It is also essential to have a thorough understanding of the mechanism of action of the conventional and investigational drugs currently being used for treatment of opportunistic infections, neoplasms, and HIV infection.

Psychosocial Problems

While managing a patient's physical symptoms, the nurse must also deal with multiple psychosocial problems. These include (Ungvarski 1988; Martin 1987):

- fear and stigma associated with the disease
- limited social support systems
- lack of adequate housing, finances, and medical insurance
- poor access to adequate health care services
- estrangement or geographic distance from families
- others in the home with HIV infection, including children
- substance abuse by the patient or by others in the home

- use of drugs not approved by the Food and Drug Administration (FDA) (obtained from foreign countries, buyer's clubs, or investigational protocols)
- depression, threat of suicide, or manipulative and noncompliant behavior
- anger directed at care givers and health care providers
- neurologic effects of the disease resulting in a decreased level of function and dementia
- blindness
- exhaustion of care givers
- dependent children at home

Since April 1988 there have been more newly diagnosed AIDS cases among IV drug users than among Gays and bisexuals, and this trend is expected to continue. IV drug use is the primary mode (72%) of transmission of HIV to the heterosexual population (CDC 1989). Approximately 7% of adult AIDS cases in the United States are women; of these women, 49% are IV drug users. Women IV drug users and female sexual partners of IV drug users frequently become infected and are the major cause of HIV infection among newborn infants (Guinan and Hardy 1987). Because most women with AIDS are in their childbearing years and may already have children, a major concern is the care of their children in the event of their disability or death (New York City AIDS Task Force 1989).

HIV-infected IV drug users tend to have poor nutrition status and a generalized deterioration of their health status even before the onset of AIDS, which leads to an increased incidence of tuberculosis, hepatitis, pneumonia, endocarditis, and other diseases (Carpi 1987). IV drug use is prevalent among poor and minority populations, which have little access to health care and health education. Problems associated with poverty such as inadequate housing, poor nutrition status, lack of health care, and lack of child care are exacerbated by the diagnosis of AIDS.

Continued substance abuse among IV drug–using AIDS patients is one of the most difficult management problems that the nurse faces. Although it is often frustrating to provide care for the patient who exhibits the manipulative and noncompliant behavior common to addiction (Carpi 1987), and expressions of anger, blame, or disappointment toward the continual abuser can impede successful nursing interventions. As the AIDS epidemic spreads to include more IV drug users, nurses must learn to identify substance abuse, to manage addictive behavior, and to differentiate the effects of drugs from the neurologic symptoms of AIDS-related infections and neoplasms.

Nursing interventions for IV drug users and their sexual partners should be aimed at teaching and supporting behavior change in the areas of substance abuse, needle use, and sexual practices. Although there is a high frequency of return to IV drug use after treatment, data on the response of IV drug users to the AIDS epidemic indicate that many are attempting to reduce their risks by reducing IV drug use or by using safer injection practices (Friedman, De Jarlais, and Sotheran 1986).

CASE MANAGEMENT

Individuals and families affected by AIDS are often so debilitated by the effects of the illness and inexperienced in obtaining access to needed services that they may be unable to seek the services they need. To ensure that the complex health and psychosocial needs of these individuals and families are met, a case management approach is necessary. The case manager must coordinate medical care and arrange for needed social services and financing. Other services that case managers may need to obtain for their cases are housing, drug treatment, volunteer services, long-term and respite care services, transportation, child care, and legal services.

Different areas of the country have designated a single or several organizations such as home care providers, drug treatment programs, or designated AIDS centers to perform case management. Depending on the agency, case managers may be nurses, social workers, drug treatment counselors, or others. Often there are several case managers at different agencies connected to the same case (New York City AIDS Task Force 1988). To provide comprehensive care for individuals with AIDS and their families, the nurse case manager must be knowledgeable about available community resources to obtain needed services as well as about the disease manifestations, conventional treatments, and current investigational protocols.

STRESS ASSOCIATED WITH CARING FOR AIDS PATIENTS

Health professionals, family, and friends all experience a high degree of stress associated with caring for AIDS patients. Health professional studies by Ross and Seeger (1988) identified the aspects causing the greatest amount of stress as the youth of the patients, the neurologic problems of AIDS, and dying patients. They also identified a need for more information about patients' emotional needs, IV drug use, depression, and anxiety.

Klein and Fletcher (1987) found that families and significant others whose support needs are not met while they are caring for the patient with AIDS experience more depression, anger, guilt, fatigue, helplessness, and illness than those who feel that their needs are met. Families identified unmet needs as inadequate social, legal, financial, or emotional supports; lack of knowledge about available community resources; limited understanding of how best to care for the patient at home; and difficulty communicating with health care professionals.

HOME NURSING CARE

On initial contact with the AIDS patient in the home setting, it is imperative that the nurse assess the patient's physical, psychosocial, and environmental status. A care plan of interventions to maximize comfort, safety, and independence can then be developed. Frequent visits for continuous patient assessment and adjustment of the care plan will be necessary during the fluctuating course of the patient's illness. Communication and collaboration with the primary physician to report any changes in the patient's condition and to obtain new treatment orders are necessary (Lieberman 1988). The nurse also supervises and instructs the home health aides or attendants in patient care, which includes assistance with ADLs, personal care, light housework, laundry, shopping, meal preparation, and infection control.

Physical Assessment

Thorough initial and ongoing assessment must be done to determine accurately the patient's needs. The following list includes elements of the physical assessment that must be examined by the nurse during each home visit (Lieberman 1988):

- a complete history of the patient's illness
- the opportunistic infections and neoplasms that the patient has had previously and ones that are current problems
- the treatments and medications that the patient is taking for these present problems as well as past treatments
- reactions to medications, including responses and side effects
- use of any non–FDA approved drugs: investigational drugs, drugs obtained from other countries, or home remedies
- the patient's neurologic status, including motor and cognitive function
- the patient's current level of function
- the anticipated effect that the course of the disease will have on the patient's future level of function
- the patient's pulmonary, gastrointestinal, genitourinary, and cutaneous status
- symptoms

During each visit the nurse assesses for sudden or subtle signs of an acute episode or exacerbation of an opportunistic illness. Prompt medical treatment may be necessary to avoid disability or death and to provide symptom relief. Symptoms to watch for include fever, dry cough, dyspnea, increased weakness, acute headache, stiff neck, mental status changes, motor dysfunction, pain, diarrhea, nausea, vomiting, and decreased visual acuity (Martin 1987).

It is often difficult to distinguish between signs of an acute illness and the patient's chronic symptoms. Any new symptoms or changes in symptoms, such as an increase in the degree of a chronic fever, must be reported to the patient's physician. Patients and their care givers must be taught to identify and report changes in physical status.

Pain, although not a major symptom, may be the most feared problem. There are many potential causes of pain: generalized debilitation and immobility; peripheral neuropathy; skin and oral lesions; edema; and chest, gastrointestinal, and central nervous system infections. Complaints of pain in the manipulative drug user are difficult to assess and manage. These patients often use medications in excess of prescribed dosages and then complain of pain and lack of caring by health care providers when their supply runs out (Schofferman 1987).

Interventions for symptom management and supportive care are based on assessments of AIDS-related illnesses and treatments and functional changes in the patient. Such interventions may include management measures to relieve shortness of breath such as encouraging rest periods, teaching semi-Fowler's position, and ordering and administering oxygen; obtaining orders for analgesia and antidiarrheals; or ordering assistive equipment (e.g., a commode, walker, tub seat, grab bars, or hospital bed). As case manager, the nurse is also responsible for determining the need for and arranging other services such as physical, occupational, and speech therapy or home health aide assistance for the physically impaired.

Psychosocial Assessment and Interventions

A psychosocial assessment is necessary for the management of a patient's care. Effective coping stems from strong social supports such as available and caring family and friends; spiritual or religious beliefs and affiliations; a sense of control to some degree over the illness; and successful coping and management of illness-related symptoms and regimens. Ineffective coping may develop as a result of weak social supports; multiple losses; feelings of guilt over past behaviors or lifestyle; substance abuse; and fears of death, disability, and loss of control. The patient may exhibit signs of sadness and depression and may become socially withdrawn and isolated (Siegel 1986).

The patient's psychosocial needs should be evaluated and appropriate interventions determined. Educating the patient in how to manage symptoms and regimens provides the patient with a greater feeling of control and may enable the patient to cope better with the disease. Other interventions may include making referrals to the following types of services:

- organizations such as the Gay Men's Health Crisis or Helping Hands (New York City) to obtain a "buddy" for the lonely, isolated patient
- counseling services for the patient who wishes to resolve such issues as guilt or anger
- psychiatric services for the severely depressed or suicidal patient
- drug rehabilitation services for the substance abuser
- day care services for family or care provider respite

The diagnosis of AIDS brings with it multiple losses for the patient and family or care givers. The patient may experience loss of health, energy, strength, and cognitive and functional ability as well as loss of job, income, feelings of control, and independence. To compensate for the AIDS patient's losses, family or friends often must assume the roles that the patient is no longer able to fulfill: care giver, financial provider, child care provider, and others (Bennett 1988).

Assessment of the needs of the family and care givers is important when establishing and maintaining home care services. To prevent "burn-out" of the care givers, the nurse must provide support, education, and referrals for counseling and additional support as needed.

Education

Education for the patient and care provider is important if the patient is to be maintained at home in comfort and safety and with maximum independence. It is an ongoing process and must focus on the patient's and care provider's learning needs during the course of the illness. Education needs include knowledge of the disease process, treatment options, and measures such as hygiene and proper food preparation for the prevention of opportunistic infections. In addition, the patient and care provider must be instructed about the patient's medications and their side effects, symptom management, and infection control. Written instructions such as *Living with AIDS: A Caregiver's Guide* (Ungvarski 1987) and *Caring for the AIDS Patient at Home* (American Red Cross and U.S. Public Health Service 1986) are useful in reinforcing the nurse's teaching and as reference tools.

Prevention and Detection of Opportunistic Infections

A major goal of nursing care of the patient with AIDS in the home is the prevention and early detection of opportunistic infections. Many of these infections are due to organisms that are already present in dormant form in the patient (e.g., mycobacteria). They emerge as the patient becomes immunocompromised and can recur even after successful treatment. Some ubiquitous organisms such as

Candida albicans cannot be avoided and may cause disease in the immunocompromised patient. There are, however, infections that can be avoided by implementing good hygiene (e.g., infection with *Salmonella* and *Cryptosporidium* organisms). Many opportunistic infections are life threatening or can cause serious tissue damage if detection and treatment are delayed (Pinching 1988). Early treatment may eliminate or reduce the need for hospitalization.

Infection control at home is needed to protect the patient from the environment and to protect the family or care giver from HIV infection. The patient must be educated in the following areas to avoid acquiring infections from the home environment (Lusby 1988):

- Use good hygiene (i.e., wash hands; bathe regularly; keep skin clean, dry, and intact; perform mouth care).
- Wash and peel fruits and vegetables.
- Cook food thoroughly; avoid raw eggs, meat, and fish.
- Refrigerate or discard leftover food.
- Use separate razors, toothbrushes, and eating utensils.
- Clean dishes and eating utensils in hot, soapy water.
- Maintain a clean home environment; clean air conditioner filters regularly.
- Avoid handling pet excreta, litter boxes, cages, or aquariums.
- Avoid contact with people who have infections.

The family and care givers must be taught how HIV is transmitted and appropriate precautions to take. Friedland (1987) found a significant reduction in frequency and closeness of interactions between family members and AIDS patients due to the fear of transmission of HIV. Once the family members were taught about the lack of transmission risk to household contacts who are not sexual partners of AIDS patients, normal personal interactions were maintained. Routine, close contact and household interactions do not pose HIV transmission risk except where direct contact with the blood and body secretions of the patient is involved. Care givers must be taught the following precautions to avoid this exposure (Lusby 1988):

- Wash hands before eating and meal preparation and after toileting.
- Wash dishes with hot, soapy water, rinse them in hot water, and dry them. They need not be separated from others in the household.
- Disinfect surfaces that have been soiled with blood or body fluids with a solution of household bleach and water (1:10).
- Clean soiled linens and clothes separately from those of the rest of the household in hot water with standard detergent and bleach.

- Wear gloves when handling blood, body fluids, and excretions and articles containing these.
- Wear masks and gowns when soiling or splashing is possible (e.g., when irrigating wounds).

Nutrition

Nutrition depletion is common as a result of a number of different problems, such as neoplasms involving the gastrointestinal tract, mycobacterium infection and candidiasis, extreme fatigue, depression, and the like. To minimize nutrition losses and subsequent weakening of the patient's condition, the following are recommended (McCaffrey 1987):

- Arrange for grocery shopping and meal preparation by friends, family, volunteers, or home health aides.
- Make Meals-on-Wheels referral.
- Encourage friends to visit during meal times to make eating enjoyable for the patient.
- Encourage soft foods, "blenderized" drinks, and nutrition supplements for patients who fatigue easily or have mouth or esophageal lesions.
- Provide relief from mouth sores with frequent mouth rinses and a topical anesthetic solution.
- Minimize nausea, vomiting, or diarrhea by obtaining orders for antiemetics and antidiarrheals as needed.
- Encourage small, frequent, high-calorie and high-protein meals.

When dysphagia or malabsorption exists, the patient may require a nasogastric tube or total parenteral nutrition (Crocker 1988).

HOSPICE CARE

Because there is no cure for AIDS, even the most aggressive medical treatments are palliative. Therefore, many AIDS patients seek experimental "curative" therapy for HIV infection or aggressive treatment for AIDS-related opportunistic infections and neoplasms. The decision to stop aggressive treatment may be made by a patient when treatment appears to have little or no benefit, when intolerable drug toxicities occur, or when death is imminent (Clark et al. 1988). Because of the early onset of dementia, it is important that treatment choices be addressed while the patient is lucid enough to make decisions. The patient should be encouraged to write a living will that communicates decisions about aggressive and palliative treatment and whether or not to resuscitate. This document should be reviewed frequently in light of the changing, developing knowledge base and advances in AIDS treatment.

Once his or her condition deteriorates, a patient may opt for hospice care at home. This provides palliative care to patients and supportive care to patients and their families or care givers during the terminal stage of life. The goal is to enhance the quality of life for the patient by providing and teaching comfort measures, pain control, symptom relief, and emotional support. Effective symptom management is essential if the patient is to be maintained at home and to die in comfort and with dignity.

The patient and care givers need help with preparing for the patient's progressive weakness and impending death. Arrangements for 24-hour nursing care as well as for equipment such as a hospital bed or oxygen may be needed. Instruction on care of the bedbound patient, incontinence care, symptom management, and signs and symptoms of impending death will help reduce patient and care giver anxiety.

After the patient's death, continued bereavement support to family and friends can help promote normal grieving. The nurse must identify the need for additional counseling and support for family and friends, especially for those who may themselves be at risk for acquiring the disease that caused the death of their loved one (Schofferman 1987).

DRUG THERAPY

Listed in Tables 13-1 and 13-2 are the drugs used to treat AIDS-related infections and neoplasms and their common side effects. Physicians may prescribe other drugs to manage infections that exhibit a poor response to currently used drug regimens. Because patients may be taking a number of medications concurrently, they are at an increased risk for adverse reactions and interactions. They must be monitored closely for side effects and taught to report any new signs or symptoms.

Home Intravenous Therapy

Because the treatment of opportunistic infections may continue for a prolonged time or even for life, IV therapy is now frequently given in the home. Besides being more cost effective, it can psychologically benefit patients by providing them greater control of their own care and the ability to maintain routine lifestyles (Garvey 1987).

Table 13-1 Drug Therapies for Opportunistic Diseases

Disease	Medication and Dosage	Side Effects
Pneumocystis carinii pneumonia (PCP)	Pentamidine isethionate (Pentam 300), 4 mg/kg/day IV (by slow infusion) or intramuscularly (IM; can cause sterile abscesses)	Hypotension, rash, glucose imbalance, neutropenia, nephrotoxicity, hepatotoxicity, hypocalcemia, thrombocytopenia, taste changes
	Trimethoprim-sulfamethoxazole (Bactrim, Septra), 20 mg/kg trimethoprim and 100 mg/kg sulfamethoxazole orally or IV every 6 hours	Rash, nausea, vomiting, neutropenia, gastritis, Stevens-Johnson syndrome, hepatotoxicity, stomatitis, fatigue, thrombocytopenia, anaphylaxis
	Dapsone-trimethoprim, 100 mg dapsone and 20 mg/kg trimethoprim orally every 6 hours	Mild bone marrow suppression, rash, nausea, vomiting
	Pyrimethamine-sulfadoxine (Fansidar), 25 mg and 50 mg, respectively, every week for prophylaxis	Rash, Stevens-Johnson syndrome, nausea, vomiting, elevation in liver enzymes and serum creatinine, fever, chills
PCP prophylaxis	Pyrimethamine-sulfadoxine (weekly), trimethoprim-sulfamethoxazole (every 12 hours, 2–7 days/week)	
	Aerosolized pentamidine (60–150 mg every week)	Bronchospasms, metallic taste
	Pentamidine (4 mg/kg every month IV or IM)	
Toxoplasmosis	Pyrimethamine (Daraprim), 100 mg loading dose, 25–50 mg orally every day	Anorexia, vomiting, leukopenia, megaloblastic anemia, glossitis, thrombocytopenia
	Sulfadiazine, 1 g orally every 6 hours	Fever, nausea, Stevens-Johnson syndrome, vomiting, urticaria
Cryptosporidiosis	No clearly active agent; spiramycin, 1 g 3–4 times a day	Nausea, vomiting, diarrhea, abdominal pain, acute colitis
	Eflornithine	Investigational
	Somatostatin analog SMS201-995	Investigational

continues

Table 13-1 continued

Disease	Medication and Dosage	Side Effects
Isosporiasis	Trimethoprim-sulfamethoxazole	See under PCP
Isosporiasis prophylaxis	Trimethoprim-sulfamethoxazole (at lower dose), pyrimethamine-sulfadoxine (weekly)	
Mycobacterium tuberculosis (TB)	Isoniazide, 10–15 mg/kg/day orally	Fever, rash, paresthesia, peripheral neuropathy, anorexia, nausea, vomiting, hepatic toxicity, malaise
	Ethambutol (Myambutol), 25 mg/kg/day orally	Reversible blurred vision, anaphylaxis, skin irritation, nausea, vomiting, fever, malaise, headache, confusion
	Rifampin (Rifadin, Rimactane), 600 mg/day orally	Urine discoloration, rash, nausea, vomiting, flulike symptoms, thrombocytopenia
	Pyrazinamide, 20–35 mg/kg/day orally in three or four divided doses	Liver toxicity, nausea, vomiting, dysuria, malaise, anorexia, fevers, gout, arthralgias
	Cycloserine (Seromycin), 250–500 mg orally twice a day	Central nervous system toxicity, nausea, headache, seizures, tremor, psychotic states, irritability, vertigo
	Streptomycin, 15–25 mg/kg IM every 12 hours	Nausea, vomiting, vertigo, itching, fever, facial numbness, elevated white blood cell count
Mycobacterium avium-intracellulare	Rifabutin (Ansamycin), 300 mg/day orally	Hepatotoxicity, rash, neutropenia, nausea, vomiting, thrombocytopenia, diarrhea, itching
	Clofazimine (Lamprene), 100 mg/day orally	Reddish-brown discoloration of skin, conjunctiva, sweat, hair, urine, and feces; abdominal pain; diarrhea
	Isoniazide	See under TB
	Rifampin	See under TB
	Ethambutol	See under TB
Candidiasis	Nystatin suspension (Mycostatin), 5–15 mL orally 4 times a day	Taste alterations, vomiting, nausea
	Clotrimazole troches (Mycelex), one troche 4–5 times/day	Taste alterations, nausea, vomiting
	Ketoconazole (Nizoral), 200–400 mg orally once a day	Hepatotoxicity, nausea, vomiting, dizziness, rash, decreased libido, drowsiness

Cryptococcosis	Amphotericin B (Fungizone), 0.5–1.0 mg/kg/day IV (begin with test dose, proceed with gradual dose escalations)	Fever, rigors, nephrotoxicity, nausea, hypotension, thrombocytopenia, anaphylaxis
	Amphotericin B	See under Candidiasis
	Flucytosine (Ancobon, 5-FC), 50–150 mg/kg orally every 6 hours	Bone marrow suppression, nausea, vomiting, rash, confusion, vertigo, headaches, sedation, hallucinations, elevated liver enzymes, dizziness
	Fluconazole, 50–400 mg/day orally	Increase in hepatic enzyme levels, nausea, bloating, skin rash
Histoplasmosis	Amphotericin B	See under Cryptococcosis
Cytomegalovirus	Ganciclovir (DHPG), 2–7 mg/kg IV every day, 5 times a week	Bone marrow suppression, nephrotoxicity, gonadal suppression, muscle aches, headache, anorexia, confusion
	Phosphonoformate (Foscarnet), 60 mg/kg every 8 hours IV (induction phase), then every day, 5–7 days/week	Nephrotoxicity, elevated liver enzymes, anemia
Herpes simplex virus (HSV)	Acyclovir sodium (Zovirax), 200–400 mg orally 5 times a day	Nephrotoxicity, elevated liver enzymes, anemia
Herpes zoster (shingles)	Acyclovir sodium, 400–800 mg orally 5 times a day	See under HSV
Progressive multifocal leukoencephalopathy	Cytarabine, cytosine arabinoside, 10–200 mg/m^2 IV every day, 1–7 days (has not been successful)	Bone marrow suppression, hepatic damage, gastrointestinal disturbances

Home Care for the AIDS Patient and Drug Therapy 225

Table 13-2 Treatment for HIV-Associated Cancers

Drug	Side Effects
Kaposi's Sarcoma	
Chemotherapy agents	
Vinblastine	Bone marrow suppression,
Etoposide	opportunistic infections,
Vincristine	gastrointestinal disturbances,
Bleomycin	alopecia, peripheral neuropathy
Doxorubicin	
Methotrexate	
Combinations	
Doxorubicin, bleomycin, vinblastine	
Doxorubicin, bleomycin, vincristine	
Vinblastine, bleomycin	
Vincristine, methotrexate	
Doxorubicin, vincristine	
Etoposide, doxorubicin, bleomycin, vinblastine	
Alpha-interferon therapy	
Recombinant interferons alfa-2a and alfa-2b	Fever, chills, chronic fatigue, malaise,
Interferon alfa-N1	anorexia, neutropenia
Interferon alfa-N1 and vinblastine	
HIV-Associated Lymphomas	
Multiple drug combinations are used that include the following in various doses, schedules, and routes	
Bleomycin	See under chemotherapy agents
Doxorubicin	
Cyclophosphamide	
Dexamethasone	
Vincristine	
Etoposide	
Methotrexate	
Nitrogen mustard	
Leucovorin	
Prednisone	
Procarbazine	

Tonnessen (1988) reviewed retrospectively the charts of patients being treated with amphotericin B for cryptococcal meningitis; no cures were found, but hospitalizations were eliminated in compliant patients. In a study of 109 patients receiving home IV therapy with ganciclovir, pentamidine, amphotericin B, total parenteral nutrition, trimethoprim-sulfamethoxazole, antibiotics, fluids, and chemotherapy, it was reported that 36% were able to remain at home for 2 months to more than 1 year between hospitalizations; 38% were able to return to their usual employment; and 82% were able to assume primary responsibility for the preparation, administration, and monitoring of the IV treatment (Carmody 1988).

The criteria for home administration of IV therapy include relative stability of the disease process, an initial successful response to the drug, and minimal or well-controlled adverse effects of the drug (Schietinger 1986). Before a patient is discharged to home on IV medications, environmental and psychosocial aspects must be assessed to ensure appropriateness of home therapy. Appropriate environment includes the cleanliness of the home and the availability of electricity, plumbing, refrigeration, and a telephone. A psychosocial assessment is done to evaluate whether the patient or care provider can or cannot learn to administer and monitor the IV therapy.

If the patient is expected to be on IV therapy for a long time, a permanent device such as a Mediport or Broviac catheter is practical to ensure venous access. Infection at the site of the venous access device often occurs, however, and the patient may require hospitalization for antibiotic therapy. It is important to monitor the patient's laboratory values for adverse effects of the drugs, such as renal and hepatic insufficiency or neutropenia, that may necessitate a decrease in the dose or complete termination of the drug. Changes in mental or visual status may require an increased dependency on nurses for the administration of the IV therapy.

The home care agency must have strict standards of practice for infection control and for the preparation and administration of the therapy. The agency must also provide for the proper isolation and disposal of equipment used (e.g., needles are never capped but are disposed of in rigid, puncture-proof containers).

Investigational Drugs

Many patients are involved in clinical trials of experimental drugs for treatment of HIV infection. These trials are established by the National Institute of Allergy and Infectious Diseases (NIAID) and are conducted by AIDS clinical trials units (ACTUs) throughout the country. The ACTUs study agents for their potential use against HIV infection or the various opportunistic infections and neoplasms that develop in HIV-infected persons. Nurses can call NIAID (303-496-5717) or the American Foundation of AIDS Research (212-719-0033) for more information. When caring for a patient involved in a clinical trial, the nurse should call the ACTU in which the patient is enrolled to get data about the drug and its adverse effects. Investigational drugs currently in clinical trials are listed in Exhibit 13-1 and Table 13-3.

Alternative Therapy

Some patients may explore unproven methods of treating their HIV-related illness in place of standard medical therapy. They may be reluctant to discuss their

Exhibit 13-1 Combinations of Drugs under Investigation

Recent studies are combining zidovudine (AZT) with other agents that may have synergistic or additive activities and toxicities that do not overlap:

- AZT alternating with dideoxycytidine (combination used to decrease toxicity)
- AZT with acyclovir
- AZT with probenecid (an antigout drug)
- AZT with interferon alfa
- AZT with interferon beta
- AZT with granulocyte colony-stimulating factor with erythropoietin
- AZT with gancyclovir (for AIDS and cytomegalovirus)
- AZT with chemotherapy with or without radiation therapy (for high-grade lymphoma)
- AZT with chemotherapy and radiation therapy (for primary central nervous system lymphoma)
- AZT with IV immune globulin (for children with symptomatic HIV infection)
- AZT with human interferon (recombinant alfa-2a and lymphoblastoid) (for AIDS and Kaposi's sarcoma)
- AZT with Foscarnet
- AZT with recombinant interleukin-2 (for persistent generalized lymphadenopathy)
- AZT with granulocyte-macrophage colony-stimulating factor (for AIDS and severe ARC)

Other drug combinations being studied in current clinical trials are:

- clindamycin and primaquine (for mild to moderate *Pneumocystis carinii* pneumonia)
- CM-CSF and methotrexate, bleomycin, doxorubicin, cyclophosphamide, vincristine, and dexamethasone (for lymphoma)
- fluconazole and amphotericin B (for cryptococcosis)
- recombinant tumor necrosis factor with recombinant interferon gamma (for ARC)
- ribavirin and isoprinosine (for asymptomatic viremic patients)
- trimetrexate with leucovorin calcium rescue (for *P. carinii* pneumonia)

use of alternative therapies with health care professionals for fear of rejection, abandonment, and withdrawal of hope. The nurse must demonstrate openness, understanding, and realistic hope while counseling patients regarding both conventional and alternative treatments. To assist the patient in making an informed decision about the use of unproven therapies, the nurse must be knowledgeable about the various alternative therapies and their potential side effects and drug interactions (Clark et al. 1988). The nurse must also advise patients against the use of products that may endanger their safety or welfare.

Table 13-3 Investigative Agents Currently in AIDS Clinical Trials Group Clinical Trials for HIV Infection

Medication	Mechanism of Action	Known Side Effects
Antivirals		
Zidovudine (AZT, Retrovir) (only drug approved by FDA for treatment of AIDS and ARC)	Reverse transcriptase (also used for HIV-associated thrombocytopenia and neurologic dysfunction)	Bone marrow suppression, nausea, severe anemia and neutropenia, myalgias, fatigue, insomnia, headache, mild confusion, agitation
AL721	Extracts cholesterol from infected T cells; virucidal	None
Dideoxycytidine	Reverse transcription inhibitor	Peripheral neuropathy, fever, rash, arthralgias, stomatitis
Dideoxyinosine	Reverse transcription inhibitor	Toxicities not yet known
Phosphonoformate (Foscarnet)	Reverse transcription inhibitor	Nephrotoxicity, elevated liver enzymes, anemia
Dextran sulfate	Blocks (in vitro) viral attachment to cell membranes	Diarrhea, mild confusion, lethargy, thrombocytopenia, leukopenia, increased liver function tests, headache
Ribavirin (Virazole)	Either reverse transcription inhibitor or false guanine analog	Headaches, irritability, gastrointestinal upset, metallic taste, fatigue, insomnia, dry mouth
Recombinant soluble T4 (also called soluble CD4)	Interferes with binding of HIV gp120 to intact CD4 molecules	No toxicities observed
Immune modulators		
Ampligen	Augments cellular immunity; also has antiviral activity by stimulating interferon production	Mild flulike symptoms
Intravenous immune globulin	Increases circulating immunoglobulin G antibody titer	No significant toxicities
Granulocyte-macrophage colony-stimulating factor	Promotes proliferation and activity of granulocytes and macrophages	Fatigue, fever, muscle aches, anorexia, headaches, diarrhea, rash
Diethyldithiocarbamate (Immuthiol)	Induces T-cell differentiation and maturation	Chest pain, nausea, vomiting, behavior change, adverse reaction to alcohol
Interleukin-2	Stimulates proliferation of T cells	Flulike symptoms, neutropenia, nausea, polydipsia, headache

continues

Table 13-3 continued

Medication	Mechanism of Action	Known Side Effects
Antivirals and immune modulators		
Interferon alfa	Inhibits transcription/translation of viral messenger RNA; also has immunomodulating effects	Flulike symptoms, neutropenia, weight loss, thrombocytopenia, renal insufficiency, confusion, paresthesias
AS101	Enhances lymphokine function	Toxicities not yet known; garlic odor, fever and chills during infusion
Inosine pranabex (isoprinosine)	Enhances lymphocyte proliferation	Nausea, elevated uric acid levels
Tumor necrosis factor	Cell membrane lysis, possible immunomodulating effects	Fever, chills, leukopenia, fatigue, headache, anemia, hyperglycemia, hypotension, inflammation at injection site, elevated liver enzymes

INTO THE 21ST CENTURY

The CDC estimates that by the end of 1991 a total of 185,000 to 320,000 people will develop AIDS. The General Accounting Office, an investigational arm of Congress, forecasts a larger number: 300,000 to 480,000 cases. As the number of AIDS patients continues to grow, home care will be an even more crucial alternative for patients and families, oncology nurses, and society as a whole.

STUDY QUESTIONS

1. The Oncology Nursing Society's position paper of 1987 identifies oncology nurses as particularly well prepared to care for people with HIV-related illnesses. Describe the roles that the advanced practice oncology nurse might assume to ensure excellence in care for people with HIV-related illnesses in the community and at home.
2. How can nurses working in the community and in home care help curb the spread of HIV infection?

REFERENCES

American Red Cross and U.S. Public Health Service. October 1986. *Caring for the AIDS patient at home*. Washington, D.C.: American Red Cross.

Bennett, J. 1988. Helping people with AIDS live well at home. *Nursing Clinics of North America* 23:731–48.

Carmody, M. 1988. Psychosocial benefits of home infusion therapy for AIDS patients. Presented at the Fourth International Conference on AIDS.

Carpi, J. 1987. Treating IV drug users—A difficult task for staff. *AIDS Patient Care*, December, 21–23.

Centers for Disease Control. 1990. *HIV/AIDS Surveillance Report. Morbidity and Mortality Weekly Report* 39:1–18.

Clark, C., A. Curley, A. Hughes, and R. James. 1988. Hospice care: A model for caring for the person with AIDS. *Nursing Clinics of North America* 23:851–62.

Crocker, K.S. 1988. AIDS-related GI dysfunction: Rationale for nutritional support. *Critical Care Nurse* 8:43–45.

Friedland, G.H. 1987. The effects of AIDS diagnosis upon close, personal interactions among family members of AIDS patients. Presented at the Third International Conference on AIDS.

Friedman, S.R., D.C. Des Jarlais, and J.L. Sotheran. 1986. AIDS health education for intravenous drug users. *Health Education Quarterly* 13:382–93.

Garvey, E.C. 1987. Current and future nursing issues in home administration of chemotherapy. *Seminars in Oncology Nursing* 3:142–47.

Guinan, M., and A. Hardy. 1987. Epidemiology of AIDS in women in the United States 1981 through 1986. *Journal of the American Medical Association* 257:2039–42.

Klein, S.J., and N. Fletcher. 1987. The importance of supportive interventions for caregiving family/friends during the AIDS crisis. Presented at the Third International Conference on AIDS.

Lieberman, J.C. 1988. Home health care and hospice for people with HIV infection. In *AIDS: Concepts in nursing practice*, eds. G. Gee and T.A. Moran. Baltimore: Williams & Wilkins.

Lusby, G. 1988. Infection control precautions and HIV infection. In *AIDS: Concepts in nursing practice*, eds. G. Gee and T.A. Moran. Baltimore: Williams & Wilkins.

Martin, J.P. 1987. Sustaining care of persons with AIDS. In *The person with AIDS: Nursing perspectives*, eds. J.D. Durham and F.L. Cohen. New York: Springer-Verlag.

McCaffrey, E.A. 1987. Meeting nutritional needs. *AIDS Patient Care*, September, 28–31.

National Academy of Sciences Institute of Medicine. 1986. *Confronting AIDS: Directions for public health, health care, and research*. Washington, D.C.: National Academy Press.

New York City AIDS Task Force. 1988. *Models of care report*. New York: New York City Department of Health.

New York City AIDS Task Force. 1989. *Report of the Needs Assessment Work Group*. New York:

Pinching, A.J. 1988. Prophylactic and maintenance therapy for opportunistic infections in AIDS. *AIDS* 2:335–43.

Ross, M.W., and V. Seeger. 1988. Determinants of reported burnout in health professionals associated with the care of patients with AIDS. *AIDS* 2:395–97.

Schietinger, H. 1986. A home care plan for AIDS. *American Journal of Nursing* 86:1021–28.

Schofferman, J. 1987. Hospice care of the patient with AIDS. *Hospice Journal* 3:51–74.

Siegel, K. 1986. AIDS: The social dimension. *Psychiatric Annals* 16:168–72.

Tonnessen, G. 1988. Amphotericin B—Outpatient therapy. Presented at the Fourth International Conference on AIDS.

Ungvarski, P.J. 1988. Home health care. In *AIDS: A health care management response*, ed. K.D. Blanchet. Rockville, Md.: Aspen Publishers.

SUGGESTED READING

Abrams, D.I. 1989. Oral dextran sulfate (UA001) in the treatment of the Acquired Immunodeficiency Syndrome (AIDS) and AIDS-Related Complex. *Annals of Internal Medicine* 110:183–188.

American Foundation for AIDS Research (Am FAR). 1989. *AIDS/HIV experimental treatment directory*, Washington, D.C.

Berkowitz, C.D. 1985. AIDS and parasitic infections including *Pneumocystis carinii* and cryptosporidiosis. *Pediatric Clinics of North America* 32:933–951.

Bloom, J.N., and A.G. Palestine. 1988. The diagnosis of cytomegalovirus retinitis. *Annals of Internal Medicine* 109:963.

Carter, W.A. 1987. Clinical, immunological, and virological effects of ampligen, a mismatched double-stranded RNA, in patients with AIDS or AIDS-related complex. *The Lancet* 1:1286–1292.

Donehower, M.G. 1987. Malignant complications of AIDS. *Oncology Nursing Forum* 14:57–64.

Forecasts of AIDS fall short, U.S. study says. 1989, 26 June, *New York Times*: B5.

Fuessl, H., and H. Heinleim. 1988. Treatment of persistent diarrhea in AIDS with the somatostatin analogue SMS 201-995. Fourth International Conference on AIDS.

Gee, G., Moran, T., and Wong, R. 1988. Current strategies in the treatment of HIV infection. *Seminars in Oncology Nursing* 4:126–131.

Gold, J.W. 1988. Infectious complications in patients with HIV infection. *AIDS* 2:327–334.

Groopman, J. 1987. Effect of recombinant human GMCSF or myeloporesis in the Acquired Immunodeficiency Syndrome. *New England Journal of Medicine* 317:593–598.

Henochowicz, S., and D. Hoth. 1988. Unproven agents in the treatment of human immunodeficiency virus (HIV) infection. *AIDS Updates* 1:1–10.

Kaplan, L.D., C.B. Wofsy, and P.A. Volbending. 1987. Treatment of patients with acquired immunodeficiency syndrome and associated manifestations. *Journal of the American Medical Association* 257:1367–1373.

Kovacs, J.A., and H. Mauser. 1988. Opportunistic infections. In *AIDS: Etiology, diagnosis, treatment and prevention*, 2nd ed., eds. V.T. DeVita, S. Hellman, and S.A. Rosenberg. Philadelphia: J.P. Lippincott Co.

Lynch, M., L. Yanes, and K. Todd. 1988. Nursing care for AIDS patients participating in a phase I/II trial of recombinant human granulocyte-macrophage colony stimulating factor. *Oncology Nursing Forum* 15:463–469.

NIAID AIDS PROGRAM: Protocols that are open or closed to accrual as of March 17, 1989. New York: New York City Department of Health.

Polsky, B., and D. Armstrong. 1988. Other agents in the treatment of AIDS. In *AIDS: Etiology, diagnosis, treatment and prevention*, 2nd ed., eds. V.T. DeVita, S. Hellman, and S.A. Rosenberg. Philadelphia: J.B. Lippincott Co.

Richman, D.D. 1988. The treatment of HIV infection. *AIDS* 2:5137–5142.

Ryan, A., B.J. Thomson, and A.D. Webster. 1988. Home intravenous immunoglobulin therapy for patients with primary hypogammaglobulinemia. *The Lancet* 2:793.

Stern, J.J. 1988. Oral fluconazole therapy for patients with Acquired Immunodeficiency Syndrome and cryptococcosis: Experience with 22 patients. *American Journal of Medicine* 85:477–480.

The Swiss Group for Clinical Studies on the Acquired Immunodeficiency Syndrome. 1988. Zidovudine for the treatment of thrombocytopenia associated with human immunodeficiency virus (HIV). *Annals of Internal Medicine* 109:718–721.

Ungvarski, P.J. 1987. Living with AIDS: A caregiver's guide. New York: National Center for Homecare Education and Research.

Varchoan, R., and S. Broder. 1988. Pharmacologic treatment of HIV infection. In *AIDS: Etiology, diagnosis, treatment and prevention*, 2nd ed., eds. V.T. DeVita, S. Hellman, and S.A. Rosenberg. Philadelphia: J.P. Lippincott Co.

Volberding, P.A. 1984. Therapy of Kaposi's Sarcoma in AIDS. *Seminars in Oncology* 11:60–67.

Chapter 14

Acquired Immunodeficiency Syndrome Patient Handbook

Jeanne Kalinoski

> The *AIDS Patient Handbook* currently used at the New York City Bellevue Hospital is reproduced in its entirety for nurse educators who need to provide practical information to people living with AIDS outside the hospital setting.

The following booklet was prepared by Jeanne Kalinoski, AIDS Education Program Coordinator, and other members of the AIDS team at New York City's Bellevue Hospital. This city hospital has long been a leader of New York City's huge municipal hospital system. Located in lower mid-Manhattan, Bellevue is one of the largest and busiest hospitals anywhere in the country. A city hospital in such a densely populated urban area is assured a continuous stream of patients, many of whom are poor, unemployed, without medical insurance coverage, mentally ill, or incarcerated. As the acquired immunodeficiency syndrome epidemic has grown in New York City, Bellevue Hospital has accepted ever larger numbers of patients. On any one day more than 140 beds are occupied by suspected or confirmed AIDS patients, and many more clinic patients come for ambulatory care visits and treatments.

The nursing staff have had to devise many new ways to cope with the demands of caring for the patient with AIDS. Instead of writing a chapter, Jeanne Kalinoski, who is also the Assistant Director of Nursing on the AIDS team, allowed us to reproduce a publication that is handed out to all AIDS patients at Bellevue. She has had requests from around the world for help in preparing AIDS patient education materials and is pleased to reproduce this booklet in full at this time. The down-to-earth details contained in the pages that follow bear testimony to the extraordinary problems facing the nurse who is trying to care for a patient with AIDS, a patient who not only is frightened but also may be poor, undernourished, alone, and a user of drugs.

We are aware that future materials need to be available in Spanish and that there should be much more additional information and tips aimed at women who are drug users or who have contracted the disease from drug users, and whose children have AIDS. This is a rapidly emerging area of need. In the meantime, this remarkable booklet addresses the major situations facing the AIDS patient and offers many practical suggestions.

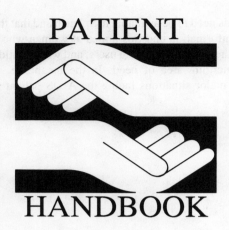

BELLEVUE HOSPITAL CENTER

AIDS PATIENT HANDBOOK

Written and Edited By:
Jeanne Kalinoski, MA, RN
AIDS Education Program Coordinator and
Assistant Director of Nursing
AIDS Team

Contributions

Keith Hanson, BS, RN
Assistant Head Nurse
12 East Unit

Dean Rakower, MS, RD
AIDS Nutrition Specialist
AIDS Team

Oliver Cole
PWA

Sharon Sageman, MD
Attending Physician
Psychiatry

Gretchen Harris
Associate Director
Patient Advocacy

Cover Design:
  Michael G. McKibbon, PWA

Illustrations:
  Rick Surmacz

Source: Copyright, 1988, New York City Health & Hospitals Corporation, Jeanne Kalinoski, in conjunction with the Bellevue Hospital Center AIDS Program. Revised 1989.

INTRODUCTION

This Handbook has been written to provide you basic information about your illness and steps you can take to be as physically and emotionally healthy as possible.

Use this Handbook with the members of your health team, and share it with family and friends.

After you are discharged, you may want to refer to the Handbook to help you remember what you learned in the hospital.

AIDS: WHAT IS IT?

AIDS is caused by a virus called HIV (Human Immunodeficiency Virus).

The AIDS virus (HIV) is spread from one person to another by contact with blood, semen, vaginal secretions, and breast milk. (The virus then must enter the bloodstream in order to live.)

Those at risk for being infected with the AIDS virus are:

—Male or female sexual partners of infected people.
—Intravenous (IV) drug users who share needles, syringes, and/or cookers.
—People who receive contaminated blood or blood products.
—Babies of infected women.
—Babies who breast feed from infected women.

After the AIDS virus gets into the bloodstream, it enters certain cells, and over a period of time it damages the immune system. The immune system helps you destroy the germs that make you sick.

When the immune system is damaged by the AIDS virus, you may experience swollen lymph nodes, fatigue, fevers, a white coating on the tongue (thrush), weight loss, and/or diarrhea. You may develop diseases known as opportunistic infections or malignancies (cancers).

When a person with suspected or confirmed AIDS enters the hospital, he/she must undergo different kinds of tests to find out what infection or malignancy is present. These tests are very important to help the doctors make a diagnosis and decide what treatment is best for you.

During your hospital stay, members of the health team will teach, counsel, and guide you so that you can learn about and cope with your illness.

COPING WITH THE AIDS EXPERIENCE

Most people who learn that they have AIDS react with feelings of anger, sadness, and isolation. They might feel unloved, unlovable, and unwanted. Some experience a sense of shame and assume they are being punished for something. It is important for you to know that all these feelings, even though they may be disturbing, are a normal reaction to learning you have a serious illness. Exploring and understanding your feelings is part of your emotional recovery.

Sometimes these feelings occur soon after the diagnosis is made, and sometimes they don't show up until you have left the hospital. Allow the feelings to be there and to wash over you, but just as important, allow the feelings to go away. A very important part of your health is your positive attitude. If you let yourself be angry or sad all the time, it can interfere with your emotional and physical well being.

Suggestions:

—Do something every day that will make you feel good in a healthful way. This could include getting some physical exercise, seeing a friend, or going to the movies.
—Reach out to your friends and family. People with AIDS sometimes push away those who truly care about them. This is neither good for you nor good for the people who love you. Your loved ones may be unsure of what to do and are waiting to hear from you.
—Most people with a long-term, serious illness report that they have "good" days and "bad" days. It is not unusual to feel "blue" or "down in the dumps." If these feelings of depression should persist for more than a couple of weeks, or if you have thoughts of hurting yourself, it is time to seek help. The staff at Bellevue is available to refer you to a mental health professional or support group.
—You will feel stronger and more in control of your life if you let your needs be known. People can't read your mind, so tell them what you want.
—Many people have found strength and comfort by exploring and developing the spiritual side of their lives. This may be accomplished by visualization, meditation, or participation in a formal religion.
—Doing the best you can to keep up your personal grooming and living area can help you feel both physically and mentally better.

YOUR BODY—CHECK IT OUT

If you are living with AIDS, it is important to examine yourself at least once a week. You should look at your entire body, note any changes, and report what you find to your health care provider.

SKIN
- Dry/Scaly
- Rashes
- Sores/Bumps
- Color Changes

LIPS
- Cracks
- Sores

MOUTH
- White Specks or Coating
- Bleeding Gums
- Sores/Bumps
- Pain

DIGESTION/EATING
- Weight Loss or Gain
- Appetite (how well you eat)
- Nausea (upset stomach)
- Vomiting (throwing up)
- Strange Taste
- Difficulty Swallowing
- Pain in the Chest when Swallowing
- Stomach Ache

BOWEL MOVEMENTS
- Diarrhea (loose stools)
- Constipation
- Pain
- Bloody Bowel Movements or Bleeding
- Loss of Control
- Changes in Regular Habits

URINATION
- Frequency (how often you urinate)
- Pain/Burning
- Bloody Urine

Loss of Control   _____

GENITALS/SEX ORGANS
Discharge from Penis or Vagina   _____
Sores/Bumps   _____
Change in Color   _____
Pain   _____

RESPIRATION/BREATHING
Shortness of Breath (at rest, while walking, after any physical effort)   _____
Cough   _____
Chest Tightness, Pain   _____

NERVOUS SYSTEM
Headache   _____
Stiff Neck   _____
Numbness or Tingling in Hands and Feet   _____
Loss of Balance   _____
Confusion, Loss of Memory, Difficulty Concentrating   _____
Slurred Speech   _____
Change in Vision, Sensitivity to Light   _____
Shaking, Twitching, Seizures   _____
Tiredness   _____
Sadness, Depression   _____

TEMPERATURE
Fever (normal is between 97° and 100°F, but some people with AIDS run higher temperatures all the time. It is significant when your temperature goes higher than usual)   _____
Chills   _____
Night Sweats   _____

HELPFUL HINT

Write down the changes you see in your body, or use this list and check them off. If you have a question, write it down, too. This will serve as a reminder for your next visit to the doctor.

HOW TO TAKE CARE OF YOURSELF

SKIN CARE

—Wash your entire body every day (if possible). Showering by standing up or sitting on a chair in the tub is preferable to baths.

—Gently pat yourself dry to avoid irritation.
—Apply lotion to the skin to prevent dryness.
—If you have to spend a lot of time in bed, do not stay in one position too long (your skin could break down and develop sores). Roll side to side occasionally. Propping a pillow against your back can help you rest comfortably on your side. It is helpful to have another person position you in bed.

MOUTH CARE

—Clean your teeth with a soft toothbrush or cotton swab (Q-Tip).
—Brush after each meal.
—Brush your teeth gently and avoid scraping sore, bleeding gums with toothbrush bristles.
—If brushing is too painful, rinse your mouth often. There are two kinds of mouthwashes you can make: (1) Add ¼ teaspoon of salt to a large glass of warm water and stir. (2) Add 2 tablespoons of baking soda to a quart of water and shake well.
—Use a lip moisturizer.

CLEANLINESS

—If your underpants or clothes become soiled with blood or body secretions, wash yourself and change your garments.
—Change and wash sheets, pillow cases, and blankets that become soiled with blood or body secretions.
—Wash your hands after using the toilet and before preparing meals. Get into the habit of washing your hands often.
—Use a tissue every time you cough, sneeze, or spit. Throw all dirty tissues into a plastic bag, and then wash your hands.

MEDICINES

—Take all the medicines your doctor has ordered for you, and follow the directions carefully.
—Members of the health team can help you learn about the reasons for, and side effects of, your medicine.
—If you think that you are having side effects from any medicine, call your doctor to find out if you should continue or stop taking the medicine.
—If you have trouble keeping track of your medicines, write down their names and make a daily list of the hour(s) you should take them. Each time you take

a medicine, check it off. This method will prevent you from either missing a dose or taking more than you need.

NUTRITION

—Eat well-balanced meals every day (see the nutrition section).

ACTIVITIES

—Get a good night's sleep, and take naps if necessary.
—Pace yourself. Do not do too much at one time.
—Get involved with physical activity that does not overtire you.
—If you are on bed rest, exercise your arms and legs by moving them up and down. If it is possible, put a board at the foot of the bed and pretend to walk on it.

SAFETY

—Put a non-skid bath mat in the tub.
—Area or "throw" rugs may cause falls—remove them.
—Do not wear "floppy" slippers or shoes.
—If you get up in the middle of the night to go to the bathroom or kitchen, do not walk in the dark—put the lights on.

SEXUAL PRACTICES

Because AIDS is a sexually transmitted disease (STD), you have to be careful about your partner's and your own safety. You do not want to be exposed to more AIDS virus, and you do not want to spread the virus to your partner. You also want to protect yourself from diseases such as herpes and syphilis, which can be spread by sexual contact.

Everybody should know as much as possible about the people they have sex with. Therefore, it is important to have an honest talk with your sexual partner(s).

If you do not have a partner, masturbation is a safe and effective way of pleasing and comforting yourself.

DO NOT HAVE SEX WHILE DRUNK OR HIGH!!!!!!!

Your judgment will be impaired, and you will end up taking sexual risks.

AVOID SEXUAL CONTACT IF YOUR PARTNER HAS SORES OR LESIONS ON THE SEX ORGANS OR OTHER PARTS OF THE BODY

Open areas may help the spread of STDs.

GUIDELINES FOR MEN AND WOMEN

SAFE (will not transmit the AIDS virus)

—Dry kissing
—Hugging
—Massage
—Body-to-body rubbing
—Masturbation with a partner while avoiding direct contact with bodily fluids
—Verbal lovemaking
—*Gentle* S/M without bruising or bleeding
—Separate sex toys

BE CAREFUL (safety cannot be guaranteed)

—French kissing
—Oral-genital contact with precautions (condoms, dental dams)
—Vaginal intercourse with a condom and a spermicide
—Anal intercourse with a condom and lubricant (K-Y jelly)

UNSAFE (can definitely transmit the AIDS virus)

—Anal intercourse without a condom
—Vaginal intercourse without a condom
—Blood contact
—Rimming (oral-anal contact)
—Oral-genital contact without a condom or dental dam

Activities such as fisting, douching, and taking enemas can damage delicate tissues and increase the risk of getting a sexually transmitted disease. Contact with urine and/or feces also is a risk.

CONDOMS

Condoms are worn to prevent semen and other body secretions from passing from one person to another. Commercial condoms (those you buy in a drugstore) should be used. Alternatives, such as plastic wrap, "Baggies," balloons, etc. are extremely unreliable.

A lubricant should be used to make the sex act easier to do, and it helps prevent the condom from breaking. Do not use lubricants that contain oil or petroleum jelly (Vaseline, baby and cooking oils, body oils sold in sex shops). They can weaken Latex and cause the condom to break. Use a water-based lubricant (K-Y jelly, spermicide).

CONDOM TIPS

—Long fingernails and rings can rip the condom. Fingernails should be trimmed, and rings should be removed.
—Put the condom on before sexual contact.
—Leave a space at the tip of the condom to collect the semen.
—Use the condom only once, and change condoms for each different sexual act (vaginal, anal, oral).
—Try to prevent the condom from slipping off during intercourse.
—When withdrawing (pulling out), hold the condom; do not let any semen spill.
—When you are finished, place the condom in a tissue or paper towel, throw it away, and then wash your hands.

Remember: Using a condom does not guarantee protection from sexually transmitted diseases!

SPERMICIDES

Spermicides should be used for added protection. Spermicides are the contraceptive foams and the jellies or creams used with diaphragms. They contain an ingredient, nonoxynol-9, that *might* prevent the spread of the AIDS virus during sexual contact.

Spermicides are not used instead of a condom; they are used *in addition to* a condom.

PREGNANCY

If a woman who is infected with the AIDS virus gets pregnant, she runs the risk of transmitting the virus to her unborn baby. A woman and a man who are either expecting a baby or considering a future pregnancy should get counseling from a health professional.

DRUG USE

Dirty needles can spread a variety of diseases, and using drugs of any kind can damage your immune system and can hurt your liver, kidneys, and heart.

If you are using drugs, we strongly recommend that you become involved in a treatment program. The hospital staff is available to assist you in finding a program.

However, if you do choose to shoot drugs again, it is very important that everything you use to inject yourself—needles, syringes, cookers, cotton, and water—be sterile. Wiping off the needle with a tissue or running a piece of wire or water through the works *is NOT good enough*!

HOW TO CLEAN YOUR WORKS

1. Separate the needle and plunger from the syringe.
2. Boil them in water for *at least* 15 minutes.

OR

1. Draw up rubbing alcohol through the needle and into the syringe. Squirt out the alcohol. Do this several times.
2. Separate the needle, plunger, and syringe.
3. Soak the works in the rubbing alcohol for at least 15 minutes.

Note: A bleach solution, instead of alcohol, may be used in this procedure.

MORE DRUG TIPS

1. *Never* share works with anyone.
2. If you buy new works, clean them anyway. Some syringes and needles are repackaged after being used and are sold as new.
3. Clean your works every time you use them.
4. Do not reuse the cotton or the cooker.
5. The area of your body that you use to inject should be cleaned with alcohol or soap and water.

246 ONCOLOGY NURSING

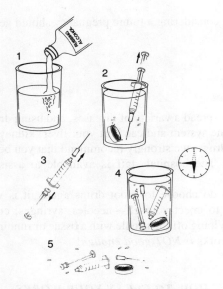

Cleaning Your Works

1) Pour rubbing alcohol or bleach solution into a clean container.
2) Draw the alcohol or bleach solution through the needle and into the syringe.
3) Separate the needle, plunger, and syringe.
4) Soak the works for at least 15 minutes.
5) Allow the works to dry before using.

Remember: Cleaning your works does not guarantee protection from the AIDS virus!

HOUSEHOLD HINTS

—Surfaces (floors, counter tops, sinks, bathtubs, toilet seats, etc.) that get soiled with blood or body secretions (feces, vomitus, urine, sputum, semen) should be cleaned with a household detergent or with diluted bleach.
—When you use bleach, dilute it (mix it) with water (small job: ¼ cup bleach to 2¼ cups water; large job: 1 cup bleach to 9 cups water). Full-strength bleach is not necessary and can irritate the skin.
—A mist bottle is a useful container for the bleach solution. Small clean-ups can be done with a spray and a wipe.
—Throw out the unused bleach solution after 1 day. The strength of the bleach will decrease after 24 hours.
—Do not mix bleach with other cleaning agents.

—Bathroom and kitchen surfaces should be cleaned regularly (at least once a week), even if they have not come in contact with blood or body secretions.
—Do not use the same sponge or cleaning cloths for the bathroom and kitchen.
—Wear reusable household gloves when cleaning areas soiled with blood or body secretions. Wash the gloves after using them: Place your gloved hands under running water, apply an agent (household detergent), rinse, remove the gloves, and allow them to dry.
—Separate dishes and eating utensils are *not* necessary.
—If you have to carry your dirty laundry to a laundry room or laundromat, use a heavy-duty plastic bag.
—When doing the laundry, set the machine on the hot water cycle and add regular laundry detergent.
—Add bleach or Lysol to the wash if any of the laundry items are soiled with blood and/or feces.
—Put *all* dirty, throw-away items into a plastic garbage bag, and tie the top of the bag when it is full.
—Dispose of needles and razors in a coffee can with a plastic lid.
—Beds can be shared unless you cannot control your bladder or bowels or if you have open sores on your body.
—Do not share toothbrushes, razors, or other personal items that could be contaminated with blood.
—Towels and washcloths should not be shared unless the items are laundered between uses.
—Wash your hands before preparing meals for yourself and others and after doing any household chores.
—Cleaning litter boxes, pet cages, and fish tanks should be avoided if possible. Ask a friend to help, or wear gloves if you do clean up after your pet.

THE CARE GIVER AT HOME

If you are caring for, or living with, a person with AIDS (PWA), you should know that there have been no cases of relatives or friends getting AIDS through casual contact—even when they live in the same household as the PWA.

—AIDS *is not spread* by the preparation and serving of food or the sharing of meals.
—AIDS *is not spread* by contact with toilet seats, door knobs, furniture, bathtubs, telephones, or any other household items.
—AIDS *is not spread* through air or water.
—AIDS *is not spread* by kissing and hugging or coughing and sneezing.

GUIDELINES

Anyone providing care to a PWA should avoid unprotected contact with blood and body secretions (feces, vomitus, urine, sputum, semen).

HANDWASHING IS DONE:

—Before and after caring for the PWA.
—If your hands accidentally come in contact with the PWA's blood or body secretions (wash your hands as soon as possible).

DISPOSABLE GLOVES ARE WORN WHEN:

—Cleaning the PWA's body, especially the rectal and genital areas.
—Touching the PWA who has open sores.
—Handling blood and body secretions.
—Emptying bedpans, urine drainage bags, or urinals.
—Giving mouth care.

NOTE: If you do not have disposable gloves, cover your hands with small plastic bags.

PLASTIC APRONS OR COVER GOWNS ARE WORN:

—Whenever your clothes might be soiled with blood or body secretions.

NOTE: Wipe the plastic apron with diluted bleach every day. Launder cloth cover gowns when they get soiled. If you do not have a plastic apron or a cover gown, fashion a plastic bag into an apron.

TAKING CARE OF THE CARE GIVER

Sometimes you might feel physically and emotionally tired. Taking care of someone who doesn't feel well can be very draining. You should and need to take care of yourself.

—Get enough rest every day.
—If possible, get a friend or relative to relieve you once in a while.
—Understand that you may experience a variety of emotions (anger, guilt, sadness). This is normal.
—Talk about your feelings to those people who care about you.

—If you start to feel overwhelmed, seek professional help. The staff at Bellevue Hospital can refer you to special organizations and support groups.
—Eat well-balanced meals. This will keep you physically strong.

NUTRITION AND AIDS

INTRODUCTION

A healthy diet is important for all people. But when you get sick, eating properly is especially important. Calories, protein, and minerals (from the food you eat) are needed to keep your body running, to prevent breakdown of body tissue, to fight infections, and to build you up again.

People with AIDS-related complex (ARC) or AIDS often lose weight. There are several reasons for this:

—Infection (calorie demands are higher).
—Poor appetite.
—Difficult or painful swallowing.
—Nausea and vomiting.
—Diarrhea.
—Inability to eat or prepare food because of fatigue or limited resources.

BASIC FOUR FOOD GROUPS

You need to eat to get calories, but you also need to include items from the Basic Four Food Groups to get enough vitamins, minerals, and proteins.

Milk Group:
At least 2 servings/day. If tolerated, try for 3 or 4 servings (1 serving = 1 cup). Milk, yogurt, cheese, ice cream, milk shakes, custard, pudding, or cottage cheese.

Meat Group:
At least 2 large servings/day (1 serving = 5 ounces). Meat, fish, chicken, turkey, eggs, nuts, beans (lentils, baked beans, split peas, dried beans).

Fruit and Vegetable Group:
At least 2 servings/day of each (1 serving = ½ cup or 1 medium piece of fruit). Include 1 citrus fruit or juice daily. Include 1 dark green or deep yellow vegetable 2 times/week.

Grain Group:
At least 4 servings/day (1 serving = ½ cup). Bread, cereal, pasta, rice, potato.

HIGH-CALORIE DIET

Putting on weight is a difficult and slow process. Do not get discouraged if you are unable to gain weight. If you can prevent *further* weight loss, you are doing O.K. On a good week, expect to gain no more than 1 or 2 pounds.

General Tips:
Eat at least 3 meals *plus snacks* each day. Start with small meals if necessary, and slowly make them bigger.

Plan your meal times. Try not to skip a meal. If you eat only a few bites, it is better than eating nothing.

Think of food as medicine. Eating helps you get better and keeps you feeling strong.

Keep snacks handy and within easy reach. Some good choices are peanut butter or cheese and crackers, nuts, leftovers, dried fruit, hard-boiled eggs, milk, granola.

Usually a lot of fat and sugar are considered unnecessary "evils" in a healthy diet. But when weight loss is a problem, fat and sugar become an important part of your diet.

Margarine, butter, oils, gravies, cream, and other fats are a good way to get extra calories without eating a lot more food. Be sure to use them in cooking *and* at the table. You can use plenty of margarine/butter on your bread. Fry foods, and use cream sauces and gravies.

Eat plenty of your favorite desserts after or between meals. Sugar and sweets, such as cookies, cakes, pastries, and candy, are high in calories.

Drink liquids at the end of your meal rather than during the meal. Coffee, tea, and broths will fill you up without adding extra calories, so avoid them. (If you do drink coffee or tea, add plenty of sugar and milk for calories.)

If you use a nutritional supplement (like Sustacal or Ensure), drink it 1 hour after a meal. Drinking it right before eating will fill you up, and you might not feel like finishing your meal.

Drink whole milk or fortified milk rather than low-fat milk. Add "instant breakfast" powder to your milk (available at any grocery store).

Make fortified milk by adding 1 cup of non-fat dry milk powder to 1 quart of whole milk for extra calories and protein.

Use milk or half-and-half instead of water when making soups, cereals, puddings, and instant drinks.

When possible, eat your meals in a relaxed and pleasant atmosphere. Have your favorite foods readily available. Take advantage of the times when your appetite is good.

Don't forget to make sure your diet is well balanced. Use the Basic Four Food Groups as a guide. Eat a wide variety of foods.

HIGH-CALORIE/HIGH-PROTEIN DRINKS

If you have a blender, here are some simple drinks you can make. Place in blender for 1 minute or until smooth.

1. 1 cup of milk
   1 banana (or ½ cup of other fruit)
   Few drops of vanilla
2. ½ cup milk
   1 scoop ice cream
   1 banana (or ½ cup of other fruit)

Other Additions:
   Chocolate syrup
   Peanut butter (2 tablespoons)
   Protein powder

(If you can't tolerate milk, substitute soy milk, soy baby formula, or soy-based ice cream.)

TOO TIRED TO PREPARE FOOD?

Keep snack foods handy. Many good foods don't need cooking or major preparation. These include cheese, nuts, granola or other cereals, peanut butter, dried fruits, boiled eggs, tuna salad.

Use convenient, ready-to-eat foods such as T.V. dinners and other frozen meals, packaged dishes such as macaroni and cheese, canned fruits, vegetables, beans, soups, chili, tuna, etc.

Buy take-out food from restaurants. However, this can be expensive.

Get your friends or family to help cook or to bring you food.

When you do cook, make a large amount at one time, separate the food into single servings, and then freeze the servings (if you have freezer space).

Try to prepare your food when you have the most energy. When you are too tired, you won't feel like cooking.

MOUTH PAIN OR DIFFICULT AND PAINFUL SWALLOWING

Prepare soft foods such as mashed potatoes, omelets, custards, cooked cereal, cottage cheese, yogurt, flaked fish, ground meat, casserole dishes, tuna or egg salad, and milk shakes. Cut whole foods in small pieces before eating.

Blenderize, mash, or strain your food. Buying a blender is worthwhile if you can afford it.

Buy baby foods if necessary. These can be diluted with milk or juices for easier swallowing. Chicken baby food mixed with milk and heated is a good-tasting cream-of-chicken soup.

To help food slide down easier, moisten the food with butter, gravy, and cream sauces. Using a cup rather than a spoon may be less painful when eating soups and cereals.

Chew your food well, and use a straw to drink liquids.

Drink fluids over ice. Milk shakes and other cold drinks may be soothing.

Avoid soda if the bubbles make it more difficult to swallow.

Stay away from very hot foods.

Avoid spicy, sour, and citrus (acid) foods like chili, tomato sauce, orange juice, and lemons if they bother you.

Avoid rough foods such as raw fruits and vegetables.

Make every bite and swallow count. Choose foods that are high in calories and protein (read the high calorie tips).

NAUSEA AND VOMITING

—Eat and drink slowly.
—Drink clear liquids between meals (broth, apple juice, grape juice, Jell-O, tea with sugar).
—Munch on dry foods (crackers, cookies).
—Instead of eating three large meals a day, eat several small meals.
—Rest after eating, but don't lie flat.
—Ask your doctor to prescribe anti-nausea medication. Take it ½ hour before meals.
—Avoid very sweet, greasy, spicy, or strong-smelling foods if they bother you.
—While you are nauseated, stay away from your favorite foods. If you eat your favorites while you feel sick, you may start to dislike them.

DIARRHEA

—Eat many small meals rather than three big meals.
—Omit greasy, fried, or fatty foods.

—Avoid high-fiber foods such as raw fruits and vegetables.
—Milk bothers some people. If you cannot tolerate milk, try yogurt.
—Drink liquids at room temperature.
—Make sure you drink plenty of liquids between meals to replace the fluid lost in the diarrhea.
—Eat bananas, apple sauce, and rice to help bind you.
—If you notice that a certain food bothers you, avoid it.
—Ask your doctor if an anti-diarrhea medication would be helpful and appropriate.

FOOD-BORNE INFECTIONS

AIDS causes your immune system to be weak, and it is difficult to fight infection. Therefore, it is necessary to avoid harmful bacteria in your food. The following measures should be taken:

Fruits and Vegetables:
—Wash all fruits and vegetables with warm water and mild soap *or* peel fruits and vegetables before eating.
—Do not use "organic" lettuce; animal feces are used in the compost.

Meats/Eggs:
—Do not eat rare meat. Medium or well-done meats have less risk of contamination.
—Avoid store-bought meat, chicken, and tuna salads made with mayonnaise. They spoil easily.
—Avoid raw eggs. Cook for at least 2 minutes to prevent salmonella infection.

Milk Products:
—Avoid raw/unpasteurized milk or milk products (read labels to identify them). They can cause salmonella infections.

Storing and Handling Foods:
—Refrigerate leftovers quickly.
—If a food seems even slightly spoiled, throw it out. Don't take chances.
—Don't use the spoon you eat with as a serving spoon.
—Don't drink or eat directly from a storage container (milk or juice carton, leftovers bowl, peanut butter jar). Bacteria from your mouth can get into the food and make it spoil faster.

MACROBIOTIC DIETS

Some people believe that a macrobiotic diet is good for PWAs. It is thought that the body is both purified and brought into balance with the spirit and environment when the diet is combined with the Eastern philosophy of *Yin-Yang*.

A macrobiotic diet allows only selected foods and liquids. It forbids dairy and wheat products, eggs, and refined sugars. The amount of liquid may be restricted.

WE DO NOT ADVOCATE THIS DIET

What is wrong with a macrobiotic diet?

1. *Low in calories and fat:*
   This diet is high in fiber, which fills you up, but it is very low in fat, and it is difficult to take in enough calories to maintain your weight.
2. *Low in many vitamins and minerals:*
   The amounts of B vitamins (especially B_{12}), calcium, and iron are very low.
3. *Low in protein:*
   If you've lost a great deal of weight, you need to build up, not decrease, the protein in your body.
4. *Fluids restricted:*
   Because fluids are restricted, you may become dehydrated. This is very dangerous.

If you do follow the macrobiotic diet, consider these suggestions:

1. Take a One-A-Day type vitamin pill with iron and other minerals.
2. Increase fluid intake.
3. Eat more fish to help increase protein and vitamin B_{12} intake.
4. If possible, incorporate dairy foods into your diet for protein and calcium.
5. If you begin to lose weight, eat more food and begin to add new foods to your diet.

NO REFRIGERATOR OR STOVE?

If you don't have a refrigerator or stove, you can still eat at home (restaurants are expensive). By planning carefully you can save money and eat a well-balanced diet.

Important Tips:
—Don't let perishable items (foods that quickly spoil or go bad) sit around. Buy single-serving sizes of canned and perishable goods.
—Keep food in a cool, dry place.
—Do not use your window sill as a refrigerator unless you are sure that the outside temperature is cold enough and that foods are *well covered* (you do not want animal droppings on your food).
—Buy a hotplate to cook on if it is allowed in your building. Make sure you turn off the hotplate after you finish cooking.
—Ask your health team about free meal programs.
—Pick foods from the following listed groups for most of your meals.

Food Choices—No Refrigerator or Stove

Milk Group
—Instant (dried) milk powder
—Canned, evaporated milk
—Single servings of:
   Milk
   Yogurt
   Cheese (¼ pound)
   Ice cream (1 cup or 1 pint)
   Canned puddings and custards

Meat Group
—Canned tuna
—Canned meats (chicken, ham, Spam, vienna sausage)
—Sliced meats (¼ pound) from the deli
—Canned beans (pinto, baked, kidney, etc.)
—Peanut butter, nuts
—Sunflower seeds

Grain Group
—Bread, rolls, crackers, bagels
—Cakes, cookies
—Granola
—Dry cereals or instant hot cereals (add hot tap water)

Fruit and Vegetable Group
—Fresh, canned, or dried fruits
—Small cans or containers of juice
—Fresh or canned vegetables

Miscellaneous (Others)
—Jelly
—Vegetable Oil
—Honey
—Vinegar
—Sugar
—Mustard

CONCLUSION

Every person with AIDS is different. The members of the health team will be planning your discharge based on your individual circumstances and needs.
Remember:
—Keep your clinic appointments.
—Tell the members of the health team if there are any changes in your physical or emotional condition or in your household situation.
—Use the phone number(s) written below to keep in touch with us:

ADDITIONAL INFORMATION

STUDY QUESTIONS

1. Which five groups are at risk for being infected with the AIDS virus?
2. Name some of the common myths about how the AIDS virus is spread.
3. Why should the person with AIDS be concerned with bacteria in food and what can be done about it?

Part III

Specialized Health Care Delivery Systems

Chapter 15

New Trends in Ambulatory Oncology Care

Randi Moskowitz

> In recent years, advances in caring for patients with cancer have contributed to the growth of outpatient oncology care. Some of the factors that have made ambulatory care more attractive include rising costs of inpatient treatment, diagnosis-related groups, shortage of hospital beds, advances in technology, increased cancer survival rates, and patient preference. In addition, to keep pace with these changes the role of the ambulatory oncology clinical nurse specialist has been expanded and broadened.

Over the past decade, care for the patient with cancer has changed dramatically. This is due, in part, to an increased understanding of the disease and an expansion of knowledge related to treatment modalities (Farley 1981). Because of the chronic nature of cancer and the advances in chemotherapy, radiation therapy, surgery, and immunotherapy, it is now possible for many patients to receive treatment in an ambulatory setting so that they can maintain as close to normal a lifestyle as possible.

Most ambulatory oncology centers offer day-long care in a specialized outpatient hospital-like facility in which the patient is offered the opportunity to return home in the evening (Clark 1986). Procedures such as the administration of chemotherapy, blood, and antibiotics and various diagnostic tests such as lumbar punctures, paracenteses, and bone marrow biopsies can be performed. Many institutions combine the treatment area with physicians' offices and clinic facilities. This improves patient flow, scheduling, and access to physician and nursing services. In this setting, nurses are generally the largest provider group; therefore, it is essential for them to become aware of the factors that have influenced the development of new trends in ambulatory care.

WHAT MAKES AMBULATORY CARE ATTRACTIVE?

Many factors have led to changes in the focus of cancer care from inpatient to outpatient services. Economic concerns include the rising costs of hospital care. Hospitalization adds considerably to the cost of chemotherapy administration, and diagnosis-related groups (DRGs) limit reimbursement and apply pressure for early patient discharge. The advanced technology available in many ambulatory care centers adds to the attractiveness of this setting.

Economic Concerns in Cancer Care

Health care is the third largest area of consumer spending in the United States (Tilbury and Fisk 1989). According to the Health Care Financing Administration (1987), it is estimated that by the year 2000 Americans will spend 15% of the gross national product on health care. This is an increase from 11.2% in 1987.

Increasing health care costs present a huge problem to patients with cancer, particularly because of the chronic nature of the illness, which may necessitate frequent hospitalizations. Hospital care expenditures account for approximately 60% to 75% of the total direct cost for cancer compared to 35% to 50% for all other diseases (Baird 1987).

The demand for health services purchased by Americans is the result of many variables, such as the size and age distribution of the population, income and price trends, and changing preferences in the quality of health care (Neal 1982). The percentage of elderly people in the population has been steadily increasing. By the year 2030, one in five Americans will be at least 65 years of age (Cangelosi and McAlhany 1989). The demand for health care increases with age; cancer is basically a disease of the elderly, so that we can expect to see an increase in this demand for care. In addition, changes in reimbursement from Medicare could negatively affect the care provided for these patients because of higher out-of-pocket costs to the patient and family.

Income and the price of health services also influence the demand for health care. A higher standard of living will enable a larger quantity of health services to be purchased (Neal 1982). On the other hand, the demand for these services is influenced by the relative price of health care compared to other goods and services (Neal 1982). If the price increases, the quantity demanded will decrease. In other words a higher income has a positive effect on the demand for health care, and a higher price has a negative effect.

The renewed awareness of wellness and illness prevention has also increased the demand for health care, as have advances in technology, which leads patients to value the services more highly.

Financial Concerns: Inpatient and Outpatient Cancer Care

It has been noted that outpatient administration of chemotherapy is less expensive than inpatient administration because of reduced fixed (overhead) and variable (staffing) costs in the ambulatory care setting (Wodinsky et al. 1987). In 1988, 1,286 cancer patient discharges were reviewed at a university-affiliated comprehensive cancer center in a large northeastern city. Inpatient hospital costs averaged $2,767 per case with a length of stay of approximately 3.88 days; this amounted to a cost of $713 per day per patient compared to a cost of $300 per day for outpatient administration of chemotherapy (R. Arons, personal communication 1989).

Diagnosis-Related Groups

The DRG approach was developed by Thompson at Yale University under a grant from the federal government (Beck 1985). The system was tested first in New Jersey and later in other states. The development of the disease categories used for DRGs was initially abstracted from *The International Classification of Diseases*, which contains 10,000 possible reasons for admission organized into 23 major diagnostic categories on the basis of body systems. These 23 categories have been further subivided into 471 DRGs (Beck 1985). Of these 471, approximately 40 contain 80% of cancer discharge diagnoses (Mortenson and Yarbro 1986).

Each hospital is notified in advance of the amount to be paid for each DRG. If the hospital provides service for less than this amount, it can keep the difference. If care costs more than the reimbursement, the hospital loses money. This is what is known as a prospective payment system (Beck 1986). Hospitals were initially reimbursed for Medicare recipients only, but now all insurance carriers reimburse by this method.

Another factor that has led to a change in the place where major care is delivered is the shortage of hospital beds. It has now become apparent that inpatient care must be utilized for the most acute episodes of illness, namely diagnosis, initial treatment, management of recurrence and oncologic emergencies, and initiation of complicated chemotherapy (Farley 1981).

Advances in Technology

The delivery of quality outpatient care is made possible because of advances in biomedical technology such as venous access devices, ambulatory infusion pumps, and more effective protocols for treatment and toxicity management. The increased knowledge and skills brought to bear in the administration of chemotherapy by highly trained oncology nurses have also influenced the choice of the ambulatory option. Physicians and patients feel more confident if they know that the nurses who are administering chemotherapy are highly skilled.

THE CHANGING ROLE OF THE AMBULATORY ONCOLOGY CLINICAL NURSE SPECIALIST

The past few years have seen the appearance of the ambulatory oncology clinical nurse specialist (OCNS), whose skill and expertise enables him or her to handle the complex needs of cancer patients and their families. As defined by the American Nurses' Association, the clinical nurse specialist is "a nurse who, through study and practice at the graduate level, has become expert in a defined area of knowledge and practice in a selected clinical area of nursing" (Kwong, Manning, and Koetters 1982, p. 427). The OCNS practices with a high level of competency in the field of cancer nursing. The OCNS is highly discriminating and definitive in identifying needs of patients and in selecting appropriate interventions. On the basis of these definitions, the role of the OCNS has been expanded to include expert clinician, teacher, role model, consultant, researcher, health policy advocate, and administrator (Navidjon and Warren 1984), whereas previously the OCNS performed tasks such as cleaning examination rooms and scheduling appointments (Tighe et al. 1985).

Direct patient care includes attending to patients and their families, coordinating clinical activities and continuing care, and administering chemotherapy. To perform these duties successfully, the nurse must have a knowledge of the physiologic and psychologic aspects of cancer. This can be assessed by documentation of the nurse's ability to problem solve, to perform health appraisals, and to develop nursing care and discharge plans.

Teaching and role modeling can be applied to staff, students, patients and their families, and the general public. The OCNS is responsible for developing a plan for individual unit orientation of nursing and allied health staff. During the process of orientation, the OCNS must identify the learning needs of staff through direct and indirect observation of their practice. Further development and refinement of the orientation program must be accomplished to meet the identified learning needs. Finally, the OCNS contributes to the growth and development of other staff nurses through counseling, support, and participation in peer review.

Patient and family education is as important as physical and emotional care. The OCNS's role is to provide patient education that is concise, current, and individualized to each particular patient and to follow up on this education. This task is completed when the patient is able to verbalize the concept of the disease process as well as medical and nursing treatments and their implications. In addition, members of the community who are seeking information must be presented with a caring, positive attitude along with answers to their questions and referrals to nearby resources.

The consultant role, wherein the nurse provides expert professional advice, is an extension of the educator role. Areas of expertise needed to fulfill this aspect of nursing include prevention and early detection, case management, primary care, and communication.

Through developing, implementing, and participating in research studies, the nurse can enhance his or her professional growth. This is accomplished by identifying researchable questions, setting priorities for unit-based research studies, establishing research methodology, developing research tasks, collaborating with physicians and patients, and communicating research findings to staff.

As noted previously, OCNSs have been assuming more responsibility for health care maintenance and continuing care. With the increase in ambulatory cancer care, it is expected that these roles will continue to be developed into the 1990s and beyond.

HOSPITAL-BASED AMBULATORY CARE AT A UNIVERSITY-AFFILIATED COMPREHENSIVE CANCER CENTER

In 1982, the National Cancer Institute awarded the Columbia University Comprehensive Cancer Center and the Presbyterian Hospital a $500,000 construction grant to develop an ambulatory oncology facility whose major goal was to provide multidisciplinary, one-class care that would further enhance clinical research in cancer. The issue of one-class care was an important one for Columbia–Presbyterian Medical Center because of its unique and diverse patient population. Most of the clinic patients live in the hospital neighborhood, are from low-income households, and are Medicaid recipients. In contrast, many of the private patients are wealthy professionals from Manhattan, northern New Jersey, and Connecticut.

A 9,000-ft^2 unit was constructed and opened for operation in August 1983. The area was divided into five related subsections, each with its own cost center. These areas include space for (1) the oncology and hematology clinics, (2) attending physician and faculty practice offices, (3) a stat hematology laboratory, (4) an ambulatory oncology day treatment center, and (5) clinical research offices. Staff members include six attending physicians and their secretaries, one clinic director (a physician), nine oncology/hematology fellows, four IV-certified oncology nurses, one anticoagulation nurse specialist, one sickle cell hematology nurse practitioner, two nursing attendants, one social worker, two clinic receptionists, two billing registrars, two phlebotomists, three laboratory technicians, one clinical trials coordinator, one clinical research coordinator, and one administrator and her secretary.

In addition to the stat laboratory, clinical facilities include six patient care suites, each consisting of a consultation room and two examination rooms. One of these suites is equipped for bone marrow biopsies and other special procedures. The Ambulatory Oncology Treatment Center, which is open from 8:00 A.M. to 6:00 P.M. Monday through Friday, can accommodate up to 13 patients at one time. Four specially trained nurses are available to administer chemotherapy and blood products. Each year since 1983 the number of patients seen on the unit has increased steadily, almost doubling over the past 5½ years.

In 1988, the Comprehensive Cancer Center's computer facility developed a software package that links information among various areas in the institution, such as the Tumor Registry, the inpatient Oncology Research Unit, the Radiation Oncology Center, and the Ambulatory Oncology Center. This program has enabled the staff to keep track of the numbers and types of treatments given, the numbers of patients seen, the numbers of patients per physician and nurse, disease categories, and other important variables. Comparisons can now be made from year to year.

All these facilities are a shared resource of the Presbyterian Hospital Department of Medical Affairs, the Columbia University Department of Medicine, and the Columbia University Comprehensive Cancer Center. All staff members work together under the direction of the administrator. It is expected that the Ambulatory Oncology Center will continue to expand over the next few years, with the addition of more physicians and the establishment of a bone marrow transplant service at the hospital.

STUDY QUESTIONS

1. Discuss three factors that have made ambulatory cancer care an attractive alternative to hospitalization.
2. Describe the major roles of the ambulatory oncology clinical nurse specialist.

REFERENCES

Baird, S. 1987. The changing economics of cancer care: Challenges and opportunities. In: *Cancer care within the context of changes in health care economics*. New York: American Cancer Society.

Beck, D.F. 1985. The hospital's financial future: DRG's and beyond. *Health Care Supervisor*, January, 1–10.

Beck, D.F. 1986. Financial strategies for the future. *Health Care Supervisor*, October, 1–12.

Cangelosi, J., and J. McAlhany. 1989. Congregate retirement communities: Exploring the importance of services and activities as viewed by residents, potential residents and administrators. *Journal of Health Care Marketing* 9:48–54.

Clark, M. 1986. A day hospital for cancer patients: Clinical and economic feasibility. *Oncology Nursing Forum* 13:41–45.

Farley, B. 1981. Primary nursing in the oncology ambulatory setting. *Nursing Administration Quarterly* 5:44–53.

Health Care Financing Administration Division of National Cost Estimates, Office of the Actuary. 1987. National health expenditures, 1986–2000. *Health Care Financing Review* 8:1–36.

Kwong, M., M.P. Manning, and T. Koetters. 1982. The role of the oncology clinical nurse specialist: Three personal views. *Cancer Nursing* 9:427–34.

Mortenson, L.E., and J.W. Yarbro. 1986. Oncology DRG research procedures: Key findings for cancer program managers and policy makers. *Journal of Cancer Program Management* 1:6–7.

Navidjon, B., and B. Warren. 1984. Documenting the activities of the oncology clinical nurse specialist. *Oncology Nursing Forum* 11:54–55.

Neal, M. 1982. *Nurses in business.* Pacific Palisades, Calif.: NURSECO.

Tighe, M.G., S.G. Fisher, C. Hastings, and B. Heller. 1985. A study of the oncology nurse role in ambulatory care. *Oncology Nursing Forum* 12:23–27.

Tilbury, M., and T. Fisk. 1989. *Marketing and nursing: A contemporary view.* Owings Mills, Md.: National Health Publishing.

Wodinsky, H.B., C. DeAngelis, J. Rusthover, I. Kerr, D. Sutherland, N. Iscoe, R. Buchman, and M. Kornigenko. 1987. Re-evaluating the cost of outpatient cancer chemotherapy. *Canadian Medical Association Journal* 137:903–906.

SUGGESTED READINGS

Ashwanden, P. 1986. *Handbook on prospective reimbursement: Effects on oncology nursing care.* New York: Columbia University Comprehensive Cancer Center.

Brandon, J.A. 1985. TEFRA: Impact on hospitals, nurses, physicians and patients. *Health Care Supervisor*, April, 70–85.

Hubbard, S.M., and C. Seipp. 1985. Administering cancer treatment: The role of the oncology nurse. *Hospital Practice* 20:167–74.

Nathanson, S.N., and D. Lerman. 1988. *Outpatient cancer centers; Implementation and management.* Chicago: American Hospital Publishing.

Spross, J., and M. Donoghue. 1984. The future of the oncology clinical nurse specialist. *Oncology Nursing Forum* 11:74–78.

Starck, P. 1983. Factors influencing the role of the oncology clinical nurse specialist. *Oncology Nursing Forum* 10:54–58.

Chapter 16

Freestanding Cancer Centers: New Trends in Nursing Care for Cancer Patients

Dolores M. Esparza and Nancy Bookbinder

> The medical and nursing services provided in a freestanding ambulatory cancer center afford patients an alternative to institutionalized treatment. These outpatient facilities may be freestanding depending on the ownership and the location of the site. A freestanding cancer center (FCC) may be owned by a hospital and be located on the hospital campus or in a geographic location distant from the hospital. Accreditation standards for FCCs are based on the criteria of the Joint Commission on Accreditation of Healthcare Organizations and other agencies. Nurses play an important role in the operations of FCCs, including such responsibilities as having input into the design and space plan of the facility, setting the policy and direction of the center, treating the patient, training the staff, and managing the departments on a daily basis.

HISTORICAL EVENTS LEADING UP TO MODERN NEEDS

Ambulatory care has come full circle from the 1600s, when patients were treated in their homes and outpatient clinics provided an alternative for patients who did not require hospitalization but who still needed medical attention (Roemer 1985; Howard 1988). The earliest documented effort to offer medical care to ambulatory patients is credited to a French physician in 1630.

Today, organized ambulatory care centers serve all populations and provide a high quality of care. In the 1940s, prepaid financing for ambulatory care gained popularity. Another significant milestone occurred in 1966, when Medicare and Medicaid legislation provided payment for medical services required by the elderly and indigent. Expanding ambulatory care service availability reflects the nation's changing economy and social trends.

The Medicare outpatient payment system is projected to take a new turn in 1990 (Koska 1988). The Health Care Financing Administration is expected to recommend changes in the pricing structure for outpatient services in an attempt to curtail medical costs. Congress intends to restructure payment methodology to hospitals for both hospital outpatient departments and physicians in the near future. The new payment system will affect the place of service for oncology care on the basis of incentives built into the new payment systems.

The recent growth of ambulatory care facilities is a direct result of increased competition among hospitals to increase their respective market share of patients. Other competitive pressures include reimbursement changes favoring outpatient settings as well as joint venture development among entrepreneurial groups, physicians, and hospitals. Finally and most influential is consumer pressure for hospitals to provide modes of service that offer an alternative to hospitalization in the communities that they serve. For cancer patients and health care providers, the freestanding cancer center (FCC) can fill this service void. Chemotherapy, radiation therapy, and support services are provided in FCCs in the ambulatory setting.

One can expect to see a great deal of change in the policies influencing outpatient care in this decade. Nurses need to be aware of all the variables affecting these changes and how they influence oncology nursing practice.

FREESTANDING CANCER CENTERS

Confusion exists about the definition of an outpatient or ambulatory cancer center. For the purposes of this chapter, an ambulatory cancer center is defined as a facility in which multimodality outpatient oncology care is delivered by a cancer care team in a physically contiguous space. This multimodality cancer care includes, at a minimum, medical oncology and radiation therapy services. In addition, surgical oncology care may be offered.

The cancer center concept was created to provide as many services required by oncology patients in one setting as possible. Provision of these services in one facility or designated area decreases fragmentation of patient care, enhances communication among members of the multidisciplinary cancer team, and decreases the inconvenience experienced by patients and their families when care is provided in multiple locations. Cancer centers also provide psychosocial support services, patient education materials and lectures, cancer screening, and rehabilitation and social work services.

Over the past 10 years the term *freestanding cancer center* has been applied to radiation therapy facilities and to hospital-based cancer programs (Meadors 1986). An FCC may be a hospital-sponsored facility. Location and ownership of the facility determine the freestanding status of the center.

An FCC owned solely by a hospital may be located in a distinct section of the hospital outpatient department, on the hospital campus, or in a location distant from the main hospital facility. As a hospital outpatient department, the FCC provides services that must meet the same criteria as other departments and be delivered by licensed personnel, as is required by the Joint Commission on Accreditation of Healthcare Organizations guidelines (Joint Commission 1989a) (for those hospitals choosing to comply with Joint Commission standards). The FCC must meet hospital outpatient building codes as mandated by state regulations in the locality where the FCC is developed. If the hospital is a party in a joint ventured FCC and if the FCC services are billed as hospital outpatient services, then the FCC must meet the same standards as a hospital outpatient department.

FCCs organized without a hospital partner are not required to meet the same standards or requirements as hospital outpatient FCCs. They may be organized as physicians' offices or clinics. Current standards for such non–hospital-based FCCs have been developed by the American College of Surgeons, the Joint Commission, and the Association of Community Cancer Centers.

CURRENT TRENDS IN AMBULATORY CANCER CENTER HEALTH MANAGEMENT

With the rapid expansion of ambulatory health care services, the need for specialized management has become increasingly apparent. Historically, hospital-based ambulatory care programs have been managed in a decentralized manner. That is, the various aspects of ambulatory care, including ancillary service departments, were managed by multiple administrators (Howard 1988). The outpatient FCC organization structure allows for a centralized management function for all services offered in the center. The ideal FCC administrator has in-depth knowledge of oncology services and the ancillary services required for cancer patients. FCC managers are responsible for a multicomponent facility that includes physician offices, a chemotherapy medical treatment area, radiation therapy, a supporting stat laboratory, and a diagnostic radiology area (Lattal 1988). The focus of the FCC is patient-oriented care delivered efficiently by a professional staff.

In an FCC organized as a hospital outpatient department, all staff should report to the FCC administrator. These staff must meet the same standards and licensure as other personnel employed in the hospital. In an FCC organized as a physicians' office or clinic, the staff may report to the FCC medical director, director of nursing, or administrator.

As hospitals, physicians, and entrepreneurs in health care seek to increase their patient market share in a competitive health care marketplace, new strategies for health care delivery have been developed. In an effort to expand medical services in communities while strengthening the relationship with local physicians, hospital administrators and physicians have entered into health care business ventures. These ventures in cancer service delivery have been structured to include hospitals and physicians, hospitals and third parties, or hospitals, physicians, and a third party. The third party in an FCC venture usually brings management expertise or financing (or both) for the building or equipment. The venture structure may be developed as a hospital outpatient department or created as a clinic or physician group practice. Although the organization structure of these ventures varies, the desired outcome of each is the delivery of ambulatory cancer services in a manner that provides convenient care for oncology patients and their families. Each setting provides challenges to nursing personnel functioning in the outpatient environment. The nursing staff in an FCC hospital outpatient department must develop criteria and standards specific to their patients' special needs while meeting hospital standards.

CONTRIBUTIONS OF FREESTANDING CANCER CENTERS TO STANDARDS OF CARE

FCCs should be designed with patients' safety and well-being as a priority. Attention to detail and the fulfillment of clinical issues must be addressed from the onset. Laboratory results, radiology results, and support services must be made available to clinicians in a manner conducive to prompt and expeditious care. Shared services with the hospital or another facility may be used to bridge the gap in services. Monitoring of the need for continuous service on off hours ensures that patients receive the medical and nursing attention that they require. If round-the-clock services are required, then the right volume of personnel must be identified and scheduled. The standard of care should be to provide safe, effective, and convenient care to the patient.

REIMBURSEMENT

As mentioned, changes in reimbursement for medical services served as a catalyst for the growth of ambulatory care. Prospective pricing of inpatient hospital services enhanced interest in and development of medical service provision in the outpatient setting. Because cancer is disproportionately a disease of the older population, most patients treated for cancer are covered by Medicare. Once the Medicare program adopted prospective pricing (i.e., diagnosis-related groups) for payment of inpatient hospital services, a rapid growth of outpatient services followed.

FCCs can bill for services under two mechanisms. Those FCCs licensed as hospital outpatient departments can bill for the technical component of care under the hospital's outpatient provider number. It is important to remember that hospital-based FCCs may be located at a site distant from the main hospital campus. The technical component of care includes staffing, facility, and equipment costs. The hospital-based FCC may also bill for physicians' professional services if the physicians providing care in the FCC are hospital-based physicians and are salaried by the hospital.

In the event that all services provided in the FCC are billed under a physician or physician group provider number, professional revenues are used to pay for the technical components of care. Physicians retain the remaining revenues after expenses as their professional income. In a joint ventured FCC that uses a physician or physician group billing number for all billing revenues are used to cover expenses, and physicians' professional fees and residual profits may be distributed to investors.

As of this writing, Medicare reimbursement for hospital outpatient technical fees is paid on a cost basis. The ancillary services provided to oncology patients in an ambulatory hospital-based setting are reimbursed according to various payment formulas. For example, Medicare uses a national fee screen for reimbursement of laboratory tests. As of 1 April 1989, radiology services, including radiation therapy, are being reimbursed under a new blended payment rate system. Hospital outpatient blended rate reimbursement for radiology is now a combination of the physician's Medicare relative value scale reimbursement and hospital technical costs for provision of service. Special procedures performed in an FCC, such as endoscopies, are paid under hospital ambulatory surgery rates. These various reimbursement formulas are considered interim payment measures while the federal government determines a new payment methodology for the ambulatory setting. Congress will decide in the next 2 years how to pay for oncology services in the outpatient setting. During the same period, Congress will select a new payment methodology for physician services furnished to Medicare patients.

ACCREDITATION REQUIREMENTS

Joint Commission

The regulation of outpatient FCCs is influenced by independent agencies. The Joint Commission has two distinct sets of guidelines and standards for accreditation of a hospital-sponsored ambulatory cancer center or an FCC (Joint Commission 1989a, 1989b). The requirements are intended to address the governance, safety, and management of a cancer center. There are many required standards of hospital-sponsored ambulatory care services, a summary of which includes the following. The first standard outlines the safety and quality of the administration and staff caring for the outpatients. A second standard provides for the education and training of the staff to ensure basic competencies. To ensure further the provision of ambulatory care services, the third standard requires written policies and procedures. The facility is an important consideration and must have provisions for safety and convenient services. Other important considerations include the medical record and its content and a quality control system that ensures the consistent monitoring of quality and appropriateness of care.

Agency Influence in Regulation

There are other regulatory agencies that specialize in surveillance of the quality of cancer patient services in ambulatory care. The American College of Surgeons (ACOS) implemented an approval system for FCCs in 1989. This ACOS accreditation program is the first such approval system for these cancer programs. Typically, hospital-sponsored ambulatory cancer centers are approved as a department of the hospital.

Another independent agency is the Association of Community Cancer Centers. This group has developed a set of guidelines parallel to the ones established by the Joint Commission. The primary objective of these guidelines is to ensure the safety of the patient.

NURSING IMPLICATIONS

Joint ventures in ambulatory care are financial survival strategies and are becoming increasingly commonplace (Bermas 1985). These contracts pose interesting challenges for nursing administrators. Nursing personnel in a ventured ambulatory cancer center that includes a hospital partner generally maintain a separate budget and nursing director. Although FCC nursing departments generally operate as hospital departments, they may be identified as a distinct unit on the hospital's organization chart.

Role of the Nurse in Freestanding Cancer Centers

Nursing practice in an FCC is dependent in part on the phase of development. In start-up FCCs the nurse should participate in the space planning, work flow design, and discussion of the clinical services to be provided (Esparza, Young, and Luongo 1989). It is the nurse who can identify the relationship of space and the rationale for proximity of services. For example, placing procedure rooms close to examination rooms will ensure the convenience and safety of the patient and improve the effectiveness of the staff's productivity.

In the implementation phase of an FCC the nurse's role entails writing policies and procedures, hiring and training staff, and ensuring that staff are credentialed in the performance of chemotherapy and other cancer therapy. Nursing also serves as the liaison among the physician, support services, and sometimes family members.

In FCCs that are in the maintenance mode the nurse serves as director of patient care and fills the role of manager. In this role he or she upgrades and monitors the standards of care, improves the equipment and environment, and enhances patient services.

Future of Clinical Nursing in Freestanding Cancer Centers

All the driving forces of medicine indicate an increasing need to use the health care system (Amara 1989). Outpatient health care is also utilized more frequently than ever before (Amara 1989). Outpatient health services are used with a frequency of 50.7% by adult females and 35.1% by adult males (Powills 1987). These economic indicators are indices on which to base predictions for the future of nurses in outpatient FCCs. The future is perhaps too clear that increased services and expanded practice will have to be delivered by nurses to serve consumers in the numbers that are being predicted.

Reporting Structure

Nursing in an FCC functions as a separate nursing department. One advantage to this structure is flexibility in effecting change. In a hospital-sponsored FCC the hospital committee structure provides a forum for a hospital reporting mechanism.

Some of the differences between a hospital-based FCC and an FCC organized as a clinic or physicians' office arise from the presence or absence of multiple layers of committees. In hospitals committees serve as the approval bodies of policies and standardized procedures. The structure of the committee varies from institution to institution depending on the bylaws of the hospital. These committees are generally required to sign off on nursing procedures. In the nonhospital setting, nursing personnel may maintain an autonomous role with greater latitude in policy making.

Liability

Separate liability insurance is a requirement for the individual nurse as well as for the FCC. The specifications of the insurance carrier should be analyzed before staff from an FCC or a hospital-sponsored center are permitted to care for patients on the inpatient units and conversely to invited staff from the inpatient facility that provide care to patients in the FCC. In addition, the details of the venture agreement should be thoroughly understood to decrease ambiguity in patient services and nursing roles.

Emergency Care Provisions

Emergency care provisions must be addressed to deal safely with emergency situations, such as cardiac or respiratory arrest. The method of providing medical staff coverage for these emergencies should be identified in writing. In these situations, generally accepted practice is to stabilize and transfer the patient to a specialized hospital inpatient unit for continued care.

Patient Service Provision

Space and staffing obviously determine the limitations of an FCC in providing patient services. Space can be a crucial variable in determining the number of patients that can be accommodated in an examination room area. The number of patients that can be scheduled for chemotherapy at any given time is influenced by the number of treatment beds. Creative scheduling is the answer to accommodating patients and maximizing space utilization. To achieve optimal space planning, it is necessary to determine, before architectural design and construction, anticipated patient volumes. Staffing correlates directly with the volume as well as the space and the layout of the design. Adequate staffing is a requirement of the Joint Commission standards.

Quality Assurance Standards

Quality assurance standards are an inherent component of any ambulatory center. This is an area that needs improvement; FCCs fall behind acute care hospitals according to the Joint Commission (Koerner 1987). It is important to establish a planned program that will systematically review and monitor the care provided. Periodic assessment of the services provided must take place to improve care. The quality assurance monitoring system must demonstrate actions taken, including the effectiveness of the actions taken as documented in the form of an evaluation. The ambulatory nurse can play a major role in establishing patient outcome standards and monitors.

Severity of Illness

There is a correlation between the increase in severity of illness of patients seen in an ambulatory facility and the increased utilization of services. Caution must be exercised in establishing the parameters of care for the treatment of outpatients. This is particularly important at a time when outpatients are sicker. Written standards, including the scope of patient care services provided in an FCC, must be adhered to.

A severity of illness index or measuring tool has not been developed for ambulatory settings (Horn, Buckle, and Carver 1988). Many attempts have been made to determine an accurate classification of the nursing time required for the different categories of patients (Jones and Frank 1986; Hastings 1987). Severity indices identify patients and group them according to the extent of the care required. For example, it may take 10 to 90 minutes of nursing time to take care of a patient who requires medications, instructions, psychosocial care, and treatment, whereas a patient with a high level of acuity needs extensive and constant monitoring and therapy. Acuity and patient classification systems for ambulatory care settings can be adapted from inpatient classification systems. It is understood that, for the most part, patients who are ambulatory maintain a greater ability for self-care and therefore have a lesser severity of illness. Some of the functions and activities are predictable; for example, patients who come for repeated visits take anywhere from 15 to 20 minutes, and a new patient takes up to 60 minutes. It is clear that a classification index for FCCs must be developed.

Ratio of Patients to Nurses

The ratio of patients to nurses is dependent on the complexity of the patient's status and the skill of the nurse. Nursing assignments are based accordingly. A mix of patient classifications, including blood transfusions, hydration, and antibiotic therapy, should be evenly distributed among the nursing staff. A patient classification ratio of four patients to one nurse is manageable.

Coordination of care requires a series of carefully planned steps (Esparza, Young, and Luongo 1989). The most important action is the process of patient selection for outpatient status, which requires evaluation of the patient's Karnofsky status. The nurse plays a significant role in the scheduling of treatments and the teaching of the family and patient regarding diagnosis and treatment. The patient can be successfully treated and supported as an outpatient in an FCC.

CONCLUSION

The expansion of ambulatory cancer services as a component of the competitive health care environment has resulted in the proliferation of FCCs. The organization structure of the FCC enhances the autonomy of the nursing role in the center. FCCs developed with hospital outpatient departments maintain a reporting relationship through the hospital structure. FCCs developed as physicians' offices or clinics may offer more latitude in defining the oncology nurse's role. The recent development of FCC criteria and guidelines by various accrediting organizations provides standards for the delivery of cancer care in the ambulatory setting. Future developments in ambulatory reimbursement will determine the financial viability of FCCs. The joint ventured FCC, structured either as a hospital outpatient department or a physicians' office, provides the opportunity for physicians, hospitals, and third parties to establish a unique oncology service while delivering coordinated care to patients and their families.

STUDY QUESTIONS

1. What accrediting body reviews hospital-sponsored and freestanding cancer centers?
2. Are hospital-sponsored ambulatory centers a department of the hospital?
3. What roles does the nurse carry out in a freestanding cancer center?

REFERENCES

Amara, R. 1989. Health care tomorrow. *Hospital Topics* 67:28–30.

Bermas, P.F. 1985. Joint ventures in ambulatory care. *Journal of Ambulatory Care Management* 8:79–87.

Esparza, D.M., N. Young, and J.A. Luongo. 1989. Effective planning for office and outpatient chemotherapy administration. *Seminars in Oncology Nursing* 5:8–14.

Hastings, C.E. 1987. Classification issues in ambulatory care nursing. *Journal of Ambulatory Care Management* 10:50–64.

Horn, S.D., J.M. Buckle, and C.M. Carver. 1988. Ambulatory severity index: Development of an ambulatory case mix system. *Journal of Ambulatory Care Management* 11:53–62.

Howard, D.M. 1988. Past experiences and future directions in ambulatory care. In *New business development in ambulatory care: Exploring diversification options,* ed. D.M. Howard. Chicago: American Hospital Publishing.

Joint Commission on Accreditation of Healthcare Organizations. 1989a. *Accreditation manual for hospitals: Hospital-sponsored ambulatory care services.* Chicago: Joint Commission.

Joint Commission on Accreditation of Healthcare Organizations. 1989b. *Ambulatory health care standards manual.* Chicago: Joint Commission.

Jones, K., and C. Frank. 1986. A special consideration: Measuring outpatient nursing services. In *Nursing productivity: The hospital's key to survival and profit,* ed. R. Spitzer. Chicago: S-N Publications.

Koerner, B.L. 1987. Clarifying the role of nursing in ambulatory care. *Journal of Ambulatory Care Management* 10:1–7.

Koska, M.T. 1988. Alternate care: HCFA examines ambulatory payment options. *Hospitals* 62:86–87.

Lattal, L.A. 1988. Operational issues. In *Outpatient cancer centers: Implementation & management,* ed. S.N. Nathanson and D. Lerman. Chicago: American Hospital Publishing.

Meadors, A.C. 1986. Radiation therapy centers: Moving into the twenty-first century. *Administrative Radiology* 5:60–62.

Powills, S. 1987. Who's using outpatient services? *Hospitals* 61:50.

Roemer, M.I. 1985. Organized ambulatory health care in international perspective. *Journal of Ambulatory Care Management* 8:1–17.

Chapter 17

Homelessness and Infection with Human Immunodeficiency Virus: What Are the Options?

Jo Anne Staats

> Homelessness is an increasing problem among persons infected with human immunodeficiency virus. Currently there are few housing options for these people. The AIDS Resource Center in New York City has developed two housing models with supportive care that address the housing and psychologic needs of persons with AIDS. The center's group residence, Bailey House, is unique in that it has on staff a nurse practitioner who coordinates all medical and nursing care of the residents.

It is estimated that nationwide there are 20,000 homeless persons with acquired immunodeficiency syndrome (AIDS) and AIDS-related complex (Hirschfeld 1988) and that by 1992 there will be 620,000 homeless persons in this country with diseases related to human immunodeficiency virus (HIV) infection. Presently, in New York City various sources state that there are 5,000 to 10,000 homeless persons with different stages of HIV infection. The city provides housing for only 3% of these individuals (Hirschfeld 1988). The rest are living in hospitals, in shelters, in single room occupancy hotels, and on the street.

The reasons for homelessness vary depending on the group affected. Many Gay and bisexual persons with AIDS are unable to pay for housing when frequent hospitalizations lead to loss of employment and income. Intravenous drug users may lose tenuous housing for the same reason, may have been homeless already, or may have families who no longer want them when they are diagnosed with AIDS. Children with AIDS may be left in hospitals by families already burdened with drug use and other family members with AIDS.

As the number of homeless people with AIDS increases, solutions to the problem are being sought by government and private agencies. Some cities, New York included, offer rent assistance and home care in an attempt to keep some people in their homes. Adult group homes, which offer minimal services, provide housing for others. There are also plans to increase the number of skilled nursing homes and health-related facilities for people with AIDS. These institutions offer various levels of care that are appropriate for disabled individuals.

In New York City the AIDS Resource Center, founded in 1983, has developed two housing models for homeless persons with AIDS. The agency's policy is that people with AIDS have better lives when they are offered decent housing with support services. By drawing on existing housing stock and community services and supplementing with services that are not available, it has been possible for the AIDS Resource Center to house more than 200 people with AIDS through its supportive housing apartment program and group residences.

The supportive housing apartment program was the first housing model developed by the AIDS Resource Center. It currently has 20 apartments (and recently received funding for 20 more) that house up to 35 individuals and families (with and without children). These apartments, in various buildings throughout the city, are rented with the knowledge of the landlords. Bailey House, the first supportive group residence for people with AIDS in New York City and the largest in the nation, houses 44 men and women in private rooms with bathrooms. Three meals a day are served in a communal dining room. These two housing models of the AIDS Resource Center receive 70% of their annual budget from contracts with the Public Health Service, the New York State Division of Substance Abuse, and the New York City Human Resources Administration. Private funds supplement these contracts and allow for expansion of services.

The AIDS Resource Center holds that these housing models are superior in many ways to other housing and institution alternatives. Institution care (health-related and skilled nursing facilities), although necessary for some people with AIDS, is inflexible and expensive. Care in a health-related facility (in New York City) costs about $225 per person per day; this is certainly less than the $800 per day in hospitals but is more than the $58 per day in a supportive housing apartment and the $125 per day in a group residence with supportive care. An adult home without supportive services is even less expensive but does not have on-site health care supervision, so that residents may require more frequent hospitalizations.

Referrals to the AIDS Resource Center come from New York City's Division of AIDS Services. The person must be homeless, have a diagnosis of AIDS as defined by the Centers for Disease Control, and be eligible for supplemental security income and New York State Medicaid. Everyone referred to the supportive housing apartment program and Bailey House is interviewed by an AIDS Resource Center staff person. For admission to Bailey House, the individual must appear to be able to live in a community, be reasonably healthy, and be drug and alcohol free. This last criterion is the most difficult to determine and points out the need for obtaining a good drug history. Before admission to Bailey House, substance users are required to enter a methadone maintenance program or a drug-free program or attend Alcoholics, Narcotics, or Cocaine Anonymous meetings.

Staffing of the supportive housing apartment program and Bailey House differs. Both models have social workers, a substance abuse counselor, a recreation therapist, a pastor, housekeepers, and administrative staff. Bailey House also has resident managers, receptionists, food service personnel, and a security guard. In addition, Bailey House has a full-time nurse practitioner, a part-time weekend nurse, a physician consultant, and personal care assistants. The personal care assistants help residents with activities of daily living.

Support services for residents of the supportive housing apartment program are provided at the agency office. Home visits are made as necessary. Residents receive medical care from local hospitals. Home attendants and visiting nurses are provided, through referral, by the Visiting Nurse Service of New York.

At Bailey House the nurse practitioner is responsible for coordinating the medical and nursing care of all residents. On admission, a history, physical examination, brief mental status examination, and some neuropsychiatric testing are performed by the nurse practitioner. This establishes a baseline for each resident. Medications and clinic appointments are reviewed at this time.

Health teaching is an important component of the program. Emphasis is placed on remaining as healthy and independent as possible. The effects of drug and alcohol on the immune system and methods of controlling their use are discussed. Safe sex is reviewed. Skin and mouth care, infection control, nutrition, exercise, rest, and stress reduction are also reviewed. Individual care plans are developed by the multidisciplinary team during weekly team meetings.

Assessment and health monitoring are done on an ongoing basis by the nurse practitioner. When necessary, the resident is referred to his or her primary medical care provider. Explaining medical treatments, medications, and alternative therapies and supporting residents in decisions that they make regarding their care are important functions of the nurse practitioner.

An attending physician from St. Vincent's Medical Center, who has extensive experience in caring for people with AIDS, consults two afternoons a week at Bailey House. At least half the residents of Bailey House receive primary medical care from this physician at his hospital-based clinic. Frequent contact between the physician and nurse practitioner has resulted in improved care for the residents (Torres and Staats 1989).

A collaborative practice agreement between the nurse practitioner and the physician delineates the responsibilities of each. Protocols of care have been adopted. The Harvard Community Health Plan's *Guidelines for Clinical Practice* (1983) are used for management of non–HIV-related medical problems. The *Criteria Manual for the Treatment of AIDS* (New York Statewide Professional Standards Review Council 1989) is used for HIV-related problems. Many medical problems, such as pneumonias, cryptococcal meningitis, toxoplasmosis, cytomegalovirus infection, and unexplained fevers, require hospitalization. Other less acute problems such as candidiasis, herpes, and diarrhea are managed on site.

The Visiting Nurse Service of New York provides additional on-site home care. These nurses administer intravenous infusions of amphotericin B and ganciclovir as well as total parenteral nutrition. They also supervise daily dressing changes and injections. Residents who are chronically debilitated and require more assistance than Bailey House staff can provide are referred to the Visiting Nurse Service for up to 24-hour home attendant care.

Multiple problems confront the residents of Bailey House. Many have been long-term substance users, have practiced prostitution, have been in prison, and have been homeless before the diagnosis of AIDS. Most come from dysfunctional families. It is not surprising when some state that AIDS is the least of their problems.

Bailey House is not a hospice, and the goal of the staff is to help residents live with AIDS. Counseling is ongoing. Narcotics, Cocaine, and Alcoholics Anonymous have on-site meetings. Acupuncture to control substance abuse is offered. The recreation therapist plans trips and entertainment. The pastor organizes frequent retreats to facilities outside the city. A resident work program allows some residents to earn extra money.

An important goal of the staff is to include family or significant others in the care of residents. Some residents request that no one be contacted when they die. Others ask, when their health begins to deteriorate, that family members be called. Some residents are rejected by family members who are afraid of AIDS. In several cases it has been possible to educate these families. Through special funds, residents have been able to visit family who live outside New York City. In a few instances family members have flown to New York City to see residents who were unable to travel. For those residents without family, the staff often serves in that capacity. On occasion, funerals and memorial services have been arranged by staff.

Another important function of the staff is to help residents face death. They are assisted with getting their wills and living wills written, making custody arrangements for children, and planning their funerals. Discussions of death are not avoided by staff, and many approaches, including listening, prayer, meditation, therapeutic touch, and humor, are used to help residents cope with their impending death and the deaths of other residents. Memorial services are held regularly at Bailey House and are attended by staff, residents, family members, and friends.

Research opportunities abound at Bailey House. There are many issues surrounding HIV infection and substance use that require exploration. The nurse practitioner evaluates the compliance of substance users in clinical trials for AIDS drugs. Assessment of the pain management needs of the substance abuser is necessary. The effects of neuropsychiatric disease on people with AIDS in a group residence has been evaluated (Staats, Hough, and Dornan 1989). It is also necessary to determine, through research, whether a supportive group residence is the best setting for persons with a chronic or terminal illness.

Drugs that control HIV-related diseases and opportunistic infections are extending the lives of people with AIDS. As a result there is an increased need for medical and nursing care, both inpatient and outpatient, and for housing. AIDS calls attention to the inadequacies of the health care system in caring for those with chronic illnesses. It also highlights the plight of the homeless. Nurses can take the lead as advocates, organizers, educators, and care givers in AIDS care.

STUDY QUESTIONS

1. Discuss the advantages of supportive housing over institution care.
2. Explore the role of the nurse in a supportive housing model.
3. How could supportive housing decrease the number of hospital admissions?

REFERENCES

Harvard Community Health Plan. 1983. *Guidelines for clinical practice*. Boston: Harvard Community Health Plan.

Hirschfeld, N. 1988. Nightmare on main street. *Daily News Magazine*, 30 October, 26–28.

New York Statewide Professional Standards Review Council. 1989. *Criteria manual for the treatment of AIDS*. Albany: New York State Department of Health.

Staats, J.A., G. Hough, and D. Dornan. 1989. Effect of neuropsychiatric signs and symptoms on homeless persons with AIDS in a group residence. Presented at the Fifth International Conference on AIDS.

Torres, R., and J.A. Staats. 1989. Primary care at a residence for persons with AIDS. Presented at the Fifth International Conference on AIDS.

Chapter 18

Cooperative Care for the Oncology Patient

Melissa Meyers

> The chapter describes the Cooperative Care Center at the New York University Medical Center in New York City. The uniqueness of cooperative care lies in how it offers reimbursable hospital care at a reduced cost by requiring the patient to come to centralized clinical services and to provide a care partner. The 104-bed center has a Therapeutic Center, an Education Center, and areas for admitting, dining, and recreation. All other services at the medical center, such as laboratory and radiology services, are available to Cooperative Care Center patients. The cost of the patient's stay averages 40% less than the typical cost of semiprivate hospitalization.

Cooperative care is an innovative form of hospital care. It prepares patients, with support from advanced practice nurses and an individual patient education program, to participate maximally in their treatment. By requiring that the patient come to the centralized clinical services and to provide a care partner, cooperative care offers reimbursable hospital services at a reduced cost.

In 1979, the first cooperative care center opened at New York University Medical Center. It comprises 104 patient rooms, a Therapeutic Center, an Education Center, and areas for admitting, dining, and recreation. All other services of the medical center available to patients in the conventional units of the hospital, such as laboratory and radiology, are also used for patients in the Cooperative Care Center. In the United States, cooperative care has been implemented in approximately 18 hospitals to date.

The cost of the patient's hospitalization, which also covers the cost of the care partner's room and board, averages 40% less than that for a patient in a semiprivate

Note: The author wishes to thank Dr. Anthony J. Grieco for his thoughtful guidance in the preparation of this manuscript.

room in the conventional part of the hospital. Cooperative care is reimbursed by third party payers as inpatient care. The minimum stay is one night.

ADMITTING

The criteria for admission to the Cooperative Care Center are the same as those for the main hospital, with one exception: patients must be mobile with the assistance of the care partner. Whether by walking or by wheelchair, everyone in the Cooperative Care Center must be ambulatory because the patient comes to the professional health care staff for assessment and treatment. A schedule of appointments is prepared for each patient daily and is delivered to the patient's room before breakfast. The care partner is usually a relative or friend whom the patient selects to enter the hospital with him or her. The care partner stays with the patient from 4 to 24 hours a day as judged necessary by the nursing staff. He or she is responsible for assisting with personal care, reporting observations of the patient's condition (such as intake and output or tolerance of medication), participating in daily activities (such as education sessions), and serving as a companion to the patient.

THE PATIENT ROOM

The patient and care partner stay together in a room that is furnished like a hotel room with twin beds. There are no hospital beds, no oxygen or suction outlets in the wall, and no electric monitoring equipment in the rooms. Only the bathroom, with its handrails and emergency call button, suggests that the room is a hospital room. Bedside telephones connect the patient and care partner to the Therapeutic Center, which is staffed by registered nurses 24 hours a day. Staff members do not routinely visit patients in their rooms but are capable of responding within seconds in the event of an emergency.

Although some patients in the Cooperative Care Center choose to wear pajamas and robes, most wear casual clothes during the daytime. There is ample space in the rooms for personal articles, and each room is equipped with a small refrigerator to store between-meal snacks and beverages. There are no restrictions on visitors in the patient rooms; privacy is ensured by a locked door.

DINING AND RECREATION

The patient and care partner go to meals in a cafeteria-style dining room, where there is greater flexibility in meal times and menu choices than in conventional hospital units. A nutritionist is available in the dining room to assist those with special needs or problems. Room service can be arranged for a patient who is temporarily unable to use the dining room because of sedation or nausea.

Each afternoon in the patient lounge the patient and care partner are invited to a "happy hour," where nonalcoholic drinks and nutritious snacks are served. In the recreation area games and crafts are provided, and movies, music concerts, or other special events are planned by the recreation therapist for the evening hours. These opportunities for patients to meet informally often lead to small group interactions that can be therapeutic for them.

THE THERAPEUTIC CENTER

The Therapeutic Center houses the clinical nursing staff and provides space for physician visits. The role of the senior nurse clinician requires experienced assessment and problem-solving skills as well as the ability to provide individual patient teaching. The minimum requirements to practice as a nurse clinician in the setting are a bachelor's degree and 3 years of acute care experience.

The average nurse-to-patient ratio is 1:15, which is appropriate because of the degree of patient and care partner involvement encouraged at the Cooperative Care Center. For example, in the self-administered medication program the patient who demonstrates adequate knowledge about his or her medications after an individual teaching session with the pharmacist can assume responsibility for self-administration. The senior nurse clinician assesses the program and all other patient and care partner activities during the nursing appointments in the Therapeutic Center.

THE EDUCATION CENTER

The Education Center houses several disciplines: nursing, social work, nutrition, pharmacy, recreation, and movement therapy. A staff of nurse educators assesses the patient's education needs on admission, recommends an education plan, and conducts individual and group classes. The minimum requirements to practice as a nurse in the Education Center are a master's degree and 3 years of acute care experience.

Although both the nursing and the social work staff assist the patient and care partner with coping, it is the role of the social worker to connect patients in the Cooperative Care Center with psychosocial support resources in the community. Nutritionists provide individual diet planning, and the movement and recreation therapists provide classes on managing stress with relaxation and recreation techniques. The Education Center also offers various audiovisual and written materials.

THE ONCOLOGY PATIENT

The Cooperative Care Center admits patients for various treatments and procedures, but approximately one-third are there to receive cancer therapy. A clinical nurse specialist becomes involved in the care of each patient on chemotherapy. The average nurse-to-patient ratio is 1:7, which reflects the complexity of care required by the population. The nurse specialist provides continuity of care from admission to admission and is available by telephone to the patient at home.

The clinical role of the oncology nurse specialist requires advanced assessment and problem-solving skills and chemotherapy administration expertise as well as experience in providing individual teaching about the disease process, treatment, and management of related symptoms. The minimum requirements to practice as an oncology nurse specialist are a master's degree, oncology nursing experience, and demonstrated teaching and leadership abilities.

A patient starting chemotherapy takes an introductory class with a nurse educator in the Education Center. Among the other classes for the oncology population are an introduction to radiation therapy, care of the Hickman catheter, and self-injection technique for interferon administration. It is the role of the nurse specialist to prepare the patient with more specific information and instructions. The patient has a scheduled appointment with the oncology nurse specialist on each day of treatment. The patient's preference for a specific appointment time is honored whenever possible. Although a 30-minute appointment is scheduled per patient, allowing time for assessment, teaching, and initiation of the treatment, the patient and care partner may remain in the Therapeutic Center for several hours while the infusion is monitored. The nurse specialist is readily accessible to address any questions or concerns that the patient or care partner may have.

The care partner's role with the patient receiving chemotherapy is to provide comfort measures, assistance with toileting, and companionship during the patient's stay in the Therapeutic Center. Once they have returned to their room, the role expands to include following safety precautions prescribed by the nurse, especially when the patient has been sedated, and summoning help by telephone if nursing assistance is needed. Of course, the care partner functions under the guidance and support of the nursing staff and may need time to develop a sense of comfort with the responsibility. If a patient cannot provide someone who is available as needed and willing to be accountable for fulfilling the expectations of the role, the staff assists the patient to a conventional hospital unit in the medical center.

Although the Cooperative Care Center was not designed only for the patient with cancer, it is particularly well suited to the needs of the oncology patient. During the diagnostic or active treatment phases of the disease, the center provides a safe and comfortable environment for patients who would otherwise be hospitalized in conventional care settings. It is not an alternative to ambulatory or day hospital care, and although in some cases the Cooperative Care Center may be appropriate for patients in the terminal phase, conventional hospital care or home hospice care is usually more suitable for those circumstances.

The center formally acknowledges the need for information and offers the patient and care partner various education resources. Although each discipline has a different focus, providing information is part of the care offered by each member of the professional staff. The daily schedule ensures that a specific amount of time each day is devoted to questions, and explanations can be repeated if necessary. The company of family and friends helps allay anxiety and enhance learning.

The Cooperative Care Center recognizes the patient's need for maintaining control. It enables patients to participate maximally in the delivery of their care. The patient receiving chemotherapy has a choice of treatment times and may assume responsibility for self-administration of oral antiemetics. Flexibility in meal times and food choices is helpful to the patient in managing nausea or anorexia. With expert professional guidance, patients develop competence in managing symptoms and gain a greater sense of overall control. The center also recognizes the family's need for control. When family members become socialized as care partners by participating in patient care decisions and activities in an environment that offers education, support, and immediate feedback, they develop a greater sense of mastery over the situation and exhibit more confidence in transferring their skills to the home setting.

The Cooperative Care Center meets the patient's need to preserve individual identity. It allows the patient to maintain individual patterns of daily living: the personal care routine, the usual sleep-wake pattern, and preferred meal schedules. Wearing their own clothes allows patients to express individuality and to preserve dignity. It supports the patient in the role of equal collaborator in care and helps discourage adoption of the sick role.

The center acknowledges the oncology patient's need for a broad base of psychosocial support. It promotes the maintenance of relationships with family and friends, especially by incorporating the care partner role into the system of care delivery. It facilitates contact with other people with cancer who are sharing a similar experience, and it offers many opportunities for developing therapeutic relationships with professional care givers.

Finally, the Cooperative Care Center helps reduce the financial burden created by multiple hospitalizations. Hospitals everywhere are striving to maintain high standards of care and at the same time to reduce costs. The cost-saving aspect of the Cooperative Care Center is particularly beneficial to oncology patients who require repeated hospital stays to complete lengthy treatment courses.

STUDY QUESTIONS

1. In what ways does cooperative care meet the oncology patient's need for safety, comfort, knowledge, self-determination, and psychosocial support?

2. How could nursing research address quality-of-life issues, reimbursement structure, and health status outcomes in the cooperative care structure?
3. Discuss the role of the cooperative care oncology nurse in case management.

SUGGESTED READING

Berg, B. 1983. A touch of home in hospital care. *New York Times Magazine*, 27 November, 90–98.

Cooperative care: Patients, partners, professionals. 1981. *Geriatric Nursing* 2:338–44.

Gibson, K., and B. Pulliam. 1987. Cooperative care: The time has come. *Journal of Nursing Administration* 17:19–21.

Grieco, A.J. 1988. Home care/hospital care/cooperative care, options for the practice of medicine. *Bulletin of the New York Academy of Medicine* 64:318–26.

Kristan, R.V. 1985. Cooperative care: Six years down a new path. *The NYU Physician* 41:52–61.

Chapter 19

The Oncology Nurse in Business

Joanne D. Hayes, Anita Nirenberg, and Randi Moskowitz

> As a result of the changing roles of men and women, increased competition in the health care field, and the expanded role of the nurse, more nurses have taken the opportunity to develop their own entrepreneurial business ventures. Therefore, it has become increasingly important for the nurse in business to have an understanding of the functions of an entrepreneur and the strategies needed for a successful marketing approach. Two oncology nurse–run businesses are described in this chapter. One business described is a consulting firm. Founded by an oncology nurse, its focus is supplying clinical expertise to clients such as hospitals and health care providers. The expertise provided may be for public and professional education, the development of cancer program components, or grant preparation and implementation required by the client. The other business is an oncology nursing agency in New York City that provides experienced, qualified oncology nurses who can deliver expert nursing skills to cancer patients in physicians' offices, hospitals, and the home.

AN OVERVIEW

Over the past decade, the number of nurses entering into business for themselves has increased greatly. This is due, in part, to the social forces that examined, redefined, and modified the status and roles of both men and women (Neal 1982). These changes have affected the nursing community, so that the number and types of jobs have begun to undergo significant restructuring as members of the profession seek entrepreneurial ventures.

Entrepreneurship and Nursing

According to Stevenson, Roberts, and Grousbeck (1985), entrepreneurship is the process of creating value by pulling together a unique package of resources to exploit an opportunity. Entrepreneurs are energetic, visionary, confident, intense, imaginative, optimistic, and courageous (Tilbury and Fisk 1989). Nurse entrepreneurs entering into business generally become dissatisfied with their career paths, not their chosen field. Two examples of innovative nurse-run businesses are discussed later in this chapter. To appreciate the impact of these programs, however, it is important to discuss further the characteristics of the entrepreneur and factors that improve marketing techniques of the business venture.

Over the past 5 years, attempts have been made to formulate a basic profile of the entrepreneur. Welsh and White (1983) have documented 11 characteristics that make up an intriguing composite of the entrepreneur:

- *Good health*. Successful entrepreneurs characteristically are free of major illness and often admit that symptoms of chronic health problems such as allergies disappear when starting their own business.
- *Basic need to control and direct*. This is not a need for power; rather, it is a need to be free to choose and to act on their individual perceptions of choices that will result in achievement.
- *Self-confidence*. Entrepreneurs are more self-confident when they are in control. Loss of control results in anger, frustration, and decreasing self-confidence.
- *Never-ending sense of urgency*. Entrepreneurs thrive on activity and achievement and have a high energy level.
- *Comprehensive awareness*. Entrepreneurs have the ability to see the entire picture as it relates to the future.
- *Realism*. Entrepreneurs accept things as they are and deal with successes and problems as they arise. Honesty and integrity are two important outgrowths of this characteristic.
- *Superior conceptual ability*. Entrepreneurs have an uncanny ability to identify relationships in complex and confused situations. This ability applies to functions and things rather than to interpersonal problems.
- *Low need for status*. Symbols of achievement and status such as clothes, office decor, and automobiles are not generally important to the entrepreneur.
- *Objective approach to interpersonal relationships*. Entrepreneurs, because of their need for control, high self-confidence, and realistic approach, generally find it difficult to become interpersonally involved. They tend to keep themselves at a distance psychologically.

- *Sufficient emotional stability.* Entrepreneurs are able to handle the anxieties and pressures of both their businesses and their personal lives. They are cool and effective in stressful situations.
- *Attraction to challenges, not to risks.* Entrepreneurs prefer situations in which they can influence the outcome; they take neither high nor low risks.

These characteristics, which are found in various degrees among all entrepreneurs, help them eventually succeed at their business ventures. Before any of this can be accomplished, however, the entrepreneur must develop a detailed marketing plan for the business as the first step.

Marketing of Services

Kotler (1988, 3), an expert in the field of marketing, defines marketing as "a social and managerial process by which individuals and groups obtain what they need and want through creating and exchanging products and value with others." Only recently has the concept of marketing been brought into the forefront of the health care business venture. Nurses who understand these concepts and the importance of marketing their services will be more successful in an increasingly competitive marketplace because they are in a good position to assess, plan, implement, and evaluate marketing strategies that influence client behavior and public perceptions (Tilbury 1989).

There are some basic tenets of marketing that are applicable to health care and nursing. The first area that must be identified is needs. Tilbury and Fisk (1989) suggest that the following factors are important in making this assessment.

- People differ in perceived needs. Factors that influence perceptions are variations in knowledge, experience, age, gender, income, and lifestyle.
- People expect their health care needs to be met with the same range of choice and level of personal attention as are provided by other non–health-related services.
- Nurses, physicians, and other health professionals have the same hierarchy of needs as patients.

People satisfy their needs and wants with products and services. All the potential clients who share a particular need or want and who are willing to engage in an exchange to satisfy that need or want constitute the market (Kotler 1988). Marketing management is a process involving analysis, planning, implementation, and control and covering ideas, goods, and services. It rests on the notion of exchange, whose goal is to produce satisfaction for the parties involved (Kotler

1988). All these factors must be taken into consideration when developing a business and marketing plan.

Types of Business Opportunities

There are many business opportunities available to the oncology nurse. Ideas for program development include education consultation (for consumers and nurses), collaborative practice with physicians, recruitment and employee searches, health promotion and screening services, administrative management consultation, publishing advisement, computer information consultation, and audio or video development. With a little ingenuity and creativity, one could develop other innovative ideas for practice.

The Oncology Nurse in Business: Moving into the 21st Century

Nurses are becoming more aware of the opportunities that are available to them in the business world. This has become evident by the numbers of nurses entering graduate business degree programs. Courses in accounting, finance, economics, marketing, and business policy have become assets in the development of business ventures.

Decisive, assertive, leadership, independent, and innovative roles are now frequently associated with women (Neal 1982). Women are being socialized into these roles, which were once the domain of men. This can only have a positive effect on the careers of nurses with business savvy.

THE NEXUS GROUP

Established in 1986, the Nexus Group is a consulting firm founded by an oncology nurse who was a former clinical nurse specialist at a community hospital in New Jersey. After the advent of diagnosis-related groups in New Jersey in the early 1980s, many hospitals began decreasing expenses by eliminating nursing positions, particularly those of clinical specialists. As is the case for many entrepreneurs, the opportunity to start a new business follows the leaving of a job, either voluntarily or as the result of budget cuts.

The word *nexus* is Latin for "linkage" or "binding." The goal of the Nexus Group is to fill the gaps in today's health care environment, many of which were caused by changes in the reimbursement system, by providing nursing expertise through the use of consultants. The major focus in oncology products such as public and professional education and management projects including development of cancer program components and grant preparation and implementation. In addition to contracting directly with clients the Nexus Group makes subcontracting arrangements, frequently with larger health care consulting firms requiring particular clinical expertise. If a request is beyond the scope of service of the principal, additional nurse consultants, usually clinical nurse specialists, are called in to deliver the service.

Establishing a new business in New Jersey starts with registering the name of the business at the County Clerk's Office. After verifying (through review of old records) that no other business in the county has the same name, a certificate is issued by the clerk for a fee of approximately $30. Incorporating the business, at least initially, was discouraged by legal counsel for two reasons: it is expensive, and it involves a lot of paper work (including quarterly reports to the government). Once the business is well established with significant revenue, incorporation is advisable.

Because the Nexus Group is a home-based business, no specific insurance is needed other than riders to the homeowner's policy to cover equipment (computer, copier, and the like). If client meetings were to be held in the home, additional liability insurance would also be required. To date, all meetings have taken place at the clients' offices.

A consulting business, because it sells a service rather than a product, is relatively inexpensive to begin. Initial capital is needed only for stationery, phone, desk, and salary for the principal. To keep overhead expenses to a minimum, no employees are on the payroll; rather, additional services (secretarial, accounting, and so forth) are subcontracted as needed.

A consultant is one who has a certain level of expertise in a specialized area and is willing to share it with a client for a specific purpose. Oncology nursing as a specialty is becoming more and more complex. There are subspecialties (surgery, chemotherapy, and radiation therapy) and subdivisions within those subspecialties (external beam radiation and brachytherapy). This complexity demands expertise in the specialty, and each nurse can carve a niche within it. On an oncology unit, for example, one staff nurse may be a venipuncture expert, one a pain control specialist, and another a wizard with dressing changes. These nurses may then call on each other as consultants to meet the needs of their patients. How can this level of consultation be translated into one that a client is willing to buy?

Scope of Service

The first step in becoming a consultant is to identify an area (or areas) of expertise. This involves taking stock of professional activities and determining what it is that one does well. Clinical practice, education, administration, and research are all areas of practice with marketing potential. Particularly in the health care professions, some clients may want to know whether expertise was developed through experience, continuing education, a formal degree program, or a combination of the three. These factors add credibility to the service being offered. Indeed, there may be some difficulty encountered in convincing potential clients that a nurse is qualified to be a consultant and does have something worthwhile to sell. Inherent in the concept of consulting is that no one can be expected to know everything.

Selling the Service

Now that the service has been identified, how is it communicated to prospective customers? Two techniques used frequently by consultants are marketing and networking.

Marketing

Although health care is one of the largest industries in the United States, it was one of the last to learn about the need for and benefits of marketing. Hospitals have only recently begun to "sell" their services to surrounding communities. Consequently, nurses have been forced to learn about this new dimension in health care. It is only recently that nursing schools have offered marketing as part of their curriculum. Today professional nurses in all settings must prove that they are worth their salaries on a daily basis.

By definition, marketing is an activity directed at satisfying perceived needs and wants through an exchange process. Similarly, nursing is a profession directed at satisfying needs and wants of patients, but the key word now is *perceived*. A consultant must perceive a potential client's needs because that client must see that the service offered will satisfy his or her need before a contract will be signed.

One of the most marketable services that the Nexus Group offers is assistance with the development of a grant proposal. These documents can be 200 to 300 pages in length; because a client has other full-time job responsibilities, developing a grant proposal can be difficult to accomplish. In this case the consultant provides the "time" necessary to write the proposal. This service has both a short- and a long-term outcome: the short-term outcome is a well-organized, comprehensive grant application, and the long-term outcome is the potential financial benefit of the final award (usually several hundred thousand dollars). To date, 90% of grants prepared by the Nexus Group have been funded.

Marketing involves an exchange process. This exchange does not necessarily have to be money; time and knowledge are other exchangeable commodities. For example, a consultant may waive the fee for a speaking engagement if the audience includes potential clients. In this case, time is being exchanged for advertising.

Kotler (1988), a prolific writer of marketing concepts, describes marketing management as demand management. The task at hand is to influence the level, timing, and composition of demand in a way that will help the organization achieve its objectives. Successful marketing management is imperative in the development and implementation of a marketing plan.

Identifying the market is the first step toward developing a marketing plan. A market is a set of actual and potential buyers of a service; in other words, who will be the purchasers of the service? These buyers may include other nurses, physicians, patients and families, the community, or even other departments in the same setting.

Because a consultant cannot be all things to all people (although some may try!), market segmentation may help target a specific size or group. Market segmentation is the subdivision of a market into distinct subsets of customers; any subset may be selected as a market target with an individual marketing plan. The purposes of segmentation are (1) to allow for better positioning to spot marketing opportunities, (2) to identify the most lucrative segment for the business, (3) to provide the ability to make finer adjustments of the service and promotion materials for each segment, and (4) to provide a clearer idea of the response to a marketing program (Kotler 1988). Segmentation may be accomplished on the basis of one or more of the following factors:

- geography—municipalities, counties, or states or the service areas of hospitals
- demographics—information such as age, sex, or income (available from the local planning board or the Census Bureau)
- psychographics—lifestyle, intelligence, traits about people, some of which are quantifiable (for example, recruiting strategies for new graduates will be different from those for experienced registered nurses)
- behaviors—the knowledge of, attitude toward, or response to the service (marketing hospice services to a physician who has previously used this service will be different from marketing those services to one who has not) (Kotler 1988).

Development and use of successful marketing strategies will enable the consultant to identify the segment that produces exceptional results, to locate high-potential areas for concentration, and to abandon markets that may be drying up or attracting too much competition.

Networking

Networking is a skill with which nurses are better acquainted than marketing. Policies and procedures are shared among nursing units, among institutions, and across the country. Job changes may also be the result of networking as one nurse identifies a good fit between a colleague and a known vacancy. For many nurses in business, networking is responsible for securing those first few clients as well as subsequent ones. This is a time-consuming process initially but if done correctly can develop into a steady stream of referrals.

Networking can best be accomplished on three levels that ideally should be developed simultaneously. First, there is professional networking. The nurse should contact colleagues in pertinent fields, by phone if possible (the personal touch is most effective) and briefly discuss the purpose of the new business and the scope of work. The nurse should follow up immediately with a letter summarizing the call and include one or more business cards and a brochure if available. It is important that potential clients have something tangible to remind them of the contact. The nurse should attend relevant professional meetings and conferences. These can be opportunities to expand the network by meeting new people. It also accomplishes two other objectives for the consultant: continuing education to stay current, and acquiring visibility. The nurse should publish in books, journals, and newsletters and stay active in professional associations either through committee work or elected office. Running for an elected office in a major professional organization is a potential way to do large-scale advertising. Simply being slated for office adds to credibility and provides national exposure as well. Finally, a widespread mailing to co-workers (including physicians, social workers, and administrators) at previous places of employment can be effective.

Personal networking is the next level. Family and friends, if not potential customers themselves, may be helpful in making contacts. Business leads can appear anywhere: at a cocktail party, the airport, and even the supermarket. The nurse entrepreneur should never go anywhere without a supply of business cards and, again, should follow up any leads with a letter.

The last level is community networking. This technique is effective because it is usually done among large groups of people: parent-teacher associations, local churches, or civic groups. The nurse should offer to give talks on health-related topics (and pass around those business cards). Public speaking provides good exposure as well as an opportunity to practice verbal communication skills. These talks are part of the community service to which every business owner commits. If the audience is charged for attending the meeting or conference, the speaker is entitled to receive a fee. If the engagement has a special value in terms of marketing, however, the speaker may decide to waive the fee.

Fee Schedules

Establishing a fee schedule is dependent on a number of factors:

- education
- the "going rate" for a particular geographic area or type of setting

- responsibility for the project (e.g., total ownership or subcontractorship for a portion of the work)

Fees may be determined as hourly or daily rates as well as on a per project basis. Travel time and expenses, preparation time, and any support services needed to complete the work (secretarial, legal, or other subcontractors) should be included in fees. Most consultants charge a minimum of $100/hour, but there is a "rule of 3" that may be used as a guideline:

$$\text{Salary} \times 3 = \frac{\text{annual revenue*}}{\text{number of hours worked/year}} = \text{hourly rate}$$

*annual revenue = 1/3 salary, 1/3 overhead, 1/3 profit

For example, a nurse consulting in pain control determines that his or her annual salary is $50,000. Therefore, the annual revenue of the business should be 3 times that amount, or $150,000, which allows $50,000 for overhead and $50,000 for profit. Dividing this figure ($150,000) by 2,000 hours of working time (40 hours/week) results in an hourly billing rate of approximately $75/hour. Although this rate may seem high, maintaining even a home-based consulting business can be expensive. Nurses are notorious for undercharging for their services and should not be afraid to ask for the fair price that the service demands.

Some clients may request services on a routine basis, such as monthly inservices on an oncology unit. It may be appropriate to request a retainer from these clients to ensure that their work takes priority among other clients. The amount is usually a portion of the estimated total billings. For example, if monthly inservices at $100 per session have been conducted at the client's institution for the past year, a retainer of that amount could be requested for the coming year, with extra charges being billed accordingly. Several retainers of this kind can ensure income and help ease the fluctuation in cash flow that is common in a consulting business.

Collecting Fees

Collecting fees is the most difficult part of operating a small business, particularly for nurses who are not used to being assertive. For large projects (the preparation for a grant proposal, for instance), it is advisable to request one-third the estimated costs when the contract is signed, one-third midway through the project (completion of the first draft), and the final third at the end of the work. Services should not begin until the first payment is made and are discontinued if the second installment is late. This may put the entire project in jeopardy if there is a deadline to meet, but it is an effective method of collecting fees on time.

Established consulting firms with good reputations frequently require payment in full before any work begins.

Billing statements should be submitted at the end of a project and then every 30 days thereafter until paid in full. Reminder notices of overdue accounts are sent at 60 and 90 days, and at 120 days the accounts are referred for collection. Late charges based on individual state law are assessed on accounts more than 30 days overdue. If the nurse is using a collection agency, he or she should investigate it thoroughly and check references. Most take 50% of the collected sum as their fee.

An alternative is taking the client to Small Claims Court for a small fee, usually $25 to $50. States vary as to the definition of small claims; most are $500 to $1,000. This is a time-consuming method but has a better return than a collection agency. Frequently a firm letter from an attorney is enough incentive for a client to settle an account.

Advantages and Disadvantages

Advantages of being a small business owner include:

- freedom to accept or reject clients and projects. A delinquent client will not be serviced more than once.
- flexibility of work schedule. Work can be performed around the demands of family, vacations, and other professional commitments.
- creativity of assignments. No two clients or projects are alike, which allows for maximum creativity.
- self-governance. There is nothing better than being your own boss!

Even self-employment has disadvantages; these include:

- professional isolation. The nature of nursing is one of working with other people; therefore self-employment can be lonely. Involvement in professional organizations such as the Oncology Nursing Society or the American Nurses' Association can help fill the void and establish that important support system.
- financial risks. Without the benefits of significant monthly retainers or guaranteed long-term contracts, the cash flow in any new business will look like a roller coaster. Planning ahead for dry spells is an absolute must.
- responsibility factor. Although other jobs may include 24-hour responsibility, a business owner has ultimate and unending responsibility. There are no more paid vacations because when the principal is away work does not get done. If a business is large enough to support a number of staff, then some of the responsibility may be shared.

- self-discipline. When the business owner has no one to report to but himself or herself, the distractions are endless. This is particularly true if one works at home. Discipline takes practice but is essential to a smooth operation.

Conclusion

Just because nurses have always worked for someone else does not mean that they always will. It is now permissible for them to talk about money, personal power, and more control over their professional lives. The nursing profession is changing, expanding, and more open to innovation. Perhaps now, instead of losing colleagues to medicine, social service, real estate, or law, the profession will be able to accommodate colleagues in the roles and environment of their choosing.

THE ONCOLOGY NURSING AGENCY

The merging or melding of the two traditionally different yet similar disciplines of nursing and business gave rise to the concept of the Oncology Nursing Agency (ONA). The disciplines are similar in their ability to provide a service to the public: one in oncology nursing, and the other in planning and facilitating all aspects needed for the corporate structure. The ONA was developed when a need to provide expert oncology nursing in various settings to people with cancer was recognized. The people who conceived and developed the agency have had long experience in the service industry; one of the principals of the company is a corporate facilities planner and the other a nurse oncologist with clinical, education, and administrative expertise. Both principals are dedicated to providing treatment, education, and financial assistance for the person with cancer as well as to producing a viable, profit-making entity. The ONA is expanding throughout the United States.

Concept of the Oncology Nursing Agency

The mission of the ONA is to provide experienced, qualified oncology nurses who can deliver expert nursing skills to people with cancer in multiple settings such as private physicians' office practices, hospitals (inpatient and outpatient settings), and the home. The ONA is responsible for properly scheduling the oncology nurse with the appropriate client and for providing the nursing agent with the scope of work in each assignment, which includes orientation to the setting, patient history, and treatment plan. The ONA provides the nursing agent with necessary supplies to provide treatment and written tools for patient education.

Benefits to the Oncology Nurse

The oncology nurse working for an agency not only removes himself or herself from the large institution but promotes self-reliance while maintaining skills and expertise in cancer nursing. In this way the oncology nurse can be his or her own time manager, which allows for flexibility and encourages self-discipline. The nurse can request work situations that correspond to personal, financial, and time requirements, thus allowing total control of the work schedule.

The oncology nurse who contracts to work for the ONA is paid by the ONA as an individual contractor. The payment schedule established by the agency is based on both the market and the special expertise required. Filing and payment of withholding taxes and Social Security payments are the nurse's responsibility. It should be pointed out, however, that there are tax advantages for individual contractors, such as certain deductions that are not allowed for salaried employees. Other benefits may include participation in the ONA's health insurance plan.

Corporate Structure

The corporation consists of three officers: the two principals of the company and the medical director. The day-to-day operation of the agency includes recruiting oncology nurses, ensuring that agency nurses have appropriate credentials, interfacing between clients and nurses, monitoring the quality assurance system, coordinating inservice education programs, developing patient and family education materials, negotiating contracts, and conducting agency administration tasks (accounting, tax, and insurance matters). Time must also be allowed for strategic planning and marketing.

Licensure and Insurance

In New York State an independent nursing agency is licensed by the Department of Consumer Affairs. Extensive regulations detailing structure, reporting requirements, and insurances that cover nursing agencies are addressed in the public health and business laws of the state. A nurses registry is an employment agency or office which recruits and hires licensed nurses for employment by the hour, day, or week.

An oncology nurse under contract with the ONA must maintain current licensure and registration as a professional nurse. Most nurses in the ONA are certified by the Oncology Nursing Society or the Intravenous Nurses Society or have other certifications from the American Nurses' Association. All nurses under contract are required to carry personal malpractice insurance coverage (minimally at the $1 million to $3 million coverage level). To be licensed by the New York

Department of Consumer Affairs, an agency must carry a $5,000 third party continuous insurance bond.

Corporate liability insurance, although not required by law, is maintained by the agency. This insures the corporation as a separate entity and protects the corporate assets as well as the personal assets of the principals of the company.

Marketing of an Oncology Nursing Agency

General marketing has been discussed earlier, but here some examples of strategies specific to this type of business are given. There are basically three target groups to whom services are marketed; each target group requires a separate marketing strategy.

Consumers

Americans spend much more time researching purchases such as automobiles or microwave ovens than health care. Given the opportunity, however, they will explore their options when it comes to choosing their medical and nursing care. The ONA's guiding philosophy guarantees the consumer of cancer therapy the right to know that the oncology nurses who administer therapies also provide education and counseling, assume the role of patient or consumer advocate, guarantee confidentiality, and have completed extensive educational and experiential oncology nursing courses. The setting in which the person with cancer receives therapy may become irrelevant when the person is assured that the hands-on nursing is professionally guaranteed.

The consumer marketing strategies include speaking at public forums, publishing articles in professional and special-interest publications, giving interviews on radio and television talk shows (public access and local), and taking part in organizations such as the American Cancer Society.

Physicians

Oncologists in private practice are involved in myriad treatment options, and their ability to deliver these treatments varies. Many private practice oncologists are in large groups and are involved in cooperative studies. Medical oncologists may deliver much of the cancer treatment in their private offices and try to keep hospitalization for their patients at a minimum. To provide complex treatments in the office setting, the medical oncologist requires the services of highly skilled oncology nursing colleagues. The emphasis on collegial practice as well as on offering advanced oncology nursing to their patient population is the basis of this marketing strategy to physicians.

The professional reputation of the ONA guarantees the oncologist in private practice expertise and quality. The physician is offered the opportunity to obtain cost savings by hiring an oncology nurse through the agency. These savings are achieved by utilizing the specialized service as required, and the physician can collaborate with the nurse regarding schedule, which avoids expensive and unproductive "down time." The physician who participates in cooperative group studies can be assured of having oncology nurses who are experienced in managing data from clinical trials as well as in providing the actual therapies. These services provided to the physician oncologist can make a difference in the physician's practice and the quality of life of patients on treatment protocols.

Hospitals

The marketing strategies for hospital contracts rely on the promotion of expertise in oncology nursing. The safe and efficient oncology nursing care delivered to the hospitalized person with cancer will enhance the overall well-being of the patient and has a positive effect on hospital costs. The experienced oncology nurse is able to detect covert changes in the patient's condition and pays attention to all problems that could result in longer hospital stays (which create bed shortages, decreasing hospital admissions, and decreasing hospital revenue). All statistics regarding these factors are maintained in the ONA computer and are presented to hospital administration during negotiation of contracts. In addition, these statistics, when analyzed, can be presented to third party payers, including Medicare, and make a difference in the delivery and costs of cancer care.

Contracts

Each client with whom the agency does business is required to sign a contract for services to be rendered. These contracts reflect individual needs and the scope of services required. The ONA has hired attorneys who have corporate and medical-legal expertise. The attorneys have drawn up contracts that reflect the scope of work on the basis of client needs. Each different type of client has a contract specific to the setting in which oncology nurses will be working. The contracts document the scope of services to be rendered, the fee schedule, and timely payment of fees. The ONA license includes antidiscrimination clauses, and a statement of such is given in the contracts.

Each of the oncology nurses who work for the ONA must sign a contract that describes agency requirements such as maintenance of a current registered nurse license, evidence of current individual malpractice insurance, and payment of fees. Renewal of nurse contracts is considered on an annual basis and may include changes in scope of services and payment schedules.

Computerization

The use of a computer in the ONA business is essential. A computer is especially needed for dispatching nurses. Listing oncology nurses, documentation of patient care, standardized care plans, patient profiles, and all laboratory results as well as generating statistical data, billing, and all information required for third party payment are standard components of this system. Data retrieval is possible at any time for review of physician or patient status. Computerized data can also be used to expand the agency and to do feasibility studies as well as for planning and management of health care facilities.

Future Projections

The ONA is in the business of "people leasing." In this high-tech, high-touch service profession, there is a need to encourage nurse contractors to be a major component of the agency's growth. Nurses who have the expertise and skills as well as the self-motivation and self-discipline needed to work as individual contractors are what the agency requires in terms of management. As it expands to other geographic locations, the agency will need to have oncology nurses committed to excellence in management skills as well as to providing quality oncology nursing care to clients. The potential for advancement in the agency is unlimited. The network structure is promoted as "consensual decision making, collective responsibility, slow evalution and promotion, implicit informal control, nonspecific career path, and holistic concerns" (Naisbitt 1982). Salaries are commensurate with skills, experience, and responsibility and may be in the range of $30/hour to $40/hour. Internal development of managers is encouraged. The network of oncology nurses as managers creates an ever-improving environment for clients. Computerized data will be used to expand the agency and to create a consulting management group to assist in feasibility studies and in planning and management of future health care facilities.

STUDY QUESTIONS

1. What are the characteristics of an entrepreneur?
2. What factors are important in identifying the needs of the client?
3. What marketing strategies were utilized for the two specific entrepreneurial ventures discussed in this chapter?

REFERENCES

Kotler, P. 1988. *Marketing management analysis, planning, implementation and control.* Englewood Cliffs, NJ: Prentice Hall.

Naisbitt, J. 1982. *Mega trends.* New York: Warner Books.

Neal, M. *Nurses in business.* 1982. Pacific Palisades, CA: Nurseco, Inc.

Stevenson, H., M. Roberts, and H.I. Grousbeck. 1985. *New business ventures and the entrepreneur.* Homewood, IL: Richard D. Irwin, Inc.

Tilbury, M, and T. Fisk. 1989. *Marketing and nursing: A contemporary view.* Owings Mills, MD: National Health Publishing.

Welsh, J, and J. White. 1983. *The entrepreneur's master planning guide.* Englewood Cliffs, NJ: Prentice Hall.

SUGGESTED READING

Books

Brown, D. 1980. *The entrepreneur's guide.* New York: Ballantine Books.

Califano, J.A. Jr. 1986. *America's health care revolution.* New York: Random House, Inc.

Connor, R.A., and J.P. Davidson. 1985. *Marketing your consulting and professional services.* New York: John Wiley & Sons.

Cooper, P.D. 1985. *Health care marketing issues and trends*, 2nd ed. Rockville, MD: Aspen Publishers, Inc.

del Bueno, D.J., ed. 1981. *A financial guide for nurses: Investing in yourself and others.* Boston: Blackwell Scientific Publications, Inc.

Dossey, L. *Space time and medicine.* 1982. Boulder, CO: Shambahala Publications, Inc.

Naisbitt, J. 1985. *Re-inventing the corporation.* New York: Warner Books.

Periodicals

Armstrong, C., and D. Thom. 1987. Create your own financial team. *Journal of the National Intravenous Therapy Association* 10:399.

Barrere, C., and L. McKinstry. 1988. Nurse exchange: An innovative approach for office nursing practice. *Oncology Nursing Forum* 15:293–295.

Getting paid for giving advice. 1985, August. *Changing Times*: 59–61.

Giglione, L. 1988. Home IV therapy—Who pays? *Journal of Intravenous Nursing* 2:294–296.

Greene, R. 1985, 21 October. Do you really want to be your own boss? *Forbes*: 86–96.

Meyer, D.K. 1987. Oncology nurses versus cancer patients' perception of nurse caring behaviors: A replication study. *Oncology Nursing Forum* 14:48–52.

Otto, S.E., and J.C. LaRocca. 1988. Nursing diagnosis: Challenge for intravenous nursing practice. *Journal of Intravenous Nursing* 11:245–249.

Shuchman, M., and M.S. Wilkes. 1989, 12 February. Asking-telling body and mind. *New York Times Magazine:* 45–46.

Weinstein, S.M. 1987. Home care forum: Cost viewpoints. *Journal of the National Intravenous Therapy Association* 10:401–409.

Chapter 20

Home Care for Cancer Patients Including Chemotherapy Administration

Cecilia Wilfinger, Robin B. Brenner, Anne Hubbard Mattson, Anne E. Belcher, Penny Ashwanden, and Randi Moskowitz

---

The focus of this chapter is the definition of home care in terms of what can be done, who is eligible to receive it, and who is best suited to provide it. Clinical, financial, and social standards are addressed. The role of the oncology nurse as care giver and patient advocate is discussed. Standards for care and outcome criteria are addressed.

Home care comprises health care services ordered by the physician, coordinated by the nurse, and delivered by an interdisciplinary team to the patient and family in their own home environment. Often home care is an alternative to hospitalization in an acute care facility or institutionalization in a long-term care facility. As Weinstein (1987) notes, there was a home care surge in the 1980s because the inception of the prospective payment reimbursement system created a natural incentive for hospitals to discharge patients to the home environment earlier and sicker. The potentially lower costs of home care combined with the superior quality of life and health care available to the patient recuperating at home have done much to stimulate the growth of home care in recent years.

Defining the home environment of the recipient of home care was much simpler at the turn of the century, when this nurse specialty was in its infancy. The home environment was traditionally where one resided in the company of family or friends. In the past the home had, at a minimum, the essential support systems for home care: utilities, heat, telephone, protection from the elements, and family members or significant others who were able to participate in the plan of care.

Today's society comprises myriad alternate homes and lifestyles. Urban and rural demographics offer many variations of the home definition ranging from the most advantaged and supportive environments to the street. Nursing homes can also be considered places of home care because the extension of acute care is often delivered in nursing homes, shelters, and residences. Nevertheless, all homes have one common element: they are the patient's territory, the domain in which he or she has ultimate control in the health care process.

Persons with cancer who traditionally have been referred for home care are those whose treatments or clinical states require skilled services for cancer-related problems. Skilled services may be needed to manage toxicity-related problems and adverse effects of chemotherapeutic regimens, to determine the correct care of mucositis, to control pain, to administer antiemetic therapies, to evaluate conditions requiring physical therapy, and to manage situations requiring the support services of paraprofessionals. The home care nurse is responsible for wound and skin care and for making assessments of the patient's nutrition status, risk of infection, potential for injury related to anemia-induced weakness, and comfort status.

New to the home care scene is the use of high technology in bringing treatment formerly administered in the hospital to the home, in particular the ability to offer infusion therapy in the home setting. Many standards for cancer chemotherapy treatment protocols and regimens incorporate continuous infusions to prevent severe toxicity and to promote tolerance of treatment dosing. The use of 5-fluorouracil for colorectal or esophageal cancer is an example. These treatments were formerly administered only in the hospital or a physician's office. The oncology patient who was to receive 5-fluorouracil boluses on five consecutive days needed to make tiring daily trips from his or her home to receive the therapy. Patients requiring continuous or intermittent intravenous infusions had to remain hospitalized for the long hours of their treatment. Terminal patients or those with chronic pain needed placement for pain control regulation. The ability to provide infusion therapy in the home setting means that all these patients can now receive their treatment at home comfortably, safely, and cost effectively.

EDUCATING THE PATIENT AND FAMILY

Providing education about various symptoms related to the disease process and treatments and about the management of drug therapies is a primary responsibility of the home care nurse. The cancer patient and the spouse or family member caring for him or her in the home setting must be willing and able to learn the therapy and the care involved in the safe administration of that therapy. One of the biggest challenges to the oncology nurse is teaching a layperson to do health care. The nurse must always be cognizant of the fact that the stress of sickness lowers a person's ability to comprehend complicated instructions. If printed learning material is used, one should be aware that the national average reading comprehension is relatively low and that the stress of an illness tends to compromise understanding. Without speaking down to the patient, therefore, the nurse must teach slowly, reiterate instructions, and do comprehensive follow-up on all the teaching that is done.

Teich and Raia (1984) review teaching and outcome measurements for a patient undergoing chemotherapy at home. Their outline covers catheter insertion and care, pump management, and patient follow-up. They indicate that, on the basis of the information provided, the patient and family must understand the rationale for treatment, details of catheter care including hand washing techniques and dressing changes, and pump manipulation and maintenance.

ELIGIBILITY REQUIREMENTS

Criteria for eligibility for home care include the establishment of a need for home care services. The patient must require pharmacy, nursing, respiratory therapy, durable medical equipment, or laboratory monitoring. The nurse responsible for administering chemotherapy or analgesia to the patient at home must determine the safety of the drug in relation to each individual patient. For example, a young person with good family support is far more likely to do well when receiving high-dose chemotherapy than a fragile elderly person who lives alone. The patient's health and social situation must be such that services can be safely administered in the home. The availability of commodities such as water, telephone, and electricity must not be taken for granted. The telephone in particular is a crucial necessity for the oncology patient at home, although one may not ordinarily think to ask whether the patient has a telephone.

For intravenous treatment patients must have adequate venous access through a peripheral, central, or right atrial line. The patient must be geographically well located to ensure timely follow-up with supportive agencies if they are needed. Today more than ever, patients may travel to metropolitan cancer centers for their primary therapy and then return to their communities to continue their treatment. Active communication and follow-up must be established between the home care oncology clinical nurse specialist and the patient and family if the patient is to return to a safe home environment. The patient and family must understand the importance of communicating feedback, in terms of side effects sustained or experienced by the patient, to the nurse to ensure the most effective treatment.

TECHNOLOGIC ADVANCES IN HOME CARE

What today's high technology has brought to the oncology patient is a wide variety of means to deliver safe, effective therapy in the home. New technology has provided such things as computer pumps, digital readouts, and safety alarm features that facilitate and enhance the care given to oncology patients. Narcotic analgesia, for example, can now be given by means of volumetric ambulatory pumps, which have a special feature called patient-controlled analgesia. This device allows the individual patient to administer bolus doses of narcotics as necessary within selected parameters set into the pump. The device keeps track of all the bolus doses administered. Subsequent changes in narcotic doses can then be determined on the basis of the number of times a bolus was given within the last 24 to 48 hours.

There are ambulatory pumps now on the market that can be programmed to circadian rhythm, which makes the administration of chemotherapeutic agents more efficacious. Pocket-sized microchip pumps in various sizes and colors have become commonplace. High technology, however, cannot be mistaken for high quality, and all equipment used or suggested for use in the home setting should be chosen with great care. The oncology nurse must choose carefully the most appropriate and reliable apparatus on the basis of pharmaceutical need, patient comfort, learning ability, and financial restrictions (Andre 1986; Feinberg 1986).

FINANCIAL CONSIDERATIONS IN HOME CARE

Although nurses have traditionally been taught not to mix money and medicine (Leonard 1988), an oncology nurse who ignores the financial impact of home care is doing a disservice to the patient (Giglione 1988). The cost of health care has risen so staggeringly that the patient's resources may already have been stretched to the limit.

Most third party insurers reimburse some home health care costs if a legitimate medical necessity is documented and, more often, if treatment is an alternative to hospitalization. Medicare and Medicaid branches of the Health Care Financing Administration (HCFA) are the largest payers for health care services in the United States today. HCFA pays for the health care needs of more than 50 million Americans who are old, disabled, or poor. Even with recent legislative reforms in payment, expenditures continue to rise. According to Davis (1985), unavoidable increases in the growth of these expenditures are due to several factors:

- the aging population accounts for more than 17% of the growth
- increases in the use of medical resources and technology account for another 33%
- the remaining 50% is largely due to inflation

The important economic factors must be determined by the patient with the assistance of the oncology nurse. Once it has been established that therapy can be delivered safely in the home, then the cost effectiveness of that therapy should be evaluated both from an overall economic point of view and from the patient's personal point of view.

It must be established whether the patient's insurance plan covers home care services, drugs, administration supplies, disposable supplies, equipment, nursing, and other professional services or paraprofessional services. The nurse must also be knowledgeable about state requirements regarding care delivered by licensed rather than state-certified agencies. The amount of coverage, deductibles, and policy limits all play a part in determining what care is planned for the patient at home. The devastating emotional impact of a diagnosis of cancer should not be compounded by another devastating factor: money. The oncology nurse must be sensitive to all these economic issues.

Most commercial insurance companies will verify a policy and benefits over the phone if adequate demographic information is presented. Home care that is immediately followed by hospitalization is often an additional criterion for home care coverage. The Catastrophic Health Act of 1988 is presently undergoing revisions but eventually should offer many Americans the chance to have therapies administered at home that previously were not covered by government insurance plans. Home chemotherapy is one such therapy that is not presently available. As the act is written, however, certain chemotherapeutic agents used in the home care market still will not be reimbursed.

Insurance companies have become increasingly reluctant to reimburse for investigational therapies (Yates 1988) even though the protocols often offer the latest state-of-the-art drugs available anywhere. Health maintenance organizations often tell subscribers that they cannot be referred or reimbursed for investigational treatments. Many third party insurance companies have clearly defined clauses that rule out reimbursement for what are considered experimental therapies not yet shown to be efficacious to the cancer patient. Ironically, these rules were initially for the protection of the consumer (i.e., to ensure payment for therapies that had been established and proven by the medical practice). For the patient with cancer, however, standard therapeutic drugs may be inferior to what state-of-the-art investigational therapies may offer in terms of treatment and cost. Although new drugs used in clinical trials may be expensive in the short term, their greater effectiveness in treating or controlling a specific cancer often results in the patient being able to return to a full and productive life sooner than with standard drugs.

THE ROLE OF THE NURSE IN THE HOME

The nurse's one visit to the patient at home often replaces the many brief visits made to a patient's bed side during the course of a day in the hospital. The nurse therefore must be well versed in physical assessment. A comprehensive physical assessment of bodily systems should follow an outlined, routine approach. In addition, a means of communication must be established with the patient and the family on a regular basis, with periodic follow-up visits or calls being scheduled as the nurse deems necessary. The nurse must have a solid knowledge of the therapeutic drugs being given and the equipment being used. If the nurse's knowledge of specific aspects is inadequate, appropriate resource material must be available. Each home care nurse should have on hand a reference guide for drugs as well as a list of telephone numbers of pharmaceutical representatives or physicians with whom to discuss the correct use of drugs and equipment.

As care giver, the home care nurse must have an innate sense of rhythmic coordination. The textbook image of a home care patient with a supportive spouse living in a suburban household is often not the scenario encountered by the visiting oncology home care nurse. The nurse's role as coordinator of all aspects of the patient's home care therefore is crucial. The home care nurse must have the ability to set priorities, to ascertain deficiencies or needs, and to determine the person most appropriate to fulfill those needs and then must be able to refer the patient or family member to the appropriate person or agency.

The nurse works closely with the physician who is primarily responsible for the patient, social service departments, insurance companies, family and friends, and, most important, the patient. In a hospital setting, one can focus on the patient; in the home, the periphery of family, friends, and environment must be taken into consideration.

THE HOME CARE NURSE AS PATIENT ADVOCATE

Taking care of the oncology patient in the home provides the oncology clinical nurse specialist with the unique opportunity of playing the role of patient advocate. The nurse is in the best position of anyone in the health care delivery system to recognize the needs of this patient population. Although the Patient's Bill of Rights applies to the patient at home as much as to the patient in the hospital setting, the home care nurse may well be the only available spokesperson for the needs, concerns, and problems of the oncology patient at home.

The home care nurse's concern for the availability, quality, and standards of treatment given to the oncology patient being treated at home is often addressed by such professional groups as the Oncology Nursing Society, the Intravenous Nursing Society, and the Home Healthcare Nurses' Association.

STUDY QUESTIONS

1. What does home care mean for the cancer patient?
2. How do oncology nurses provide therapy safely, cost efficiently, and with a positive outcome clinically, psychologically, and economically?

3. Does home care provide an alternative to hospitalization that is safe, efficacious, and efficient, or are home care nurses, as some critics contend, merely providing a substitute for an overburdened medical system that may or may not meet the needs of the oncologic population?

REFERENCES

Andre, J.-A. 1986. Home health care and high-tech medical equipment. *Caring*, September, 9–12.

Davis, C.K. 1985. Health care economic issues: Projections for oncology nurses. *Oncology Nursing Forum* 12:17–22.

Feinberg, M. 1986. High-tech pharmacy and home care: A sophisticated partnership. *Caring*, September, 35–38.

Giglione, L. 1988. Home IV therapy—Who pays? *Journal of Intravenous Nursing* 11:294–96.

Leonard, A.M. 1988. Reimbursement for home infusion therapies. *Horizons in Home Health Care* 2:4–6.

Teich, C.J., and K. Raia. 1984. Teaching strategies for an ambulatory chemotherapy program. *Oncology Nursing Forum* 11:24–28.

Weinstein, S.M. 1987. Regulatory concerns: Home care. *Journal of the National Intravenous Therapy Association*, May/June, 175–84.

Yates, J.W. 1988. Reimbursement in clinical cancer research: Current issues. *Biotherapy and Cancer* 1:1.

Part IV

Computers, Videos, and the Oncology Nurse

Chapter 21

Computers and Oncology Nursing

Janet B. Kelly, Gerry Hendrickson, and Luanne Citrin

> Computers assist oncology nurse specialists in their roles as care integrators and care givers for their patients. Computers assist nurses in their role as care integrators through communications with ancillary departments and other professionals and collecting, organizing, and storing data. Computers can assist nurses in their role as "care givers" through automated care planning, discharge planning, patient monitoring and by tracking patients' educational, therapeutic, comfort or other needs. Nurses are able to document their assessments, interventions and patient outcomes while receiving cues and reminders concerning policies, procedures and standards of care. In the future oncology nurse specialists can expect to see a spread of today's computer technology to more hospitals as well as a host of new developments, such as more intelligent systems, nursing and medical knowledge online, documentation at the bedside, and use of patient databases in education and research.

Nurses act as care integrators as well as care givers for their patients (McClure and Nelson 1982). As care integrators, nurses manage communication and the coordination of activities of physical therapists, social workers, dietitians, physicians, and a host of other professionals in ancillary departments. This role is vitally important because it ensures that services from different departments come into play at the appropriate time for the benefit of the patient. Carrying out this role involves many routine clerical tasks, however, such as writing requisitions or telephoning an ancillary department to convey, clarify, or track down some piece of information. The hospital computer system can help nurses manage this communication of information, relieve them of some routine aspects of the role, and enable them to integrate care more efficiently and accurately. Computers can also assist nurses in their role as care giver. Through automated care planning, discharge planning, and patient monitoring and by tracking patients' education, therapeutic, comfort, and other needs, computers assist nurses in providing patient care.

Computer systems offer particular benefits for the oncology nurse specialist because of the nature of care for oncology patients. Oncology patients often present with multisystem problems and thus require the involvement of many hospital services in their care. Furthermore, the care of these patients often spans many years and takes place in multiple settings (hospital, clinic, and home). The computer's ability to track and integrate information from many sources, to store this information, and then at a later time to retrieve and transmit it to a specified location is especially needed in the care of these patients. In addition the communication and decision-support capabilities of computers make it possible for the oncology nurse specialist to plan, direct, and evaluate care given by another care giver such as a staff nurse, an aide, or even a family member.

This chapter describes the capabilities of a hospital information system, information flow, nursing process application, printouts and reports, confidentiality issues, and future directions.

GENERAL CAPABILITIES OF A HOSPITAL INFORMATION SYSTEM

Traditionally, when a patient enters a hospital a complex communication system powered by large numbers of forms and requisitions goes into effect. Many departments must be notified almost immediately of the new patient's admissions and location. The patient's diagnostic and therapeutic course is affected by many different health care professionals, who must move into action to provide testing, treatment, and supportive services individualized for each particular patient. An admission notice is sent to dietary, radiology, pharmacy, social work, pastoral care, laboratories, patient accounts, and numerous other departments. These forms generally are transmitted through an internal mail system, sometimes in a timely manner, sometimes not, and occasionally not at all. It is not unusual for newly admitted patients to find that no food tray has arrived for their first hospital meal. Nor is it unusual for it to take 2 days for their television to be turned on because the television service was never notified of their admission. It has also happened that the physician has ordered a medication to which the patient has an allergy because, although the question was asked (and perhaps documented), a transcription error caused it to be omitted from a medication requisition.

These examples illustrate problems in information handling encountered in most hospitals, especially in large, complex ones. A basic hospital information system is designed to solve problems such as these. The primary functions of a hospital information system are to support communications and to collect, organize, and store data. Thus with a patient's admission into the hospital information system, the computer takes over the communication process, sending information about the patient's admission and location and selected demographic and clinical data (such as allergies) to all departments and personnel with a need to know. This communication process can be accomplished by the computer in seconds with no lost requisitions on the way.

Figure 21-1 is a schematic representation of a typical hospital information system. Variations in information systems exist in various hospitals (Pryor et al. 1983; Bleich et al. 1985; Blum 1986; Albrecht and Lieske 1985; Greene et al. 1982), but most have online admission/discharge/transfer, charge capture, and billing capability. Some hospitals have full information systems like the one depicted in Figure 21-1, which provide the ability to enter orders and to review results from nursing units as well as automation of all or some portion of the ancillary services.

In hospitals with full information systems, orders or requisitions are entered from the nursing unit and routed by the computer to the appropriate ancillary department. Results are entered into the computer in the ancillary departments as soon as the test is completed or the action taken, and they can then be viewed from the nursing unit, the physician's office, or any other terminal that is part of the system. If an appointment is required, as would be the case for a radiology test, it

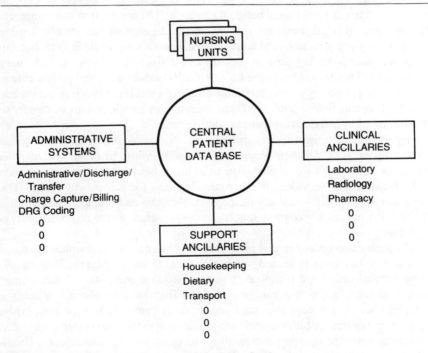

Figure 21-1 Schematic of a Basic Hospital Information System

can be scheduled automatically without a separate telephone call. Charges for the tests are captured automatically and become part of the patient's bill. If the patient is transferred to a different floor or discharged, the nurse or unit clerk enters this information into the computer, and it is then broadcast to the appropriate ancillaries automatically.

COMMUNICATING ORDERS AND RESULTS BETWEEN NURSING UNITS AND ANCILLARY DEPARTMENTS

The order-entry and results-reporting capability is often one of the earliest applications to go on line. No manual system, however efficient, can begin to equal the speed with which new medical orders entered into a computer are sorted and printed in various ancillary departments. Computerized entry eliminates lost requisitions and provides the ancillary department with all the information that it needs to complete the test. For example, a request for a diagnostic radiology examination automatically includes demographic and clinical information from the patient's computerized database. For information not already in the patient's database, the ordering screens of the computer can be designed so that all necessary data must be entered before the order will be accepted by the computer. In this way, all requisitions not only reach the department but are also legible (because they are printed by the computer) and contain complete information. In addition, there is no lag time in pick-up and delivery to or from the ancillary department. Thus turnaround time for test results is shortened, and patient care is enhanced. The oncology nurse specialist awaiting a test result, such as a complete blood cell count, before initiating chemotherapy can gain access more rapidly to this information and decrease patient waiting time.

Physicians enter their orders directly into the computer in some hospitals (Anderson et al. 1988; Schroeder and Pierpaoli 1986). In these systems, the computer "knows" a given physician from his or her log-on identification code and password and provides an electronic signature for subsequent orders. The computer supplies automatically the physician's name and title to printed orders. Accrediting agencies recognize this computer signature as the physician's legal signature.

Although direct order entry by physicians exists in only a few hospitals, in those in which it has been instituted some real benefits have resulted. First of all, computerized orders are complete. Every medication order, for example, must specify dosage, route of administration, and frequency of administration; the computer will not accept the order unless all information is supplied. Errors inherent in the transcription process are eliminated; the oncology nurse specialist no longer needs to interpret handwriting, to make assumptions about a chemotherapy or radiation therapy dose or schedule, or to call the physician to complete an order. Moreover, the time spent in transcribing, deciphering handwriting, or telephoning to clarify an order is saved.

Physicians receive information and "alerts" directly if they enter their own orders. For example, if a physician orders a medication to which the patient is allergic or one that is contraindicated, in some systems he or she is alerted to the fact immediately. The action needed to override an alert differs according to the policies of the hospital. The alert may serve merely as a reminder, allowing the physician to continue with the order in the usual way. In other systems, physicians may be required to document the reason for overriding the alert. Orders for oncology drug therapy automatically carry appropriate precautions, such as those for medications that are vesicants. Chemotherapeutic protocols may be programmed so that they are correctly ordered and each patient receives appropriate hydration and antiemetic therapy (Exhibit 21-1).

Orders are transmitted electronically to the appropriate ancillary department, where they are printed out as requisitions or schedules. After work is completed, results are entered into the computer in the ancillary department. For example, an order for a laboratory test is entered by a physician at a computer terminal at the nursing station or perhaps at the bedside and is electronically transmitted to the laboratory computer. When the blood is received in the laboratory, computerized

---

Exhibit 21-1 Chemotherapeutic Protocol as Displayed on a Computer Screen

PHYSICIAN ORDERING SCREEN **ONCOLOGY** (ABVD)
ADRIAMYCIN INJ _____ MG, IV, BOLUS VESICANT PRECAUTION: GIVE SLOW PUSH VIA RUNNING IV, START ON 05/30 2 PM, × 1 DAY
BLEOMYCIN INJ _____ U, IV, BOLUS START ON 05/30 2 PM, × 1 DAY
VINBLASTINE INJ _____ MG, IV, BOLUS VESICANT PRECAUTION: GIVE SLOW PUSH VIA RUNNING IV, START ON 05/30 2 PM, × 1 DAY
CHEMO INFUSIONS . . . . START D5/W 500 CC, W/DACARBAZINE _____ MG, IRRITANT PREC: DILUTE IN IV FLUID & GIVE SLOW DRIP, RATE: 250 CC/HR × 1 BAG, THEN D/C IV, START ON 05/30 AT 2 PM

blood analyzers run the test and automatically feed the results to the laboratory computer, which sends the results to the hospital information system. Once a test is completed, the results are available almost immediately both in the laboratory computer and at computer terminals throughout the hospital. The nursing staff can be alerted to abnormal and stat results by an alarm as they are printed out. Nursing has access to up-to-the-minute results from laboratories, radiology, nuclear medicine, electroencephalography, electrocardiology, and any other automated diagnostic department. Nursing may also have access to progress notes from reporting ancillaries such as social work, nutrition, quality assurance, and physical therapy if these are entered into the computer.

Because nurses as care integrators are at the hub of the information flow, they are affected strongly by the presence of an information system. A computerized information system benefits nursing by saving time and reducing the potential for errors, both of which are important benefits in a time of shortage. The computer helps save staff time by assuming the clerical and communication burden associated with all tasks from origination of a medical order to documentation of its completion as well as tasks associated with processing discharges and transfers (Barrett et al. 1975; Schmitz, Ellerbrake, and Williams 1976; Blackmon et al. 1982). The tasks that were formerly accomplished through routine paperwork or telephone calls are done on line, with many categories such as patient identification, age, sex, and allergies being filled in automatically from information already in the patient database. The time-consuming process of copying information from chart to form and form to form is taken over by the computer. The time spent rectifying an error caused by miscommunication between the unit and ancillary department as well as the time spent in tracking down the piece of paper that occasionally gets lost can also be saved.

Errors occur when information is improperly transferred, when time demands are so great that nurses cannot do all they need to do, and when pertinent information is simply overlooked. Because computers do not lose or forget, and because they can print out organized lists of orders and other activities to be done, they have great potential to help reduce errors, particularly errors of omission. Computers can also flag out-of-bounds values, which can prevent overlooking an exception. Out-of-bounds flagging can occur with both orders and results. For example, the computer can flag an order for a higher than normal dose of a given medication. The physician, pharmacist, and nurse are then alerted to double check the order. Although the oncology nurse specialist is familiar with many regimens for chemotherapy protocols, the unit nurses may not be. During the development of such standard protocols, input from the oncology nurse specialist is essential to facilitate appropriate care by nurses throughout the hospital.

NURSING PROCESS APPLICATION

In addition to the benefits that nurses derive as care integrators from the demographic, psychosocial, and clinical data entered by other disciplines, computer applications are available to facilitate their role as care givers in carrying out and documenting the nursing process itself (Bailey 1988; Hinson and Bush 1988). The oncology nurse specialist as well as the staff nurses caring for the oncology patient are able to document their assessments, interventions, and patient outcomes while receiving cues and reminders concerning policies, procedures, and standards of care of the nursing department.

Assessment

Computer screens are designed with menus offering the nurse selections for retrieving previously entered assessments or progress notes. The nurse can then build an admission assessment from history and demographic information already in the database, from the patient's therapeutic course from previous outpatient and inpatient visits, and from his or her current presenting status. In most systems today the retrieval of previous data is passive in the sense that the nurse must decide whether and what kind of data to review. In the future this retrieval will be active, or intelligent, because the computer will automatically present pertinent data from its history bank on the basis of defined norms or abnormalities of a disease process or a patient's expected clinical course.

Care Planning

The oncology patient population generally presents with multisystem problems or needs, which demands that an individual plan of care be developed by the oncology nurse specialist. Although oncology nurse specialists strive to manage patients on a primary care basis, it may not be possible for them to provide all direct patient care. The hospital computer system enables the oncology nurse specialist to develop the individual care plan and to communicate to various health care providers exactly how the plan is to be implemented and by whom. This provides each patient with 24-hour managed care by the oncology nurse specialists, even in their absence.

Computerized care planning systems are commonly the first nursing application to be requested by nursing departments and the first part of the nursing process to be computerized. Care planning modules may be contained in a hospital information system and integrated with the rest of a system, or they may be a stand-alone application. Today care planning is done passively. The nurse is presented with a list of problems or nursing diagnoses from which he or she selects the pertinent ones. Subsequent menus list expected outcomes and nursing orders, and the nurse selects, without computer prompting or assistance, the appropriate ones. In more advanced systems, which are also available today, the computer guides the nurse through interventions appropriate for a specific nursing diagnosis, thereby communicating to the nurse a standard of care. In the future, there will be more computer assistance in care planning. For example, by using decision-making logic the computer might actually offer suggestions to the nurse that are based on information that had been previously entered about a particular patient.

Thus a computerized patient care planning system offers today, at a minimum, an efficient means of documenting a plan of care. In the future, it will provide the nurse with an efficient tool that cues, communicates, and assists in producing a high-quality, individual plan of care.

Documenting Care

Charting against the plan of care and documenting the patient's progress toward an expected outcome are also possible on the computer. Because computers can structure the input fields, the documentation is more complete and more uniform and contains fewer charting omission errors. In addition, computerized charting is more legible, dated and timed more frequently, and more compliant with criteria for documentation (Johnson et al. 1987; Bailey 1988; Greene et al. 1982; Beckmann, Cammack, and Harris 1981). Some systems allow charting of medications, vital signs, weights, intake and output, intravenous drug administration, and other functions tied to physician orders. Still others allow charting against the nursing plan of care.

Today this charting is done in several ways. It may be a typed-in, narrative charting entry, or it may entail entering data stating that an intervention was completed or an outcome reached. It may also be done through charting menus that allow practitioners to select descriptive phrases pertaining to interventions carried out and to the progress of a patient toward an expected outcome. In the future, intelligent systems may cue or query the nurse by using the patient's database and standards of care and practice to guide the documentation process in an interactive mode.

Discharge Planning

Computerized charting capabilities also extend to discharge planning. The ability of the computer to accept and store information from many disciplines and its ability to organize and sort data allow for the development of effective and efficient discharge planning systems. From the point of admission until patients leave the hospital, the ability of patients to care for themselves, ongoing evaluation of their support systems, and their anticipated needs on discharge can be continually tracked. Data entered by the primary nurse, the oncology nurse specialist, the physician, the social worker, the chaplain, and the patient services representative are all available to be reviewed by the discharge planning unit. The patient's need for equipment, supplies, medications, and home care services can be evaluated and progress in securing these services for the patient tracked through the computer. Home care professionals can also receive summary documents and orders produced by the computer to make the patient's transition from hospital to home as smooth as possible. In intelligent systems, the computer can plot the patient's critical path and alert nurses to any deterioration in clinical or performance status.

Once the patient is discharged, the database continues to be available to the oncology nurse specialist caring for the patient as an outpatient. This feature is especially important to the oncology nurse responsible for the ongoing and possible long-term care of the patient.

PRINTOUTS AND REPORTS

An enormous amount of data about the patient is stored in the computer as diagnostic testing is performed and therapeutic interventions are carried out. These data, which include the medical and nursing plans of care, can be organized, sorted, and printed for timely reports that can support and facilitate the role of the nurse. Furthermore, reports documenting activities already performed and the patient's response to these interventions can be printed for inclusion in the patient's permanent medical record. Figure 21-2 shows some of the reports that help nurses organize their patient care activities. Together they give a comprehensive view of the needs of each patient and help organize the numerous needs and interventions required by a group of patients.

Electronic Kardex

An example of an electronic kardex for a typical oncology patient is shown in Exhibit 21-2. When the attending physician enters specific orders into the system, such as the chemotherapeutic agents and the premedications used for a specific protocol, that information is stored in the computer and is available to be organized and printed in work documents for the nurse. In addition, when the primary nurse or oncology nurse specialist enters information into the nursing plan of care, that information is stored in the computer and is also available to be printed in work documents. The electronic kardex then contains the physician's orders along with typical administration instructions and indications for testing and procedures. It might also include pertinent information from the patient's history as well as teaching and discharge needs. As results are entered into the computer or as documentation entries are made, the electronic kardex is automatically updated to indicate testing and treatments completed and results available.

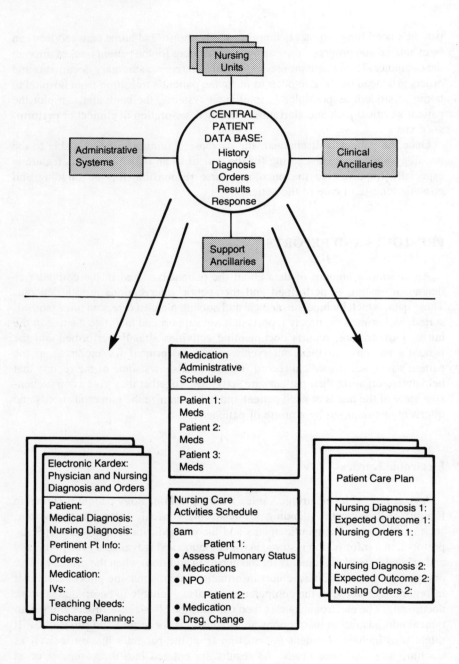

Figure 21-2 Printouts and Reports

Exhibit 21-2 Electronic Kardex

ELECTRONIC KARDEX

Medical Diagnosis: Hodgkin's Disease
Nursing Diagnosis: Mouth Pain secondary to Chemo-Induced Stomatitis

GENERAL PATIENT INFORMATION: Patient admitted for second cycle IV chemo for stage III HD. Patient uses ice cap to minimize alopecia. Patient has mediport. Oncology nurse specialist: Jane Jones.

ASSESSMENTS: Inspect oral cavity QD for regression or progression of lesions.

DIET & FLUID BALANCE:

    DIET: Regular, soft as tolerated.
        Encourage po fluids to 750 cc QD.
        Diet Consult: Determine diet tolerated best by patient (i.e., soft foods), and determine food likes/dislikes. Indication—5 lb wt loss within 1 month after IV chemo; stomatitis.

    IV:
        Periph line #1 . . . Start N.S. 250cc Rate: for infusions with chemo bolus.
        Chemo infusions . . . Start D5W 500 cc, with decarbazine 400 mg irritant prec: Dilute in IV fluids and give slow drip, 250 cc/hr × 1 bag (then D/C IV) on 05/30 at 2 pm.

MEDICATIONS:

Adriamycin inj. 40 mg IV bolus: Vesicant precaution: give slow IV push via running IV start on 05/30 2 pm × 1 day.
Vinblastine inj. 10 mg IV bolus: Vesicant precaution: give slow IV push via running IV start on 05/30 2 pm × 1 day.
Bleomycin 12 units IV bolus start on 05/30, 2 pm × 1 day.
Hep lock soln. 3 cc IV mediport flush prn.
Ativan 2 mg IV prior to chemo; may be given IM Q4h prn.
Benadryl 50 mg IV prior to chemo.
Compazine 10 mg IM prior to chemo and Q8h prn.
Decadron 20 mg IV prior to chemo.
Mylanta, lidocaine, Benadryl susp. "cocktail" 10 ml po. Swish and swallow Q8h prn for mouth pain.

MISC MD ORDERS: D/C patient in a.m. after being seen by ONS and MD.

TEACHING NEEDS: Patient requires reinforcement of mouth care instructions and need for increased po fluid intake.
                      Instruct patient on use of stomatitis "cocktail" before meals.

TESTS:
    PFT (indication IV bleomycin), schedule today 05/30.
    CXR (indication: mediastinal tumor) schedule today 05/30.

DISCHARGE PLAN: Plan to contact patient by telephone within 1 week of discharge to determine status of oral cavity.

Patient Care Plan

An example of a patient care plan for a typical oncology patient is shown in Exhibit 21-3. This example shows how individual nursing interventions developed by the primary nurse or oncology nurse specialist in response to the nursing diagnosis are incorporated with more generic nursing interventions. The patient care plan becomes part of the patient's permanent record, with progress toward

Exhibit 21-3 Example of a Patient Care Plan

PATIENT CARE PLAN

Jane Smith   Rm1735
4865865   00187   04/03/61   27   F
  DOE, JOHN MD

05/30/89   04:00 PM

PRIMARY DIAGNOSIS: —HODGKIN'S DISEASE . . .

NURSING DIAGNOSIS
  05/30 MOUTH PAIN SECONDARY TO CHEMOTHERAPY-INDUCED
         STOMATITIS

EXPECTED OUTCOMES		DEADLINE
05/30	—1) RESOLUTION OF PREEXISTING ORAL LESIONS	06/05
05/30	—2) MINIMUM OF 750 CC PO FLUID INTAKE QD	06/05
05/30	—3) DECREASE OF/RESOLUTION OF MOUTH PAIN	06/05

NURSING ORDERS		SCHEDULE
05/30	—1) ARRANGE FOR DIET CONSULTATION TO DETERMINE DIET TOLERATED BEST BY PATIENT (IE: SOFT FOODS), AND DETERMINE FOOD LIKES/DISLIKES.	05/30
05/30	—2) INSTRUCT PATIENT AND SIGNIFICANT OTHER ON MOUTH CARE, ESPECIALLY BEFORE AND AFTER MEALS. AVOID USE OF COMMERCIAL MOUTHWASHES; USE OF SALINE OR BAKING SODA SOLUTIONS SHOULD BE ENCOURAGED.	05/31
05/30	—INSTRUCT PATIENT ON USE OF STOMATITIS "COCKTAIL" BEFORE MEALS TO MINIMIZE PAIN AT MEALTIMES.	05/30
05/30	—INSPECT ORAL CAVITY QD FOR REGRESSION OR PROGRESSION OF LESIONS.	QD

Jane Jones, RN, ONS

LAST PAGE

achievement of the expected outcomes being included in the patient care notes. In addition, the components of the patient care plan are organized and sorted in a timely manner to appear on work documents such as the electronic kardex and the nursing care activities schedule.

Medication Administration List and Nursing Care Activities Schedule

Examples of work documents that organize care activities across a group of patients are the medication administration list and the nursing care activities schedule (Exhibit 21-4). These documents, produced automatically by the computer, are organized by time: they list by the hour nursing tasks such as medications to be administered, assessments to be made, and treatments and procedures to be done for a given group of patients. These lists help primary nurses organize care for all their patients so that conflicts can be quickly identified, tasks rearranged, and priorities set. Work documents such as these can also be produced for oncology nurse specialists on the basis of their particular patient load.

Computer-Produced Reports for the Chart

The reports described so far are all temporary work documents, the contents of which change as the patient's needs and interventions change. They are updated,

Exhibit 21-4 Nursing Care Activities Schedule

NURSING CARE ACTIVITIES SCHEDULE

9 AM
 PATIENT 1:
   Inspect oral cavity
   Reinforce mouth care instructions
   Instruct on use of stomatitis "cocktail"
 	
 PATIENT 2:
   Start IV line
   ABCD premeds
   IV chemo meds
 	
 PATIENT 3:
   Begin discharge teaching
 	
 10 AM
 PATIENT 4:
   Chemo meds via Hickman
   Instruct Hickman catheter care

usually at regular intervals, and the previous documents are discarded. This is not the case, however, with the permanent chart documents produced by the computer for inclusion in the medical record. Because computer technology has not yet reached the stage of development to allow easy storage and retrieval of all patient information, the paper chart continues to be the main repository of information concerning patients. Computers, however, have taken over the work of producing much of this record. Appropriate clinical information entered into the computer is printed at some point on documents that become part of the permanent medical record. As previously described all data carry the name and title (automatically generated from the log-on identification code and password) of the person who enters them, and this is recognized as a legal signature.

CONFIDENTIALITY ISSUES

Because computers hold vast amounts of medical, social, and demographic information concerning patients, special precautions and procedures must be in place to ensure the right of patients to confidentiality. The technology of any computer system must be such that access to the information it contains is regulated and selective. Entry into the computer system can be regulated in a number of ways. One way is through sign-on codes, which are unique and known only to those with the right of entry. Another method involves the use of cards with magnetic strips containing identifying information that is read by the computer.

To enhance security further, some systems limit entry by creating levels of accessibility. Once entry into such computer systems is obtained, access is limited to the information necessary to do one's job. For example, a nurse's aide who is using a computer system has no need to know the patient's financial insurance information and thus should not have access to it. Safeguards and audit trails should also be in place in these systems to alert computer operators of attempts by unauthorized personnel to enter the system (as well as attempts by authorized personnel, who might be tempted to "browse" through patient information).

The same attention paid to on-line confidentiality should also be paid to the hardcopy or report documents produced by the computer. Computers produce paper, most of which contains information about the patient. The time of the printing, the printout location, the content, and the people for whom the documents are intended must all be carefully evaluated and regulated. Again, the "need to know to perform the job" maxim usually guides the decision making.

Special attention must also be paid to the disposal of these documents. In contrast to manual systems, in which one kardex for a patient's entire period of hospitalization is updated by erasure of outdated information and pencilling in of new data, computers now print a new, updated kardex 2 or 3 times each day before the start of each new shift. Numerous temporary work documents printing on nursing units and in ancillary departments creates the need for safe, confidential disposal of paper. In most instances, shredding and recycling of paper or burning is the disposal method in use.

THE FUTURE

The future will spread today's computer technology as well as a host of new developments to more hospitals. In the future, more hospitals are likely to have computerized information systems. Oncology nurse specialists of the very near future will need to learn a computer system at some point in the course of their career. This computer system may include terminals at the bedside with built-in expert advice to assist nurses with their patient care activities. Furthermore, the large patient databases and knowledge bases developed for clinical use have considerable potential as tools in education and research.

Education Potential

One of the most exciting potentials that computers offer is in the area of education. Computers will figure in the education process in several ways. First, students will use computers to learn about computers. For example, students in nursing programs will be offered programs in basic computer programming and in the use of various commercially available word processing, spread sheet, and database software programs. It will be important for nursing professionals in management or research positions to be familiar with these tools. Second, students will use computers to learn about nursing by using software programs especially developed for nursing education. Computer technology advances such as color, audio, light pens, improved graphics, touch screens, windowing, and interactive video (which uses both computer and video technology) make using computers to learn about nursing especially promising. Students may arrive at computer laboratories as their schedules permit and review lectures, search the literature, examine articles, and study topics of interest. Simulations, graphics, and interactive video systems help students begin to learn how to apply their knowledge in clinical areas.

For practicing oncology nurses, computers offer an easy and convenient way of staying abreast of advances in the field in their own practice settings. Testing for recertification of chemotherapy administration, review of oncologic emergencies, review of safety guidelines for handling chemotherapeutic agents, learning about new products and methods of administration, and orientation in large medical centers can all be accomplished at computer terminals through the use of programs carried on diskettes. The education session takes place when it is convenient for the nurse at the nearest computer terminal.

Finally, the databases and knowledge bases used in patient care can also be used for education (see Appendix L in Clayton et al. 1989 for a discussion of the use of knowledge bases for education purposes). For example, the knowledge base of rules that allow the computer to prompt or guide a nurse through care planning or discharge planning can also be used to teach principles of care and discharge planning.

Research Potential

The research potential that computers offer is considerable. Just as the patient database used for patient care can also be used for education purposes, so can it be used for research. Today several research databases have been set up, including the clinical database of 1,103 advanced cancer patients that is being used to investigate the experience of advanced cancer (Gray et al. 1988), but the potential for retrospective research by use of the clinical patient database is largely untapped. In the future, it will be possible to use the vast amounts of data stored in computers about patients' medical and nursing histories to investigate many clinical questions in a given hospital and among several hospitals. For this research potential to be realized, the clinical database must contain items of interest coded in a way that computers can retrieve without compromising patient confidentiality.

The ability to conduct research is greatly enhanced by a project to standardize the collection of essential nursing data in a minimum dataset of common elements (Werley and Zorn 1988; Werley, Devine, and Zorn 1988). As part of this project, investigators have defined elements in three broad categories: nursing care, patient demographics, and service elements concerning the patient's hospitalization. Hospitals would need to add to this core set of elements, of course, but if these elements were present in a number of hospitals nationwide then data could be combined and research questions investigated in multiple settings.

If such standards were adopted, the benefits for nursing from capturing these data on discharged patients nationwide would be enormous. It would provide a database of uniform information from which nursing research could take place and would also have implications for nurses in practice, administration, and education. Nurses would document care for the first time according to a nationwide standard, thus facilitating continuity of care from one patient setting to another. This information would be used by health care administrators, nursing administrators, and health care policy makers in measuring nursing care, plotting trends, and investigating nursing and patient care issues and various other issues that could advance the profession of nursing.

Policies for safeguarding confidentiality of patient data in a research setting need to be developed. Confidentiality issues are different in patient care and research. For the former, issues concern access to the patient database. For the latter, an extract of patient data is taken and given to the researcher instead of patient data being obtained by browsing the database. The policies that need to be developed involve developing criteria for approving a request for data, procedures for stripping identifiers, and procedures for storage and access to data once they are in the researcher's hands. Since the Institutional Review Board (IRB) has been involved with establishing procedures for gaining access to patient data in chart form for research purposes, it is likely that the IRB will be the focus for developing and implementing policies for handling data in electronic form.

Bedside Terminals

Bedside terminals are being used and evaluated in only a few hospitals nationwide (Arnoti 1987; Soontit 1987; Childs 1988; Pesce 1988; Yero 1988; Halford, Burkes, and Pryor 1989), but they have the potential for reducing errors and promoting timely documentation. When terminals are located at the nursing station, nurses record actions and observations at the site of care (frequently on computer-generated forms), take these notes to the centrally located terminals, and enter the data well after the care has been provided. This delay increases the chance for errors: The paper might get lost, or the nurse might not be able to decipher a quickly written note or might simply neglect to record one of the notations. On the other hand, when terminals are located at the bedside nurses can document directly into the computer when they deliver care.

Bedside terminals are too new to have been subjected to careful research by independent investigators. Early studies reported that nurses do seem to document care as it is given and do not leave charting for the end of the shift (Peat, Marwick, Main and Company 1988). Some hospitals are reporting a decrease in incidental overtime as a consequence. The few studies examining the effect of bedside documentation on errors have shown a decrease in medication errors both in hospitals moving from no computerization to bedside terminals (Yero 1988) and in those moving from centrally located to bedside terminals (Peat, Marwick, Main and Company 1988).

Bedside terminals look quite promising, but some questions need to be resolved before hospitals will be willing to install them in large numbers. Cost is a major obstacle. Bedside terminals vary in cost, depending in part on their versatility, from $2,000 to $10,000 per bed (*Health Technology* 1988). Early studies indicate that savings in overtime may offset the initial capital costs, but there are too few of them to be conclusive (*Health Technology* 1988; Childs 1988). The effect on patients of having such devices in the room is also an unknown. The noise and light from the screen may be distracting or annoying to the patient. Finally, questions of how best to protect patient confidentiality need to be resolved. This includes deciding on placement of the terminal so that visitors cannot see data that the nurse is entering or viewing.

More Intelligent Systems

In the future, the oncology nurse can expect to use intelligent systems. A few systems have been developed in oncology, but they are primarily aimed at physicians to assist with their decisions in the care of oncology patients. One of these is the Oncology Clinical Information System (OCIS), which contains information about all patients admitted to the Johns Hopkins Oncology Center inpatient or outpatient units. OCIS is an information system designed to support medical decision making in this setting. Although it does not support artificial intelligence decision-making tools, it does produce protocol-directed care plans (Blum 1986).

A second system is an expert system that uses artificial intelligence to help manage the treatment of oncology patients. This system, called ONCOCIN, is a chemotherapy protocol advisor used experimentally in the oncology clinic at Stanford University (Shortliffe et al. 1984; Hickam et al. 1985). ONCOCIN offers advice about drug selection, dosing, and test selection. In intelligent systems such as this one, the computer will be able to check a given action against information it already "knows" about the patient from history, laboratory results, and medications and will use this to make comments or suggestions about the action. For example, the computer might routinely check white blood cell count, renal function, and other bodily functions before a chemotherapy treatment and suggest modifying the dosage if one or more values are abnormal.

A few decision support systems are being developed currently for nursing (Ozbolt 1988). For example, one system alerts nurses to those patients who are at risk for falls (Blaufass and Tinker 1988), and another involves pain management (Heriot et al. 1988). In the future one can expect to see greater use of such systems and intelligence applied to oncology nursing. Intelligent systems could be of particular importance in the management of oncology patients as they undergo various tests, the results of which determine decisions about treatment regimens, dosages, and frequency of administration. For example, after a gated pool scan is completed and the ejection fraction result is entered into the system, an intelligent computer system would print out specific instructions for adjusting the doxorubicin dose on the basis of that specific test result. Another example of how an intelligent system could be utilized in oncology nursing is in the management of treatment-induced side effects. As the oncology nurse specialist enters specific side effects experienced by a patient into the system, appropriate nursing measures for each sign or symptom would automatically become part of that patient's care plan.

Reference Material On Line

In the future, an increasing amount of nursing and medical knowledge will be on line and brought to bear on clinical decisions. Already a number of important reference materials are available in computerized form. For example, some important references have been put on a compact disk read-only memory (CD-ROM) disk, called *OncoDisc* (available from Lippincott Information Services, Philadelphia, PA), including texts on oncology such as *Cancer—Principles and Practice in Oncology* (DeVita et al.), *Important Advances in Oncology* (DeVita et al.), and the *Manual for Staging of Cancer* (Beahrs/American Joint Committee on Cancer). Individual hospitals are putting on line such standard references as the *Physicians' Desk Reference* or the hospital formulary.

The reference material mentioned thus far would most likely be on the hospital's own computer. At the same time, other large databases are being created and maintained externally and are accessible through dial-out modems. An example of such a database is the PDQ (Physician Data Query), a clinically oriented database produced by the National Cancer Institute that contains current information about state-of-the-art cancer treatment as well as a directory of information about physicians and organizations providing cancer care that can be retrieved by city, state, and ZIP code (Hubbard and DeVita 1985). Bibliographic databases such as MEDLINE and CANCERLIT (Kjellander, Olsson, and Zajicek 1985; Tancredi et al. 1976) are accessible by modem. Some hospitals are making subsets of MEDLINE available locally either on CD-ROM disks or on a mainframe computer.

Although oncology nurse specialists may make use of this reference material, it is oriented toward physicians and designed to assist in the decisions that they make. In the future nurses can expect to see more and more nursing knowledge in general, and oncology nursing material in particular, on computers. For example, standards of care developed for specific oncology patient diagnoses, such as those developed by the Oncology Nursing Society, could be easily retained for quick reference. Similarly, reference resources of oncology agencies and organizations, including those that are nationwide as well as those for a particular hospital, could be available for patient and family use.

Another major development for the future is being able to bring this store of knowledge to bear automatically on a clinical decision. At present the users consult on-line information at their own initiative. Thus users need to know that they do not know. In the future, actions by physicians or nurses will cause the computer to cross-check its store of knowledge and to present pertinent portions. Such systems are under development now (Clayton et al. 1989). An example will illustrate how such a system might work for oncology patients. For the patient receiving doxorubicin, a fall in the ejection fraction from the gated pool scan test requires the initiation of new patient assessments, monitoring, and education by the oncology nurse specialist. The computer system would supply the nurses with alerts, such as "observe for shortness of breath, peripheral edema, chest pain," and in addition would direct the nurse to appropriate on-line references that address this specific problem. Such references might include texts or articles as well as a specific patient care plan dealing with monitoring the patient with impaired cardiac status.

CONCLUSION

In summary, in the future nurses can expect more support from computers in their roles as care integrator and care giver. As more patient information becomes available on line and as the ability to communicate information consequently increases, nurses will become better care integrators. As hospitals provide more on-line databases, decision-making support systems, and nursing applications, nurses will be better supported in their role as care givers.

STUDY QUESTIONS

1. What advantages or problems would a hospital information system bring to your hospital?
2. What reference material would you want to have on line in your practice setting? How would you use it?
3. What are some of the alerts that an oncology nurse specialist might want to receive?
4. What steps would need to be taken to safeguard patient confidentiality in a computerized system?

REFERENCES

Albrecht, C.A., and A.M. Lieske. 1985. Automating patient care planning. *Nursing Management* 16:21–26.

Anderson, J.G., S.J. Jay, S.J. Clevenger, D.R. Kassing, J. Perry, and M.M. Anderson. 1988. Physician utilization of a hospital information system: A computer simulation model. In *Proceedings of the Twelfth Annual Symposium on Computer Applications in Medical Care*, ed. R.A. Greenes. Washington, D.C.: IEEE Computer Society Press.

Arnoti, B. 1987. Computer terminals: The new bedside manner at the Toronto Hospital. *Canadian Medical Association Journal* 137:189–90.

Bailey, D.R. 1988. Computer applications in nursing: A prototypical model for planning nursing care. *Computers in Nursing* 6:199–203.

Barrett, J.P., R.A. Barnum, B.B. Gordon, and R.N. Pesut. 1975. *Evaluation of the implementation of a medical information system in a general community hospital* (NTIS #PB 248 340). Columbus, OH: Battelle Columbus Laboratories.

Beckman, E., B.F. Cammack, and B. Harris. 1981. Observation of computers in an intensive care unit. *Heart and Lung* 10:1055–1057.

Blackmon, P.W., C.A. Marino, R.K. Aukward, R.E. Bresnhan, R.G. Goldenberg, J.M. Hiller, G.A. Lowke, and J.T. Patterson. 1982. *Evaluation of the medical information system at the National Institutes of Health Clinical Center*, vols. I, II, VI (NTIS #PB82-190083, PB82-190091, PB82-190122). Arlington, VA: ANSER.

Blaufass, J.A., and A.K. Tinker. 1988. Computerized falls alert—A new solution to an old problem. In *Proceedings of the Twelfth Annual Symposium on Computer Applications in Medical Care*, ed. R.A. Greenes. Washington, D.C.: IEEE Computer Society Press.

Bleich, H.L., R.F. Beckley, G.L. Horowitz, J.D. Jackson, E.S. Moody, C. Franklin, S.R. Goodman, M.W. McKay, R.A. Pope, T. Walden, S.M. Bloom, and W.V. Slack. 1985. Clinical computing in a teaching hospital. *New England Journal of Medicine* 312:756–64.

Blum, B.I. 1986. *Clinical information systems*. New York: Springer-Verlag.

Childs, B.W. 1988. Bedside terminals: Status and the future. *Health Care and Computing*, May, 12, 14.

Clayton, P.D., R.K. Anderson, P. Bourne, G. Conklin, T.J. Garrett, G. Hendrickson, G. Hripesak, S.J. Johnson, A. O'Toole, N. Roderer, S. Sengupta, S. Shea, and R. Sideli. 1989. *Integrated academic information management system*. New York: Columbia–Presbyterian Medical Center. Mimeo.

Gray, G., D. Adler, C. Fleming, and F. Brescia. 1988. A clinical data base for advanced cancer patients: Implications for nursing. *Cancer Nursing* 11:77–83.

Greene, R., H. Kerr, N. Likely, and P. Stephenson. 1982. Computers and patients: The user system. *The Canadian Nurse*, October, 24–26.

Halford, G., M. Burkes, and T.A. Pryor. 1989. Measuring the impact of bedside terminals. *Nursing Management* 20:41–42, 44–45.

Health Technology. 1988. Bedside computers: Do they really improve the quality of patient care? *Health Technology* 2:140–47.

Heriot, C., J. Graves, O. Bouhaddou, M. Armstrong, G. Wigertz, and M. Ben Said. 1988. A pain management decision support system for nurses. In *Proceedings of the Twelfth Annual Symposium on Computer Applications in Medical Care*, ed. R.A. Greenes. Washington, D.C.: IEEE Computer Society Press.

Hickam, D.H., E.H. Shortliffe, M.B. Bischoff, A.C. Scott, and C.D. Jacobs. 1985. The treatment advice of a computer-based cancer chemotherapy protocol advisor. *Annals of Internal Medicine* 103:928–36.

Hinson, D.K., and C. Bush. 1988. Corporate standards for nursing care: An integral part of a computerized care plan. *Computers in Nursing* 6:141–46.

Hubbard, S.M., and V.T. DeVita. 1985. PDQ: An innovation in information dissemination linking cancer research and clinical practice. In *Important advances in oncology*, eds. V.T. DeVita, S. Hellman, and S.A. Rosenberg. Philadelphia: J.P. Lippincott.

Johnson, D.S., M. Burkes, D. Sittig, D. Hinson, and T.A. Pryor. 1987. Evaluation of the effects of computerized nurse charting. In *Proceedings of the Eleventh Annual Symposium on Computer Applications in Medical Care*, ed. W.W. Stead. Washington, D.C.: IEEE Computer Society Press.

Kjellander, E., P.O. Olsson, and E. Zajicek. 1985. Usefulness of the on-line data base CANCERLIT: An evaluation study based on consecutive searches in CANCERLIT and MEDLINE for oncologists. *Journal of the National Cancer Institute* 74:1351–53.

McClure, M.L., and M.J. Nelson. 1982. Trends in hospital nursing. In *Nursing in the 1980's: Crisis, opportunities, challenges*, ed. L.H. Aiken. Philadelphia: J.B. Lippincott Co.

Ozbolt, J.G. 1988. Knowledge-based systems for supporting clinical nursing decisions. In *Nursing informatics*, ed. M.J. Ball, K.J. Hannah, U.G. Jelger, and H. Peterson. New York: Springer-Verlag.

Peat, Marwick, Main and Company. 1988. *TDS healthcare systems corporation bedside terminal study*. Photocopy.

Pesce, J. 1988. Bedside terminals: Medtake. *MD Computing* 5:16–21.

Pryor, T.A., R.M. Gardner, P.D. Clayton, and H.R. Warner. 1983. The HELP system. *Journal of Medical Systems* 7:87–102.

Schmitz, H.H., R.P. Ellerbrake, and T.M. Williams. 1976. Study evaluates effects of new communication system. *Hospitals* 50:129–134.

Schroeder, C.G., and P.G. Pierpaoli. 1986. Direct order entry by physicians in a computerized hospital information system. *American Journal of Hospital Pharmacy* 43:355–59.

Shortliffe, E.H., A.C. Scott, M.B. Bischoff, A.B. Campbell, W. van Melle, and C.D. Jacobs. 1984. ONCOCIN: An expert system for oncology protocol management. In *Rule-based expert systems: The MYCIN experiments of the Stanford Heuristic Programming Project*, eds. B.G. Buchanan and E.H. Shortliffe. Reading, MA: Addison-Wesley.

Soontit, E. 1987. Installing the first operational bedside nursing computer system. *Nursing Management* 18:23–25.

Tancredi, S.A., R.H. Amacher, J.H. Schneider, and B.M. Vasta. 1976. CANCERLINE: A new NLM/NCI database. *Journal of Chemical Information and Computer Sciences* 16:128–130.

Werley, H.H., E.C. Devine, and C.R. Zorn. 1988. The nursing minimum data set: Effort to standardize collection of essential data. In *Nursing informatics*, ed. M.J. Ball, K.J. Hannah, U.G. Jelger, and H. Peterson. New York: Springer-Verlag.

Werley H.H., and C.R. Zorn. 1988. The nursing minimum data set: Benefits and implications. In *Perspectives in nursing—1987–1989*. New York: National League for Nursing.

Yero, M. 1988. St. Francis Hospital goes bedside and beyond. *Health Care and Computing*, January, 48, 50, 52.

Chapter 22

New Instruction Technologies for Cancer Education: The Oncology Nurse Educator's Role

Susan Bloch, Penny Ashwanden, and Dianne M. Howser

> New education technologies may provide cost-effective means for providing individual and flexible learning opportunities. The chapter reviews developments and trends in the use of instruction technologies and explores the potentials inherent in the most effective education modalities, including computer-assisted instruction, instruction video, cable television, satellite teleconferencing, and interactive videodisc systems.

With the rapid changes that are occurring in the health care industry, the oncology nurse educator is in a position to be a creative facilitator of the professional growth of nurses involved in the care of the cancer patient. New education technologies (including computers, video, cable television, interactive video, and satellite teleconferencing) can become the nurse educator's partner in the development of effective instruction methods (McDonald 1983; Nielsen and Miaskowski 1987; Sinclair 1985). Such technologies can enhance oncology nurses' acquisition of essential skills and information. For example, the independent learner can now gain access easily to education information available on computers and videodiscs. By using such technologies, the oncology nurse can take responsibility for charting his or her own course through the sea of new information necessary to remain current in cancer care. The educator's role is evolving from that of a transmitter of information to a facilitator of the nurse's independent professional growth. Nurse educators and practicing nurses must discover how new education technology can provide innovative solutions to current education problems.

In this chapter recent developments in education media and technologies are highlighted, and the opportunities they offer to the oncology nurse educator are

---

Note: The authors would like to thank Dr. Dorothy Fishman for her help in preparing this chapter.

discussed. The educator is presented with options for assisting the practicing oncology nurse and oncology nursing student to meet their specific education objectives. Much of the fear and apprehension surrounding the use of new education modalities will disappear when nurse educators discover how these instruction methods can help oncology nurses work and learn better and more efficiently (Magnus 1985).

With a sound working knowledge of the strengths and limitations of various instruction technologies, the oncology nurse educator will be able to select the apropriate modality not only for enhancing care of the person with cancer but also to meet patient education and public education goals. Education media will not replace conferences, college courses, or clinical experience; they will, however, offer an efficient and effective supplement with which to meet identified education needs.

In choosing any of the education modalities described in this chapter, the oncology nurse educator should follow the instruction design model discussed below. Where appropriate, assistance should be solicited from instruction designers, curriculum designers, education computer experts, and education video specialists. The instruction design approach to the development of education modules involves five distinct phases: analysis of the needs of the learner, development of performance outcomes and objectives, selection of a modality (e.g., computer, video, live demonstration, or panel discussion), incorporation of adult learning theories and principles into the education design, and testing and revision of the education modules on the basis of formative and summative evaluations. Whether one selects a commercially available videotape and follows the viewing with discussion or opts to develop an interactive computer-assisted instruction package, the educator will have to consider the characteristics and needs of the learners and the desired level of instruction as well as cost and time factors (Billings 1985; Chang 1986; Day and Payne 1987).

COMPUTER-ASSISTED INSTRUCTION

What is Computer-assisted instruction?

Computer-assisted instruction (CAI) refers to the process in which a computer serves as a tool for the transfer of information from a computer program to an individual or a group of learners. It often provides remediation and facilitates development of problem-solving skills. It is a highly interactive learning device that makes the learner a partner in the learning process. The computer program contains written and visual information presented at a pace and sequence that responds to the needs of the individual learner.

Computers have a remarkable ability to store, collect, retrieve, and manipulate information with speed and efficiency. In view of current nursing shortages, the rising cost of education and professional training, the increasing call for accountability and quality assurance, and rapid changes in oncology nursing practice, CAI offers a cost-effective and desirable means of assisting learners to meet education goals.

CAI programs can be divided into four categories: drill and practice, tutorials, games, and simulations. The quality of the instruction is directly related to the design of the courseware, not to the program category selected. The program can range from a conversational problem-solving format, which places the student in real-life situations (simulations), to simple question-and-answer (drill-and-practice) designs. Drill and practice is particularly effective for teaching such basic skills as the application of drug information and dosage calculation of medications. In all types of CAI, the student is judged by the answers given or by the outcome of the action taken rather than by the subjective evaluation of an instructor (Howard 1987). In more sophisticated interactive programs, there are numerous "branching" opportunities that enable the student to jump ahead, pause, escape, or review previously learned information on the basis of demonstrated needs and knowledge level (Greipp 1987). Such programs are referred to as *interactive* because of their capacity to adjust the presentation of information on the basis of responses from the user.

Development of Computer-Assisted Instruction in Nursing

The development of the computer as an education tool began during the 1960s as an outgrowth of teaching by programmed instruction (Mahr and Kadner 1984). Although interest in CAI for medical and nursing education has been slow to evolve, the development of microcomputers in the 1980s served as a catalyst for the expansion of computer use in the health care industry, including nursing. Nurses and hospitals are using computers for storage of medical information, diagnostic testing, basic and applied science, patient monitoring, and education. Nurse educators are beginning to integrate the use of the cost-effective microcomputers into their instruction and education programs. During the past decade, CAI has been used increasingly at all levels of nursing education, from baccalaureate and graduate programs to continuing nursing education (Felton and Brown 1985; Gaston 1988).

Benefits and Limitations of Computer-Assisted Instruction

CAI offers numerous advantages over traditional classroom instruction. Because it is learner centered, CAI allows for increased feedback and interactivity between the student and the material presented. It is self-paced, provides information tailored to student needs, prompts the reinforcement of learning, and standardizes instruction delivery and performance evaluation. CAI is neither limited by classroom schedules nor dependent on time constraints, instructor availability, or skill of individual instructors. It provides students with an opportunity to review and experiment without embarassment or fear of potentially harming a patient. Students can update knowledge and skills in their own specialty area or in other general areas at their own convenience. Clinical instructors are not limited to providing experiences that are based on the available clinic population because the student can gain experience with any simulated patient condition (Brose 1984; Hodson et al. 1988; Yoder and Heilman 1985).

CAI can integrate various media and graphics, thereby providing a rich sensory experience (de Tornyay and Thompson 1987). The most rapid developments during the past 5 years have been the incorporation of computer graphics and multimedia into CAI programs, which provides visual reinforcement to textual information.

Barriers to the expansion of CAI in nursing education include the lack of adequate software, fear and resistance on the part of nursing faculty and nursing educators regarding its use, time, the cost of purchasing hardware, and the lack of human interaction in the learning process (Anderson 1986; Murphy 1987; Sinclair 1985). Many nursing school faculty members resist utilizing CAI because the techniques are not universally accepted as a viable education tool by nursing educators and because there have been limited opportunities for faculty training in CAI (Thomas 1985).

In nursing, the availability of well-designed CAI packages remains a serious problem. Practicing nurses and nursing school faculty are rarely rewarded for their efforts in developing, debugging, evaluating, and testing CAI materials. Because the design and implementation of CAI programs take a considerable amount of time, effort, and funding, nursing has been slow to become involved in CAI project development.

There are fewer incentives for faculty members on the tenure track for CAI development compared to traditional research and writing (Thomas 1985). Faculty who have little or no direct experience with computers are not comfortable with relinquishing the control of instruction to machines. One misconception held by some faculty and nurse educators is that the computer replaces the instructor. On the contrary, there will always be a need for instructors to guide students, to help them meet goals, and to help them manage the development of individual learning objectives (Anderson 1986). Recently, however, many nursing school administrators have supported development of their faculty's computer literacy skills, particularly knowledge and skills in CAI. There have been an increasing number and variety of workshops on CAI and nursing ranging from basic overview courses to advanced program development.

Effectiveness of Computer-Assisted Instruction As a Teaching Tool

Studies of the effectiveness of CAI in medical and nursing education have revealed that students learn 15% to 50% faster than they do with the lecture format (Anderson 1986; Bitzer and Bitzer 1973; Deignan and Duncan 1978). Studies have also demonstrated equal or greater retention (Conklin 1983; Murphy 1984; Pogue 1982) and greater transfer of learning to actual clinical situations with CAI instruction (Huckabay et al. 1979) in comparison with traditional teaching methods. Although research regarding retention of information learned with CAI compared to traditional methods is limited, studies do indicate generally equal retention rates and an improved ability to transfer skills learned to the clinical setting (Chang 1986). Students have identified the benefit of immediate feedback in learning new skills through CAI. CAI generally provides more effective direct reinforcement than other instruction formats (Murphy 1984; Schleuterman, Holzermer, and Farrand 1983).

Student Attitudes toward Computer-Assisted Instruction

Some studies (Chang 1986; Neil 1985) have focused on student attitudes toward CAI instruction, although Chang (1986) notes that few have included really well-constructed attitudinal scales. Most studies have used student rating forms to evaluate CAI, and generally positive subjective statements have been obtained (Bitzer and Bitzer 1973; Pogue 1982; Timke and Janney 1981). One must be cautious in drawing conclusions from these types of ratings, however; one cannot generalize across different studies, and extraneous factors may also affect student responses on these forms. Chang (1986) notes that students' positive attitudes toward trying any novel method of instruction or the social desirability of using computers for instruction may have influenced some of the findings. She proposes using an analytical model for evaluating CAI designs that looks at the intervening and extraneous variables that affect outcome variables.

The Future: User-Friendly Computers Offer Help in Program Design

It is no longer necessary for oncology nurse educators to gain computer programming skills before initiating a CAI project. Authoring systems are now built into some software packages. These provide educators with a complete framework for writing and delivering computer-aided instruction (Hodson et al. 1988). The educator may use such software packages to write step-by-step lessons, to test students, and to evaluate and record student progress. Some packages include "branching" or alternative paths that provide students with more individual instruction. Authoring systems limit the flexibility provided when a program is designed from scratch by a programmer, however.

Nurse educators will profit from recognition of the value of CAI in enhancing teaching effectiveness. Becoming involved in advanced technologies such as the development of CAI materials is vital to developing autonomy and self-direction in nursing education and nursing practice (Hassett 1984). CAI allows the learner to make decisions and choices on the basis of personal interests, abilities, and existing level of knowledge. Participation in CAI in response to nurses' own perceived needs, at their own speed, and at convenient times can promote increased motivation to learn and a more positive attitude toward independent learning.

TELEVISION AND VIDEO

Development of Education Television

In the 1960s video was utilized to bring expert lecturers and instructors from outside geographic areas into classrooms and meetings, often as substitutes for live guest lecturers. Since that time, the decreasing cost of portable video cameras and the availability of easy-to-use editing equipment has enabled educators with little technical expertise in television production to develop effective instructional video materials with little or no professional help.

In medicine and nursing, video is now used to dramatize clinical situations or to allow practice and analysis of interviewing techniques. Video provides health care professionals an opportunity to learn skills and to acquire important information in a simulated setting before confronting life-threatening situations in an actual clinical setting.

Benefits and Limitations of Education Television

Video is an extremely versatile education medium that is simple to use and transportable. It offers relatively low software costs and standardized education, and it is a highly visual medium that is widely accepted by the general public. It is an excellent medium for demonstration, provides an opportunity to view specific sequences or the entire content more than once, has unique abilities in capturing simulated and live events, and often triggers discussion (Rollant and Siler 1984).

Television teaching has several advantages that are not available to the classroom teacher. Videotapes are inexpensive and available to students at any time; thus they can reduce staffpower requirements and can help avoid scheduling conflicts. Both audio and visual components are recorded simultaneously on magnetic tape and are available for immediate viewing. Editing of tapes allows the instructor to incorporate graphic materials such as slides, photographs, and animated and nonanimated graphics, which increases user acceptance and learning of the program content. Through the editing process, the instructor can summarize key concepts and prioritize the content for the learner.

Taping an instructor at a podium delivering a lecture with one fixed camera can be a waste of the medium. Colorful graphics, slides, or live footage from clinical settings contribute to making a lecture program interesting and stimulating for the audience. Viewers who are accustomed to high-quality broadcast television will not tolerate poorly produced programs.

Besides the purchase costs of the player/recorder and television monitor, a more serious limitation to standard linear video is lack of interaction between the learner and the presenter. To review the lesson materials, students can only rewind the tape and hope to gain a better understanding through a second viewing. Other drawbacks include the fact that video cassette players tend to break down, particularly if they are in constant use, and they require regular care and maintenance. Videotapes must be handled gently and stored in clean and well-ventilated shelving because they are easily damaged.

Instructors who deliver quality traditional classroom lectures may not present well on television. Demonstrating a high level of comfort, spontaneity, and creativity on television may require rehearsal time to gain "camera awareness" skills (Millonig 1988).

Closed-Circuit Television

Closed-circuit television has emerged as a cost-effective alternative to traditional forms of continuing nursing education. It allows nurses to keep current in their field of expertise, to develop new skills, and to earn institution- or state-mandated continuing education credits without leaving their work place (Tribulski and Frank 1987).

Many hospitals already have closed circuit television systems as supplements to more traditional modes of patient education. There are now computerized "director" systems that function like a jukebox, playing individual videotapes in a specified sequence. A computer timer selects and plays each tape at its programmed time. Nursing units, waiting rooms, and conference areas can be linked into the system by cable and a video monitor/receiver.

Tribulski and Frank (1987) note that closed-circuit television nursing education increases positive attitudes toward independent learning and that self-learning modules effectively replace traditional lecture-style classroom activities. The tapes decrease the need to have instructors available at all hours of the day to reach all staff. Increasing the availability of flexible, round-the-clock, continuing education opportunities can serve as an important factor in staff retention and recruitment, which makes closed-circuit television quite attractive to departments of nursing.

The drawbacks of closed circuit television are frequently related to the high initial installation costs. System malfunctions and service and repair fees also add to the expense of maintaining this method of nursing education.

Satellite Television

Another exciting technology that can be linked with a closed-circuit video system is satellite television. Through a receiver dish on the roof of a building, a health care facility can receive a signal from a distant location by means of a satellite located more than 22,000 miles above the earth (Nierenberg 1987). Time can be rented on an available satellite and specialized programming transmitted to selected viewing sites across the country through a relay that receives signals and beams them back to Earth. Satellites provide a means for transmitting signals across long distances on frequencies that are not used by standard radio and television stations.

The Hospital Satellite Network (HSN) is the largest of several medical satellite television networks that provide continuing education programming for nurses as well as physicians, managers, allied health professionals, and patients. HSN also provides cancer-related programming free of charge to the 21 national Comprehensive Cancer Centers and the National Cancer Institute.

Satellite television eliminates the cost and need for nurses to travel for continuing education opportunities while offering various education programming. Satellite television also links small rural and community hospitals with experts from leading medical institutions.

Video Teleconferencing

Another advance in the satellite television market is video teleconferencing, an innovative high-tech method that links a presenter or a panel with individuals at many different geographic locations through one- or two-way video and audio channels (Byrne 1982). Satellite teleconferences can be arranged in multiple locations all over the country through the use of receiving equipment known as "down-link" dishes (Figure 22-1). The host site or receiving site can rent a specially equipped mobile van to receive the televised signal. The signal can then be sent by cable to be projected on a large screen or a standard television monitor.

Video teleconferences can be used to broadcast important education information to large numbers of people in a wide geographic area. The National Cancer Institute, for example, sponsored its first live interactive teleconference, Consensus Development Conference on the Management of Clinically Localized Prostate

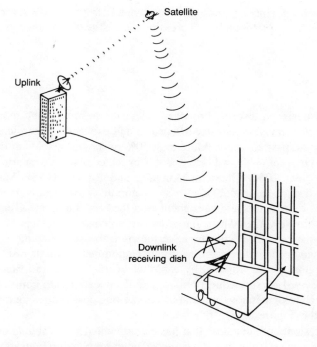

Figure 22-1 Dish Configuration for Satellite Video Conference

Cancer, over 3 days in 1987. The program included more than 24 formal presentations covering staging, radiation therapy, surgery, and adjuvant therapy and concluded on the third day with an official consensus statement of the conference.

Videoconferencing has become widely accepted in the health care fields. Nurses in particular have become increasingly interested in participation in videoconferencing, noting the cost effectiveness of this method of education in view of the present costs of travel and down-time in staff productivity incurred with national conferences (Limon, Spencer, and Henderson 1986).

At present, satellite teleconferences are relatively expensive to produce. Video teleconferences require technical expertise to coordinate audio and visual signals at each viewing site. Technical difficulties in either picture or sound quality as well as program content and the presentation skills of the presenters directly contribute to the effectiveness of the program. For this type of program, it is best if a large-screen projector or multiple small monitors are used for the audience's comfort in viewing.

Videoconferences require adequate planning, good technical and production support, interaction between learners and presenters, a local moderator, and good support materials (Fink 1987). Recent developments in digital fiberoptic communications allowing voice, visual, and computer data to be sent over a single telephone line have contributed to decreasing the costs of video teleconferencing.

Cable Television

Originally designed to bring broadcast television to remote and mountainous areas, the cable television industry has grown and expanded its services dramatically during the past 15 years. More than 50% of the households in the United States were wired for cable in 1985, and it is expected that the proportion will be 90% by the year 2000 (Heinich, Molenda, and Russell 1985). Many cable channels are designated as public access or community stations. Numerous local cable stations rent studios and equipment on a fee basis for single events or on a weekly basis. In New York City some cable stations charge as little as $25/hour for public access use, and all citizens have the right to use the studio. Education institutions and health care organizations are beginning to avail themselves of the education opportunities provided by cable television (Banks and Banks 1988). Bringing televised nursing education and public education into homes and work places is a technologic innovation that offers exciting possibilities for the creative nurse educator (Figure 22-2).

One professional organization that has experimented with cable television for continuing education is the Inter-Collegiate Center for Nursing Education (ICNE) in the state of Washington. ICNE developed a series of continuing nursing

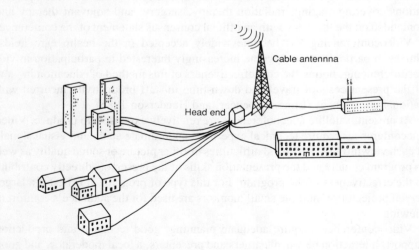

Figure 22-2 Configuration for Cable Television

education courses for cable transmission in the state (Clark and Cleveland 1984). Production costs were defrayed by grants and registration fees.

Difficulties with this mode of education delivery that were reported by ICNE included transmission problems, program scheduling difficulties, and low enrollment. Lack of familiarity with this new system and a tendency among nurses to select more traditional modes of continuing education contributed to somewhat disappointing results (Clark and Cleveland 1984). Nevertheless, evaluation of several of ICNE's televised courses revealed that 90% of the nurses who participated liked taking a course through television and that 85% felt that the course objectives had been met.

Several schools of nursing and medical centers have begun utilizing cable television for delivering information about health maintenance and disease prevention to their communities (Timke 1984). At the Milwaukee County Medical Complex in Milwaukee, Wisconsin, for example, an institutionally funded cable television series was launched in 1981 for public education. The program is hosted weekly by nurses who focus on various health topics, including cancer. Tapes of the programs are used at community health fairs and programs for staff education and other purposes. The programs are also seen on the hospital's closed-circuit television channel on a rotating schedule. The video programming offers major benefits for both community and professional education. It is also an attractive marketing tool for the institution. With continuing education costs rising and innovations in cable television allowing for a new interaction between sender and receiver, the future of cable television as a viable instruction method for transmitting new health information appears to be encouraging.

Videodisc

Developed in the late 1970s and hailed as the vanguard of interactive instruction technology, videodisc has emerged today as a viable medium in education and training (Mitchell and Bolles 1987). Videodiscs offer rapid access to large quantities of high-quality audio and visual material on durable 12-in plastic disks or laser film and can merge the "branching" power of CAI with the visual appeal of video (Rizzolo 1989).

Videodiscs store a large quantity of coded information on hard disks that resemble a phonograph record. Although standard or linear videotape is made of magnetic tape, videodisc is made of a special plastic with visual and audio information encoded in the concentric grooves with proximal frames placed just micrometers apart (Sweeney and Gulino 1988). When in play, the videodisc grooves or tracks are read by a sensitive laser beam. With a storage capacity of 54,000 visual frames on each side and two separate audio tracks, one disk can hold the information contained in several hundred books and about 1,000 filmstrips (Heinich, Molenda, and Russell 1985).

The videodisc is usually controlled by a computer that directs the sequencing of images stored on the disk from one frame to the next according to the needs of the user. In less complex systems, the videodisc is controlled by the directions of the learner through a keyboard without a computer interface. A videodisc player that is controlled by a computer is known as an interactive videodisc system (Figure 22-3) (see below). Frames can be shown at regular speed, in fast forward, in slow motion, in reverse, or frozen frame by frame. The user can cause the imaging to jump from one point to another for review or to go directly to a part of the program containing the specific information desired. The learner can control the movement of the videodisc program by selecting an option from a directory (e.g., "Review" or "Test") or by causing the computer to search the entire disk in seconds for the desired information.

Interactive Videodisc Systems

Of all the new instruction technologies, interactive videodisc systems are perhaps the most exciting because of their ability to combine any type of visual image (television film segments, three-dimensional graphics, and animation) with modern computer capabilities. In this system the videodisc player, which is linked to a microcomputer through an interface, allows for true interactivity between instruction and the learner (Morariu and Marcia 1988). This configuration provides the greatest range of capabilities, including complex instruction designs; combinations of computer graphics, text, and sound; the greatest number of "branching" opportunities; and even student recordkeeping. The external microcomputer controls the videodisc player by input from a touch-sensitive screen or a

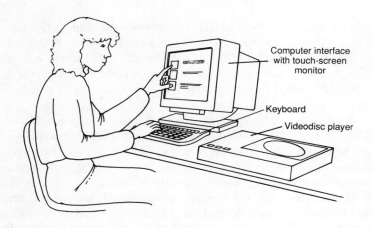

Figure 22-3 Interactive Videodisc System

keyboard. Software programs and authoring systems can be purchased to allow the user to design interactive instructions for specific videodisc players.

The full potential of interactive videodisc technology is now being realized in a number of exciting systems developed for medical education. One of the best known and tested is the cardiopulmonary resuscitation (CPR) system developed by David Hon of the American Heart Association (Hon 1982). This system uses a videodisc player, a random access audio player, a monitor, a microcomputer, and a sensored mannequin that is wired to the computer. The sensors in the mannequin monitor the accuracy of the learner in applying specific CPR techniques. Feedback from the computer allows learners to progress through the course at their own rate and desired sequence. A study to evaluate the efficacy of this system found no significant learning differences between the experimental interactive video group and a control group that had received traditional CPR instruction from on-site instructors (Edwards and Hannah 1985).

Several pharmaceutical companies have underwritten the development of videodisc systems for continuing medical education (Bolles 1988). The National Library of Medicine and a number of medical schools have already developed useful interactive videodisc systems for the study of pathology, radiology, anatomy, and other health sciences topics. Recently, several special grants have become available to nurse educators interested in developing interactive video instruction programs. The Division of Nursing of the Public Health Service and several large computer companies have provided funding, and several exciting programs are now in the development stages.

Use of Interactive Videodisc Systems in the United States

A recent survey by the American Journal of Nursing Company of videodisc utilization in hospitals and schools of nursing revealed that only 11% of those surveyed presently use videodisc technology, mostly because of the time and costs involved. Nevertheless, 49% of the respondents said that they planned to purchase interactive videodisc systems in the near future (Rizzolo 1989). There is little in the nursing literature about how to produce programs or how to utilize commercially available materials effectively for academic training, continuing education, or patient education. Nurses who want to become involved in this technology need to read journals, join organizations, and attend conferences designed specifically for interactive videodisc users.

Advantages and Limitations of Interactive Videodisc Systems

Major advantages of interactive video are that animation, text, audio, slides, photographs, sound, and video or film footage can all be incorporated into one instruction system. Videodisc systems are particularly effective in nursing education for demonstration or simulation of a technique, concept, or assessment of a patient condition. The user practices important clinical decision making on the basis of information presented. If the wrong decision is chosen or the wrong test performed, the system can be designed to provide remediation and review.

Recently, interactive video hardware and software systems have remained state of the art for only 2 or 3 years before being overtaken by newer, faster, or easier to use systems. The lack of standardization of equipment, the speed of change occurring in the biomedical world, and the cost of producing or purchasing a videodisc system all tend to curb expansion of this technology.

When educators more fully appreciate the range of knowledge and skills that students can acquire through videodisc, use of this technology will inevitably expand. The videodisc can be a most cost-effective medium for demonstrating large visual collections (for example, of pathology slides) and for interactive programs in which clear visualization and simulation are essential. Hundreds of slide trays can be stored on one side of a disk, and a single image or frame can be held constant, resulting in a freeze frame. Another intriguing capability of the videodisc is its ability to hold two completely separate sound tracks, which is useful in incorporating instructions in two different languages.

Effectiveness of Interactive Videodisc As a Teaching Tool

Interactive video programs, particularly highly interactive programs with numerous "branching" alternatives, are expensive to produce. With dwindling resources for nursing education and increasing needs for accountability, it has become imperative to determine whether interactive video instruction is more effective than other, less expensive forms of education. To date, research on the effectiveness of interactive instruction has been limited. Fishman (1984) designed a study at Massachusetts General Hospital comparing interactive video instruction with traditional lecture and linear videotape methods of cancer chemotherapy instruction for nurses. Results of this study demonstrated that the interactive video learner obtained a significantly higher level of mastery on posttests and retention tests than either the linear video group or the traditional lecture group. More recently, Levenson and Morrow (1987) conducted a study to determine the effectiveness of and differences between interactive and noninteractive video instruction about smokeless tobacco. In this study, the interactive video group demonstrated more accurate and comprehensive recall. In addition, although both groups felt positive about their method of instruction, the interactive group was more willing to promote cessation. It is clear that more research is needed to justify expansion of interactive video.

FUTURE TRENDS

New developments in communication technologies will continue to shape the future of education media during the remainder of this century. Increased operating speeds of microcomputers allow for new capabilities such as voice synthesis. The expanded use of computerized voice simulators will help humanize the learning process of interacting with a computer rather than with an instructor. After feeding in a response on a computer-assisted or interactive video instruction system, the learner is given verbal feedback from the computer about the correctness of the response and is encouraged to try again if an error was made. Computers that are capable of providing verbal feedback offer supportive guidance throughout the education experience by prompting and reinforcing the learner with verbal cues each step of the way as the learning progresses (Byrne 1982).

Another recent development that will have a strong impact on education technology in the next decade is compact disk read-only memory (CD-ROM), which is an exciting method of storing vast quantities of data on a 12-cm plastic disk. One CD-ROM can hold up to 300,000 single-spaced, typewritten pages, or the equivalent of close to 1,000 800K floppy disks (Tizes 1989). A CD-ROM is capable of storing any digitized information including graphics, sound, animation, and illustrations, all of which can be cataloged and archived. CD-ROM technology promises scientific and medical educators an optimal method of managing voluminous quantities of information on huge databases that are accessible at incredible speeds.

Voice synthesis and CD-ROM technologies are expensive and not yet widely available. In the years to come, however, educators will be able to explore the potential benefits of these systems and how to integrate them into current instruction programs.

The use of advanced education technologies in nursing education is now a reality. The rate and scope of change in the professional environment continue to escalate as new technologies are introduced and others are replaced. As new technologies mature, they gradually become more user-friendly and less expensive in terms of both hardware and software development costs.

Although it is easy to get caught up in the excitement of the newest developments, nurse educators still need to evaluate their students' needs to select appropriate, creative, and cost-effective solutions to match identified instruction goals. Nurse educators need institution support to allow them to expend the time and effort necessary to develop the best education materials. The time has come for faculty and nurse educators to explore the potential benefits of developing and using CAI, video, and interactive video systems in cancer education.

STUDY QUESTIONS

1. How does instruction design theory affect the selection of one type of education modality over another?

2. How can computer-assisted instruction supplement the development of clinical problem-solving skills for the practicing nurse?
3. What are the benefits and limitations of television teaching, that is, using videotapes instead of live classroom instruction?
4. What makes an interactive videodisc system interactive, and why has this method of instruction been more effective than traditional modes of instruction in terms of both knowledge and retention?

REFERENCES

Anderson, K. 1986. Computer-assisted instruction. *Journal of Medical Systems* 10:163–71.

Banks, M.J., and M.E. Banks. 1988. The evolution of health programming on cable television. *Health Values* 12:21–27.

Billings, D.M. 1985. An instructional design approach to developing CAI courseware. *Computers in Nursing* 3:217–23.

Bitzer, M., and D. Bitzer. 1973. Teaching nursing by computer. *Computers in Biology and Medicine* 3:187–204.

Bolles, J.R. 1988. The videodisc in health sciences education: A perspective on a powerful medium. *Journal of Biomedical Communications* 15:2–5.

Brose, C.H. 1984. Computer technology in nursing: Revolution or renaissance? *Nursing and Health Care* 5:531–34.

Byrne, R.B. 1982. Toward the year 2000: An overview of probable communication futures. *Mobius* 2:13–21.

Chang, B.L. 1986. Computer-aided instruction in nursing education. *Annual Review of Nursing Research* 4:217–33.

Clark, C.E., and T.L. Cleveland. 1984. Alternative ways of offering CE: The media and the mode. *Journal of Continuing Education in Nursing* 15:168–72.

Conklin, D. 1983. A study of computer assisted instruction in nursing education. *Journal of Computer Based Instruction* 9:98–107.

Day, R., and L. Payne. 1987. Computer managed instruction: An alternate teaching strategy. *Journal of Nursing Education* 26:30–36.

Deignan, G.M., and R.E. Duncan. 1978. CAI in three medical training courses: It was effective! *Behavior Research Methods and Instrumentation* 10:228–30.

de Tornyay, R., and M. Thompson. 1987. *Strategies for teaching nursing.* New York: John Wiley & Sons.

Edwards, M.J., and K.J. Hannah. 1985. An examination of the use of interactive videodisc cardiopulmonary resuscitation instruction for the lay community. *Computers in Nursing* 3:250–52.

Felton, G., and B.J. Brown. 1985. Application of computer technology in two colleges of nursing. *Journal of Nursing Education* 24:5–9.

Fink, D.J. 1987. Outstanding examples of innovative CME methods. *Mobius* 7:79–86.

Fishman, D.J. 1984. Development and evaluation of a computer assisted video module for teaching cancer chemotherapy to nurses. *Computers in Nursing* 2:16–23.

Gaston, S. 1988. Knowledge, retention and attitude effects of computer-assisted instruction. *Journal of Nursing Education* 27:30–34.

Greipp, M.E. 1987. Grant application strategies for computers in nursing education. *Computers in Nursing* 5:20–23.

Hassett, M.R. 1984. Computers and nursing education in the 1980's. *Nursing Outlook* 32:34–36.

Heinich, R., M. Molenda, and J.D. Russell. 1985. *Instructional media.* New York: John Wiley & Sons.

Hodson, K.E., C. Brigham, A. Hanson, and K. Armstrong. 1988. Multi media simulation of a clinical day. *Nurse Educator* 13:10–13.

Hon, D. 1982. Interactive training in cardiopulmonary resuscitation. *Byte* 7:108–38.

Howard, E.P. 1987. Use of a computer simulation for the continuing education of registered nurses. *Computers in Nursing* 5:208–13.

Huckabay, L., N. Anderson, D.M. Holm, and J. Lee. 1979. Cognitive, affective, and transfer of learning consequences of computer-assisted instruction. *Nursing Research* 28:228–33.

Levenson, P.M., and J.R. Morrow, Jr. 1987. Learner characteristics associated with responses to film and interactive video lessons on smokeless tobacco. *Preventive Medicine* 16:52–62.

Limon, S., J.B. Spencer, and F.C. Henderson. 1986. Video-teleconferencing by nurses—For nurses. *Nursing and Health Care* 7:313–317.

Magnus, M.M. 1985. Issues and concerns in computer technology in nursing education. *Journal of the New York State Nurses Association* 16:56–60.

Mahr, D.R., and K.D. Kadner. 1984. Computer-aided instruction: Overview and relevance to nursing education. *Journal of Nursing Education* 23:366–68.

McDonald, C.J. 1983. Computer technology and continuing medical education. *Mobius* 3:7–12.

Millonig, V.L. 1988. Television: An alternate delivery method in continuing education. *Journal of Continuing Education in Nursing* 19:54–57.

Mitchell, P.H., and J. Bolles. 1987. The generic videodisc: An innovative technology in nursing education. *Journal of Nursing Education* 26:74–77.

Morariu, J.A., and W.A. Marcia. 1988. Videodisc technology and biomedical communications. *Journal of Biomedical Communications* 15:6–9.

Murphy, M.A. 1984. Computer-based education in nursing. *Computers in Nursing* 2:218–33.

Murphy, M.A. 1987. Preparing faculty to use and develop computer-based instructional materials in nursing. *Computers in Nursing* 5:59–64.

Neil, R.M. 1985. Effects of computer-assisted instruction on nursing student learning and attitudes. *Journal of Nursing Education* 24:72–75.

Nielsen, B.B., and C.A. Miaskowski. 1987. The influence of an oncology nursing continuing education program on nursing practice. *Journal of Continuing Education in Nursing* 18:193–99.

Nierenberg, J. 1987. New technology for educating nurses. *Journal of Continuing Education in Nursing* 18:17–19.

Pogue, L.M. 1982. Computer-assisted instruction in the continuing education process. *Topics in Clinical Nursing* 4:41–50.

Rizzolo, M.A. 1989. What's new in interactive video? *American Journal of Nursing* 89:407–408.

Rollant, P.D., and R.B. Siler. 1984. Videotape production: An inexpensive way to teach nursing skills. *Association of Operating Room Nurses Journal* 39:1136–40.

Schleuterman, J.A., W.L. Holzermer, and L.L. Farrand. 1983. An evaluation of paper-and-pencil and computer-assisted simulation. *Journal of Nursing Education* 22:315–23.

Sinclair, V.G. 1985. The computer as partner in health care instruction. *Computers in Nursing* 3:212–16.

Sweeney, M.A., and C. Gulino. 1988. From variables to videodiscs. *Computers in Nursing* 6:157–63.

Thomas, B.S. 1985. A survey study of computers in nursing education. *Computers in Nursing* 3:173–79.

Timke, J. 1984. Television—A resource for nurse educators to teach the community about health maintenance and disease prevention. *Journal of Nursing Education* 23:217–18.

Timke, J., and C.P. Janney. 1981. Teaching drug dosages by computer. *Nursing Outlook* 29:376–77.

Tizes, B. 1989. Billions and billions of bytes. *MacGuide Magazine* 2:134–38.

Tribulski, J.A., and C. Frank. 1987. Closed circuit TV: An alternate teaching strategy. *Journal of Nursing Staff Development* 3:110–15.

Yoder, M.E., and T. Heilman. 1985. The use of computer assisted instruction to teach nursing diagnosis. *Computers in Nursing* 3:262–65.

Part V

The Future: Moving into the 21st Century

Chapter 23

What's Next for Oncology Nursing?

*Anne E. Belcher, E. Anne Hubbard Mattson,
Randi Moskowitz, Penny Ashwanden, and Nancy E. Riese*

The challenges for the future of oncology nursing reflect the challenge to the greater health care system (Mauksch 1989; Haddon 1989; King 1989; Lynaugh and Fagin 1988). In 1987 Dr. Otis Bowen, Secretary of the Department of Health and Human Services, commissioned a 19-member panel to look at the entire health care system, to report on the nation's shortage of registered nurses, and to recommend measures to prevent the recurrence of the problem.

The commission concluded that the nursing shortage was due to (1) increasing demand for nurses to supply increasingly technical, complex, and cost-effective patient care; (2) changes in the delivery, organization, and financing of health care; (3) various trends, including an aging population, new technologies and treatment possibilities, legislative changes, and the emergence of new diseases such as acquired immunodeficiency syndrome; and (4) fewer potential entrants into nursing because of an overall decline in college enrollments and because the profession is not viewed as an attractive career alternative for those entering college as a result of low salary levels and low prestige. The commission noted that these societal and health care industry changes have had a profound effect on the practice of nursing and on the ability to retain and recruit nurses (Commission on Nursing 1988).

The challenge in oncology nursing is for nurses to understand these changes and trends and to develop innovative and efficient delivery systems for nursing care. These systems should include creation of more hospital-based patient care units that develop into professional nursing practice centers, design of nursing practice protocols that incorporate reimbursable clinical services, development of primary care teaching and counseling and screening programs for patients, promotion of entrepreneurial nursing that generates revenues, and identification of high nursing care costs and actions to lower them.

These innovative practice patterns are not new in the oncology nursing arena. This book is filled with creative options to meet the challenges of the future. The challenge today is to recognize our strengths and to capitalize on them. Oncology nursing has been at the forefront of developing innovative, alternative delivery systems through an ability to recognize those patient populations that have special delivery-of-care needs. With development of health promotion and disease prevention protocols, oncology nurses can provide reimbursable, cost-effective screening and health counseling. Zander (1988) identifies case management protocol development as a means to achieving autonomous, cost-effective, professional nursing care with a focus on quality of patient outcomes.

Autonomy in nursing practice is not a new concept (Mundinger 1980; Rudolf 1989), but it continues to be the hallmark of professional practice. Oncology nurse entrepreneurs have taken it upon themselves to practice autonomous nursing by assuming the management and risk of a business, by market research and analysis of potential clients, by effective marketing strategies, by product promotion, by identification and lowering of costs, by fee setting and efficient accounting systems, by paying strict attention to legalities, and by continued assessment of consumer satisfaction. The entrepreneur is in the position to market the status and prestige of the profession.

The Commission on Nursing has identified trends in the health care industry and society leading to the nursing shortage as well as general measures to address the current position of nursing and where it should head in the future. Oncology nursing has already begun to address some of these measures. The education system and practice must continue to adapt to be successful in the future.

ONCOLOGY NURSES AS ADVOCATES

As Nelson (1988, 136) indicates, the nurse as advocate "has moved from a posture of interceding, supporting, or pleading a case for the client to acting as guardian of the client's rights to autonomy and free choice." This has occurred in spite of nurses' perceived obligation to be loyal to a physician, to an employer, or to personal values and beliefs. This change has presented a unique challenge to the oncology nurse, who is often expected to recruit patients into research protocols that may require time and money and involve discomfort on the part of the subject. As patients become more knowledgeable about cancer and its treatment as well as about their rights, they are asking more questions and expecting nurses' support for their informed decisions.

In an effort to assist patients and their families to make these informed decisions, the National Cancer Institute published a brochure about clinical trials written in lay terms (Nealon, Blumberg, and Brown 1985). The use of this brochure by prospective subjects will challenge oncology nurses and physicians alike to provide clear explanations, to answer questions, and to accept patients' negative as well as positive decisions.

Rights of patients identified by Annas (1974) as having particular relevance to nurses' advocacy of persons with cancer are:

- knowledge of research and experimental protocols
- complete and accurate information regarding medical care and procedures
- clear, concise explanations of all proposed procedures, including risks, mortality, and probability of success
- clear, complete, and accurate evaluation of one's condition and of the prognosis without treatment
- opportunity to refuse any drug, test, procedure, or treatment

Kohnke (1982) identifies two essential aspects of nurses' protective advocacy for patients: informing patients adequately so that they can make knowledgeable decisions, and supporting them in whatever decisions they make. She also reminds the nurse advocate that patients have the right not to know, if this is their wish.

Issues that must be addressed before nurses can serve as true patient advocates are as follows (Miller, Mansen, and Lee 1983):

- redefinition of the role of the physician as sole authority and decision maker
- redefinition of the role of the nurse as care giver or implementer of the physician's plan of care
- colleagues' concern regarding nurse advocates as encouraging patient resistance and noncompliance
- lack of nurse authority or power (personal, invested, and delegated)

To serve as more effective advocates, oncology nurses must be aware of these issues and address them in a systematic manner. Nelson (1988) recommends that nurses clarify the meaning of advocacy and the extent of nurses' commitment to its practice, thereby clarifying their image as advocate to the public. Nurses also need to understand better the bureaucracy in which they practice, thereby becoming more socially and politically active. Nurses' practice acts should be revised to safeguard the role of the nurse as advocate. Now as never before, oncology nurses must address their commitment to this role as more persons, especially the elderly, are diagnosed with cancer, as patients and their families become more knowledgeable about cancer and more concerned about self-care, and as technologic advances generate such ethical concerns as do not resuscitate orders.

QUALITY ASSURANCE

In 1985, the Joint Commission on Accreditation of Healthcare Organizations recognized that health care institutions must change their focus from addressing short-term solutions to isolated problems to identifying key areas related to delivery of quality care that could be monitored over longer periods of time. The revised quality assurance standard stated "there is an ongoing quality assurance program designed to objectively and systematically monitor and evaluate the quality and appropriateness of patient care, pursue opportunities to improve patient care, and resolve identified problems" (Joint Commission 1988, 235). This change in perspective on quality assurance offers oncology nurses the opportunity to identify departmentwide studies of standards of care as well as to develop and monitor unit-specific (i.e., oncology) standards of care.

Oncology nurses at health care institutions throughout the country are developing unit-based quality assurance programs. For example, Coyne and Killien (1987) described the development of projects that addressed structure, process, or outcome criteria such as nurses' compliance with medication administration protocols and the rate of actual medication errors, assignment and implementation of primary nursing responsibilities, and patient body temperature during surgery. It was noted that unit representatives and their staff nurse colleagues often gained knowledge and skills in, as well as generated ideas for, nursing research projects.

Specific examples of this transition from unit-based quality assurance to unit-based research are described by Gaits et al. (1989). They delineate the role of the oncology nurse in the central nursing quality assurance program, unit-based quality assurance forums, and unit-based research forums. Projects described include a comparative study of habit retraining and rigid toileting in patients with urinary incontinence, factors affecting nursing time spent administering oral nonabsorbable antibiotics in a laminar airflow environment, comparison of arterial line and venipuncture for obtaining partial thromboplastin times, and the effect of parental visitation in the postanesthesia care unit on the perioperative experience of pediatric patients.

Oncology nurses have ever-growing opportunities to affect quality of care through quality assurance. How better to ensure that the American Nurses' Association (ANA) and the Oncology Nursing Society (ONS) *Standards of Oncology Nursing Practice* (1987) as well as institution and unit-based standards of care are attained and maintained than through the development and implementation of quality assurance projects?

SPECIALIST AND GENERALIST

Oncology nursing has matured as a specialty; this was highlighted by the formation of the ONS in 1975. Nurses can now seek certification as oncology certified nurses, and position statements on both generalist and advanced nursing practice have been issued by the ONS. Debate now centers on the concept of advanced certification: who is eligible for it, what its content is, and whether the focus should be on subspecialization (e.g., radiation therapy, chemotherapy, or bone marrow transplantation). One effort to deal with the issue of subspecialization has been the formation of special-interest groups, to which any member of the ONS can belong by paying an additional membership fee.

Diers (1985) notes that characteristics of advanced practice include professional authority, accountability, responsibility, and collegiality with others. Specialist practice is defined in terms of "what one needs to know in order to give good, specialized patient care (Diers 1985, 43). The kinds of knowledge needed to prepare for advanced practice are clinical judgment, scholarly inquiry, and leadership. This preparation should occur at the master's level, and there should be multiple opportunities for practice.

The ANA's *Statement on Graduate Education in Nursing* (1978) defines the nurse generalist as "one who has a comprehensive approach to health care and can meet diversified health concerns of individuals, families, and communities" (p. 1), whereas the nurse specialist is one who "functions within a specified and clearly designated field, drawing upon scientific knowledge and extensive experience" (p. 1). Reed and Hoffman (1986, 49) identify factors that shape advanced practice now and will do so in the future as "current and potential needs for health care services, trends and roles of master's prepared nurses; assumptions about health problems; current perspective and future trends in graduate nursing education; mission, purpose, and philosophy of the educational institution; availability of resources; faculty characteristics, including philosophy, interest, and ability; and organization and structure of existing programs."

Chickadonz and Perry (1985, 80) indicate that "the issue is not clinical specialization versus generalization, but the preparation of a clinical nurse specialist capable of autonomous independent functioning." At a 1984 invitational conference hosted by the Cancer Nursing Service at the Clinical Center, National Institutes of Health, the recommendations for clinical practice for the oncology certified nurse covered the areas of cost containment, aging population, practice standards, consumerism, role development, and professional issues. Recommendations for education and administrative support were also delineated (Donoghue and Spross 1985).

As the field of oncology continues to expand, nurses will have to develop expertise not only in treatment modalities but also in the disease continuum (prevention and early detection through terminal care), disease process across age groups (pediatrics to geriatrics), site-specific diseases (e.g., breast, lung, or colorectal), setting (e.g., acute care or hospice), and symptom management (e.g., pain or nutrition). There will be continuing challenges to oncology nursing as a specialty arising from the growth of knowledge and skills and also in terms of roles (i.e., clinician, manager, researcher, consultant, and teacher) and relationships (employee or entrepreneur). Oncology nurses with a diversity of education and experience are needed to address these challenges in the years to come.

ONCOLOGY NURSES IN PREVENTIVE EDUCATION

The role of the oncology nurse in preventive education has assumed increasing importance in recent years as knowledge regarding prevention has grown and as the public's quest for healthful living has accelerated. Although nurses are frequent volunteers for health fairs and screening clinics, they often overlook opportunities for education in acute care settings. For example, Cole and Gorman (1984) found that nurses in hospitals could not be assumed to serve as role models and health educators because of their lack of knowledge of or their emotional reactions to the practice of breast self-examination (BSE). On the other hand, nurses have been actively involved in the development of prevention education programs.

Smeltzer and Vrba (1986) describe their program in a cancer detection center where public education lectures were held, drawing large numbers of participants. The H. Lee Moffitt Comprehensive Cancer Center in Tampa, Florida has a nurse-operated cancer screening and detection van that provides specific assessment services as well as education. Such projects as these provide oncology nurses with the opportunity to assume a leadership role in preventive education. The challenge is to give nurses the knowledge and an appreciation of the importance of their role in cancer prevention.

ONCOLOGY NURSES IN CRITICAL CARE AND REHABILITATION

Nurses in critical care settings are now identifying the need for knowledge and skills in oncology nursing as more persons with cancer experience critical episodes that require immediate nursing intervention (Chernecky and Ramsey 1984). These episodes include neurologic, gastrointestinal, renal and electrolyte, endocrine, and bone marrow complications as well as infection, shock, and multisystem organ failure (Howland and Carlon 1985). Oncology nurses in all settings must be prepared to identify patients at risk, to monitor them for complications, and to intervene quickly and effectively. The changing nature of cancer and its treatment indicates a growing need for oncology nursing to develop expertise in critical care nursing.

Oncology nurses are also focusing more time and attention on the rehabilitation of persons with cancer. In fact, the ONS recently issued "Rehabilitation of Persons with Cancer: An ONS Position Statement" (Mayer and O'Connor 1989). The development of this statement reflects the increasing number of cancer survivors who are living with cancer. As a result, the structure, process, and outcome of rehabilitation are being applied to the care of persons with cancer. Oncology nurses should initiate rehabilitation interventions as soon as the diagnosis of cancer is confirmed. Issues of survivorship must also be addressed through research so that persons with cancer can achieve optimal functioning within the limits imposed by their disease (Carter 1989).

PREPARATION FOR ONCOLOGY NURSING AS A SPECIALTY

Oncology nursing, like many other specialties in the nursing profession, evolved in the context of on-the-job education and experience, including orientation, inservice education, and staff development, as well as through direct care experience and, in more recent years, continuing education and graduate education. The ONS differentiated between generalist and advanced practice levels in its *Standards of Oncology Nursing Education* (1989). Both generalist and advanced level standards address faculty, resources, curricula, the teaching-learning process, and the learner. Although there is no education requirement for the oncology nurse generalist, this person is defined as "a registered nurse who possesses general knowledge and skills applicable to diverse health concerns of clients" (ONS 1989, 17), whereas the advanced oncology nurse is one "with master's, doctoral, or post-doctoral education who applies theoretical knowledge in a specialized field" (ONS 1989, 16).

Efforts to hire licensed practical nurses into the ONS as associate members have been aborted twice at national congresses, the second time by a narrow margin. Perhaps members opposed to recruiting these nurses into the organization are concerned with the difficulty of defining yet another level of practice. No doubt there will be continuing debate on this controversial issue.

With regard to advanced and specialty education in oncology nursing, the American Cancer Society and the ONS collaborated on *The Master's Degree with a Specialty in Oncology Nursing* (1988). This document is useful as a curriculum guide for faculty and students in identifying outcome objectives and course content basic to advanced oncology nursing practice.

The development of certification in oncology nursing has occurred at a rapid and challenging pace for the ONS. Thousands of nurses now use *OCN* (oncology certified nurse) after their names, and more are registering for the examination at the annual congress each spring as well as at regional sites each fall. Plans are now underway by the ONS to begin exploring the possibility of advanced or subspecialty certification. Certainly the growth of special-interest groups indicates the need for careful study before expansion of the certification program.

The ONS is now an ANA-accredited and approved provider of continuing education. This development reflects the specialty's commitment to basic preparation for and maintenance of competence and growth of oncology nurses.

REFERENCES

American Cancer Society and Oncology Nursing Society. 1988. *The Master's degree with a specialty in oncology nursing*. Pittsburgh: ONS.

American Nurses' Association Commission on Nursing Education. 1978. *Statement on graduate education in nursing*. Kansas City, Mo.: ANA.

American Nurses' Association and Oncology Nursing Society. 1987. *Standards of oncology nursing practice.* Kansas City, Mo.: ANA.

Annas, G.J. 1974. The patient rights advocate: Can nurses effectively fill the role? *Supervisor Nurse* 5:21–25.

Carter, B.J. 1989. Cancer survivorship: A topic for nursing research. *Oncology Nursing Forum* 16:435–437.

Chernecky, C., and P. Ramsey. 1984. *Critical nursing care of the client with cancer.* Norwalk, Conn.: Appleton-Century-Crofts.

Chickadonz, G.H., and A.M. Perry. 1985. Clinical specialization versus generalization: Perspectives for the future. In *Current issues in nursing*, ed. J. McCloskey and H. Grace. Boston: Blackwell Scientific Publications.

Cole, C.F., and L.M. Gorman. 1984. Breast self-examination: Practices and attitudes of registered nurses. *Oncology Nursing Forum* 11:37–41.

Commission on Nursing. 1988. *Report to the Secretary of Health and Human Services.* Bethesda, Md.: National Institutes of Health.

Coyne, C., and M. Killien. 1987. A system for unit-based monitors of quality of nursing care. *Journal of Nursing Administration* 17:26–32.

Diers, D. 1985. Preparation of practitioners, clinical specialists, and clinicians. *Journal of Professional Nursing* 1:41–47.

Donoghue, M., and J. Spross. 1985. A report from the First National Invitational Conference. *Oncology Nursing Forum* 12:35–73.

Gaits, V., R. Ford, R. Kaplow, G. Bru, A.E. Belcher, M. Brown, and M. Bookbinder. 1989. Unit-based research forums: A model for the clinical nurse specialist to promote clinical research. *Clinical Nurse Specialist* 3:61–65.

Haddon, R.M. 1989. The final frontier: Nursing in the emerging health-care environment. *Nursing Economics* 7:155–66.

Howland, W.S., and G.C. Carlon, eds. 1985. *Critical care of the cancer patient.* Chicago: Year Book Medical Publishers.

Joint Commission on Accreditation of Healthcare Organizations. 1988. *Accreditation manual for hospitals.* Chicago: JCAHO.

King, M.G. 1989. Nursing shortage circa 1915. *Image: Journal of Nursing Scholarship* 21:124–27.

Kohnke, M.F. 1982. *Advocacy: Risk and reality.* St. Louis, Mo.: C.V. Mosby Co.

Lynaugh, J.E., and C.M. Fagin. 1988. Nursing comes of age. *Image: Journal of Nursing Scholarship* 20:184–89.

Mauksch, I.G. 1989. Understanding our past to rebuild our future. *Oncology Nursing Forum* 16:483–87.

Mayer, D., and L. O'Connor. 1989. Rehabilitation of persons with cancer: An ONS position statement. *Oncology Nursing Forum* 16:433.

Miller, B.K., T. Mansen, and H. Lee. 1983. Patient advocacy: Do nurses have the power and authority to act as patient advocate? *Nursing Leadership* 6:56–60.

Mundinger, M.O. 1980. *Autonomy in nursing.* Rockville, Md.: Aspen Publishers, Inc.

Nealon, E., B. Blumberg, and B. Brown. 1985. What do patients know about clinical trials? *American Journal of Nursing* 85:807–10.

Nelson, M.L. 1988. Advocacy in nursing. *Nursing Outlook* 36:136.

Oncology Nursing Society. 1989. *Standards of oncology nursing education: Generalist and advanced practice levels.* Pittsburgh: ONS.

Reed, S.B., and S.E. Hoffman. 1986. The enigma of graduate nursing education: Advanced generalist? Specialist? *Nursing and Health Care* 7:43–49.

Rudolf, V.M. 1989. Oncology nursing protocols: A step toward autonomy. *Oncology Nursing Forum* 16:643–47.

Smeltzer, C.H., and P.D. Vrba. 1986. Education and cancer screening. *Nursing Management* 17:64–66.

Zander, K. 1988. Nursing case management: Strategic management of cost and quality outcomes. *Journal of Nursing Administration* 18:23–30.

Index

A

"ABCD" method, 21
Absorption, of drug in older patient, 156
Accreditation, of freestanding cancer center, 270–271. *See also* Joint Commission on Accreditation of Healthcare Organizations; Licensure
Acetaminophen, use following bone marrow transplantation, 110
Acquired immunodeficiency syndrome (AIDS)
　CDC definition of, 173–174, 195
　evidence of progression to, 177–179
　home care. *See* Home care; Home nursing care
　homeless population and, 276–280
　indicator diseases, 179–189. *See also individually named diseases and infections*; Opportunistic infections
　nature of, 173–174
　neurologic complications in, 184–185
　ONS position paper, 189
　in pediatric population. *See* Pediatric AIDS
　prevention and early detection of, 14
　HIV antibody testing and counseling, 174–177
　HIV screening and, 17
　school and community education programs, 208
Active biotherapy, specific and nonspecific, 79
Active nonspecific therapy. *See* Immunotherapy
Activities of daily living (ADLs)
　in Cooperative Care Center, 285
　home nursing care and, 213
　suggestions for AIDS patients, 221
ACTUs. *See* AIDS clinical trials units (ACTUs)
Acyclovir sodium
　in treatment of HSV and HZV infections, 225
　use following bone marrow transplantation, 99, 110
ADC. *See* AIDS dementia complex (ADC)
ADLs. *See* Activities of daily living (ADLs)
Admission process
　for bone marrow transplantation patient, 103–104

hospital information system and, 314
Adolescents, AIDS and. *See* Pediatric AIDS; Pediatric HIV infection
Adoptive immunotherapy, 81
Adriamycin, cardiotoxicity of, 154
Adult group homes, as homelessness solution, 277
Advanced cancer, patient with. *See* Terminally ill patient
Adverse effects
　of bone marrow transplantation
　　immediate, 109–115
　　long–term, 115
　of cytoreduction, 105, 106
　in older patient
　　drug therapy, 156
　　radiation therapy, 155
　of screening program, 17
Advocacy
　defined, 8. *See also* Patient advocate
　for health policy, 29–30
　oncology nurses and, 356–357
　risk taking and, 9
Aerobic training, nursing research into, 69
Aerosolized pentamidine, as prophylaxis for *Pneumocystis carinii* pneumonia, 223
Agency services. *See* Oncology Nursing Agency (ONA)
Aging, 142–145
　demographics of, 141–142
　experimental cancers and, 144–145
　immunological changes associated with, 152
　morphologic lesions of, 143, 144
　population profile. *See under* Elderly
　process of, 142–143
　theories of, 143–144
AIDS clinical trials units (ACTUs), 227
　current investigative agents, 229–230
AIDS dementia complex (ADC), 185
　impact on patient, 186
　nursing interventions in, 187

AIDS Home Care Program, eligibility for, 213
AIDS Patient Handbook
　copy of, 236–256
　preparation and use of, 234–235
AIDS-related complex (ARC)
　homeless population and, 276–280
　pediatric population and, 193
　　characteristics, 195
AIDS Resource Center (New York City), homelessness solutions by, 277
Alcohol, intake guidelines, 26
"Alerts", on computer system, 317
Allogeneic bone marrow transplantation, 103
　results of, 98
Alpha-interferon therapy
　action and side effects of, 230
　for Kaposi's sarcoma, 226
Altered fractions, in radiation therapy, 64–65
Alternate homes, defining home environment and, 303–304
Alternative therapies, AIDS patients and, 227–228
Ambulatory care
　attractiveness of, 260–262
　centers for, definitions of, 267. *See also* Freestanding cancer center
　development and organization of, 266–267
　growth of, 1
　HIV antibody testing programs, 177
　hospital–based, examples of, 263–264
　nurse's role in, 3
　　as clinical specialist, 262–263
Ambulatory Oncology Treatment Center (New York), 263–264
American Academy of Pediatrics (AAP), AIDS educational policy recommendations, 208
American Cancer Society, oncology nursing specialty recognition and, 361
American College of Surgeons (ACOS), and freestanding cancer center accreditation, 271

American Foundation of AIDS
    Research, 227
American Hospital Association, *A
    Patient's Bill of Rights*, 52
American Nurses' Association (ANA)
    Code for Nurses, 7–8
    *Code for Nurses with Interpretive
        Statements*, 52
    *Human Rights Guidelines for Nurses
        in Clinical and Other Research*, 52
    quality assurance and, 358
    *Standards of Oncology Nursing
        Practice*, 52
    *Statement on Graduate Education in
        Nursing* (1978), 359
3-amniopropylaminophosphorothioic
    acid, as radioprotector, 66
Amphotericin B
    home care administration of, 279
    in treatment of candidiasis, 225
    in treatment of cryptococcosis, 225
    in treatment of histoplasmosis, 225
Ampligen, action and side effects of, 229
Analgesics, absorption in elderly, 156
Ancillary departments, and nursing units,
    communicating via computer,
    316–318
Ancobon. *See* Flucytosine
Anesthesia
    in cancer pain treatment, 131
    risk to elderly associated with, 149
Ansamycin. *See* Rifabutin
Anti-infectious agents, use following
    bone marrow transplantation, 99–100
Antibiotics
    pediatric AIDS patient and, 196
    use following bone marrow
        transplantation, 110
Anticonvulsants, in cancer pain
    treatment, 131
Antisense RNA inhibition of oncogene
    expression, 51
Antiviral agents, current investigative
    trials, 229–230
Appointments, scheduling of, 315–316
ARC. *See* AIDS–related complex (ARC)

Argon-pump dye lasers, in PDT, 48
AS101, action and side effects of, 230
Assessment
    computer system as aid in, 319
    health care needs of terminally ill
        patient, 165–169
    for home nursing care of AIDS
        patients
        physchosocial, 218–219
        physical, 217–218
    parameters for patients receiving
        BRMs, 95
    for surgery in elderly patients, 150
Autologous bone marrow
    transplantation, 100, 102
    results of, 98
Automated care planning. *See* Care
    planning, automated
Autonomy, in nursing practice, 356
AZT. *See* Zidovudine (AZT)

B

B-cell acute lymphocytic leukemia, in
    HIV-infected patients, 188
B-cell tumors, in AIDS patients, 186
Bacillus Calmette-Guerin (BCG)
    HIV-infected children and, 200
    immune modulation and, 78, 79
Bacteremia, gram-negative, in older
    patient, 151–152
Bacterial opportunistic infections, in
    AIDS patients
    adult, 180, 182
    pediatric, 195–196
Bailey House, for homeless HIV infected
    population, 277–278
    problems encountered, 279
BCG. *See* Bacillus Calmette–Guerin
    (BCG)
Bed-side terminals, 329
Behaviors
    high-risk, 204–205
    illness, in elderly, 145–146
    as market segmentation factor,
        293

Bellevue Hospital, *AIDS Patient Handbook*, 236–256
Bereavement support, AIDS patient survivors and, 222
Beta-carotene, as radioprotector, 66
Bibliographic databases, 331
Billing statements
  computerization and, 301
  from consulting business, 296
  recording charges for, 316
Bioimplantable, self-powered pump reservoir systems, in intrahepatic artery chemotherapy, 47
Biologic needs, of terminally ill patient, 166–167
Biologic response modifiers (BRMs)
  current status of, 81, 83–87. *See also individually named modifiers*
  defined, 79
  mechanisms of, 81
  nursing implications, 87
    patient assessment parameters, 92–95
    symptom management, 88–90
  side effects frequency, 84
  tumor immunology and action of, 79, 80
Biologic therapy
  biotherapeutic agents classification, 82
  classifications of, 79, 81
  described, 78
Biomedical technology
  economics of cancer care and, 261–262
  in home care setting, 304
    advances in, 305–306
  innovative, 2
  nurse and, 6
Biotherapeutic agents
  classification of, 82
  side effects of, 87
    management of, 88–90
Bleeding, as bone marrow transplant complication, 109–110
Bleomycin fibrosis, risk in older patient, 154

Blood
  computerized analysis of, 317–318
  pediatric AIDS patient care precautions, 200–201
BMT. *See* Bone marrow transplantation (BMT)
"Boarder babies," 206
Body composition, and drug vulnerability in older patient, 156
Body fluids, pediatric AIDS patient care precautions, 200–201
Body heating. *See* Hyperthermia
Body image, nursing research into, 70
Bone marrow
  harvesting of, 107
  infusion of, 108–109
  preparation of, 108
Bone marrow transplantation (BMT)
  complications of
    immediate, 109–115
    long-term, 115
  discharge teaching and planning for, 116
  disease types treated with, 99
  donor bone marrow types, 100, 102–103
  economic issues in, 116–117
  engraftment period, 109
  future trends, 117
  nursing diagnoses and clinical problems related to, 101–102
  obstacles to, 99–100
  pretransplant period, 103–105, 106
  rationale for, 100
  results of
    allogeneic, 98
    autologous, 98
  transplantation period, 105, 107–109
Brachytherapy, 60, 63–65
Brain implants, for glioblastoma, 63, 64–65
"Branching," in computer-assisted instruction, 337, 339
  videodisc and, 345
Breast cancer
  risk factors, incidence and screening recommendations, 17–18

risk in elderly population, 147
Breast self-examination
  nurse involvement in, 360
  recommendations for, 18
Bromodeoxyuridine (BUdR), as radiosensitizer, 66
Buccal drug delivery route, 128
BUdR. *See* Bromodeoxyuridine (BUdR)
Business
  oncology nurse in, 290. *See also* Nurse-run business
  opportunities in, 290
  setting up, mechanisms for, 291
Business plan, 289–290

C

Cable television, as educational tool, 344–345
CAI. *See* Computer-assisted instruction (CAI)
Calvary Hospital (Bronx, NY)
  nursing ethics group at, 171
  patient care program at, 164
Cancer Control Objectives for the Nation: 1985–2000, 35–36
Cancer pain. *See* Pain
Cancer prevention
  community-based strategies for, 28–29
  counseling interventions, 24–28. *See also* Counseling
  and early detection, 14–15
    carcinogenesis initiation, 15–16
    in elderly populations, 146–148
    nursing research in, 68–69
    screening benefits, 17
    screening recommendations, 17–24. *See also individually named cancers*
    target provisions, 41
  health promotion and, 13–14
  nurse's role in, 4, 359–360
  primary, secondary and tertiary, 14, 16
  research agenda, 30–31
CANCERLIT, 331

Cancer(s)
  acute versus chronic pain experience directly from, 126–127
  in HIV-infected patients, 188
  initiation and promotion of, 15–16
  therapy for. *See* Treatment modalities
  warning signals for, 16
Candida spp., as bone marrow transplant complication, 110
Candida albicans infection, in AIDS patients, 182
Candidiasis, in AIDS patients
  drug therapies for, 224–225
  oral form, 182
Capsaicin, in cancer pain treatment, 130
Carbon dioxide laser, in PDT, 49
Carboplatin, 52
Carcinogenesis
  phases in, 15–16
  risk factors in. *See* Risk factors
Carcinoma. *See* Cancer(s)
Cardiopulmonary resuscitation (CPR), interactive videodisc system and, 347
Cardiotoxicity, of Adriamycin, 154
Cardiovascular assessment parameters, for patients receiving BRMs, 92–93
Care. *See also* Health care
  of active patients. *See* Ambulatory care
  after hospitalization. *See* Continuing care
  critical, oncology nurses in, 360
  documentation of, 320
  of dying patient. *See under* Terminally ill patient
  in emergency, provision for, 273
  in the home. *See* Home care
  nursing activities schedule, 325
  palliative. *See* Palliative care
  planning of. *See* Care planning, automated
  quality of, 4
  of self. *See* Self care
  of skin, 70
  supportive. *See* Supportive care

Care giver
  for AIDS patient, 247–248
  care of, 248–249
  computer assistance for, 313–314
  education about HIV transmission and prevention of infection, 220–221
  nurse support for, 4
  responsibility of, 165
Care manager, nurse's role as, 3
Care partner
  in cooperative care, 281, 282
  role of, 284
Care planning, automated, 313–314
  and documentation, 320
  in nursing process, 319–320
  report generation, 324–325
Caring for the AIDS Patient at Home, 219
Carmustine. *See* Methyl CCNU
Case management, AIDS patients, 216
  New York City's Human Resources Administration approach to, 213
Catheter occlusion, implantable pumps and, 47
Catheters, in hyperthermia, 61–62
CD-ROM. *See* Compact disk read-only memory (CD-ROM)
CDC. *See* Centers for Disease Control (CDC)
Cell, death and repair potential of, 60
Cellular mediated reponses, in biotherapy, 79, 80
Centers for Disease Control (CDC)
  AIDS definition
    adult, 173–174, 195
    pediatric, 195
  AIDS educational policy guidelines, 207–208
  HIV infection spectrum, 179
  pediatric AIDS statistics, 193
  schoolchildren's beliefs about AIDS, data on, 179
Central nervous system (CNS)
  abnormalities in pediatric AIDS, 197
  toxicity, nursing research into, 70
Certification, of oncology nurses, 361

Cervical cancer, risk factors, incidence and screening recommendations, 19
Cervical intraepithelial neoplasia (CIN), carbon dioxide laser use in, 49
Charges, recording of, 316
Charting
  computer information system and, 320
  computer-produced reports for, 325–326
Chemotherapeutic agents
  in elederly patient, 152–154
  toxicity of, 153, 158
  in Kaposi's sarcoma treatment, 226
Chemotherapy
  in Cooperative Care Center, 284
  delivery techniques, 46–48
  in home care setting, 304
  new agents for, issues concerning, 51
    informed consent, 51–54
    quality-of-life, 54–55
  and older patient
    physiologic factors, 152–154
    psychologic and psychosocial factors, 154
  protocols via computer screen, 317
Chest radiography, as screening procedure, recommendations about, 20
Children
  with AIDS. *See* Pediatric AIDS; Pediatric HIV infection
  beliefs about AIDS, CDC data on, 179
CIN. *See* Cervical intraepithelial neoplasia (CIN)
Clinical nurse specialist. *See* Oncology clinical nurse specialist (OCNS)
Clinical trials
  informed consent for, 51–54
  of new drugs. *See* AIDS clinical trials units (ACTUs)
Clofazimine, in treatment of *Mycobacterium avium-intracellulare* infection, 224
Clonidine, in cancer pain treatment, 130

Closed-circuit television, as educational tool, 341–342
Clotrimazole troches, in treatment of candidiasis, 224
CNS. *See* Central nervous system (CNS)
Cognitive behavioral approaches, in cancer pain treatment, 131–132
Colitis, CMV, in AIDS patients, 184
Collaborative care. *See* Cooperative care
Collaborative practice, 1, 3
  cancer prevention and detection, 15
  in supportive housing apartment program, 278–279
Collaborative research, 56
Colony-stimulating factors (CSFs)
  cells producing, 86–87
  granulocyte-macrophage, action and side effects of, 229
  toxic effects of, 84, 87
Colorectal cancer
  home administration of 5-fluorouracil in, 304
  risk factors, incidence and screening recommendations, 18–19
  risk in elderly population, 147
Columbia-Presbyterian Medical Center, ambulatory oncology facility development, 263–264
Columbia University Comprehensive Cancer Center, 263–264
Combination drug therapies
  for HIV-associated lymphomas, 226
  investigational, 228
  for Kaposi's sarcoma, 226
Commission on Nursing, future nursing trends, 355–356
Communication, within hospital, 314–316. *See also* Computer system
Community
  defined, 28
  prevention programs in, stages of, 28–29
Community networking, in business, 294
Compact disk read-only memory (CD-ROM)
  capacity of, 349
  reference material on, 331

Compatibility. *See* Histocompatibility
Compliance, drug vulnerability and, 156
Computer-assisted instruction (CAI), 335–336
  benefits and limitations of, 337–338
  categories of, 337
  described, 336–337
  development in nursing, 337
  effectiveness as teaching tool, 339
  potential of, 327–328
  student attitudes toward, 339
  user–friendly, 339–340
  videodisc coupled with, 345. *See also* Videodisc systems
Computer programs, as educational tools. *See* Computer-assisted instruction (CAI)
Computer system
  for automated care planning, 313–314
  bed-side terminals, 329
  benefits of, 314
  communicating orders and results via, 316–318
  confidentiality issues, 326–327
  education potential of, 327–328. *See also* Computer-assisted instruction (CAI)
  general capabilities of, 314–316
  intelligent systems, 330
  in nursing agency business, 301
  nursing process applications, 318–319
    admission assessment, 319
    care documentation, 320
    care planning, 319–320
    discharge planning, 320–321
  printouts and reports from
    permanent chart documents, 325–326
    temporary work documents, 321–325
  reference material on-line, 330–332
  research potential of, 328–329
  schematic of, 315
Condoms, recommendations about, 244
Confidentiality, 7
  computer information systems and, 326–327

in research setting, 328–329
disclosure and, 53
for HIV infected children, 207–208
Confusion, postoperative, in elderly patients, 150
Conscience, patient's wishes and, 170
Consultant, nurse as, 3
Consulting business, 290–297. See also Nexus Group
Consumers, nursing agency services and, 299
Continuing care
in cancer pain treatment, models of, 132–133
clinical nurse specialist role in, 133
Control, by patient of care delivery, 285
Conventional bone marrow transplantation, allogeneic, 103
Cooperative care
center for. See Cooperative Care Center
concept of, 281
cost of, 281–282
history of, 281
Cooperative Care Center
admission criteria, 282
dining and recreation facilities, 282–283
Education Center in, 283
and the oncology patient, 284–285
patient and care partner room in, 282
Therapeutic Center in, 283
Coping skills
for children and adolescents with AIDS, 206–208
nursing research into, 72–73
suggested strategies, 238
of terminally ill patient, 167
Corporate structure, of Oncology Nursing Agency, 298
Corynebacterium parvum, immune modulation and, 78, 79
Costs. See Economics of cancer care
Counseling
effectiveness of, 24
lifestyle change, 27–28
nutrition, 25–27
tobacco usage prevention, 24–25
Cover gowns, in AIDS patient care, 248
Criteria Manual for the Treatment of AIDS, New York Statewide Professional Standards Review Council 1989, 278
Critical care, oncology nurses in, 360
Cruciferous vegetables, intake guidelines, 26
Cryopreservation, of bone marrow, 109
Cryptococcosis, in AIDS patients, drug therapies for, 225
Cryptococcus neoformans infection, in AIDS patients, 182
Cryptosporidiosis, in AIDS patients, 180
drug therapies for, 223
symptoms and nursing care considerations, 181
Cured food, intake guidelines, 26
Cyclophosphamide, prior to bone marrow transplantation, 104
high dose, 105
Cycloserine, in treatment of *Mycobacterium tuberculosis* infection, 224
Cytarabine, in treatment of progressive multifocal leukoencephalopathy, 225
Cytomegalovirus (CMV)
in AIDS patients, 184–185
drug therapies for, 225
and interstitial pneumonia following bone marrow transplantation, 110–111
Cytoreduction, general side effects of, 105, 106
Cytosine arabinoside, in treatment of progressive multifocal leukoencephalopathy, 225
Cytoxan. See Cyclophosphamide

D

Dapsone–trimethoprim, in treatment of *Pneumocystis carinii* pneumonia, 223

Daraprim. *See* Pyrimethamine
Data capture, and research potential, 328
Data retrieval, by computer, 301
Databases
  educational use of, 328
  in hospital information system, 321, 322
  as on-line reference material, 331
Day care centers, CDC guidelines for AIDS patients, 207
Death
  patient approaching. *See* Terminally ill patient
  preparation for, 279
Decision making, for terminally ill patient, 170–171
Decision support systems, 330
Decontamination, prior to bone marrow transplantation, 104
Demand management, in marketing, 292–293
Demographics, as market segmentation factor, 293
Deoxycoformycin, 52
Detection
  of AIDS–related disease
    evidence of progression, 177–179
    indicator diseases, 179–189. *See also* Malignancy(ies); Neurologic disease; Opportunistic infections; Wasting syndrome
  of cancer. *See under* Cancer prevention
Developmental delays, in pediatric AIDS patients, 204
Dextran sulfate, action and side effects of, 229
DHE. *See* Dihematoporphyrin ether (DHE)
DHPG. *See* Gancyclovir
Diagnosis-related groups (DRGs), 261
Diagnostic tests, ordering and receiving results via computer, 316–318
Diarrhea, pediatric AIDS patients and, 202

Dideoxycytidine, action and side effects of, 229
Dideoxyinosine, action and side effects of, 229
Diet. *See also* Food preparation; Nutrition
  guidelines for, 25–27
  recommendations for AIDS patients, 249–256
  in pediatric setting, 202
Diethyldithiocarbamate, action and side effects of, 229
Digital rectal examination, recommendations about
  colorectal cancer detection, 19
  prostate cancer detection, 20
Dihematoporphyrin ether (DHE)
  administration of, 49
  as photosensitizing agent, 48
Dimethoprim-sulfamethoxazole, use following bone marrow transplantation, 110
Dining, in Cooperative Care Center
  facilities, 282–283
  flexibility, 285
Diphtheria, tetanus, and pertussis vaccine (DTP), HIV-infected children and, 200
Discharge planning, computer information system and, 320–321
Disclosure, elements of, 52–53
Disease prevention. *See* Cancer prevention
Dish configuration, for satellite video conference, 343
Disinfection, pediatric AIDS patient care precautions, 201
Disposable gloves, in AIDS patient care, 248
Disposal, of computer-produced documents, 326–327
Distribution, of drug in older patient, 157
DNA
  hyperthermia and, 61
  radiation damage to, 60
DNR. *See* Do not resusciate (DNR) status

Do not resusciate (DNR) status, 4, 169
Documentation
   computer information system and, 320. *See also* Printouts, from computer information system
   disposal issues, 326–327
Donor
   for bone marrow transplantation, 100, 102–103
   compatibility with bone marrow recipient, 103
   marrow harvesting from, 107
Dose, establishing level for biologic response modifiers, 87
Dose-limiting toxicities, biologic response modifiers and, 87
Downlinking, for satellite conferencing, 342–343
DRGs. *See* Diagnosis-related groups (DRGs)
Drill and practice, in computer-assisted instruction, 337
Drug abuse
   Bellevue Hospital *AIDS Patient Handbook* recommendations, 244–246
   and cancer-related pain, 127
Drug adversity. *See under* Adverse effects; Toxicity
Drug apparatus, cleaning recommendations for, 244–246
Drug delivery
   automated systems for, 47–48
   oral, 128
   routes for, 128–130
Drug–induced illness, in older patient. *See* Polypharmacy
Drug kinetics, in elderly patient, 155–158
Drug therapies, for AIDS patients
   alternatives to, 227–228
   for HIV-associated cancers, 226
   home intravenous therapy, 222, 226–227
   under investigation, 227, 228–230
   for opportunistic infections, 223–225

Drug vulnerability, of older patient, 156–158
DTP. *See* Diphtheria, tetanus, and pertussis vaccine (DTP)
Dying patient
   care of the. *See under* Terminally ill patient
   severe pain in, 127
Dysmorphic syndrome, in pediatric AIDS, 197, 199
Dyspnea, nursing research into, 70

E

EBV. *See* Epstein-Barr virus (EBV)
Economics of cancer care, 1–2
   ambulatory versus inpatient concerns, 260–261
   bone marrow transplantation, 116–117
   cooperative care and, 281, 285
   diagnosis–related groups, 261
   future models, 14
   technological advances, 261–262
Education
   about AIDS, in school and community, 208
   computer as tool in, 327–328. *See also* Computer–assisted instruction (CAI)
   for disease prevention, oncology nurses in, 359–360
   nursing research into, 71–72
   in pain management, 134
   of primary care providers, 41
   via television. *See* Education television
Education Center, in cooperative care facility, 283, 284
Education television
   benefits and limitations of, 340–341
   closed-circuit, 341–342
   development of, 340
   future trends, 348–349
   via cable, 344–345
   via satellite, 342
   and video teleconferencing, 342–344

videodisc and, 345–348. *See also* Videodisc systems
Eflornithine, in cryptosporidiosis treatment, 223
Elderly
 cancer detection in, 146–147
 cancer incidence and mortality (over 65 years), 142, 143, 145
 chemotherapy for, 152–154
 future health care concerns, 158
 life-threatening infections in, 150–152
 nursing implications, 148
 polypharmacy and, 155–158
 population profile and disease pattern, 145
 psychologic and social dimensions of, 145–146
 radiation therapy for, 154–155
 surgical treatment and, 148–150
Elective surgery, versus emergency surgery, 149
Electronic kardex, 321, 323
ELISA. *See* Enzyme-linked immunosorbent assay (ELISA)
Emergency care, provisions in freestanding cancer center, 273
Emergency surgery, elective surgery versus, 149
Engraftment period, in bone marrow transplantation, 109
Enteritis, CMV, in AIDS patients, 185
Enterobacter spp., 151
Entrepreneur
 characteristics of, 288–289
 nurse as, 1. *See also* Nurse-run business
Entrepreneurship, and nursing, 288–289
Environmental exposure, cancer rates and, 14, 16
Environmental Protection Agency, pesticide safeguard recommendations, 30
Enzyme-linked immunosorbent assay (ELISA), HIV antibody testing by, 174–176
 in pediatric population, 194

Epidural drug delivery route, 130
Epstein-Barr virus (EBV), in AIDS patients, 185
Error handling, in computerized information system, 318
Escherichia coli, 151
Esophageal cancer, home administration of 5-fluorouracil in, 304
Ethambutol
 in treatment of *Mycobacterium avium-intracellulare* infection, 224
 in treatment of *Mycobacterium tuberculosis* infection, 224
Ethical issues
 challenges to nurse, 4, 11
 patient advocacy and, 8–9
 reflection on, 6
 technology and, 9–10
 and terminally ill patient, 169–171
Ethics
 ANA code of, 7–8
 definition of, 6
 International Code of (1950), 7
Ethics group, nursing (Calvary Hospital), 171
Etoposide, toxicity associated with, 153
Exchange process, in marketing, 292
Excretion, of drug in older patient, 157–158
Exercise, health promotion and, 68, 69
Expert systems, computer information system and, 330
Expertise, consulting service and, 291–292
External beam therapy, 59–60

F

Faith, terminally ill patient and, 168
Family
 education of
  about HIV infection transmission and prevention, 220–221
  in home care setting, 304–305
  of pediatric AIDS patient, 199

Family member(s)
evaluating cognitive function in older patient, 150
impact of AIDS on, 205–206
Family member(s)
changes in traditional roles of, 7
contributing to cancer pain problem, 124
Fansidar. *See* Pyrimethamine-sulfadoxine
Fatigue
biologic response modifiers and, 91
nursing research into, 69
Fats, intake guidelines, 26
5-FC. *See* Flucytosine
Fecal occult blood testing, recommendations about, 19
Fees, consulting business and
collecting, 295–296
setting, 294–295
Fluconazole, in treatment of cryptococcosis, 225
Flucytosine, in treatment of cryptococcosis, 225
Fluid balance, cytoreduction side effects involving, 106
5-fluorouracil
toxicity associated with, 153–154
use in home care, 304
Food preparation. *See also* Diet; Nutrition
for older patient undergoing radiation therapy, 155
recommendations for AIDS patients, 251
to alleviate or prevent symptoms, 252–253
possible infections from, 253
Food storage, recommendations for, 254–256
Foscarnete. *See* Phosphonoformate
Freestanding cancer center
accreditation of, 270–271
concept of, 267
health management trends in, 268–269
nurses' role in, 271–272
nursing structure and policies in, 272–274
organization of, 267–268
reimbursement of, 269–270
standards of care and, 269
Frustration, 4
Funeral, planning for, 279
Fungal opportunistic infections, in AIDS patients, 182–183
Fungizone. *See* Amphotericin B

G

Games, in computer-assisted instruction, 337
Gamma-globulin, in passive biotherapy, 81
Gancyclovir
home care administration of, 279
in treatment of CMV infection, 184, 225
use following bone marrow transplantation, 99
Gastrointestinal system
assessment parameters for patients receiving BRMs, 94
cytoreduction side effects involving, 106
graft versus host disease and, 112
Gene replacement therapy, 50–51
Generalization, specialization versus, 358–359
Geography, as market segmentation factor, 293
Geriatric oncology, 3
Glioblastoma, brain implants for, 63, 64–65
Graft rejection. *See* Rejection
Graft versus host disease (GVHD), bone marrow transplantation and, 99, 111–114
clinical severity grading, 113
nursing diagnoses, 112
staging system, 114
Gram-negative bacteremia, in older patient, 151–152
Grant proposal, development and preparation of, 292

Granulocyte-macrophage colony-
stimulating factor, action and side
effects of, 229
Grieving, support during, 222
Group homes, for homeless adults, 277
Guidelines for Clinical Practice (1983),
by Harvard Community Health Plan,
278
*Guidelines on Withdrawing or
Withholding Food and Fluid* (ANA
1988), 9–10
GVHD. *See* Graft versus host disease
(GVHD)

H

Haemophilus influenzae, 151
Haemophilus influenzae type b vaccine,
HIV-infected children and, 200
Hand washing, in AIDS patient care,
220, 248
pediatric setting, 201
Harvard Community Health Plan,
Guidelines for Clinical Practice
(1983), 278
Harvesting, of bone marrow, 107
HbCV. *See Haemophilus influenzae*
type b vaccine
Health care
active versus palliative, 9. *See also*
Palliative care
in advanced disease, options
available, 132–133
automated planning of. *See* Care
planning, automated
caregiver and, 4
economics of. *See* Economics of
cancer care
future concerns for elderly, 158
innovative delivery modes, 3
marketing of, 292
patient participation in. *See*
Cooperative care
quality of, 4
restructuring of, 1
standards of, 4

Health Care Finance Administration,
1
Health care system
contributing to cancer pain problem,
124
cost-effective models for, 14
Health education, nursing research into,
71–72
Health management trends, in
ambulatory care setting, 268–269
Health policy, advocacy for, 29–30
Health professional. *See also* Oncology
nurse(s); Physician contributing to
cancer pain problem, 123
*Health Promoting Behavior: Testing a
Proposed Model*, 68
Health Promoting Lifestyle Profile,
subscales of, 69
Health promotion, 13–15
in cancer patients, 68
research agenda, 30–31
Health responsibility, health promotion
and, 69
Hematologic assessment parameters, for
patients receiving BRMs, 94
Hepatitis B recombinant vaccine, HIV-
infected children and, 200
Herpes simplex virus (HSV) infection, in
AIDS patients, 184
drug therapies for, 225
Herpes zoster virus (HZV) infection, in
AIDS patients, 184
drug therapies for, 225
High-calorie diet, recommendations for
AIDS patients, 250–251
High-calorie/high protein drinks,
recommendations for AIDS patients,
250–251
High-fiber foods, intake guidelines,
26
High-risk behavior, HIV-infected
adolescents and, 204–205
Histocompatibility, tests to determine,
103
Histoplasma capsulatum infection, in
AIDS patients, 182–183

Histoplasmosis, in AIDS patients, 182–183
  drug therapy for, 225
HIV. *See* Human immunodeficiency virus (HIV)
HLA. *See* Human leukocyte antigen (HLA) typing
Hodgkin's disease, in HIV-infected patients, 188
Home care
  for AIDS patients, 212
    caregiver stress, 216
    case management, 216
    children, 201
    disease complexity and, 214
    by nurse. *See* Home nursing care
    psychosocial problems, 214–216
  for cancer patients, 303–304
    eligibility requirements, 305
    financial considerations, 306–307
    nurse's role, 307–308
    patient/family education, 304–305
    technologic advances, 305–306
  growth of, 1
  for terminally ill, 10
Home environment, defining, 303
Home nursing care, for AIDS patients, 217
  drug therapy, 222–230
  education for patient, 219
  nutrition, 221
  opportunistic infection detection and prevention, 219–221
  psychosocial assessment, 218–219
  physical assessment, 217–218
  Visting Nurse Service, 279
Homelessness
  HIV infection and, 276–280
  reasons for, 276
  solutions to, 276–277
Hospice care, 132
  for AIDS patients, 221–222
Hospital-based ambulatory care, 263
Hospital formulary, as on-line reference material, 331

Hospital information system. *See* Computer system
Hospital Satellite Network (HSN), 342
Hospitalization, of HIV-infected children, precautions, 200–201
Hospitals, nursing agency services and, 300
Housekeeping, recommendations for AIDS patients, 246–247
Housing, for HIV-infected population, 277–278
HSV. *See* Herpes simplex virus (HSV) infection
Human immunodeficiency virus (HIV)
  antibody testing
    in pediatric population, 194
    pre-test counseling content, 178
    reasons for initiating, 174, 175
    sample programs in ambulatory care, 177
    types and significance of results, 174–176
  homelessness and, 276–280
  infection prevention counseling, 27
    for family and caregiver protection, 220
    nurse's knowledge and skills for, 177
    reasons for, 174, 175
  infection progression monitoring, 177–179
  investigational drugs, 227, 229–230
  malignancies related to, 188
  in pediatric population. *See* Pediatric HIV infection
  screening effectiveness, 17
Human leukocyte antigen (HLA) typing, prior to allogeneic bone marrow transplantation, 103
Humoral mediated reponses, in biotherapy, 79, 80
Hybridoma technology, 78
  in monoclonal antibody production, 86
Hygiene, in AIDS home care, 220–221
  suggestions for, 240–241

Index

Hyperthermia
  clinical use of, 61–63
  PDT and, 48
Hypoxemia, in older patient, 150
HZV. *See* Herpes zoster virus (HZV) infection

I

ICNE. *See* Inter-Collegiate Center for Nursing Education (ICNE)
Idarubicin, 52
Identity, maintaining patient's, 285
Ifosfamide, 52
IL-2. *See* Interleukin-2 (IL–2)
Illness, drug-induced, in older patient. *See* Polypharmacy
Illness behavior, in elderly, 145–146
Illness severity, in freestanding cancer center, 273–274
Image, of oncology nursing, 4
Immune globulin, intravenous administration of, 229
Immune modulators, current investigative trials, 229–230
Immune system
  abnormalities in pediatric AIDS, 194
  aging and, 152
  modulation of. *See* Immunotherapy
Immunization Practice Advisory Committee, recommendations for HIV-infected children, 200
Immunizations, in HIV-infected children, 199–200
Immunosuppression, prior to bone marrow transplantation, 104
Immunotherapy
  adoptive, 81
  early work with, 78–79. *See also* Biologic therapy
Immuthiol. *See* Diethyldithiocarbamate
Implant therapy. *See* Brachytherapy
Implant(s)
  for chemotherapy delivery. *See* Pumps
  of radioactive source. *See* Brachytherapy

Inactivated polio vaccine (IPV), HIV-infected children and, 200
Incorporation, of business, advantages and disadvantages of, 291
Index, severity of illness, 273–274
Indicator diseases, of AIDS, 179–189. *See also individually named diseases and infections*; Opportunistic infections
Infants, AIDS and. *See* Pediatric AIDS; Pediatric HIV infection
Infection(s). *See also individually named infectious agents*
  after intraoperative radiation, 66
  following bone marrow transplantation, 110–111
  prevention of, 99–100
  food-borne, recommendations for AIDS patients, 253
  implantable pumps and, 47
  life-threatening, in elderly patient, 150–152
  opportunistic, in AIDS. *See* Opportunistic infections
  precautions against, in bone marrow transplantation, 103–104
Information, flow within hospital, 314–316. *See also* Computer system
Informed consent
  for clinical trials, 51–54
  and surgical risk, 148–149
Infusion, of bone marrow, 108–109
Inosine pranabex, action and side effects of, 230
Institution Review Board (IRB), and research into patient data, 329
Instruction, computer-assisted. *See* Computer-assisted instruction (CAI)
Insurance, liability and. *See* Liability
Integration, of care, nurses and, 313–314
Integrity of nursing, 8
Intelligent systems, computer information system and, 330
Inter-Collegiate Center for Nursing Education (ICNE), cable television programming through, 344–345

Interferon(s)
  actions, indications and dosage recommendations, 83
  alpha-. *See* Alpha-interferon therapy
  functions of, 81, 83
  in passive biotherapy, 81
  side effects/toxicities associated with, 83–84
Interleukin-2 (IL-2)
  action and side effects of, 229
  as biologic response modifier, 85
  toxic effects of, 84, 85
International Association for the Study of Pain, 71
International Code of Ethics for Nursing (1950), 7
Interpersonal support, health promotion and, 69
Interstitial pneumonia, as bone marrow transplant complication, 111
Intrahepatic artery chemotherapy, 47
Intranasal drug delivery route, 129
Intraoperative radiation, 65–66
Intrapersonal skills, of terminally ill patient, 167
Intrathecal drug delivery route, 130
Intravenous administration
  of drugs, 129–130
    hydration therapy, home nursing care and, 213
  of immune globulin, action and side effects of, 229
Investigational drugs, for HIV infection, 227, 229–230
Iododeoxyuridine (IUdR), as radiosensitizer, 66
IPV. *See* Inactivated polio vaccine (IPV)
IRB. *See* Institution Review Board (IRB)
Isolated regional limb perfusion, 46
Isoniazide
  in treatment of *Mycobacterium avium-intracellulare* infection, 224
  in treatment of *Mycobacterium tuberculosis* infection, 224
Isoprinosine. *See* Inosine pranabex
Isosporiasis, in AIDS patients, drug therapies for, 224
Isotope therapy, 60
IUdR. *See* Iododeoxyuridine (IUdR)

J

JC virus, 184
Johns Hopkins Oncology Center, shared governance model, 3
Joint Commission on Accreditation of Healthcare Organizations
  care quality criteria, 4
  freestanding cancer center and, 270–271
  quality assurance issues, 357–358

K

Kalinoski, J., *AIDS Patient Handbook*, 234
Kaposi's Sarcoma (KS), 185–186
  drug therapies for, 226
  sites, 188
  ulcerative form, symptoms and nursing care considerations, 181
Kardex system, 321, 323
Ketoconazole, in treatment of candidiasis, 224
Klebsiella pneumoniae, 151
Knowledge bases, educational use of, 328
KS. *See* Kaposi's Sarcoma (KS)

L

Lactose intolerance, pediatric AIDS patients and, 202
LAF. *See* Laminar airflow (LAF) sterile technique
LAK cells. *See* Lymphokine-activated killer (LAK) cells
Laminar airflow (LAF) sterile technique, 104
Lamprene. *See* Clofazimine

Lasers, in PDT, 48
Length of stay, 2
Leukemia, B-cell acute lymphocytic, in HIV-infected patients, 188
Levamisole, immune modulation and, 79
Liability
  in freestanding cancer center, 272
  Oncology Nursing Agency and, 298–299
Licensure. *See also* Accreditation
  for nursing agency, 298–299
  and recruiting of nurses to ONS, 261
Life, quality of. *See* Quality-of-life
Life expectancy, limited. *See* Terminally ill patient
Lifestyle
  counseling for change in, 27–28
  defining home environment and, 303–304
Living with AIDS: A Caregiver's Guide, 219
Local hyperthermia, 61, 63
Lung cancer
  risk factors, incidence and screening recommendations, 20–21
  risk in elderly population, 147
Lymphadenopathy, persistent generalized, HIV infection progression and, 178
Lymphocytes, tumor infiltrating. *See* Tumor infiltrating lymphocytes (TILs)
Lymphokine-activated killer (LAK) cells
  administration of, 85
  in biotherapy, 79, 80
  toxic effects of, 84
Lymphoma(s), HIV-associated
  drug therapies for, 226
  non-Hodgkin's, 186–187
  primary central nervous system (P-CNS), 187–188
  T-lymphoblastic, 188

M

Macrobiotic diets, recommendations for AIDS patients, 254

Malignancy(ies)
  AIDS-related
    adult, 185–188
    pediatric, 196
  HIV-related, 188
Malignant melanoma, in elderly, 148
Market, identification of, 293
Market segmentation, 293
Marketing
  of consulting service, 292–293
  of nursing agency, 299–300
Marketing management, 292–293
Marketing plan, 289–290
  and market identification, 293
Master's Degree with a Specialty in Oncology Nursing, The (1988), 361
Maturation factors, 78
Maximum tolerated dose, biologic response modifiers and, 87
Meal preparation. *See* Food preparation
Measles, mumps, and rubella vaccine (MMR), HIV-infected children and, 200
Medicare reimbursement, of freestanding cancer center, 270
Medication administration list, automated, 325
MEDLINE, 331
Melanoma, malignant, in elderly, 148
Membranes, damage from PDT, 49
Mental status
  examination in older patient, 150
  of terminally ill patient, 167
Metabolic assessment parameters, for patients receiving BRMs, 95
Metabolism, of drug in older patient, 157
Metastases, advanced cancer designation and, 163
Methanol extraction residue, immune modulation and, 79
Methotrexate, toxicity associated with, 153
Methotrimeprazine, in cancer pain treatment, 131
Methyl CCNU, toxicity associated with, 153–154

Misonidazole, as radiosensitizer, 66
Mitochondria, PDT damage to, 49
Mixed leukocyte culture (MLC), prior to allogeneic bone marrow transplantation, 103
MLC. *See* Mixed leukocyte culture (MLC)
MMR. *See* Measles, mumps, and rubella vaccine (MMR)
MoAbs. *See* Monoclonal antibodies (MoAbs)
Mobile van unit, continuing care and, 132
Models
　of continuing care, 132–133
　of cost-effective health care, 14
　in radiation oncology nursing, 67–68
　of shared governance, 3
Molecular biology recombinant genetics, 78
Monoclonal antibodies (MoAbs)
　in passive biotherapy, 81
　production of, 86
　toxic effects of, 84, 86
　uses of, 81, 86
Moral issues. *See* Ethical issues
Moral questioning, 6
Mortality
　achieving reduction in, 14–15
　　objectives, 39–41
　from cancer in elderly, 142, 143, 145
Mouth, routine examination of, recommendations about, 23–24
Mucositis, as cytoreduction side effect, 106
Multichannel programmable pumps, 47–48
Multimodality cancer care center, defined, 267
Multiple myeloma, in HIV-infected patients, 188
Musculoskeletal assessment parameters, for patients receiving BRMs, 95
Myambutol. *See* Ethambutol
Mycelex. *See* Clotrimazole troches

Mycobacterium avium-intracellulare infection, in AIDS patients, 182
　drug therapy for, 224
Mycobacterium tuberculosis infection, in AIDS patients, 180, 182
　drug therapy for, 224
Mycostatin. *See* Nystatin suspension
Myelosuppression, risk in older patient, 153–154

N

Narcotics, terminally ill patient and, 170
National Cancer Institute (NCI)
　Cancer Control Objectives for the Nation: 1985–2000, 35–36
　satellite conferencing and, 342–343
　What Are Clinical Trials All About? A Booklet for Patients with Cancer, 53
National Center for Nursing Research, research support from, 31
National Institute of Allergy and Infectious Diseases (NIAID), experimental AIDS drug trials, 227, 229–230
Navelbine, 52
NCI. *See* National Cancer Institute (NCI)
Needles, cleaning recommendations for, 244–246
Neodymium:yttrium aluminum garnet (YAG) laser, in PDT, 49
Neoplastic diseases, risk factors, incidence and screening recommendations for, 16–24. *See also individually named cancers*
Nerve fibers, pains and, 125
Networking
　in business, 293–294
　　levels of, 294
　suggestions for, 73
Neumann's general systems model, 68
Neurologic assessment parameters, for patients receiving BRMs, 92
Neurologic disease, in AIDS patients, 184–185
　pediatric form, 203–204

Neuropathic pain, 125
Neurosurgical approaches, in cancer pain treatment, 131
New York City AIDS Task Force, 189
  AIDS incidence predictions, 213
New York City Human Resource Administration, AIDS case management approach of, 213
New York Statewide Professional Standards Review Council 1989, *Criteria Manual for the Treatment of AIDS*, 278
New York University Medical Center, cooperative care concept of. *See* Cooperative Care Center
Nexus Group
  advantages and disadvantages, 295–296
  collecting of fees, 295–296
  establishment of, 290–291
  fee schedules, 294–295
  scope of service, 291–292
  selling the service, 292–294
NIAID. *See* National Institute of Allergy and Infectious Diseases (NIAID)
Nitrites, intake guidelines, 26
Nizoral. *See* Ketoconazole
Nociceptive pain, 125
Non-Hodgkin's lymphoma, in AIDS patients, 186–187
Nonmalignant pain, patients experiencing, 127
Nonnitromidazole compounds, as radiosensitizers, 66
Nonnociceptive pain, 125
Nosocomial pneumonia, in older patient, 151
Nurse. *See* Oncology clinical nurse specialist (OCNS); Oncology nurse(s)
Nurse-run business
  examples of
    agency services, 297–300. *See also* Oncology Nursing Agency (ONA)
    consulting, 290–297. *See also* Nexus Group
  opportunities for, 290

Nursing agency. *See* Oncology Nursing Agency (ONA)
Nursing practice
  computer system application to, 318–321
  current environment, 1–2
  defined, 13
  as health promotion, 13–14
  innovative changes in, 355–356
Nursing research, 55–56
  into health education, 71–72
  opportunities at Bailey House, 279
  in radiation oncology, 67–68
    coping and stress management, 72–73
    facilitation of, 73
    pain control and management, 71
    patient or health education, 71–72
    prevention and detection, 68–69
    symptom management, 69–70
Nursing units, and ancillary departments, communicating via computer, 316–318
Nutrition. *See also* Diet; Food preparation
  AIDS patients and
    adults, 221
    children, 202
    recommendations for, 249–256
  counseling for, 25–27
  cytoreduction side effects involving, 106
  health promotion and, 69
Nystatin suspension, in treatment of candidiasis, 224

O

Obesity, avoidance counseling, 25–26
OCIS. *See* Oncology Clinical Information System (OCIS)
OCN (Oncology certified nurse), 361
OCNS. *See* Oncology clinical nurse specialist (OCNS)
On-line reference material, 330–332
ONA. *See* Oncology Nursing Agency (ONA)

ONCOCIN, as expert system, 330
OncoDisk, 331
Oncogenesis, 15
Oncology certified nurse (OCN), 361
Oncology Clinical Information System (OCIS), 330
Oncology clinical nurse specialist (OCNS)
  in Cooperative Care Center, 284
  versus generalist, 358–359
  role in ambulatory care, 262–263
  role in pain management, 133
Oncology nurse(s)
  advocacy and, 356–357. *See also* Patient advocate
  benefits of computer system to, 318
  benefits of nursing agency to, 298
  in business, 290. *See also* Nurse-run business
  in a business setting. *See* Nexus Group; Nurse-run business; Oncology Nursing Agency (ONA)
  as care integrator, 313–314
  certification of, 361
  as consultant, 3
  in pain management, 133
  in critcal care and rehabilitation, 360
  in freestanding cancer center
    patient ratio, 274
    role, 271–272
  as HIV counselor, 177
  image of, 4
  as patient advocate. *See* Patient advocate
  practising environment for, 1–2. *See also* Nursing practice
  in prevention education, 359–360
  primary nursing resposibilities of, 8
  research opportunities for. *See* Nursing research
  role in pain management, 134
  role of, 1–4
    changes in, 7–9, 11
    shortage of, 355
Oncology nursing
  care activities schedule, 325
  challenges in, 355
  entrepreneurship and, 288–289. *See also* Nurse-run business
  models, 67–68
  primary responsibilities in, 8
  as a specialty, 361
Oncology Nursing Agency (ONA)
  benefits to nurse, 298
  computerization in, 301
  concept of, 297
  contracts with, 300
  corporate structure of, 298
  development of, 297
  licensure and insurance requirements, 298–299
  marketing of, 299–300
Oncology Nursing Society (ONS), 2
  AIDS position paper, 189
  outcome standard for cancer nursing education, 68
  quality assurance and, 358
  rehabilitation and, 360
  research priorities (1988), 68
  specialty recognition and, 361
  Standards of Oncology Nursing Practice, 52
ONS. *See* Oncology Nursing Society (ONS)
Opportunistic infections
  in AIDS patients, 179–180
    bacterial, 180–181
    fungal, 182–183
    and neurologic disease, 185
    prevention and detection of, 219–221
    protozoal, 180, 181, 203
    viral, 183–184
  and HIV infection, 173–174
Optimal immunomodulating dose, biologic response modifiers and, 87
OPV. *See* Oral polio vaccine (OPV)
Oral cancer, risk factors, incidence and screening recommendations, 23–24
Oral drug delivery route, 128
Oral examination, recommendations about, 23–24

Oral polio vaccine (OPV), HIV-infected children and, 200
Orders, routing of, 315–316
  between nursing unit and ancillary department, 316–318
Orem's model of self care, 67–68
Ovarian cancer, risk factors, incidence and screening recommendations, 22–23

P

P-CNS lymphoma. *See* Primary central nervous system (P–CNS) lymphoma
Pain
  in AIDS patients, 218
  classification of
    by mechanism, 124–125
    by patient group, 126–127
    by syndromes, 126
  contributing factors
    health care system related, 124
    health professional related, 123
    patient and family member related, 124
  control and management of, nursing research into, 71
  control of, nursing research into, 71
  evaluation, 134
  management of
    by clinical nurse specialist, 134
    ethical issues affecting terminally ill patient, 170
    future directions, 134–135
  treatment of
    cognitive behavioral approaches, 131–132
    continuing care in, 132–133
    drug delivery routes, 128–130
    neurosurgical approaches and anesthetic techniques, 131
    new uses for old drugs, 130–131
  undertreatment of, 122–123
Pain consultant, nurse as, 133
Pain syndromes, classification of, 126

Palliative care, 132
  active care versus, 9
  for terminally ill patient, 165
Pancreatic cancer, risk factors, incidence and screening recommendations, 23
Papanicolau smear testing, recommendations about
  cervical cancer detection, 19
  ovarian cancer detection, 22–23
Parenteral nutrition, home care administration of, 279
Parents, impact of AIDS on, 206
Passive biotherapy
  adoptive, 81
  specific and nonspecific, 79, 81
Pathogenesis, pain classification by, 124–125
Patient advocate
  ANA code and, 7–8
  nurse as, 8, 356–357. *See also* Advocacy
  in home care setting, 308
  for terminally ill, 170–171
Patient education
  for AIDS sufferers
    CDC guidelines, 207
    and their care providers, 219
    hygeinic precautions, 220
  Bellevue Hospital *AIDS Patient Handbook*, 236–256
  for bone marrow donor, 107
  in home care setting, 304–305
  nursing research into, 71–72
  via closed-circuit television, 341–342
Patient: Nurse ratio, in freestanding cancer center, 274
Patient(s)
  admission process prior to bone marrow transplantation, 103–104
  assessment of. *See* Assessment
  Bellevue Hospital *AIDS Patient Handbook* for, 236–256
  care plan for. *See* Care planning, automated
  as consumer of cancer therapy, 299

contributing to cancer pain problem, 124
in Cooperative Care Center, 284
grouping by pain experience, 126–127
older population. See Elderly
participation in own treatment. See Cooperative care
rights of. See Rights of patients
service provisions for, in freestanding cancer center, 273
A Patient's Bill of Rights (AHA), 52
Payments. See Reimbursement
PCP. See *Pneumocystis carinii* pneumonia (PCP)
PDQ. See Physician Data Query (PDQ)
PDT. See Photodynamic therapy (PDT)
Pediatric AIDS, 192–193
and adolescent high-risk behaviors, 204–205
care program for, 197–199
coping strategies in, 206–208
disease process, 194–197
education for prevention, 208
epidemiology, 193
family education and, 199
HIV testing, 194
home care and, 201
immunizations in, 199–200
impact of, 205–206
in-hostpital precautions for, 200–201
management issues, 202
neurologic abnormalities, 203–204
nutrition, 202
respiratory tract infections, 203
transmission methods, 193–194
Pediatric HIV infection, 192
antibody testing, 194
CDC definition, 195, 197
classification of, 195, 198
coping strategies in, 206–207
signs and symptoms, 198
supportive care in, 199
Pelvic examination, recommendations about
cervical cancer detection, 19
ovarian cancer detection, 22

Pender's health belief model, 68
Pender's health promotion model, 68–69
Pentamidine isothionate, as treatment/prophylaxis for *Pneumocystis carinii* pneumonia, 223
"People leasing," business of. See Oncology Nursing Agency (ONA)
Persistent generalized lymphadenopathy (PGL)
HIV infection progression and, 178
lymphoma risk in, 187
Personal networking, in business, 294
Pesticides, safeguard recommendations for, 30
PGL. See Persistent generalized lymphadenopathy (PGL)
L-phenylalanine, toxicity associated with, 153
Phosphonoformate
action and side effects of, 229
in treatment of CMV infection, 225
Photodynamic therapy (PDT), 48–50
Photosensitizing agent, for PDT, 48
Phototoxicity, as PDT complication, 50
Physicians' Desk Reference, as on-line reference material, 331
Physician Data Query (PDQ), 331
Physicians
and computer interraction, 316–317
nursing agency services and, 299–300
PII. See Dihematoporphyrin ether (DHE)
Planning
of care. See Care planning, automated
for discharge, 320–321
Plastic aprons, in AIDS patient care, 248
PML. See Progressive multifocal leukoencephalopathy (PML)
Pneumococcal vaccine, HIV-infected children and, 200
Pneumocystis carinii infection, as bone marrow transplant complication, 110
Pneumocystis carinii pneumonia (PCP),
in AIDS patients, 180
drug therapies for, 223
pediatric form, 203

symptoms and nursing care considerations, 181
Pneumonia
 in AIDS patients. *See Pneumocystis carinii* pneumonia (PCP), in AIDS patients
 interstitial, as bone marrow transplant complication, 111
 in older patient, 150–151
Pneumonitis, CMV, in AIDS patients, 185
Polio vaccines, HIV-infected children and, 200
Polypharmacy, in older patient, 155–156
Population, age distribution in, 7
Practice. *See* Collaborative practice; Nursing practice
Precautions, in pediatric AIDS patient care, 200–201
Predictive value, of screening tests, 17
Prednimustine, toxicity associated with, 153
Pregnancy, Bellevue Hospital *AIDS Patient Handbook* recommendations, 244–245
Presbyterian Hospital (New York), 263–264
Prevalence of disease, screening program and, 16–17
Prevention. *See* Cancer prevention
Primary central nervous system (P-CNS) lymphoma, in AIDS patients, 187–188
Primary prevention, defined, 14, 16
Printouts, from computer information system, 321, 322
 electronic kardex, 321, 323
 medication administration list, 325
 nursing care activities schedule, 325
 patient care plan, 324–325
Privacy. *See under* Rights of patients
Problem-solving skills, 336
Proctosigmoidoscopy, recommendations about, 19
Professional networking, in business, 294

Programming, of implantable pumps, 47–48
Programs, as educational tool. *See* Computer-assisted instruction (CAI)
Progressive multifocal leukoencephalopathy (PML), in AIDS patients, 185
 drug therapy for, 225
Promoting Health/Preventing Disease: Year 2000 Objectives for the Nation (1989), 30, 39–41
Prospective payment
 elderly patients and, 158
 initiation of, 1
Prostate cancer
 risk factors, incidence and screening recommendations, 20
 risk in elderly population, 147–148
 teleconference on, 342–343
Protective clothing, recommendations about, 21
Protective environment, patient orientation to, 103–104
Proteus spp., 151
Protozoal opportunistic infections, in AIDS patients, 180
Pseudomonas aeruginosa, 151
Psychographics, as market segmentation factor, 293
Psychosocial issues
 AIDS patients and
  adults, 214–216
  assessment and interventions, 218–219
  children, 204
 Cooperative Care Center and. *See* Cooperative care
 cytoreduction side effects and, 106
 elderly patients and, 145–146
  chemotherapy, 154
 terminally ill patient's needs, 167–168
Pump oxygenator, in isolated regional limb perfusion, 46
Pumps
 for chemotherapy delivery
  in home care setting, 306
  implantable, 47

multichannel programmable, 47–48
Pyrazinamide, in treatment of *Mycobacterium tuberculosis* infection, 224
Pyrimethamine, in toxoplasmosis treatment, 223
Pyrimethamine-sulfadoxine, as therapy/prophylaxis for *Pneumocystis carinii* pneumonia and, 223

Q

Quality assurance, 357–358
  standards in freestanding cancer center, 273
Quality of care, defining, 4
Quality-of-life
  chemotherapeutic protocols and, 56
  and pain management, 135
  and pain relationship research, 71
  terminally ill patient and, 165
  therapeutic success as measure of, 54–55

R

Radiation oncology. *See* Radiation therapy
Radiation therapy, 59
  altered fractions, 64–65
  application and incidence of use, 67
  brachytherapy, 63–64
  delivery techniques, 59–61
  goals of, 67
  hyperthermia, 61–63
  intraoperative, 65–66
  nursing research in. *See* under Nursing research
  in older patient, nursing considerations, 154–155
  prior to bone marrow transplantation, 104
  sensitizers and protectors, 66–67
Radioactivity, of brachytherapy patients, 63–64

Radioisotopes, 60
Radiopharmaceutical therapy, 60
Radioprotectors, 66–67
Radiosensitizers, 66–67
Radiotherapy. *See* Radiation therapy
Recombinant immunomodulator factors, availability of, 78
Recombinant soluble T4, action and side effects of, 229
Recreation facilities, in Cooperative Care Center, 283
Recruitment, 4
Rectal drug delivery route, 128
Reference material, on-line, 330–332
Referral patterns, cancer prevention and detection, 15
Reflective thinking, 6
Regional hyperthermia, 61, 63
Rehabilitation, oncology nurses in, 360
Rehabilitation of Persons with Cancer: An ONS Position Statement, 360
Reimbursement. *See also* Economics of cancer care
  of freestanding cancer center, 269–270
  hyperthermia treatment and, 61
  prospective, 1, 158
  unpaid, recourse for, 296
Rejection, of bone marrow transplantation, 99, 114
  decreasing incidence of, 103
  syngeneic transplant and, 102–103
Relapse, following bone marrow transplantation, 99, 115
  autologous transplant, 100, 102
Relaxation training, in cancer pain treatment, 132
Religion, terminally ill patient and, provisions for, 164
Renal assessment parameters, for patients receiving BRMs, 93
Reporting structure, in freestanding cancer center, 272
Reports, automated. *See* Printouts, from computer information system

Reproductive function, nursing research into, 70
Reprogramming therapy, 50
Requisitions, routing of, 315–316
Research
   chemotherapy toxicity, 158
   computer usefulness in, 328–329
   facilitation of, suggestions for, 73
   factors influencing productivity, 55–56
   nursing staff involvement in, 55–56. *See also* Nursing research
   oncology nursing issues, 10–11
   ONS priorities (1988), 68
   pain management findings, 134–135
Respiratory assessment parameters, for patients receiving BRMs, 93
Respiratory tract infections, in pediatric AIDS patients, 203
Restructuring of health care, 1
Results, routing of, 315–316
   between nursing unit and ancillary department, 316–318
Retinochoroiditis, in AIDS patients, 185
Retrovir. *See* Zidovudine (AZT)
Ribavirin, action and side effects of, 229
Rifabutin, in treatment of *Mycobacterium avium-intracellulare* infection, 224
Rifadin. *See* Rifampin
Rifampin
   in treatment of *Mycobacterium avium-intracellulare* infection, 224
   in treatment of *Mycobacterium tuberculosis* infection, 224
Rights of patients
   nurses' advocacy of persons with cancer, 356–357
   privacy, 7. *See also* Confidentiality
   for HIV infected children, 207–208
Rimactane. *See* Rifampin
Risk factors
   in carcinogenesis, 37–38
      breast, 17
      cervix, 19
      colon and rectum, 18
      lungs, 20
      mouth, 23–24
      ovaries, 22
      pancreas, 23
      prostate, 20
      skin, 21
      testicles, 21
   in elderly population, 147–148
   reducing, population targets, 39–41
Risk taking, advocacy and, 9
Risk(s)
   behavior of HIV-infected adolescents, 204–205
   surgical, in older patient, 149–150
Room, for patient and care partner, 282
Roy's adaptation model, 68
"Rule of 3", for setting consulting fees, 295

S

Safe sex, recommendations for, 242–244
Safety, Bellevue Hospital *AIDS Patient Handbook* suggestions, 242
Salt-cured food, intake guidelines, 26
Satellite conferencing, 342–344
Satellite television, as educational tool, 342
Schoolchildren, beliefs about AIDS, CDC data on, 179
Schools
   AIDS education in, 208
   CDC guidelines for AIDS patients, 207
SCID. *See* Severe combined immunodeficiency (SCID)
Screening programs
   for elderly populations, 146–148
   for HIV antibody. *See* under Human immunodeficiency virus (HIV)
   for neoplastic diseases
      general issues, 16–17
      specific types, 17–24. *See also individually named cancers*
Secondary prevention, defined, 14, 16
Secretary's Commission on Nursing (1988), 2–3

Security, in computer information systems, 326–327. *See also* Confidentiality
Segmentation, of market, 293
Self-actualization, health promotion and, 69
Self care
  Orem's model of, 67–68
  predictors of, 72–73
Self-employment, advantages and disadvantages of, 296–297
Self-examination, recommendations for
  breast, 18
  skin, 21
  testicles, 22
Seromycin. *See* Cycloserine
Serratia spp., 151
Services, target provisions, 41
Severe combined immunodeficiency (SCID), bone marrow transplantation and, 97
Severity of illness index, 273–274
Sexual activity
  Bellevue Hospital *AIDS Patient Handbook* suggestions, 242–244
  HIV-infected adolescents and, 204–205
Sexual function, nursing research into, 70
Shared governance, Johns Hopkins model, 3
Shingles. *See* Herpes zoster virus (HZV) infection
Shortage, of nurses, 355
Siblings, impact of AIDS on, 205–206
Side effects. *See* Adverse effects; Toxicity
Sigmoidoscopy, recommendations about, 19
Simulations, in computer-assisted instruction, 337
Skin
  assessment parameters for patients receiving BRMs, 94
  care of, nursing research into, 70

  cytoreduction side effects involving, 106
  graft versus host disease and, 112
  hyperthermia effect on, 63
  self-examination of, recommendations for, 21
Skin cancer
  risk factors, incidence and screening recommendations, 21
  risk in elderly population, 148
Slim's disease. *See* Wasting syndrome
Small business owner, advantages and disadvantages of being, 296–297. *See also* Nurse-run business
Small Claims Court, unpaid fees and, 296
Smoked food, intake guidelines, 26
Software
  as educational tool. *See* Computer-assisted instruction (CAI)
  for implantable pumps, 47–48
Solid tumors, in HIV-infected patients, 188
Soluble CD4. *See* Recombinant soluble T4
Somatic pain, 125
Somatostatin analog SMS201-995, in cryptosporidiosis treatment, 223
Specialization, versus generalization, 358–359
Specialty, oncology nursing as, 361
Spermicides, recommendations about, 244
Spiramycin, in cryptosporidiosis treatment, 223
Spiritual needs, of terminally ill patient, 168–169
Spirituality, terminally ill patient and, 168
Sputum cytology, as screening procedure, recommendations about, 20
Squamous cell carcinoma, YAG laser use in, 49
Staffing levels, 2
  and nurse shortage, 355

Index 391

Standardization, of nursing data, 328
Standards of care, 4
  data capture and, 328
  freestanding cancer center
    contributions to, 269
Standards of Oncology Nursing Education, 361
Staphylococcus aureus, 151
Statement on Graduate Education in Nursing (ANA 1978), 359
Stereotyping, and changing role of nurse, 7
Sterilization, pediatric AIDS patient care precautions, 201
Stool blood test, recommendations about, 19
Streptococcus pneumoniae, 151
Streptomycin, in treatment of
  Mycobacterium tuberculosis infection, 224
Stress management
  health promotion and, 69
  nursing research into, 72–73
  reduction techniques, in cancer pain treatment, 132
  in those involved with AIDS patients
    adults, 216
    children, 206
Subcutaneous drug delivery route, 129
Sublingual drug delivery route, 128
Sulfadiazine, in toxoplasmosis treatment, 223
Sun exposure, reduction in, counseling for, 27–28
Sun screen preparations, recommendations about, 21
Support networks, terminally ill patient and, 168
Support system, in decision-making, 330
Supportive care, 132–133
  elderly patients and, 158
  for pediatric HIV-infected patients, 199
Supportive housing apartment program, 277
Surgery, in elderly patients, 148–149
  postoperative confusion, 150

preanesthetic evaluation, 149
preoperative nursing assessment, 150
risks associated with, 149–150
"Swinging door" policy, 10
Symptom management
  in AIDS patients, 218
  following biotherapeutic agent administrations, 87, 88–90
  nursing research in, 69–70. *See also individual symptoms*
  by patient, 285
Symptoms
  cryptosporidiosis, 181
  HIV infection progression, 178
    Bellevue Hospital *AIDS Patient Handbook* checklist, 239–240
  management of. *See* Symptom management
  of pediatric HIV infection, 198
  Pneumocystis carinii pneumonia (PCP), 181
  ulcerative Kaposi's Sarcoma, 181
Syndrome(s)
  pain, classification of, 126
  wasting, as AIDS manifestation, 188–189
Syngeneic bone marrow transplantation, 102
Syringe, cleaning recommendations for, 244–246

T

T-cell depletion techniques, 99
  allogeneic bone marrow transplantation, 103
T-helper cells, HIV infection progression and, 178
T-lymphoblastic lymphoma, in HIV-infected patients, 188
T lymphocytes, HIV infection progression and, 178
Tamoxifen, toxicity associated with, 153
TB. *See* Tuberculosis (TB)
TBI/TLI. *See* Total body irradiation (TBI)/Total lymphoid irradiation (TLI)

Team approach. *See* Collaborative practice
Technology. *See* Biomedical technology
Teenagers, AIDS and. *See* Pediatric AIDS; Pediatric HIV infection
Teleconferencing, by satellite, 342–344
Teletherapy, 59–60
Television, for education. *See* Education television
Terminal care. *See under* Terminally ill patient
Terminally ill patient
 continuing care options, 132–133
 ethical issues affecting, 169–171
 health care needs of
  nursing assessment, 165–169
  program example (Calvary Hospital), 164
 hospital versus home care, 10
 severe pain in, 127
 status designation, 163
 technology and, 9
Terminals, bed-side, 329–
Tertiary prevention, defined, 14
Testicles, routine versus self-examination, recommendation for, 22
Testicular cancer, risk factors, incidence and screening recommendations, 21–22
Tests, ordering and receiving results via computer, 316–318
Therapeutic Center, in cooperative care facility, 283, 284
Therapy. *See* Treatment modalities
Thermistors, in hyperthermia, 61, 62
TILs. *See* Tumor infiltrating lymphocytes (TILs)
TNF. *See* Tumor necrosis factor (TNF)
Tobacco, counseling to prevent use of, 24–25
Total body irradiation (TBI)/Total lymphoid irradiation (TLI), prior to bone marrow transplantation, 104, 105
Toxicity
 of biologic response modifiers, 83–84
 and symptom management, 87, 88–90

of chemotherapeutic agents in elderly, 153–154, 158
Toxoplasma gondii infection, in AIDS patients, 180
Toxoplasmosis, in AIDS patients, 180
 drug therapies for, 223
Transdermal drug delivery route, 129
Treatment modalities. *See also individually named therapies*
 AIDS drug therapies. *See* Drug therapies, for AIDS patients
 intravenous. *See* Intravenous administration
 medication administration list, 325
 new developments in, 45–46
  for cancer pain, 127–133. *See also under* Pain
 nursing research applications, 55–56
 ONCOCIN as protocol advisor, 330
 for opportunistic diseases, 223–225
 pain syndromes associated with or unrelated to, 126
 by radiation. *See* Radiation therapy
 surgical. *See* Surgery
Treatment planning, in radiation therapy, 60
Tricyclic antidepressants, in cancer pain treatment, 130
Trimethoprim-sulfamethoxazole
 in treatment of *Pneumocystis carinii* pneumonia, 223
 in treatment/prophylaxis of isosporiasis, 224
 use following bone marrow transplantation, 99
Tuberculosis (TB), in AIDS patients, 180, 182
 drug therapy for, 224
Tumor infiltrating lymphocytes (TILs), in biotherapy, 79, 80
Tumor necrosis factor (TNF)
 action and side effects of, 230
 as biologic response modifier, 84
 in passive biotherapy, 81
 toxic effects of, 84
Tumor(s)
 B-cell, in AIDS patients, 186

pain syndromes associated with, 126
  solid, in HIV-infected patients, 188
Tutorials, in computer-assisted instruction, 337

U

Ulcerative Kaposi's Sarcoma, symptoms and nursing care considerations, 181
Uncertainty, 6
  technology causing, 9
Universal precautions, in pediatric AIDS patient care, 200–201
Uplinking, for satellite conferencing, 342–343

V

Vaccines
  in biologic therapy, 79, 81. *See also individual vaccine agents*
  HIV-infected children and, 200
Veno-occlusive disease (VOD), as bone marrow transplantation complication, 114
Video, as educational tool. *See* Education television
Video teleconferencing, 342–344
Videodisc systems, as educational tool, 345–346
  advantages and limitations, 347–348
  effectiveness of, 348
  examples, 346–347
  use in USA, 347
Vinca alkaloids, toxicity associated with, 154
Viral opportunistic infections, in AIDS patients, 183–184
Virazole. *See* Ribavirin
Visceral pain, 125
Visiting Nurse Service of New York, HIV infection on-site home care, 279
Vitamins
  intake guidelines, 26
  as radioprotectors, 66

VOD. *See* Veno-occlusive disease (VOD)
Voice synthesis, on CD-ROM disks, 349

W

Wasting syndrome, as AIDS manifestation, 188–189
Western blot analysis, HIV antibody testing by, 174–176
  in pediatric population, 194
Wills, writing of, 279
Wisconsin Cancer Pain Initiative, 122–123, 134
Withdrawal/withholding treatments, 9–10, 169–170
Works, cleaning recommendations for, 244–246
Workshop on the Community and Cancer Prevention and Detection, proposed research agenda of, 30–31
World Health Organization (WHO), Cancer Pain Relief Program, 123
Wound healing, delayed, after intraoperative radiation, 66
WR-2721 CS-2. *See* 3-amniopropylaminophosphorothioic acid

Y

YAG laser. *See* Neodymium:yttrium aluminum garnet (YAG) laser

Z

Zidovudine (AZT)
  action and side effects of, 229
  drug combinations with, investigative studies, 228
  use in AIDS dementia complex, 185
  use in HIV infection, 178
  use in *Pneumocystis carinii* pneumonia, 178
Zovirax. *See* Acyclovir sodium